בס"ד

QUESTIONS *On Any* SUBJECT

Rav Avigdor Miller ZT"L

Book 2

Published by:

Toras Avigdor

Adar 5785

This book is dedicated by

Michael and Tanya Farah

In honor of our Parents:

Dr. Bijan Farah & Judith Franks-Farah

Joseph Manoochehri A"H & Nadia Azizi

And in memory of our Grandparents:

Yechezkel Ben Yair & Devorah Bat Mashallah

Farahmandpour

Eliezer Ben Yehuda & Esther Leah Bat Charna

Franks

Yadollah Ben Yaakov & Farangeez Bat Brachas

Azizi

Yaakov Ben David & Devorah Bat Sarah

Manoochehri

In honor of our children:

Yosef Avraham, Lielle Devorah, Eliana

May their Ahavat Hashem and their

Yirat Shamayim grow endlessly

This book is dedicated by

Michael and Tanya Farah

To the Rabbanim who guided us
and who were instrumental to our growth:

Rishon Letzion HaRav David Yosef

Rabbi Michael Azoze

Rabbi Meir Chai Benhiyoun

Rabbi Asher Brander

Rabbi Daniel Cavalier

Rabbi Yosef Cohen

Rabbi Yitz Jacobs

Rabbi Shmuel Laniado

Rabbi Mordechai Lebhar

Rabbi Tal Perez

And a special Hakarat HaTov to:

Rabbi Shalom Garfinkel

Rabbi Shlomo Yisraeli

Rabbi Hertzel Yitzhak

Who, without them, we would not be who we are today.

And of course,

Rav Avigdor Miller zatzal

whose Torah has touched our lives
and inspires us every day to be closer
to Hakadosh Baruch Hu.

Questions On Any Subject - Book 2

ISBN: 978-1-60763-441-6

Email: *info@TorasAvigdor.org*

Telephone: *732.844.3670*

Address: *1273a 46th Street Brooklyn NY 11219*

Manufactured in China

Contents

Quotable Quotes

"Ladies, I'm happy to see that tonight you're active. You're asking good questions but it will take me until 1:00 tonight to answer them."

"Now I want to tell you people; you need not ask just pious questions. You can ask impious questions here too, contrary questions. Don't be afraid. You won't lose status with me. I'll argue with you. It doesn't mean I'll agree with you."

"You know the good questions; they wait until a few minutes before half past ten. That's a very good question and I spoke about it already; it's treated in my first book. However, in three minutes I won't be able to answer. So next time, come next week and at 10:15 or at the beginning of the hour, don't be bashful! Be the first one to ask and I'll be glad to answer you. I told you that last week. Give me time. I can't answer in three minutes."

"Anybody have any questions? Anybody? Don't be bashful."

Preface

Thirty years ago, I was introduced to the Torah tapes of Rav Avigdor Miller, *zt"l*. On that day, I acquired for myself not only a *rebbe*, but a new way of thinking, a new way of living. The recorded Thursday night lectures were unlike anything I had heard before, and I recognized almost immediately that I was listening to someone who was capable of taking the deepest ideals of the Torah and making them suitable for practical Torah living.

The almost endless topics and ideas that the Rav spoke about covered the full gamut of Torah living. His ability to present them clearly and cogently was incredible. The Rav spoke to me like no one else had before. I, along with thousands of others, are eternally grateful to Hakadosh Baruch Hu for planting the Rav in our generation and giving us that gift for so many years.

While the full lectures were the focus of the Thursday night gathering in the shul, it's hard to deny that the 'Questions and Answers' session at the end of the lecture was equally important to many of the attendees and listeners of the tapes. The Rav opened up the floor for his famous "And now, questions on any subject!" period during which we, from both the men's and women's sections, were able to ask whatever we wanted – either by raising our hands and being called on, or anonymously by writing our questions on slips of paper and passing them up to the front.

Putting aside the almost unbelievable sight of a person willing to take questions on any topic and then capable of presenting clear answers on the spot, it was the opportunity to acquire a Torah *hashkafah* that wasn't limited to certain areas of life. All of a sudden, a new panorama opened up for us, an opportunity to approach the totality of Torah living with understanding. Personally, I know that much of my *hashkafah*, the way I view, process, and understand most of the world around me, whether in my personal life or in the wider world around me, is built upon those Q&A sessions.

Hundreds, thousands, of questions that had floated around in and out of my head for years were suddenly being dealt with – and not superficially. And it was actually an intense joy, because אֵין שִׂמְחָה כְּהַתָּרַת הַסְּפֵקוֹת – *There's no happiness like having doubts resolved.*

Anyone who listened – just to the Rav's Q&A sessions – slowly but surely acquired a Torah mind, a mind capable of looking at the world with the confidence that he or she was seeing things and interpreting them from a Torah perspective. And because the Rav taught us that acquiring a Torah mind is one of the most valuable acquisitions in this world, every answer we heard from his mouth was another step in that direction.

Over the many years – from the early 1970s until the Rav passed away in 2001 – the Rav answered more than 15,000 questions for the public, and Toras Avigdor is dedicated to making each of those Q&As available to the public. As we transcribe them, we intend to make them easily accessible, whether on our website, app, or published books. That was the primary intent of the Rav; his dream was to make a 'Torah Mind' available to Klal Yisroel, and we at Toras Avigdor strive to help fulfill his dream.

So why this *sefer?* How is this *sefer* different from the Q&A email that is sent to tens of thousands of subscribers every day? How is it different from the Q&As that are available on our app and website?

The answer is that although the Rav's answer on each individual question can be studied and understood independently of any other Q&A – even when on the same topic – the fact is that at different times, he would approach the same questions from different angles. It depended on various factors – the listeners, the time, and sometimes even the lecture he had just given.

Consequently, many times when we share Q&As with the public – by daily email, on our website, and in our Toras Avigdor *parsha* booklets – we receive follow-up questions from readers asking for more clarity. "But what about this?" "Why didn't the Rav mention so and so in his answer?"

Simultaneously, as we began to transcribe and categorize the Q&As we noticed that what the Rav said in 1973 could be augmented and better understood if you heard, for example, his answer to a similar question in 1993. Although each one is a *davar shaleim* on its own, each Q&A brought even more clarity to the subject.

And so, the idea was born. We were going to make use of the Q&As that had already been transcribed, and select various answers on the same topic that would complement each other, and thereby give readers a 'bigger picture.'

Now, while arranging the Q&As by subject matter will help one get a clearer and better overall understanding of the subject than having just one Q&A, it's important to note that there is much more available than what is in this *sefer*. For every Q&A we selected, there were another few that were not used due to space constraints or other considerations. We did our best to choose a selection of answers and order them in a way that would create a chapter with a progression of ideas that would help add clarity to the subject. Many hours were invested in choosing Q&As, editing them, and classifying and ordering them. A team of *talmidei chachamim*, *talmidim* of the Rav, sat together and struggled to make the right choices, attempting to create chapters that would be composed of the words of the Rav from various years, and would flow from one Q&A to another, and in totality, give the reader a complete understanding of the subject.

However, as much as we've attempted to do our best in providing the reader an enjoyable and educational reading experience, we have no doubt that many readers will be left with questions, with a certain lack of clarity in how to best assimilate and apply the Rav's answers. And so, it's always important to keep the following rule in mind as you learn this *sefer* or access any of the Rav's Q&As on our other formats: The Rav intended to give over what he understood to be true unadulterated Torah ideology. As far as applying it to a certain situation, everyone was welcome to approach him or their own *rav* in private, but he wanted the proper Torah *hashkafah* to be heard and assimilated into the consciousness of the Am Yisroel.

Another important point: The Rav was speaking to 'healthy' people, people of sound mind who are capable of understanding how to best assimilate and apply his answers or of knowing when to ask further questions of their *rebbeim*. For those who misinterpret and misapply the Rav's words, the answers would have been better left unsaid. But the Rav never held back from teaching us the Torah-true *hashkafah* because unhealthy people might take advantage to misuse it. In regard to this, he would always quote the Navi, צַדִּיקִים יֵלְכוּ בָם וּפֹשְׁעִים יִכָּשְׁלוּ בָם – *The righteous will walk in these ways while the wicked will trip up on these same ways* (*Hoshea* 14:10), and he would tell us to look in *Bava Basra* (89b) where Rabbi Yochanan ben Zakai applied this *pasuk* to a similar situation. In fact, one of his last lectures, less than two months before his *petirah*, was about this subject.

Our intention at Toras Avigdor is to present the Rav's answers precisely as he delivered them in public – in the most authentic way possible. Contrary to what many claim, the Rav did not intend his responses for a small crowd of a certain type. He recorded the tapes, reviewed them afterwards, and sent them around the world to be listened to. His dream was that they should spread far and wide. And so, even though we sometimes receive emails and letters from readers with personal opinions about what they believe should be sent out and what not, we and the *rabbanim* we speak to are not willing to act as filters for the Rav's words, nor do we think we should. Like the measured words of any *tzaddik* and *talmid chacham*, the Rav's words are valuable and should be studied, not cancelled.

We tried as much as possible to provide you with a date on the bottom of each Q&A (in case we did not have an accurate date on record, we provided an estimate) so that the reader can appreciate when it was said and bring that to the attention of their local *rav*, *rebbi*, *rosh yeshiva* or whomever they turn to with questions, and discuss how to apply the Rav's words in their own life.

And so, we present to you this volume of the Rav's answers to Questions On Any Subject, and we daven to Hashem that his words should penetrate the consciousness of the Am Yisroel and help us create for ourselves Torah minds.

Rabbi Amichai Markowitz,
Rosh Chodesh Kislev 5784

Preface Volume 2

It is with immense gratitude to Hakadosh Baruch Hu that I am able to take part, along with the rest of the Toras Avigdor staff, in presenting to the Torah *tzibbur* a second volume of Questions On Any Subject, culled from the Rav's Q&A sessions that took place over a more than thirty-year period.

It is an especially emotionally charged time for me because only a few days ago, my precious daughter, Menucha Chaya, was *nifteres,* and it was her birth that had brought me especially close to Rav Avigdor Miller.

When Menucha required hospitalization soon after birth my wife and I turned to the Rav for advice, *brachos*, emotional support, and guidance. In his inimitable way, he provided all of it for us. It was especially comforting being able to walk with the Rav and have my own personal Q&A sessions with the Rav, asking him my most important questions, and knowing that the answers I was getting were coming from a man who spent his entire life dedicated to creating a Torah mind.

His practical words kept me grounded always, and everything that my wife and I did during Menucha's twenty-eight years in this world in caring for her while raising another nine children was grounded in the Torah of the Rav.

I am *mispallel* to Hakadosh Baruch Hu that all of the authentic Torah *hashkafah* that Toras Avigdor was *zoche* to give over to the world and continues to give, should be a *zechus* for Menucha Chaya bas Amichai. She was always proud of what Toras Avigdor was accomplishing, and now that she's with Hakadosh Baruch Hu again, I'm sure she's even more proud, knowing that it was she who was the catalyst for all that Toras Avigdor has become.

Rabbi Amichai Markowitz,
Chodesh Adar 5785

Quotable Quotes

“You can ask any question at all. Questions of *emunah*, *kefirah*. Anything you want – you can ask. Here is your chance. There is no charge.”

“Questions on anything. If there won’t be any questions, I’ll supply my own topics. Anything at all, Eskimos, lampshades. Anything.”

“And now, questions on any subject at all. And you don’t have to hesitate, you can't pull any punches on me, I can punch back, too.”

“Now don’t ask such stupid questions. Some people ask meaningless questions. So think before you’re going to ask. Don’t get up and think. Think before you get up.”

“Now, in case people will fall short of questions, I’ll supply the questions, but I’m just listening in order to give you an opportunity.”

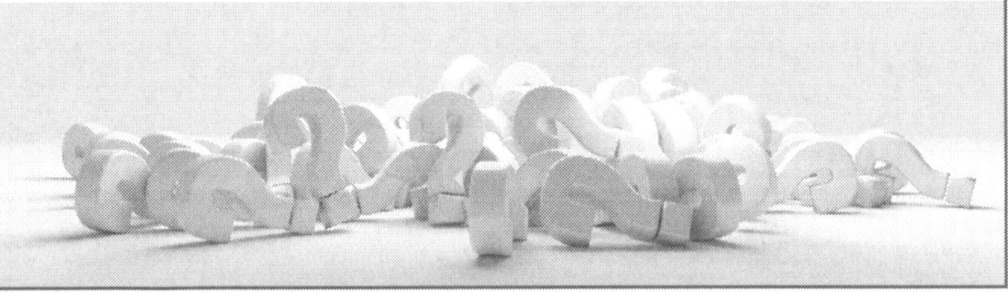

QUESTIONS *On Any* SUBJECT

Chapter 1

Becoming Jewish

Chapter Sponsor

לעילוי נשמת

ר' **דוד אברהם** ז"ל

בן ר' **שרגא גרשון** הי"ו

Dedicated by the Kazlow Family

Contents

Chapter 1

Converts

Bringing In Gentiles

Q/ If a Jewish man is married to a gentile woman and she is interested in learning about Yiddishkeit, is it permissible to bring the couple into your home to be *mekarev* her with the intent of having her convert eventually?

A/ The answer is, we are not interested in converting gentiles. That's a fatal error. There's no mitzvah to convert any gentiles. And although if that gentile would become a *ger tzedek*, a sincere convert, it's a good thing – no question it's a good thing – but to us it would be a bigger accomplishment if you could get him to break off with her. And if you can't, you shouldn't give any recognition to their relationship; you shouldn't sanction their union by inviting them together to your home.

Now, I understand that this is against the trend of the times, but what can we do? The reason we are an eternal people is because we go against the trend of the times.

And I must commend the local Sefardi *kehillah*. The local Sefardi *kehillah* has a principle that they do not countenance any conversions at all – even with the best of intentions*). And they are smart, because we are a nation who can't

A ger who maintains relations with his family, that's not a full ger; that's a big error. There are cases like that, and they think they are perfect geirim.

afford to risk our franchise of living forever; it means playing around with extinction. And although if there is a righteous convert, we welcome them here and they are welcome in most places, we do not encourage the furtherance of proselytizing. Because that is not our business in this world; we are the Chosen Nation. Only if a person will be stubborn and insist on becoming a *ger*, then we take him.

There's a *ger* who once came here; he was interested in converting. We didn't encourage him, but some time passed and finally he decided to become a *ger*. He came to me and he asked me, "What do I do?"

I said, "You go to a rabbi who does conversions."

So he went and the rabbi told him, "It's going to cost you 300 dollars." He almost hit the ceiling when he heard that, because he had good intentions and 300 dollars in those days was a small fortune. But I didn't raise a finger to help him. We have to make it as hard as possible in order to give him the acid test. There have been cases where I regretted that I encouraged those becoming *geirim*. Later, I regretted it. And therefore, you have to make it hard for him.

If he is persistent, and he finally goes through everything – it costs him money and it also costs him a minor operation, and then he has to say farewell to his family too. Because a *ger* who maintains relations with his family, that's not a full *ger;* that's a big error. There are cases like that, and they think they are perfect *geirim*. No; a *ger* has to say goodbye to his family. He has to turn his back on his relatives, even on his

---

*) **Q:** What do you think about the Sefardic custom in Brooklyn of not accepting converts?

A: The Sefardic custom of not accepting converts you must know, is a necessary and important *tikun* because a careless system has become the norm to accept anybody as a convert.

December 1985

father and his mother, and look only to Hakadosh Baruch Hu as his Father. Then, we accept him!

But we don't encourage it. That's not our business; we stand aloof. Hakadosh Baruch Hu is going to make us prosper only because of that. The Reformers, because their ranks are dwindling – their children are intermarried and are going lost – they went out on a big campaign; they embarked on a campaign to bring in converts. You already understand what kind of converts they have. They are converted by a piece of paper; the converts don't have to do anything.

Their purpose is to swell the ranks of the Reform Temple, but the end is extinction. They are headed to destruction. They won't last because of that – just because of that. It's only those Jews who are aloof from the nations of the world and don't encourage *geirim*, these are the ones who are going to persist – that's the Am Hashem.

April 1979

Dissuading Converts

Why is it that we always push away goyim from becoming geirim?

Q/ **Why is it that we always push away *goyim* from becoming *geirim?***

A/ The answer is, because we have been disillusioned too frequently. And that's because there are a lot of unsettled people who like to dabble in religion.

You know, if you would set up a *geirus* center in Harlem, you'd be mobbed. The truth is that even without a *geirus* center, they already have 'synagogues' and 'synagogues.'

Once, a man came to me from one of these places. He said he's a Jew, a Reverend So-and-So of a synagogue, but

Hagar was a gem; Hagar was a diamond.

he wants to convert properly. Well, his name sounded not Jewish to me – it sounded like one of the apostles – so I said, "What's the name of your synagogue?"

He said, "We are called The Church of the Holy Body."

So I saw that he had some way to go before he became a *ger.* We have to be careful. We have to be very careful, because once you get a fifth columnist in, there's a great deal of harm. They can cause plenty of harm.

But when somebody is sincere and persistent and goes through the process despite the difficulties, then not only do we not discourage him, we take active steps to be *mekarev* him.

May 1976

Genuine Geirim

Q/ I heard that the purpose of *galus* is to pick up *geirim* from the gentile nations. What do you say to that?

A/ The Gemara says in one place that, לֹא הִגְלָה הַקָּדוֹשׁ בָּרוּךְ יִשְׂרָאֵל לְבֵין הָאֻמּוֹת אֶלָּא כְּדֵי שֶׁיִּתּוֹסְפוּ עֲלֵיהֶם גֵּרִים – *Hakadosh Baruch Hu sent us among the nations in order that converts should join us* (*Pesachim* 87b). When there was a famine in the land (*Bereishis* 12:10) and Avraham Avinu was sent because of the famine to Eretz Mitzrayim, he came back with Hagar. Hagar was a gem; Hagar was a diamond.

When we went into Mitzrayim and then the *geulah* came in the days of Moshe Rabbeinu, גַּם עֵרֶב רַב עָלָה אִתָּם *– a great admixture of the best of the Egyptians came up with us.* When there was a famine in the days of the Shoftim, and Elimelech, the husband of Noami, took his family to Eretz

Moav; the purpose was to bring back Rus. And even when the Jews went through the *galus* of Poland, the purpose was to extricate Count Potocki from the gentile environment and make him a *ger tzedek*. לֹא הִגְלָה הַקָּדוֹשׁ בָּרוּךְ יִשְׂרָאֵל לְבֵין הָאֻמּוֹת אֶלָּא כְּדֵי שֶׁיִּתּוֹסְפוּ עֲלֵיהֶם גֵּרִים.

But does that mean that is the only purpose? And what about the Rema and what about the Gra and what about all the *kehillos hakodesh*? They were just *tafel,* what they accomplished in exile? They went into exile just to bring in Count Potocki?

The answer is that that is not the only purpose; it doesn't mean the only purpose was that *geirim* should be added to them. Hakadosh Baruch Hu has many purposes, but it means this purpose is one of them.

And so, as we wander among the nations, we pick up here and there some gems from the nations of the world who have become *geirim* and we appreciate them. Rabbi Akiva came from *geirim*. Shmaya and Avtalyon came from *geirim*. And therefore, that is one of the purposes of our wanderings in exile. But it is not the only purpose.

We appreciate them. Rabbi Akiva came from geirim. Shmaya and Avtalyon came from geirim.

August 1986

A Difficult Process

Q/ Chazal say (*Pesachim* 87b) that one of the purposes of *galus* is to cause *geirim*. So why do we discourage them when they want to join our nation?

A/ We are supposed to discourage *geirim* only for the purpose of ascertaining who the good *geirim* are. That's all. If you make it hard to become a *ger* until he persists, that's the test, and then we accept him.

There is no question that a ger is an achievement; a good ger is a big achievement.

If a *ger* had to take out 300 dollars from his pocket – at least it's something.

That's why I don't believe in a society to finance *geirim*. You shouldn't make it easy; it should be hard. Here comes a penniless person; his family has disowned him, he doesn't have a nickel and he wants to become a Jew. So we tell him the good news that it costs 300 dollars. He hits the ceiling! He is astounded!

When he comes to me, I tell him calmly – of course I never do the *geirus* – but I tell him that I know the process and it costs 300 dollars. He hits the ceiling! Okay, just let him subside.

He goes away. If he comes back again and he says, "Alright," then I know he means business.

Of course, it's only if he doesn't have a girlfriend. If he has a Jewish girlfriend somewhere and that's why he wants to become a *ger*, it may be worth 300 dollars to him. So we're not talking about that.

So it depends on the circumstances. But there is no question that a *ger* is an achievement; a good *ger* is a big achievement.

April 1975

Improper Intentions

Q/ If the initial intent for conversion is done for the sake of marriage and then the intent changes for the sake of wanting to become a Jew and it's done in the proper way, is it acceptable halachically?

A/ If somebody converts for the purpose of marriage without being sincere, it's accepted by *halachah* anyway.

If somebody converts for the purpose of marriage without being sincere, it's accepted by halachah anyway.

We can't do it; we wouldn't encourage or accept them but once it's done they are *geirim* anyhow. כֻּלָּן אַף עַל פִּי כֵן כֻּלָּן גֵּרִים – They're *geirim* anyhow (*Yevamos* 24b). If they went through *geirus* they're *geirim*. Only we don't like that kind of *ger*.

So therefore, if you ask halachically – halachically we don't accept unless it's sincere. For the purpose of a marriage, we don't accept. But if it was done, even though it was done improperly, meaning with *tevilah* or *milah*, whatever is necessary, but not with the right intentions, *b'dieved,* it's a *geirus*.

Now, if that *ger* will later become more sincere, certainly it's good. But that doesn't mean that the people who accepted him did right. It is wrong to accept a *ger* who converts for marriage or other ulterior motives.

December 1978

Born Again

Q/ Why do you insist that a *ger* brings along with him his baggage from when he was a gentile? Isn't it true that a גֵּר כְּקָטָן שֶׁנּוֹלַד דָּמֵי – *a convert is like a newborn baby*?

A/ No. When a gentile converts to Judaism, he's considered like a newborn person only for technical things; his relatives are no longer considered relatives to him and so on. It's only for technicalities. But there's

You can never expel all the impressions of your youth from your mind.

no question that he brings with him all of his traits and all of his habits.

Let's say a dope addict gentile becomes a *ger*; he still has to break the habit. It's a fact; he's an addict. It won't change just because he converted. Same thing, all his childhood impressions are still with him. Merely by becoming a *ger* – even a sincere *ger* – he's not changing his personality, you understand that.

And the *Kuzari* tells us that you can never expel all the impressions of your youth from your mind. It's a fact; it's there. And as my *rebbes* added, even in the next world you won't be able to get rid of those impressions. Of course, you have a right to differ with this *chiddush* of my *rebbes,* but surely in this world, your past baggage will not change merely by becoming even a *tzaddik*. Surely it won't change by becoming a *ger*.

January 1971

Loving Converts

Q/ Were the *geirim* from Egypt responsible for making the Golden Calf, and is that a sign of the trouble that converts might cause?

A/ The question is: Were the *geirim*, the *erev rav* who came from Egypt, the ones who were responsible for the golden calf?

Now, this we know from sources, from the sages, and the Rambam sums it up: "All the ten incidents in the *midbar* were caused by the *erev rav*." The Rambam states that. And so, wherever it states that the people did this or did that, we have to know that it was due to the influence of converts.

Now, converts are welcomed and converts are a liability. It's both. We love converts. There's a mitzvah to love *geirim* with a double love. First of all, there's a love that you have to love a Yisroel, and then there's a special love for converts. It's remarkable how some of our *gedolim* of today go out of their way to help and to show their love for converts. I can tell stories about that.

We love converts. There's a mitzvah to love geirim with a double love.

But we have to know that they are a liability too because they bring with them outside concepts that sometimes are difficult to contend with. But we can't help ourselves.

The same is also true about *baalei teshuvah* who come from the outside world. We must be patient with them. We want more and more *baalei teshuvah*, but there's no question that a *baal teshuvah* always brings in problems. Not only problems of observance, but problems of even being decent and being civilized. It takes a lot of patience to deal with them, but that's our job. We have to welcome them and bring in more and more, and be more and more patient.

June 1980

Marrying Converts

Q/ Based on what the Rav spoke about tonight, about how Avraham Avinu was careful to take a wife for Yitzchak only from his family and not from any of the converts he had made, would the Rav say that it's proper to avoid being *meshadech* with a *giyores?*

A/ Let me tell you something. To my knowledge, there have sometimes been cases of *giyoros* who have produced the best families of *talmidei chachamim*. Many fine, beautiful families began with a *giyores*.

Some-times, the best shidduch will be the giyores who has chosen out of her own free will to join our People.

Only that Avraham Avinu, at that time, was concerned with the future of a nation that didn't even exist yet. He was creating a new nation. And therefore, it was imperative that he choose the best mother possible to be the mother of that entire nation.

But today, the nation exists already. The Am Yisroel already exists, and therefore it's different. Rus is the model of a *giyores* that produced one of the best. If not for Rus, you wouldn't have Tehillim and you wouldn't have the Beis Hamikdash. It was Dovid Hamelech who was the one who made the plans for the Beis Hamikdash. And if not for Rus, you wouldn't have Shlomo and you wouldn't have *Mishlei*.

So many of the wonders of our nation – *Mishlei, Koheles, Tehillim, Shir Hashirim,* are all because of a *giyores*. And many other achievements as well.

So today, there's no problem with marrying a *giyores*. And many times you'll find that she was one of the best. The very best!

However, if all things are equal and there are plenty of other choices and you can marry a girl who comes directly from Avraham Avinu, then naturally, that's first. That's the first choice. But sometimes, the best *shidduch* will be the *giyores* who has chosen out of her own free will to join our People. And you'll be successful raising a fine family with a wife who is a *giyores*.

November 1998

Descendants of Amalek

Q/ Why was the Amaleiki nation worthy of having *geirim* as their descendants? The Gemara says that the

descendants of Haman converted and learned in the yeshivos.

Every human being is capable of endless greatness.

A/ The answer is that Hakadosh Baruch Hu wants to demonstrate the inherent greatness in human beings. מַיִם עֲמֻקִּים עֵצָה בְלֶב אִישׁ – *There are deep waters of counsel and wisdom in every man's heart* (*Mishlei* 20:5). Every human being is capable of endless greatness. When Hakadosh Baruch Hu breathed into humans His breath, the breath of life, the soul, He breathed from Himself. Which means that endless nobility and wisdom were breathed into the human breast by Hashem. It's waiting there. It's waiting to be drawn out.

And even Haman, had he become a *baal teshuvah,* a *ger,* he could have become a *rosh yeshiva.* Imagine! Haman becoming a *rosh yeshiva.* He could have become a *tzaddik hador.* Everybody, up to a certain stage, has free will. Haman probably was deprived of his free will after he passed a certain point, but his grandchildren, his great-grandchildren, weren't deprived.

Now, had our nation been able to fulfill the command of מָחֹה תִמְחֶה, to wipe out the Amalekim, then nobody would have remained to become *geirei tzedek.* And that would have been alright too; Hakadosh Baruch Hu gave that sentence that they should wipe them out. But since they didn't do so, those who survived still had a chance.

Same thing with the Germans. I don't like the German people at all and I believe they are deserving of a very great punishment, Hakadosh Baruch Hu should wipe them out, just like the descendants of Amalek for what they did to our people.

And nevertheless, if a German becomes a *ger tzedek* and he is *misnaheg,* he acts, according to the Torah, we have the greatest respect for him. And he could become a *gadol b'Torah.* I know such a case. A son of a German *ger* who

I know such a case. A son of a German ger who was a tzaddik gamur.

was a *tzaddik gamur.* Because every man possesses endless greatness within his capabilities.

June 1982

Chosen Souls

Q/ How is it that Moshe, the greatest man who ever lived, married a Midyanite woman, the daughter of Yisro?

A/ You must understand, number one, a very great principle; that Hakadosh Baruch Hu is most interested in a person's character. רַחֲמָנָא לִבָּא בָּעֵי – *Hashem wants the heart* (*Sanhedrin* 106b). And Yisro was a most remarkable man with a remarkable heart. He was a man who made a break with his past. Yisro was a priest of idolatry, and he was enthusiastic about it too. שֶׁפִּטֵּם עֲגָלִים לַעֲבוֹדָה זָרָה – *He used to fatten the calves for the idols* (*Rashi*, *Yisro* 25:1). When he had a 'mitzvah' of offering a calf, he refused to bring it right away; instead he spent time fattening it so that it should be a *'mitzvah min hamuvchar.'* He was an enthusiastic idolater.

And when this man finally discovered the truth, he became an enemy of idolatry. He became enthusiastic about fighting idolatry. And because of that, he was ostracized by his people. He was in danger. Nobody would even help him. And the *midrash* tells us that because of that, his daughters had to go out and tend his sheep. And they were persecuted until Moshe came and he rescued the daughters from the persecutors. So we see that Yisro was a man who suffered for his principles.

Now, when a man demonstrates greatness of soul, we don't care what nation he's from. And therefore, Tzipora was certainly a fit wife for this great man, Moshe Rabbeinu. Because he too was able to ignore his environment. He was born in a palace and he had all privileges, and yet, he forsook it to go out to help his downtrodden brothers. And so, there's no question that this was a perfect match, and there's nothing to criticize in the *shidduch* of Moshe Rabbeinu.

Rus became great because she forsook her nation and joined ours.

Now, why did it turn out just like this? It could be it was the *hashgacha* of Hashem, that He wanted to teach this great lesson that the nations of the world can attain greatness if they're willing to overstep the boundary between them and us.

And that's what happened to great people in every generation. Rus became great because she forsook her nation and joined ours. And if you look further, you find that Shmaya v'Avtalyon, the great teachers of our people, also came from converts. And if you look further, you find that even Rabbi Akiva is descended from converts. Rabbi Akiva was the main teacher of our people in the period of the Tana'im. From the times of the Beis Hamikdash until the *milchemes Beitar,* all that we have came through his mouth. And he was the son of converts.

You see this with Onkelus Hager too. He made *Targum Onkelus*, and his work is in the Chumash. It's even printed in the Chumash above *Rashi Hakadosh*, right next to the Torah itself.

And therefore, that's a great principle, that the doors are open for the chosen souls of the nations of the world. And therefore, when you look at this inspiring story that Tzipora, a *giyores*, was married to Moshe Rabbeinu, that's a tremendous lesson for the world. The door to greatness is open for everyone.

March 1983

A tremendous lesson for the world. The door to greatness is open for everyone.

Superior Souls

Is the Jewish soul superior to the non-Jewish soul?

The answer is, absolutely. No question about it.

Now, even if a non-Jew becomes converted to Judaism and he is accepted as one of the whole Klal Yisroel, nevertheless, there remains a difference. I would like to grant him everything because he deserves credit, but there remains a difference.

Like the *Kuzari* (1:25–43) says, he can be accepted among us, but he remains a little bit less than us. It doesn't mean he can't become very great, but there is something in the Am Yisroel that causes the Shechinah to rest on them, לִהְיוֹת לְךָ לֵאלקִים וּלְזַרְעֲךָ אַחֲרֶיךָ – *to be Elokim to you and your seed after you* (*Bereishis* 17:7). And seed means only those who are born of the *zera* of the Avos. So the Shechinah rests only on the *zera ha'Avos.*

So can a *goy* become as great as a Jew? A *goy* can never become the best. Even if he becomes a *ger,* a *ger* is never on the same degree as the *zera Avraham,* the seed of Avraham. That's what all the Rishonim say. Although *geirim* are certainly privileged and beloved; וַאֲהַבְתֶּם אֶת הַגֵּר – there's a special commandment to love the convert, but no, he cannot be equal to a Jew who has the same perfection.

March 1977

The Greatest Soul

If a person becomes a ger, is converted voluntarily, is he better than somebody who is born into Judaism?

Q/ According to what the Rav said tonight about the greatness of going beyond the line of duty, it sounds like if somebody is a *ger* and is *mekabel* the Torah of his own will, it would be better than somebody who is born a Jew?

A/ Question: If a person becomes a *ger*, is converted voluntarily, is he better than somebody who is born into Judaism?

And the answer is as follows. All of us live by the merit, the *zechus,* of Avraham. Avraham was the great *ger;* he was the first one. And he had the most difficulty. Nobody ever encountered as much difficulty in being loyal to Hashem. וּמָצָאתָ אֶת לְבָבוֹ נֶאֱמָן לְפָנֶיךָ – Only Avraham's heart was found loyal (*Nechemiyah* 9:8). He had the most loyalty of all hearts. So Avraham was the *ger* par excellence. He's called *ger tzedek*, par excellence.

So Hakadosh Baruch Hu said, "I swear to you that because you are such a good *ger* and you did it voluntarily – you weren't born into it; you were born into a house of Terach, of idolaters. And you fought against your family's idolatry. You're the real *ger*. So all of your children are going to have the merit of being real *geirim*. I give them the merit of you."

Avraham's *zechus* is so much that it's enough for his children afterwards.

So now any other person who comes – let's say a man comes from Yefes or from Cham and he wants to become a Jew – we accept him and it's a *zechus*, but he doesn't have the *zechus* of that great *ger* Avraham Avinu. We have the *zechus* of that *geirus*. That's what Hakadosh Baruch Hu promised forever.

And therefore, no matter how great it is for an individual to become a *ger*, he can never overshadow the greatness of our *geirus* because we are sharing in the merit of Avraham's free will when he became a *ger*. Think that over.

June 1983

Adopting Foreigners

Q/ Is it permitted to adopt a non-Jewish child from Asia or Japan?

A/ And from Sweden? And from America? Should you adopt a gentile child from any country? That's the question.

And the answer is no. What do you need it for? It's a mitzvah to take Swedes into your home?! Since when is it a mitzvah to bring gentiles in?

If a gentile becomes inspired, he becomes a man of spirit, so when people of spirit come to us, we're more than happy to welcome them. Certainly. It's a glorious thing. But we're not going to kidnap little gentiles and make them into Jews without asking them. What kind of mitzvah is that?

We're not going to kidnap little gentiles and make them into Jews without asking them. What kind of mitzvah is that?

I'll tell you stories and stories that I know of from personal experience, people eating the bitter bread of disappointment. They took into their homes gentile girls and they raised them as Jews. They made *tevilah* or whatever was needed and raised them as Jews. Subsequently, the girls discovered that they're not of Jewish parentage, and so, in today's climate you understand what that means, they chose not to follow Jewish ways.

And now you have a frum father and mother with a big girl who is not keeping Shabbos. In the house she obliges, at least, but outside, she does what she wants and they are eating their hearts out. Sooner or later, they'll have to get rid of her. This story happens again and again, and it serves them right for doing such a stupid thing.

Aren't there plenty of gentiles in the world, even more than Jews?

When you adopt, you must know whom you're adopting, even a Jewish child. It may be a *mamzer.* It's a child that's not fit to marry into the Jewish people. If it's a child that a girl had from her brother, that's a *mamzer.* He can't marry into the Jewish people. If it's a child who a married woman had by adultery and therefore she gave him away for adoption – you can't adopt such a child. What to do with it? Let others worry about it. You'll take her and put her into the Bais Yaakov school and then that child will grow up to be a frum girl and then someday the secret might be out. She might be a mother already or a grandmother, and tragedy of tragedies. You're ruining families. And therefore, adoption must be done only with consultation and great deliberation.

July 1982

Wasted Adoptions

Q/ Why have you said that it's not right for Jews to adopt and to raise non-Jewish children who have no homes? Isn't it a *kiddush Hashem?*

A/ The answer is, it's stupidity. Let me explain something to you. What mitzvah is it for a Jew to raise up gentile boys? You mean to say that the gentiles don't have institutions for them? Aren't there plenty of gentiles in the world, even more than Jews? Aren't there gentile millionaires who have plenty of money for that purpose? Aren't there so many Jewish institutions that need your dollars, and you're wasting your money on these children – money that these children can get without you?

So here's a fool. This fool, he takes two or three children from *goyim;* he adopts them and he works like a horse all his life to support them. And what happens eventually? They become delinquents. One is a dope addict, a tramp; and the father weeps his eyes out for his son, who is going on the '*derech hayashar.*'

And here's a yeshiva man who had no children, so he adopted two gentile girls. The older one, when she was eighteen, discovered that she's a gentile, so she threw everything away. She still lives in the house because her stepmother loves her too much to let her go, to let her darling go.

So these *shotim* are spending their money, and when they die, these adopted children are going to inherit all their money. Instead of their money going to yeshivos, where they might get a little Olam Haba for all the labor that their wasted lives were spent on, instead all their money goes out of the family. It's a wasted life, a ruined life.

when they die, these adopted children are going to inherit all their money.

February 1984

Complete Separation

Q/ The Rav said tonight that for a *ger tzedek,* a convert, to succeed at being a servant of Hashem, he must disentangle himself completely from his former family and lifestyle. But how can you really expect that from a convert, if even Chazal tell us that a convert and his descendants are naturally sensitive to remarks about their previous lifestyle

and family ties for as much as ten generations (*Sanhedrin* 94a)?

A/ Look, if a *ger* has a sensitivity, if he has feelings for his former life, his former family, up until a certain amount of generations, it doesn't mean we are going to praise him for that. No, not at all. Look, it's a natural thing. But it's nothing to be proud of. The truth is, the less sensitivity that he has for them, the better off he is.

Separation from his life as a gentile is of utmost importance.

That's going to be one aspect in the service of Hashem that the *ger* will have to make progress in. Separation from his life as a gentile is of utmost importance. That's actually a criterion for the genuineness of his *geirus.* If a *ger* is sharply sensitive about remarks, then he's still far away from us. Joining the Jewish People means distancing yourself from your gentile family and gentile lifestyle. There's no way around that. It can't be any other way.

July 1999

Polite Separation

Q/ **Does a convert still have the duty of respecting his parents?**

A/ And the answer is, he has no parents. A *ger* has no parents. However, it's recommended that he should be respectful to everyone, because even if you're disrespectful to a horse – let's say you're mean and vicious to your horse – it will turn out that you're vicious to other people too.

Like the *Chovos Halevavos* says, you shouldn't talk *lashon hara* even about a dead carcass in the street. The *Chovos Halevavos* says that a wise man was walking with his student,

So the wise man said, "Why don't you say, 'How white her teeth are?'"

and the student, when he saw a dead cow in the street, said, "How foul this carcass is!" So the wise man said, "Why don't you say, 'How white her teeth are?'"

Because when you're accustomed to belittling and accusing everybody, you'll do it to your fellow Jews too. So be nice to *goyim* too. Practice being nice to gentiles and it will help you be nice to Jews. Anybody who is mean to gentiles, you should know, will be mean to Jews too.

June 1992

QUESTIONS *On Any* SUBJECT

Chapter 2

Lost Jews

Leilui nishmat

David ben Reina

Hilda Yafa bat Yamile

Aharon ben Jamile

Contents

Chapter 2

Lost Jews

Who is a Jew? 1

Q/ Does a person have a right to call himself a Jew if he's an atheist and doesn't practice Judaism at all?

A/ We'll approach this question in two different senses. In a certain sense, worse than an idolater; the Rambam says that an *oved avodah zarah*, an idol worshiper, is better than an atheist (*Rambam*, *Maamar Kiddush Hashem*). So this Jew doesn't deserve anything. He doesn't deserve to live even.

I'm not talking now about the question of *tinok shenishbah l'bein ha'akum*, when somebody is not to blame. But the truth is that if he's an atheist, even though he's *nebach* an atheist, he's still an atheist. It makes no difference why he's an atheist. If a person is a criminal, an adulterer, so even though it's not his fault, he never learned otherwise, he's still an adulterer. He's still a wicked man.

However, יִשְׂרָאֵל אַף עַל פִּי שֶׁחָטָא יִשְׂרָאֵל הוּא – *A Jew who sins is still a Jew* (*Sanhedrin* 44a). So if this wicked man had a child from a Jewish woman, the child is a Jew with a Jewish father. The child can become a *tzaddik;* he can become a *gadol*, a *rosh yeshiva*. It can happen.

To be a part of the Am Yisroel means that you behave like the nation of Hashem is expected to behave.

So therefore, technically, he's a Jew, but spiritually, he's worse than a *goy*. You have to understand it in two different senses. יִשְׂרָאֵל אַף עַל פִּי שֶׁחָטָא יִשְׂרָאֵל הוּא means only in the sense that he technically is a Jew; but if he's a very big *chotei*, then he loses his right even to exist.

May 1990

Who is a Jew? 2

Q/ Do the references to the Am Yisroel in Tanach, which speak about their uniqueness in the world, refer only to observant Jews or to all Jews?

A/ The answer is that it refers to the Am Yisroel. The Am Yisroel, however, is a specific term. It's not a general term for all of the people who are technically Jews. The Gemara says that Am Yisroel means עוֹשֶׂה מַעֲשֵׂה עַמְּךָ – those Jews who behave like the Am Yisroel behaves. To be a part of the Am Yisroel means that you behave like the nation of Hashem is expected to behave.

Like Rabbeinu Saadya Gaon said: אֵין אֻמָּתֵנוּ אֻמָּה אֶלָּא בְּתוֹרָה – *We are bound together as a nation only by the Torah* (*Sefer Emunos V'deios* 3:7). And when Moshe Rabbeinu wrote the Torah and he handed it to the people, he said: "הַיּוֹם הַזֶּה נִהְיֵיתָ לְעָם – *Today you became a people*" (*Devarim* 27:9). Which means, without the Torah, we're not a people. So those Jews who are outside the Torah are not included in the Am Yisroel.

Now, it doesn't mean they're not a Yisroel. יִשְׂרָאֵל אַף עַל פִּי שֶׁחָטָא יִשְׂרָאֵל הוּא – *A Jew who sins is still a Jew* (*Sanhedrin* 44a), which means that he still remains responsible to fulfill everything and he'll be punished for everything that he disregards. And also, if he repents he's still a Jew. Or if, let's say, an irreligious couple have a daughter and the daughter is a frum girl, so she's a *kosher bas Yisroel*, because her parents are Yisroel. אַף עַל פִּי שֶׁחָטָא יִשְׂרָאֵל הוּא. But they don't belong to the Am Yisroel unless they behave like a Yisroel. To be included in the Am Yisroel, a person has to be together with the Am Yisroel in keeping the Torah, and there are no two ways about that.

January 1978

It's a fundamental error. You cannot be good without Torah.

Good Lost Jews?

Q/ What do you say to a nonreligious Jew who says, "What do I need religion for? It's enough to be a good person."

A/ Let me tell you. I go in the streets every day and I watch the people at the fruit stores, the customers. They stop and they eat cherries; just to taste them and they don't buy them. They pick grapes; they eat them and don't buy them. They pick peanuts and eat them and don't buy them. Apricots! They taste them, eat them, and don't buy them.

So the whole world is a world of crooks. The irreligious are *mamash ganavim*. You have to learn that to take a fruit – a peanut today costs a penny – is *gezel*. Without learning Torah, without *yiras Shamayim*, you will never know how to be a decent person. It's a fundamental error. You cannot be good without Torah. You do harm to your fellow man all the time.

And therefore, you have to learn *Bava Kama* to know not to damage other people's property. You have to learn *Bava Metzia* to learn that if you find something you have to return it. All kinds of *bein adam l'chaveiro* have to be learned.

You have to take a little boy and start teaching him to have respect for other people's money.

Ona'as devarim. *Dinim* of *nezikin*. And that you can never know.

And that's why it's so good when they start teaching little boys *Bava Kama*. Once a man complained: "My little son," he said, "they're making a lawyer out of him in the yeshiva. In *Bava Kama* they're teaching him laws."

I said – it's not my own – I said to him what an *adam gadol* once said. "You have to take a little boy and start teaching him to have respect for other people's money. If you don't teach him when he's little, he'll never learn. So start with the little boys *dinei mamanus*. They'll learn how to respect other people's money. You have to start as early as possible because later in life, people who didn't learn Torah and start learning later in life, will find it difficult to think about that."

A man once walked into our *shul*, a *baal teshuvah* boy, he wanted to open the window so he pushed his hand against the glass and he pushed out the pane. He broke the pane. So I told him, "You have to pay for it." It was a big *chiddush* to him. "I have to pay? It was an accident." A man is *chayav* even *b'shogeg* if he was *mazik*. But he never learned that. "I didn't mean any harm," he thinks.

So he did me a favor and he said he'll give me some money. I said, "Don't give me money. I have to go get a glazier now? I can't find a glazier. Maybe you should do it yourself." So he had to go find a glazier to put in the pane because he broke it.

And therefore when you don't learn, nothing means anything to you in *dinei mamanus*. You'll always have excuses. There is no such thing as being good without Torah.

January 1996

Great Lost Jews

An irreligious Jew has concealed in the depth of his nature all the good qualities of the Jewish people

Q/ You speak here often about recognizing the greatness and the holiness of the observant Jews. What about the irreligious Jews?

A/ When we speak about irreligious Jews, we must speak about the *potential* that they possess. Today he may be hostile to you but you might be surprised; someday he might turn out to be a *tzaddik*.

I'll tell you some incidents from my experience. There was a boy that I considered a bum when he was in the yeshiva. He was sixteen years old and he was critical of *talmidei chachamim*. He was *chutzpadik*. I lost any connection with him. Years passed by. And then when I met him again he had a black hat and a beard. And he was a good learner. It amazed me! I saw what could happen to a bad boy. He became such a fine *talmid chacham*. You can never know.

An irreligious Jew has concealed in the depth of his nature all the good qualities of the Jewish people; only there's a sediment on top – *goyishe* ways, wrong ideas. But there's no question that given the right environment, the right influence, he could develop.

I'll tell you even more. You'd be surprised but there are plenty of *goyim* who can develop into nice frum *tzaddikim*. And it happened already! There are gentiles who became Jews and became heroes for Judaism! Some gave their lives for the Torah! Yes! Count Potocki, a Polish count, became a Jew in secret. And then the gentiles discovered him and the church had him burned at the stake. He refused to recant. He died a frum Jew. Count Potocki, yes. Also Lord Gordon in England. Lord Gordon was a frum Jew, a *ger*, converted. Certainly! You can never tell. Everybody has certain qualities within him.

The Jew certainly is a goldmine of good qualities. And it's a tragedy when he wastes his life and doesn't bring all of the greatness which he possesses to the surface.

Of course, *l'havdil*, the Jew certainly is a goldmine of good qualities. And it's a tragedy when he wastes his life and doesn't bring all of the greatness which he possesses to the surface.

July 1992

Distant Jews 1

Q/ Doesn't Hashem also go with the non-frum Jews? יִשְׂרָאֵל אַף עַל פִּי שֶׁחָטָא יִשְׂרָאֵל הוּא – *Even though he sinned, he's still a Yisroel?*

A/ And the answer is, absolutely not. כִּי הִנֵּה רְחֵקֶיךָ יֹאבֵדוּ – *Those who are far away from You, go lost* (*Tehillim* 73:27).

Who are those who are far away? Those who don't think about Hashem, they are far away from Him. And Hashem is not with them.

He's a Yisroel? That means he has the same potential as a Yisroel. Let's say somebody is about to be born. He's not a Yisroel yet. You can't count him with a *minyan;* he's not born yet.

So this person also, he's also a potential Yisroel. If he does *teshuvah* then he's a Yisroel. But otherwise, the Shechinah does not rest on *resha'im* at all. If ten *resha'im* come together, the Shechinah is not there.

And therefore, don't make any mistake about it, Hashem is close לְעַם קְרוֹבוֹ, to the people who are close to Him (ibid. 148:14); only to the *shomrei Torah.* And when you see one of the *shomrei Torah* you should know that the Shechinah is walking with him.

July 1994

Distant Jews 2

If "All Yisroel have a share in the World to Come", how could some be shut out from the World to Come?

Q/ If כָּל יִשְׂרָאֵל יֵשׁ לָהֶם חֵלֶק לְעוֹלָם הַבָּא – *All Yisroel have a share in the World to Come*, how could some be shut out from the World to Come?

A/ And the answer is, it's like a yeshiva that's making a Chanukah party. So they give each *talmid* a ticket for himself and for his family too.

And so when he comes home he tells them, "We're going to a Chanukah party next Sunday and here are tickets!"

Then after a while, he gets into a fight with his younger brother and out of spite, he tears up all the tickets! And now the family remains home next Sunday.

And so, you have to keep hold of your tickets. If a Jew loses the ticket, if he stops saying *Krias Shema Shacharis v'Arvis* or wearing tefillin or keeping Shabbos or *taharas hamishpacha*, or all the other things – they're all tickets that we must hold onto – he's going to lose his admission to what he was rightfully entitled to have.

December 1978

Distant Jews 3

Q/ Is there any hope that the Jews who do *aveiros* constantly because they're completely lost from us, that they will be *zocheh* to Olam Haba?

A/ Now you cannot ask such a question wholesale. Every person is a story by himself.

Why is it that you see so many of the youth who are attracted to Far Eastern religions?

Did he have an opportunity to learn and neglected it?

Did he come from a family against which he rebelled and he refused to be trained in the proper way?

It depends. Very many people, you should know, had access to Torah instruction and so, it's not an excuse.

Why is it that you see so many of the youth who are attracted to Far Eastern religions? Why is it that when you see the Moonies and you'll hear the names of some of their executives, they're Jewish names? Or Jews for Yoshke. Why are there Jews interested in such things? Why didn't they turn first to their own people?

Now, these people are not going to be excused at all. If you're looking for something, what about us? After all, we're an old established business. Judaism is an old firm; we're not newcomers. Give us a chance too. If you turn your back on us and you go to queer outlandish things, it shows there's something rotten here. That's a character of disloyalty. Loyalty is an inborn quality. Why don't you love your own people first?

I told you a story. I was standing on a corner on Kings Highway and two Moonies were standing and trying to attract people. So two gentile boys, you could see they were gentile boys, Irishmen, walked by. They said to the Moonies, "We have our own religion."

That's the way to talk. They're loyal to their religion.

So why is it that there are so many Devoras and Friedmans and Rubins now in the Moonies' clasps, in the Moonies' claws? The answer is, it's disloyalty. And disloyalty is not an excuse.

A young man who comes here sometimes told me that for some time he was in the Buddhist monastery in Los Angeles before he did *teshuvah*. In a Buddhist monastery. And he used to come late to *'tefillas Shacharis'* in the monastery so the chief Buddhist, the '*rosh yeshiva*,' called him and asked him. He was a Jew, the chief Buddhist. And he asked him why he comes late to 'davening.'

In the end, he was expelled because he didn't keep all the '*dinim*' of the monastery. He became a *baal teshuvah.*

So I asked him, "What's the matter with you? How did you come to do such a thing? You lived in Boro Park. You went from Boro Park to a Los Angeles monastery? You're crazy?"

You lived in Boro Park. You went from Boro Park to a Los Angeles mon-astery? You're crazy?

He said that to him, Judaism was nothing at all.

Isn't that a tragedy? So therefore, I can't be *melamed zechus* on him at all.

It could be that people who had no opportunities at all and their parents were no good either, it could be that Hakadosh Baruch Hu will have pity on them and won't send them to Gehinom.

Now, they can't go to Gan Eden. For Gan Eden you have to have some positive achievements. Even if He'll forgive their sins – I don't know if He would forgive their sins because some of the sins are inexcusable. Even a good *goy* wouldn't do some of the sins that they do – immorality of the worst kind. Even a good gentile wouldn't do such things. So I don't know if Hakadosh Baruch Hu will excuse him.

But even if you could excuse him and he'll be excused from Gehinom, who says he's worthy of Gan Eden? I don't know what to say about that. I'll leave it to Hakadosh Baruch Hu, but I'm quite pessimistic.

And therefore, when we want to view this subject in general, we'll be frustrated because every person is a problem by himself and it's וְלוֹ נִתְכְּנוּ עֲלִילוֹת – *all of a person's deeds are weighed by Hashem* (*Shmuel I* 2:3). He's the only One capable of weighing them.

October 1987

Now, if you wish to do something, subscribe to Orthodox newspapers and magazines for him

Distant Jews 4

Q/ **A *tinok shenishbah* – who is in that category?**

A/ Now, that's a question I don't want to discuss because *tinok shenishbah* is not a clear-cut concept. There are many people who could have become loyal Jews, but they chose not to. But exactly to know who yes and who not, I'm not capable of telling you.

But we know the general rule is this: If a person is a *tinok shenishbah* and he is an *apikores,* we follow Reb Chaim Brisker, *zichrono livracha,* who says, "*Nebach an apikores is fort an apikores.*" If he doesn't believe in Hashem, then he doesn't belong to us at all. If he believes in Hashem only he doesn't know exactly what to do, that's something else.

August 1993

Respect From a Distance

Q/ **How do you deal with a close relative who is an *apikores,* and yet, he acts respectful to his Orthodox relatives?**

A/ First of all, have nothing to do with him. הַרְחֵק מִשָּׁכֵן רָע – Keep away from relatives who are *apikorsim* because your association with them is not going to do you any good.

Now, if you wish to do something, subscribe to Orthodox newspapers and magazines for him; that way, every week the mailman will be bringing propaganda to him.

All kinds of Orthodox Jewish newspapers or periodicals you can send him. Send him books too. Let him read. Maybe, in the course of time, it'll have some influence.

Let him cut you off. You're lucky if he does.

But you and your family should not be identified *at all* with irreligious relatives; it is important that they should not come into your home and that your family should not visit them. The mere knowledge that there are irreligious relatives in the background is already not healthy.

November 1988

Breaking Off 1

Q/ **If a close relative threatens to cut off relations with me if I don't attend a Reform *bas mitzvah* on Shabbos, what shall I do?**

Let him cut you off. You're lucky if he does.

October 1993

Breaking Off 2

Q/ **If a Jew *chalilah* marries a gentile, how do we react to such a person?**

A/ We react like the person doesn't exist. We have nothing to do with that person at all, and if you pass him on the street, he's a zombie, he's a ghost, he's a dead man. You don't see him.

That always was the system of Jews and it should remain the system forever.

And you don't see his mother and his father either. If the mother and father maintain relations with him, if he takes his *shiksa* and visits his parents, then you forget about his parents. You don't know them.

Anybody who harbors these people, who has personal relations with them, you should have nothing to do with them. That always was the system of Jews and it should remain the system forever.

A woman once told me, a pious woman, that her mother lives with a *goy*, somewhere in the South. So I said, "Then you don't have any mother."

She gasped on the telephone. There was silence.

I said, "That's it. You don't have any mother. A mother who lives with a *goy* is not your mother. You should never call her or write to her or even recognize that she's alive."

A man told me that his father ran away with a gentile woman. So forget about him. He's not your father. You never knew him.

That's our reaction to them. And there shouldn't be any weakness in this. You choose Hakadosh Baruch Hu or you choose the other one.

September 1976

Breaking Off 3

Q/ If a person has a friend who is engaged to be married to a *shiksa,* is it worth it to try to push him to break it off even if it means the friction I cause might mean me losing that friend?

A/ If a person can be separated from a gentile union, is it worth exerting efforts to do it?

By all means! No question about it! You're saving his life!

October 1993

Dodging Obligations

Should you attend a wedding of a close relative where they serve oysters?

Q/ **Should someone attend a wedding of a close relative where there's mixed dancing?**

A/ Now this question we can rephrase. Should you attend a wedding of a close relative where they serve oysters?

Now, mixed dancing is worse than oysters. Oysters, if somebody points a gun at your head and says, "Eat these oysters," then eat oysters to save your life. If he points a gun at your head and says, "Dance with that girl over there," tell him to shoot. Or take the gun away from him and shoot him. It's יֵהָרֵג וְאַל יַעֲבֹר! Immorality – a man should give his life rather than commit immoral things.

The question is what to do if you're invited and you don't want to lose that relative. So here's what you do. First of all, you have to try to be away. Even if you have to go to Eretz Yisroel at that time, it pays. What does it cost, $500? If you can afford it, do it. If not, go to Chicago. That's a pretty good excuse.

In case you can't go anywhere else, come into the lobby, and come early and be conspicuous so when your relative comes into the lobby, he should see you loafing there all the time. And when the dancing begins, quietly slip out and go

How should we react to the news that the Pope made a Jewish nun a saint?

home. And if they say “Why didn't you come?” you say “I was there!”

“Why didn't you sit down and eat?”

“I had stomach trouble. I had to go home.”

April 1985

Lost Nuns

Q/ How should we react to the news that the Pope made a Jewish nun a saint?

A/ What the Pope does is none of our business. Only it’s a great pity on a Jewish soul that went lost. That’s all.

The saint is now in Gehinom and is getting the treatment that all the *poshei Yisroel* get. Because we say, “You wanted to be a saint? So why weren’t you a frum Jewish woman? You had to forsake your people?”

And therefore, the whole subject is alien to our minds. It’s one more soul that went lost.

So just because she’s a Catholic saint, what of it to us? And suppose she was a drug addict in a cellar, drugged with narcotics, is she any better off to us? And therefore, it’s a pity on all of them.

May 1987

Lost Cultists

"You wanted to be a saint? So why weren't you a frum Jewish woman?"

Q/ What can you do for a man who joins a cult, and now he's trying to take other people with him into the cult?

A/ A person who becomes a *meisis u'meidiach,* who tries to persuade Jewish children to leave their faith, the first thing is, we should pray to Hakadosh Baruch Hu that he should get killed. You should pray to Hashem that he should die as soon as possible.

Q/ I was told by one rabbi that I could cut off his tongue and cut off his right hand so he couldn't speak and he couldn't write. What do you think about that, Rabbi?

A/ I don't know what you can do to him right now. Legally, I can't tell you anything.

March 1999

Lost Forever 1

Q/ In today's generation, will everyone merit the Geulah when Mashiach comes? I mean, will it be like Mitzrayim where some were left behind, or will today be different?

A/ Absolutely not! No, it won't be different. In order to be *zocheh* to the Geulah, you have to want the Geulah. If people are facing Hawaii, if they're facing far away, then Hashem says, "Stay there." Now, it

When the time will come, it'll be too late then.

could be that the people who were born in Hawaii, they don't know, they're *tinokos shenishbah,* so מְקַבֵּץ נִדְחֵי עַמּוֹ – *Hakadosh Baruch Hu will gather them together.* He'll gather them together. But those who are trying to get lost will succeed in getting lost.

And therefore, it's so important to make sure that you get found without waiting until it's too late. When the time will come, it'll be too late then. Just like in Mitzrayim; when they went out of Mitzrayim, those who had to remain behind said, "I changed my mind. I want to go out." Ha, nothing doing. You missed the boat. They missed the boat. When the time comes to go out, you have to be ready for the call. You have to be prepared.

April 1997

Lost Forever 2

Q/ How can we explain that up until recent times, the Jewish nation was always the Torah nation, whereas today the percentage of Torah Jews is so much smaller?

A/ How can we explain the decline in Torah loyalty among the Jewish people today?

Now, a simple overall reason we immediately can say, and that's the advent of tolerance and emancipation. The Jewish nation thrives on persecution. But when the sun of equal rights began to shine upon our people, then they began to yield their principles.

And it's a *mashal;* it's compared to a certain fable that the sun and the wind once had a wager if they could make a man take off his coat. So the wind said, "I'll try." And the wind began to blow with violence. It became cold and the man buttoned up his coat even more tightly and he refused to let the coat be blown off of his shoulders.

Now the sun said, "You failed. I'll take over," and the sun began to shine. It became very hot and the man began to unbutton his coat, one button after the other. And finally, he took off his coat entirely.

And so, in the olden days when they persecuted the Jews, the Jew became even more loyal as a result of *tzaros*. The more they attempted to force him to give up his Judaism, the stronger he clung to it.

But when the time came for tolerance – it was about 1750 and onward – all over Europe the winds of the Renaissance began blowing more strongly; intellectualism began rising, the Church began losing its power, and there grew up a class of intellectuals. And the spirit of tolerance began to spread; one government after another gave edicts of emancipation to the Jews, and so the Jewish backbone began softening and rotting away. And that's the general reason why we have the situation today. The Jew thrives on *tzaros*.

If it's possible for a Jew to utilize emanci-pation, it's a glorious oppor-tunity to have freedom.

If it's possible for a Jew to utilize emancipation, it's a glorious opportunity to have freedom. You can build more Torah. You can accomplish more perfection in *avodas Hashem*. That's the very greatest of achievements. And that's why the Orthodoxy of today is the most successful, the most praiseworthy. In spite of all the opportunities to go out and mix among the gentiles, we still have *frumme* people who are really frum, men and women who are idealists.

Today, we're lucky to be alive! We're passing the test that the old generations didn't have. Despite all the opportunities and all the blandishments that are trying to lure us away, still, we have staunch frum men and women, boys and girls. That's our pride!

Today, we're lucky to be alive! We're passing the test that the old generations didn't have.

But not enough. Every nation has a lot of weaklings and hangers-on. Yet even these weaklings and hangers-on became strong when the storm winds of persecution were blowing. Even the most uneducated, even the most coarse, the most brutal kind of a Jew used to give his life in stubborn obstinacy and opposition to those who tried to force him to bow down to idols and to kiss the cross.

But when the sun of tolerance began to shine, then the lower elements yielded. We're left today only with the intellectuals, the smartest and the best people.

However, that's a general picture. If time would permit, we could see much more in this, but right now that'll suffice. And it'll teach us that what's going to happen is going to be a reversal of history. The sun of tolerance is going to grow dim all over the world. We're going to go back again to an era of intolerance. Things won't remain this way.

And Hakadosh Baruch Hu is going to bring His people in their entirety back to Torah. They'll be forced back into it. Of course, the lucky ones are the ones who are doing it today without being forced, but eventually all Jews will be forced back.

What happened in Russia is just a picture. In Russia, the Jews were given an acid test and they yielded. The worst Communists, the worst haters of the Torah were the Yevsekas, the Jews themselves. People don't realize. The Yevsekas, the accursed Yevsekas persecuted Judaism more than the Communists in Russia. And then the Jews yielded, and they thought that now they could get lost in the lap of Mother Russia.

But no. Now the Russians began to change and they began to show discrimination, and now it's so bad that a lot of Jews are trying to escape from Russia and they're coming back to Jewish communities.

As a result of that, winds of antisemitism are blowing everywhere. Hitler was just a portent. Hitler is not the end. It's because Jews yielded that Hakadosh Baruch Hu fulfilled what the Gemara says, הַקָּדוֹשׁ בָּרוּךְ הוּא מַעֲמִיד לָהֶם מֶלֶךְ קָשֶׁה כְּהָמָן – *Hashem will raise up a king as wicked as Haman,* וּמִיָּד הֵן עוֹשִׂין תְּשׁוּבָה – *and He'll bring them back* (*Yerushalmi Taanis* 1:1).

It's not irreversible that there has to be democracy. America is losing out on all fronts to the Communists.

Of course, if all of us today exerted all our efforts in bringing back Jews – we're not doing it at all, but if we would do that, a massive national effort to bring back Jews to Judaism, then it wouldn't be necessary to use any exterior means. But it's not being done, except on a very small scale here or there, and there's no question that the wheel of history is going to turn back.

It's not irreversible that there has to be democracy. America is losing out on all fronts to the Communists. The Panama Canal is now in the possession of a tyrant, a dictator. The Suez Canal is being given over to dictators. Soon Russia is going to have control of two canals. There are countries after countries that the careless, reckless American president and the careless, reckless American legislators are yielding to the Communists. All over the world they're gaining footholds. Democracy is not going to spread. It has no backbone anymore. It's *min haShamayim*.

Why are Americans so crazy that they've gone mad over immorality, over adultery, and over homosexualism? A people like that are not able to rule themselves anymore. They give the mandate over to wicked, selfish politicians and the end is, the country is losing out.

The SALT agreement is an agreement whereby America ties its hands in making its defenses and it gives Russia full power to go ahead. Because Russia makes promises that they're going to limit their armaments. But Secretary of State Vance – I think Vance is his name – *ah vantz*. This

There are laws now that they passed lately that there must be freedom of information. Hakadosh Baruch Hu is doing it only because of His people Yisroel, only because of us.

Mr. Vantz said – he didn't say it publicly, but he made this statement privately: "We have no way of checking on Russia here." So we're going to promise to limit our armaments – and we're going to do it because we're open. All the liberals don't permit us to keep any secrets anymore. There are laws now that they passed lately that there must be freedom of information. Anybody could spy on the government and can spread news about secret information, and you can't do anything.

How did President Nixon lose out? Because he tried to stop a Jewish psychologist in Washington from peddling secret news. He tried to stop by breaking in illegally. What could he do? He couldn't help himself. So there was a big fuss and they threw him out of office and now there are no secrets.

So the Russians will know everything about America. They know all of our secrets that cost billions in research! They know right away! We haven't the slightest idea what's doing in Russia. So we're making a SALT agreement with them; it's as stupid as could be. They promise and we promise. So America will keep its promise. They won't keep anything. The democracies are rotting away!

And Hakadosh Baruch Hu is doing it only because of His people Yisroel, only because of us. Because the time has come for a great change. He can't afford to lose any more Jews. And if Jews are not going to go back, the world will go back. There's no question about it. You mark my words! You'll see changes all over.

And that's why it behooves us today to get busy and to bring in as many Jews as we are able to bring back! That's our self-preservation.

July 1979

Coming Back

Move back to Brooklyn, send your children to the very frummest yeshivos,

Q/ If assimilation is worse than death, and most American Jews are assimilating, what shall we do?

A/ And the answer I told you already. Move back to Brooklyn, send your children to the very *frummest* yeshivos, and Hakadosh Baruch Hu will give you so much *nachas*, not only in the next world – but in this world too. And you'll remain forever with the Jewish people and your great-great-great-great-great descendants will continue to be with the Klal Yisroel and with Hakadosh Baruch Hu. That's the way to do it.

December 1995

Chapter 3

Bringing Back Lost Jews

Chapter Sponsor

Leilui nishmat

**Yechiel Mechel
Ben Eliyahu**

Contents

Chapter 3

Coming Closer

Time for Kiruv

Q/ How much time should a person give away to help others come closer to Torah and to Yiddishkeit?

A/ Now that's a question that I have been concerned with for at least forty years, and I never found an answer.

Tentatively, we say as follows: As long as you're interested in learning, you have an hour that you want to spend on learning, do it for yourself.

But keep in mind that there are hours that you do waste. Many people need some recreation. It's fun to be *mekarev rechokim*, and there is plenty of wasted time. I'll give an example. If you're a yeshiva man, Fridays, after the *seder,* if you would sit in the *beis hamedrash* while they're sweeping up and you'd sit in the dust and you'd continue to learn – some people do that until the last moment; just before Shabbos you run home to take a bath, then I say don't budge. Keep on learning. But if you're going to waste time Friday afternoon, then waste it on *kiruv rechokim* and get Olam Haba in your spare time.

There's a lot of time wasted by everybody. Some people need a little rest from learning or a change. But the rule is – and it may sound selfish, but I

The truth is that if a person really has something in his heart, he would express it by deeds.

wouldn't budge from that. If you have an hour to learn, do so and don't give it away for any other purpose.

May 1979

Resistance to Kiruv

Q/ What do you say about a Jew who responds to our trying to convince him to do mitzvos by saying, "But I am a Jew in my heart and that's enough"?

A/ Many times you experience that; you urge somebody to do this or not to do that, and he says, "But I am a Jew in my heart."

So imagine that this 'heart-Jew' went swimming. And he went out a little bit beyond his depth and now he has cramps and he is shouting for help. And the lifeguard is sitting on the beach and looking on.

So you say to the lifeguard, "A man is drowning!"

He says, "Is that so?"

So you tell him, "Don't you want to help?!"

And he says, "Sure I want to help him. I want to help him!"

With a heart you are not going to save anybody's life. Just because you want to help, a person is not going to be saved from drowning.

Life is expressed by deeds. The truth is that if a person really has something in his heart, he would express it by deeds. The fact that he doesn't do those deeds, that itself demonstrates that he is a nothing Jew – that is the very best evidence that it's not in his heart. A man can't look on while his fellow man is crying for help and say, "I really intend to help you."

And so, the criterion of a person is not what he claims is in his heart, but what *actually* is in his heart. And the only way that a man can know if he is deceiving himself or not deceiving himself is how he expresses that Jewishness.

Now, if a person is a Jew in his heart, but he supports let's say the UJA – so he is a UJA in his heart; he is not a Jew in his heart. Supporting UJA doesn't make you a Jew. If a person likes knishes and that is how he expresses his Judaism, that doesn't demonstrate that his heart is in the right place.

And therefore, the heart is only meaningful when it is expressed in actions. And when the actions contradict it, that demonstrates as clearly as can be that in his heart, he is a nothing.

November 1981

Every week the newspaper will come to their door. That's what you should do.

Shabbos Invites

Q/ Is it proper to invite an intermarried couple to a meal for Shabbos in order to maybe be *mekarev* them?

A/ A mixed couple?! Absolutely not! No – you should not give their relationship any formal recognition by inviting them to a *seudah* as a couple. No. Absolutely not. No such thing! That would already be a concession, and it would mean that you are yielding to the wickedness of the times.

But you could do this. You could order a subscription to the Jewish Press and have it mailed to them every week. That might have a good effect on them. You want to buy a different newspaper for them? Okay. Every week the newspaper will come to their door. That's what you should do.

Or if you wish, you can invite them to your home for a talk when there are no children around. Only when there

If you're a good swimmer and you know how to save lives, jump in.

are no children around. And you can talk to them. Maybe you can accomplish something. But don't bring them into your home in any official manner as guests and give them that recognition. No. You must always remember to make a protest – an open demonstration protest – against the wickedness of intermarriage. Intermarriage is worse than death. It's worse than a thousand deaths.

June 2000

Kiruv Professionals

Q/ Someone who is an *apikores* – should I try to be *mekarev* him to Yiddishkeit or just avoid his bad influence?

A/ Is it better to walk away from somebody who has a bad influence or to try to correct him?

We'll take an analogy. Somebody fell off a pier into the water and you happen to be there. Is it better to jump in to save him or to remain where you are?

And the answer is, if you're a good swimmer and you know how to save lives, jump in. Otherwise, stay where you are because both will go down.

If you're an expert in dealing with *apikorsim*, with people who know nothing, or atheists, then by all means. Certainly. After a while, when you see that he's stubborn and he wants to carry out his point, let him drown. What can you do? But you have to at least try to save him.

But if you're not adept, which most people are not – very few people are trained in the ways of combating *apikorsus* –

so you're safest by staying away, by keeping to yourself. Most people are advised to keep away from the wicked.

July 1980

Kiruv How-To 1

"Do one mitzvah," tell him. "One mitzvah! You won't be sorry."

Q/ How could I *mekarev* somebody who isn't interested in doing mitzvos?

A/ The first thing to tell them is, "Are you interested in your own benefit? Then you should know, my friend, that mitzvos, once you've practiced mitzvos, you'll discover that the mitzvos are מְתוּקִים מִדְּבַשׁ וְנֹפֶת צוּפִים – *sweeter than honey and the drippings of the honeycomb.*"

Tell him that. If you yourself don't feel it yet, say it anyhow as a sales talk. מְתוּקִים מִדְּבַשׁ וְנֹפֶת צוּפִים – It's better than honey. The truth is – that's the truth.

There are so many people who began like nobodies and they ended up by being *tzaddikim gemurim*. Tell him that. Little by little, persuade him. It's for his benefit. "Do one mitzvah," tell him. "One mitzvah! You won't be sorry."

And little by little, step by step, you can attract a person into the circle of the *shomrei mitzvos.*

November 1996

Kiruv How-To 2

Q/ In the course of my business, I sometimes come across assimilated Jews who practice *avodah zarah*. Should I try to influence them to do *teshuvah*?

Watch out, only men with men and women with women.

A/ The gentleman is asking a question: Should you try to influence Jews against worshipping idols? I think so. You should influence Jews for any good thing that you can, certainly. You can buy them a subscription to a frum Jewish newspaper or a Jewish magazine; that's the best way to do it. Little by little, it might work – they can't throw it into the garbage every week, after all, so one day while they're eating breakfast, they'll be reading it, and maybe something will come into their minds.

May 1987

Kiruv How-To 3

Q/ Shouldn't one be *mekarev rechokim* by speaking to them personally, verbally?

A/ Should one attempt to bring people close to Judaism by personal contact with them?

In a certain manner, yes. If you speak to them outside or even in your own home, and you see that they're the kind that wish to learn, then it's easier to bring them into your house. If they're contentious and they wish to argue, then keep them out of your house and try your best.

But, in any case, don't spend much time with anybody. Because everybody is vulnerable to wrong influences.

Now sometimes there's a *rachok*, somebody who is not close to Judaism, who is an idealist of good character and he's not going to spoil you. On the contrary, all your good qualities will rub off on him. If you understand that, then you can do that.

Watch out, however. Only men with men and women with women. A man should never be *mekarev* a female. If you're a woman, never try to be *mekarev* a man. Because the results are not going to be good. It never works. Things happen.

But when you know how to do it, if you're a professional, you can be *mekarev* people without injuring yourself. But most people are not professionals, and therefore, they should keep others at arm's length. To send them materials by mail, like I said before, you can do to everybody.

May 1986

The emotions are so violent and so beautiful that people are picked up

Kiruv How-To 4

Q/ The frum community has little real association with the ninety percent of other Jews. How can people be brought back if we avoid them out of fear of their influence?

A/ That's a good and legitimate question. But first let me explain.

In case you're not a good swimmer, you're advised never to try to save somebody who is drowning. He's sure to pull you down. If you're a good swimmer, then you can swim over to him and give him a good punch and knock him out so he won't struggle anymore, so you can drag him to dry land.

Now, what does that mean in today's words? You don't punch anybody to make him a *baal teshuvah.* But if you can drag him, let's say, to a Lubavitcher *farbreng;* a thousand people are standing on their feet, there's no place to sit down. A thousand are standing on their feet and they're all singing together, that's a punch in the head. He is knocked out. He can't think anymore. The emotions are so violent and so beautiful that people are picked up and carried by the wave of the ocean of feeling and many people have been brought back to Judaism just by that.

Start teaching him the Gemara right away. Get him involved in Gemara

I remember almost sixty years ago, a boy came from the West to our yeshiva; he didn't know anything, and one of my *chaveirim* wanted to influence him, so he started from the beginning; to prove that there's Hashem, *brias ha'olam, yesh mei'ayin*, all the *yesodos ha'emunah*.

I said, "That's not the way to do it. If you're going to start from the beginning with him, he'll challenge you at every step. No. He's been brought up the other way. He wasn't brought up to be a *maamin*. You'll start teaching him *emunah*? No. Start teaching him the Gemara right away. Get him involved in Gemara. Once he gets into the spirit of the Gemara, there's a *kasha,* and he feels he is accomplishing, he's learning well, then he becomes identified with the Gemara, and even without thinking, he becomes a defender of the Torah. That's the way to do it."

You don't achieve *teshuvah* by teaching people to believe in Hashem, that He created the world out of nothing. The world was nothing at the beginning. Even energy particles didn't exist. And Hashem said, "*Yehi* – let it be," and energy came into existence and the particles came together at Hashem's command and created this and created that. That's the truth and that's the way the Chumash talks, but that's not how you'll make him a *baal teshuvah.*

If you want to win over a *baal teshuvah*, how do you win him over? If not with learning Gemara, sometimes with music, frum music. With *melaveh malkas*. With emotions, with happiness and *simcha* and friendship. Give him a good Shabbos meal. Let him sing *zemiros* together with you. That's the way to win people in.

After all, how are people taken away from Judaism? Is it by logic? When you see these boys come out of the subways, twenty boys with saffron robes and long pigtails, who are these monks? Not a single Italian or Irishman among them.

All Jews! How did that happen? Did they sit down and study the Torah and reject the Torah? No, they didn't study anything. It's emotions.

You can bring in Jews by the thousands if you really intend to do it.

So many are going lost only because of emotions, and so let us use emotions to bring them back again! Friendship, happiness; certainly.

Now the question was, according to what you heard here, that you should isolate yourself, then how can you go out and show friendship to other people?

You must know, חַיֶּיךָ וְחַיֵּי חֲבֵרְךָ חַיֶּיךָ קוֹדְמִין – *If it's a question of your life and your friend's life, your life comes first* (*Bava Metzia* 62a). Your life comes first. If you're going to bring into your house somebody who has non-Jewish behavior and you have children in the house, forget about it. You can't afford to do that. You must go out to them in an organized way.

And I'll tell you how to do it. If you yourself try to contact people on the street, you can do that. You can hand them literature. Find out where they live. Send them subscriptions to Orthodox newspapers. Send them Orthodox pamphlets. Little by little, the message comes in every week by the mailman instead of you coming personally.

Now, after a while, if you want you can call up and find out how things are going, and on an individual one-to-one basis you can be *mekarev* them. Or, you bring them in groups. Not in your home, but in groups. And you teach them. It's being done. Many places are doing it.

It's not being done enough. You can bring in Jews by the thousands if you really intend to do it. Most people, however, are not interested. And therefore, it's not being done.

I have to add, however, that you have to be very careful to do it right. Here's a case of a young man who tried to convert an Italian girl. Well, he converted her, but she converted him

You're dealing with a patient, a sick person, and you have to see what's effective for him.

too. I don't want to say what happened subsequently. She ruined him.

Like it says in the *midrash*, אַבְרָהָם מְגַיֵּר אֶת הָאֲנָשִׁים וְשָׂרָה מְגַיֶּרֶת אֶת הַנָּשִׁים. Now, Avraham was converting men, not women. Don't convert women! Keep away from women! And women, don't try to convert men! Women should convert women. Otherwise, who knows what's going to happen? They might drag you down into the ocean and you'll drown together.

And therefore, it's possible to save Jews without sacrificing your family, but it doesn't mean you have to associate with irreligious people. If you see a sincere young man, or you're a woman and see a sincere young woman and they have an interest in Judaism, you can be friendly with them. You can invite them to your home sometimes, if they'll cooperate and behave properly and dress properly. And little by little, that's how many have been drawn in.

But just to give up all principles and let them associate with you and you associate with them, no. It's impossible to do that because your life is number one on the agenda. חַיֶּיךָ קוֹדְמִין.

February 1989

The Correct Attitude

Q/ If someone is *mechalel Shabbos* in his business despite the urging of others to close his store, should we nevertheless treat him as an equal or should we disdain him?

A/ And the answer is that you're dealing with a patient, a sick person, and you have to see what's effective for him. You have to treat the sick patient with wisdom. Of course, in your heart, there's no question what you think. A person who is *mechalel Shabbos,* הֲרֵי הוּא כְּעַכּוּ"ם, he's like a gentile. A *mechalel Shabbos* is כְּעוֹבֵד עֲבוֹדָה זָרָה, he's like an idolater. He's a lost soul. There's nothing to talk about! There's nothing to debate!

In your mind you have to know that a mechalel Shabbos is a very ruined and broken person.

But it's not the proper way to show that to him if you intend to continue your efforts. And therefore, you must do whatever is necessary.

Now, that doesn't mean that when he comes, let's say, into the congregation, that you should be according him the same deference that you'll give to a decent, frum Jew. You can't do that. But you can treat him with wisdom, why not?

But whatever you do, however you're going to treat him, in your mind you have to know that a *mechalel Shabbos* is a very ruined and broken person. No question about it. And you shouldn't have any doubts where he stands in your mind.

June 1980

Don't Give Up

Q/ How can one influence his brothers to become frum? It seems to be impossible.

A/ It's impossible if you sit here and sigh and say, "It's impossible." Did you try doing anything about it?

"I tried talking to them," you say.

But you're not able to talk! So here's what you should do. Although I'm not saying The Jewish Press is for *bnei Torah* to sit and read, at least buy a subscription to The Jewish Press

It certainly will have a good influence on him. He might start thinking about eating kosher.

for your brother. Let him get a copy of The Jewish Press once a week.

It certainly will have a good influence on him. He might start thinking about eating kosher. He might start thinking about keeping Shabbos. After all, it's in the environment; he sees such a newspaper.

Did you buy him books? There are books that you can buy. Today there are so many English books. At least try that.

And therefore, we shouldn't merely give up, because there are so many ways today of approaching people that we didn't have in the past.

January 1984

Men and Women

Q/ **How can I be *mekarev*, it means draw close to Yiddishkeit, an unmarried girl of thirty-five?**

A/ So if you're a young man or a man, the first thing to do is to run away as far as you can. Have no business with any girls at all. By being *mekarev* a girl to yourself, you're just putting yourself in the situation where who knows what can happen.

Now, this is said from experience. There have been people who were *mekarev* girls, even having them Shabbos at their tables week after week, and the end of one situation I can tell you about was that he and the girl eloped; he left his frum wife with her six children.

And so, don't be *mekarev* girls. It says אַבְרָהָם מְגַיֵּר אֶת הָאֲנָשִׁים וְשָׂרָה מְגַיֶּרֶת אֶת הַנָּשִׁים. Men should concentrate on men and women on women. Avraham wasn't *megayer* any women. That's our principle.

And therefore, הֱוֵי בּוֹרֵחַ מִן הָעֲבֵרָה – you should run away from an *aveirah* as if you're running away from fire. If there's a fire, you won't flirt with it. And a sin is also a fire.

August 1982

You should run away from an aveirah as if you're running away from fire.

Youth and Kiruv

Q/ Considering the fact that so many Jews are going lost, does the Rav feel that the Jews in the frum community should utilize a major part of their resources to be *mekarev* our estranged brethren, or should we use our resources to strengthen our own people and to build up the frum communities themselves?

A/ Our resources are limited. We don't have much money. We don't have many millionaires. And we don't have too much time – most of us have to work too. So the time and the money that we have – should we devote more time to help the lost Jews who wandered away from the Torah, or should we say no, we want to learn more Gemara and become bigger *lamdanim,* learn more *mussar seforim*, become bigger *maaminim, ohavei Hashem.* What should we concentrate more on?

Now first of all, when you're young, concentrate on yourself. Give all your time to put into yourself as much as you can. If you go out into the world before you're fully ripe, it's like taking a green apple off the tree, and it's not so useful to the world. If you remain in the yeshiva until you're ripened, then the world has more use out of you. So in general, we'll say charity begins at home. You come first. חַיֶּיךָ וְחַיֵּי חֲבֵרֶיךָ חַיֶּיךָ קוֹדְמִים – you come first.

If you can do it in a way that will not endanger your progress, your success, your shleimus, you should do it.

However, if it's not too much of a loss of time for you, you should try to help your fellow man. There are some people who are not going to spend their days learning, and with a little bit of money and encouragement, they'll go out and do the job for you. So therefore, let your money work for you. You put in all the time you have for yourself – there are plenty of frum young men who would like to go out and be active bringing back, being *machzir b'teshuvah* the lost Jews. They wouldn't sit and learn anyhow, so let them do that. Let them be *osek* in *hatzalah* of all the lost Jews. And we can raise enough money on a small scale for that. At least something we could do.

But there's no question that your *neshamah* comes first. You don't have any resources? Then think about yourself.

But one thing I have to warn you. Don't go out yourself and try to save the irreligious Jews. If you're not able to swim, don't jump in to save a drowning man. He might pull you down too. If you're not a *shaleim* in *avodas Hashem* and you try to associate with the non-*frumme,* they might spoil you. And don't think it's not a possibility.

And therefore, חַיֶּיךָ קוֹדְמִים. If you can do it in a way that will not endanger your progress, your success, your *shleimus,* you should do it.

October 1997

Kiruv in Brooklyn

Q/ Would it not be a noble and righteous endeavor for *bnei Torah* to go out of town and be *mekarev* youth rather than remain in New York City and make progress fortifying themselves?

A/ And the answer is, when somebody, *chalilah*, falls into the ocean – it happens sometimes; you were walking on the pier and somebody fell overboard from the boat nearby. Wouldn't it be a good deed for you to dive in?

The answer is, if you cannot swim, better not to try it. Because it will be two people going down. Don't try to save anybody if you're not a good swimmer.

To make a rescue at sea is suicide unless you are able to swim well. If you are able to throw the drowning man a line, if you are able to stretch a long pole to him like an oar, or maybe push out a boat to him, yes. But otherwise, you must stand by and say, "It's just too bad." You can shed tears if you wish, but you cannot ruin your life.

Now, to go out of town to a college campus, or even in town on a college campus, if you are not ready for the task, it's almost suicide.

Therefore, take your time and ripen on the tree of life in the yeshiva. Wait until you're ready to go out.

Take your time and ripen on the tree of life in the yeshiva. Wait until you're ready to go out.

However, in some cases it's advisable if you are under the strict supervision of a *rebbe*. For instance, Lubavitcher boys – when they're sent out by the Rebbe, he's in contact with each one. He doesn't just send them out and say "Go!" and then forget about them. Therefore, he's holding a lifeline for them, they're not swimming independently.

Let's say he sends someone to Australia to bring back Jews. He keeps them in mind, and after one or two years he says, "Come back to New York." That's what he does; that's a different story.

But otherwise, if you go out like a regular yeshiva man, your *rosh yeshiva* is so loaded down with worries about how to pay his *rebbes*, that as soon as you walk out of the door he forgets about you. If you call him up and he remembers your

There is plenty of work around. You don't have to go far afield.

name, that's already a good thing. You can't blame the poor man.

But the Lubavitcher Rebbe doesn't have the worry of supporting Lubavitch – there's someone else who worries about that. The poor *roshei yeshiva* can't think about you, so therefore they're not sending you out because they can't take responsibility for you.

So you must remain where you are. If you want to be *mekarev* – right next door to you! You don't have to go out of town. Right next door to you, if you live in Brooklyn, in the Bronx, in Bensonhurst, in Queens, wherever you are, right next door there are opportunities. On the way to yeshiva, stop, pat a young fellow on the back, and say, "Why don't you go to yeshiva?" Things like that. If you are a girl, speak to girls, ask them to go to a Bais Yaakov, to some special Torah classes. There is plenty of work around. You don't have to go far afield.

February 1976

Kiruv Outside of Brooklyn 1

Q/ **If you follow what the Rav said before that we stay only in a *makom Torah,* are we not in a sense consigning two-thirds, a half, three-fourths, of the Jewish nation to be forgotten about and to go lost?**

A/ The question is, by me saying that you should remain in a place of Torah, aren't I not consigning a great mass of the Jewish people *chas v'shalom* to go lost?

The answer is as follows. The *rabbanim* who settled far away – not only in small communities but even in Boston and in Baltimore – lost their children.

These people should know, first and foremost, never to let loose of their lifeline, and that is their home in the Torah community.

In order to save somebody who is drowning, you must be an expert swimmer. It doesn't pay for two people to drown when only one man is drowning.

We don't realize how perilous it is to go out in a small community. And even if you're there for a short time, when you finally leave them, you don't realize that you're castrated forever. You're ruined forever.

I don't want to speak too much, but I know from experience. People who have been in small communities and then finally they settle in big communities, they have lost out. They're ruined. Especially the wife. The first lesson that a *rebbetzin* learns, a young *rebbetzin* learns, is not to have babies. That's lesson number one. And this lesson she never forgets even after they move back into a good Torah community.

Now the question is, if we're going to be busy saving ourselves, what will we do with the masses of Jews out there?

And the answer is, if we really mean business, we have to send out people whose base of operations is a big city, a Torah community. We have to send them out on missions, but they should come back quickly. They can go out on a month-long tour, speaking, searching out *neshamos*, making *shidduchim* in small towns, urging people to move, trying to open frum services, kosher butchers, and so on. But these people should know, first and foremost, never to let loose of their lifeline, and that is their home in the Torah community, back in the big cities. That's of utmost importance because חַיֶּיךָ וְחַיֵּי חֲבֵרָךְ חַיֶּיךָ קוֹדְמִים. If there's a question of your life or somebody else's life, your life comes first.

May 1984

If a Jew moves out of town to do kiruv rechokim work, does he deserve to be praised or criticized?

Kiruv Outside of Brooklyn 2

Q/ If a Jew moves out of town to do *kiruv rechokim* work, does he deserve to be praised or criticized?

A/ If a person moves away from a Jewish center, a center of Jewish life, for a real sincere purpose, let's say to save Jews, would we criticize him?

It depends. If he does it because of a salary, then it's only an excuse. If a person, let's say, moves to a small town, and he says he does it for *kiruv rechokim,* so we ask him one question: Suppose they wouldn't pay you that salary, would you go there for *kiruv rechokim*? By no means. So that's insincere. It means he's selling his *neshamah* for the sake of a few extra dollars, and the *neshamos* of his children.

If there is a person who is willing to donate, let's say, a week or two weeks of his life to go outside and bring in Jews without any profit, so he's sincere; certainly.

Even then, however, he has to be under some guidance of a mentor. Let's say it's a young fellow, he might be like the swimmer who is trying to save a drowning man, but he himself is not capable of keeping himself afloat together with somebody else on his back. So it's better not to attempt the rescue if he can't swim by himself.

May 1979

Kiruv and Bribery

Q/ How can you counteract the disdain of the lost Jews towards the *frumme* and Yiddishkeit?

A/ One way is to show them affection and to honor them. Another way is to bribe them with certain forms of good times and happiness in order to make them want to come.

Now I'll explain how each one of these is being used.

Affection and honor: If you're *mechabed* every person, if you honor every man, he cannot help being bribed by you. You show affection for him, you treat him with respect, and that's the first step to being *mekarev* him.

If you honor every man, he cannot help being bribed by you.

A second way is to bribe him with good times. Now this is what Lubavitch does when they make an encounter of college people with Lubavitch – "An Encounter With Chabad," they call it.

So you might think that the college boys and girls come carrying philosophical books under their arms, and Chabad comes to greet them with *seforim* like *Chizuk Emunah* and *Kuzari* and *Moreh Nevuchim,* and there's a philosophical encounter. No, it's nothing like that. Here's the encounter. They all sit together and they hear a tune sung, a *niggun*. And as a result of this *niggun*, there are a number of people who have come over and become *baalei teshuvah.*

Now, it may seem silly to you but that's how people are. If you would come head-on in an intellectual collision with these people, you've accomplished nothing because they don't have any sense anyhow. Don't think college people have sense. How do you think they became bums? They yielded to their environment. He went to college, and all around him was nothing but overalls and barbarianism, so he yielded to them. Now they're in Lubavitch and they're listening to a *niggun* and so they're overwhelmed by emotion and they yield this way. Emotion is a very big factor.

And therefore, there are ways of bribing people and getting them to like you and that may overcome, to some

You must show friendship. You must show character. You must show idealism.

extent, this barrier of hatred. If you try to win over Jews, you could win them over.

Now this doesn't mean that you shouldn't use intellectual explanations for people. But don't rely on that alone, because it's not effective in and of itself. You must show friendship. You must show character. You must show idealism. And then that person may listen to your intellectual approach too. And then he can become sympathetic to your cause.

April 1973

Calling All Jews

Q/ Can we rightfully conclude from what you said tonight that a mass outcry to Hashem by all of Orthodox Jewry in *galus* today would bring the Geulah much more quickly?

A/ Absolutely, absolutely! But the Orthodox Jews are not enough – we need *all* of Jewry. There are not enough Orthodox Jews. We are judged by the majority of Jews, and the Reformers are Jews. And we are suffering because of them, make no mistake about it. כָּל יִשְׂרָאֵל עֲרֵבִים זֶה לָזֶה, We are all responsible for each other and these *resha'im* must be converted by us. If they'll die out quickly we'll be *patur* from them, but as long as they're still here, it's our job to convert them. We have to save them because if they are the majority, then *chas v'shalom,* who knows what can happen! And they *are* the majority!

Now, crying out always helps and we should cry as much as we can, but the crying out should not be by Orthodox Jewry alone. All Jews must unite and cry out. And therefore, Koch [*Ed: Ed Koch, an irreligious Jew, was the mayor of New*

York City at the time] has to come to a *beis hamedrash* and stop being an *oisvorf*; he has to become a *baal teshuvah.*

And all the liberals and Reform rabbis, all of them together have to do *teshuvah*, because we are responsible for the Jewish gays too! You can't ignore them – their sins are on the heads of the entire Jewish people. כָּל יִשְׂרָאֵל עֲרֵבִים זֶה לָזֶה! We're talking now, of course, about the fundamental requirement that we have to be worthy in order to bring the Geulah. If *chas v'shalom* they don't do *teshuvah*, then Hakadosh Baruch Hu has a different method; but we prefer the first method.

You can't ignore them – their sins are on the heads of the entire Jewish people.

March 1989

Chapter 4

Chassidim & Misnagdim

Chapter Sponsor

L'iluy nishmas

Shulamit Samara bat Tzvi Hirsch

Yocheved bat Tzvi Hirsch

Dedicated by the Sneider Family

Contents

Chapter 4

Chassidim and Misnagdim

How it Began

Q/ **What was the main cause of the split between the *chassidim* and the *misnagdim*?**

A/ Now, if you're a *chassid,* listen carefully and don't be offended. The main cause of the split was the *chassidim.*

I'll tell you why the main cause was the *chassidim.* Because up until then, there were no *chassidim* in Europe; all the Jews in Europe followed *nusach Ashkenaz*; they all prayed in one way. There was a certain *nusach Sefard* in Oriental countries, but in Europe they all followed *nusach Ashkenaz.* Even Italians had a *nusach Italiani*, which is a *nusach Ashkenaz.*

So when the Baal Shem Tov came and he instituted for his disciples a different form of *tefillah*, he adopted mostly the *nusach Sefard* format and it caused an upheaval. Because among Jews, any change in *minhagim* is considered extremely serious. It caused a revolution. And so, if the *chassidim* hadn't done that, there wouldn't have been such *machlokes.*

They said, "Who knows where this is going to lead us to?!" And therefore, they came out and opposed it.

When the *chachmei haTorah* saw a new movement and how they were changing *minhagim*, they became alarmed, because this wasn't long after Shabtai Tzvi and the Frankists who had caused a lot of trouble; they ended up in *shmad*. And so they said, "Who knows where this is going to lead us to?!" And therefore, they came out and opposed it. But in the end they were satisfied because they saw that the results were not harmful.

January 1983

The Gaon's Cherem

Q/ **How are we to view the *cherem* placed upon the *chassidim* by the Vilna Gaon?**

A/ Now this question I would never be able to answer if not for a *sefer* called *Zichron Yaakov*.

The *Zichron Yaakov* was written by Harav Lifshitz who lived in Kovno, and he was the secretary of Rav Yitzchak Elchanan. Rav Yitzchak Elchanan was the Kovner Rav before World War I. He was a national Torah authority and Rav Lifshitz was his secretary, his right-hand man.

This Rabbi Lifshitz wrote *Zichron Yaakov,* and he describes among other things, the struggle between the Vilna Gaon and the *chassidim*. And he explained it as follows. He said he himself was not capable of understanding the situation until an old *rav*, a Lithuanian *rav* from the previous generation, explained it to him.

When the *chassidim* began, it was a revolutionary movement. The introduction of a different *nusach*, *nusach Sefard* and then *nusach Ari* which is also *nusach Sefard*, in Europe created a great fear that a reform will take place.

Now other people could also come and make new *nuschaos.* The ancient system of davening was regarded as sacred and untouchable. And now here came a group and they changed it.

There was a tendency to belittle the learning of the yeshivos and even the gedolei Yisroel.

Also, at that time among the *chassidim,* there was a strong tendency to belittle the *lamdanim* of the non-*chassidishe* people, because they were considered not enthusiastic enough in *avodas Hashem,* and also that their Torah was *shelo lishmah;* therefore there was a tendency to belittle the learning of the yeshivos and even the *gedolei Yisroel.*

The Gra was alarmed by this, and therefore the Gra was sent by Hakadosh Baruch Hu to come out and to blast the *chassidim.* He came out with *kol koreis* against them. He warned people against them.

Now, when the *chassidim* saw that they were being attacked, their reaction was to show that the accusations against them were groundless. "But we *are* for learning Torah! But we *are* for fostering yeshivos!" And therefore, as a result, they began to spend more and more time on studying Torah and after a little while, the *chassidishe* places had as much Torah learning as many yeshivos, as there was in the non-*chassidishe* places.

So the *Zichron Yaakov* said it was a result of the criticism. Because the *chassidim* were being attacked, they wanted to show that they were just the same as anybody else when it comes to the love of Torah; and the *misnagdim* began to bring *mussar* into their camp to show they were no less than anybody else when it comes to *avodas Hashem.*

So therefore, the mutual criticism was *min haShamayim,* so that all sections of the populace became more aware now of the necessity of spreading *lomdus* and more aware of the necessity of spreading *hislahavus* and the study of *yirah* and true *avodas Hashem.*

And therefore it was a מַחְלֹקֶת לְשֵׁם שָׁמַיִם – *a dispute that was fought l'sheim Shamayim* and סוֹפָהּ לְהִתְקַיֵּם – *it had permanent results* (*Avos* 5:17). As a result, the world of Torah became greater and the world of *avodah* became greater.

And so, if we look back and we see the *yad Hashem*, we see everything was done for a purpose that culminated in the complete benefit, the full benefit of the Am Yisroel.

January 1985

The Gaon's Foresight

Q/ Was the Vilna Gaon aware of what the *chassidim* were when he opposed them? Or was he deceived?

A/ Now that question is not simple because you have to have the mind of the Vilna Gaon to understand that. The Vilna Gaon was a unique phenomenon, and he saw ahead into the future what we don't see even today. And so, even though people today say that now it's אִגַּלַּאי מִלְּתָא לְמַפְרֵעַ, it's retroactively revealed that he was in error, it's not so. The Vilna Gaon knew his business.

The Vilna Gaon was a unique phenom-enon, and he saw ahead into the future what we don't see even today.

However, I'm going to tell you what one writer said that's pertinent to this subject. Now, it may be that others won't be happy with this – they'll disagree – but this is what Reb Yaakov Lifschitz said in the *Zichron Yaakov* and he heard it from *gedolei Yisroel*.

He said that if the Vilna Gaon had not stepped in at that moment to oppose the *chassidim*, who knows what would have happened to some of their sects? Some of the groups of *chassidim* might have gone far away, but because the Gaon came out with thunder and lightning against them, so now they tried their best to show that they are really good Jews. As a result, the *chassidim* took upon themselves to study Torah, and today in the *chassidishe* world, there's a great deal of Torah that might not have been.

I'll give a similar example. In Kelm, Reb Simcha Zissel, *zichrono livracha,* was the man who preached *mussar* all the time. And he criticized those who didn't study *mussar*. *Mussar* is the study of the fear of Hashem. He had opponents in Kelm; they were opposed to his *shitah*. He had bitter opponents. Finally, Reb Simcha Zissel passed away and Reb Lazer Gordon said a *hesped* on him. At the funeral oration, Reb Lazer Gordon said as follows:

He said Reb Simcha Zissel had a great effect on the people who followed him – they studied *mussar* and they became better – and a great effect on his opponents because his opponents tried their best to show that without *mussar* you can also be *tzaddikim*.

And so that's the opinion – not my opinion, the *Zichron Yaakov* says that; he actually says that in the year תקנ"ל there were some *chassidim* who were going wild and even the *rebbes* criticized them. They're called *chassidei talak;* they made antics, wild antics – I can't describe them but they did wild things. Some of them used to stand on their heads in the middle of davening to show that they were full of happiness with Hashem. And they were rebuked by the *rebbes*; they were rebuked.

Some of them used to stand on their heads in the middle of davening to show that they were full of happiness with Hashem.

So things could have gone off on a tangent. That's what the *Zichron Yaakov* said he heard from *gedolim*; that when the Gra came out and he scolded them in a loud voice, it brought things to a halt, and they, instead of giving up – didn't give up the *dveikus* and the *simcha,* but they added now other things that used to be considered the province of the *misnagdim;* Torah and so on.

And so, the *Zichron Yaakov* says that because the *gedolei Yisroel* came out full blast against the *chassidim* then, the *chassidim* wanted to show that the suspicions were unfounded, so the *chassidim* betook themselves to learning more and more. And therefore, Torah learning began to increase among the *chassidim* to a very big extent. And in the course of time, the *chassidim* learned almost as much Torah as the *misnagdim*. And therefore, the *chassidim* improved as a result.

Whether you like it or not, it's not my opinion; I'm quoting from the Zichron Yaakov.

Whether you like it or not, it's not my opinion; I'm quoting from the *Zichron Yaakov*.

September 1976

A Middle Ground

Q/ What do you mean when you say that the *misnagdim* and *chassidim* are different today only in superficial things?

A/ One man once gave a *mashal*. He said that a man had two sons-in-law. One son-in-law liked *milchigs*. This was a rich man, a very wealthy man. So for a *milchige* son-in-law, he had a special *milchige* kitchen. And he hired a cook who cooked all day *milchige* things. Potatoes with cream and other things, fish. A *milchige* kitchen.

The other son-in-law liked *fleishigs*. And for this son-in-law, he hired a special cook and built a special kitchen; every day *fleishigs*. The sons-in-law couldn't eat together. Here was a *milchige* son-in-law and here was a *fleishige* son-in-law. They ate at separate tables.

After a while, the father-in-law became poor and he couldn't afford to give so much milk and cream, so he started giving the *milchige* son-in-law water with potatoes instead of milk and potatoes. Instead of the cream, he gave substitutes, *pareve* substitutes.

Today we can all eat together at one table. We're all the same today.

And for for *fleishige* son-in-law, he started giving him cheaper things; less meat and more potatoes.

So the potatoes increased here and the potatoes increased there. The milk decreased here and the meat decreased there. And finally, the sons-in-law were both eating only potatoes. So one day, they said to each other, "Once upon a time, I was *fleishigs* and you were *milchigs* so we ate separately. But today, I'm potatoes and you're potatoes. Let's eat together!"

So in the olden days, *misnagdim* learned Torah day and night; they learned Torah day and night. Everybody took a son-in-law for ten years *kest* among *misnagdim*. Ten years *kest*! Torah was the life of the nation.

And the old *chassidim* were *fierdik!* Old *chassidim* were on fire! Once upon a time there were *fierdik chassidim*; they burned with *avodas Hashem* once upon a time. They danced and sang!

They stood long *Shemoneh Esreis* too. Some of them used to stand for seven hours davening *Shemoneh Esrei*! I had a *rebbe*, a *chassid;* one of my *rebbes*. He was from Lubavitch; he came from the old town of Lubavitch. He told me there was a man there who davened *Shemoneh Esrei* for seven hours in the olden days – that's seventy years ago. Seven hours of *Shemoneh Esrei* in Lubavitch! Have you ever heard of such a *Shemoneh Esrei*?

And therefore, here was Torah and here was *avodah*. But after a while, the Torah began to diminish and the *avodah* began to diminish. So today we can all eat together at one table. We're all the same today.

Of course not everybody will say that, but more or less, all the Jews today are one people. So therefore, the old feud is long forgotten and we are one people. מִי כְּעַמְּךָ יִשְׂרָאֵל גּוֹי אֶחָד

Those who are chassidim should remain chassidim. We need them. Believe me, we need them.

בְּאָרֶץ – *We are one nation in the world.* 'One nation' means *echad,* together. There's not much difference anymore.

By the way, there is a difference. And I say each should maintain his differences. They shouldn't become one. Hakadosh Baruch Hu wanted all the *shevatim* to be separate *shevatim.* Reuven separate, Shimon separate. Each *shevet* had its own characteristics. Every *shevet* had its *maalos.*

Those who are *chassidim* should remain *chassidim.* We need them. Believe me, we need them. *Misnagdim* who are all for learning Torah; they should keep learning Torah and building *yiras Shamayim*. Each one should improve. It could be eventually they'll all become the same; they'll all become *tzaddikim gemurim* eventually – very good. But in the meantime, don't give up the idiosyncrasies because Hakadosh Baruch Hu loves all the *shevatim;* He loves Reuven and loves Shimon. He loves *chassidim* and He loves *misnagdim.* He loves them all. *Ken yirbu v'chen yigdelu.*

September 2000

Chassidim Live On

Why don't *chassidim* today follow the way of the Baal Shem Tov?

A/ We must know that they do, to some extent. Of course, in the course of time, the *chassidim* cool off and the *misnagdim* cool off – everybody cools off as time goes on – but the contribution that these great men made is still among us.

There's no question about it, because there's a certain spirit among *chassidim*. That's why in Europe, when among the Lithuanian Jews, the practices were already becoming weaker and weaker and a big part of the youth had forsaken the Torah, among the *chassidim,* although it wasn't the same as it used to be, there was a greater percentage of loyalty than among the *misnagdim*.

And Rav Chaim Ozer, *zichrono livracha,* said, "They daven later than we do." You know the *chassidim* were blamed for davening too late in the morning. So Rav Chaim Ozer said, "The *chassidim* daven later than the *misnagdim.* But their *eineklach* daven later than our *eineklach.*" Which means the grandchildren of the *misnagdim* stopped davening, but the grandchildren of the *chassidim* still continue to daven. He said, "Their *eineklach* daven later than our *eineklach.*" Lithuania's children stopped davening, and the *chassidishe* children continued to daven.

They had a tremendous influence that lasted to this day, and it lasts forever.

And that spirit still remains. They had a tremendous influence that lasted to this day, and it lasts forever.

October 1993

Misnagdim Live On

Q/ Is it true that today there exist no more real *litvakkes*?

A/ I have to explain that question. People have an idea that all the *yiras Shamayim* today was learned from the *chassidim* and the children of the old *litvishe*, either they went lost or they are influenced by the *chassidim,* and that causes them to survive.

Now, it's not a silly question, because to a large extent, everybody has been influenced by the *chassidim* – no question

Baruch Hashem, we say that the contribution of the litvaks and the contribution of the chassidim together are building up our people.

about that. Because not long ago, I met an old rabbi – he's a *chashuve talmid chacham*, but he has almost no beard. He's clean shaven except for a little patch on the chin.

And I was thinking, nowadays, when even people who are moderate *shomrei mitzvos* many times have beards, and here's a famous rabbinical figure with a little patch on the chin, it's anachronism – for thirty years ago, forty years ago, maybe.

This man is a leftover from the *litvishe* days when people didn't wear beards and they could still be big *rabbanim*. Today any *chashuve rav* has a beard, if he's a *rav* or some public figure.

There's no question that the *chassidish* influence has been quite extensive.

However, I'll give a humble suggestion. The *litvish* influence on the *chassidim*, that's also been extensive, because who founded Mesivta Chaim Berlin? Who founded the Mirrer Yeshiva? Who founded Lakewood? Who founded Baltimore? Who founded the Chicago Yeshiva? All these were *litvishe roshei yeshiva*. And so, you cannot say that their influence is small. There are thousands upon thousands of *talmidim* who themselves are *rebbeim* today, as well as *rabbanim* and frum Jews.

And so, *baruch Hashem*, we say that the contribution of the *litvaks* and the contribution of the *chassidim* together are building up our people.

And then we have to mention the contribution of frum Germans. The *frumme* German community has contributed a lot too! It shouldn't be underrated. Everybody who does something good is contributing.

October 1981

Friendly Opponents 1

Today there are different customs, that's all. They're all minor things.

Q/ **What causes the unfriendliness between *chassidim* and *misnagdim*?**

A/ And the answer is nothing. We're quite friendly.

Look, I consider myself a full *misnaged.* And not only I, but my *rebbes.* We don't practice anything of *chassidus.* Yeshiva men today practice a lot of *chassidishe* things, but I don't and my family never did. They couldn't even pronounce the word *chassidim.* They used to say *s'chidim.* They couldn't pronounce the word correctly. They didn't have them in their districts in Europe.

But my *rebbe*s weren't unfriendly.

There was just one short period at the beginning when *chassidus* began to rise that the Gra, *zichrono livracha,* was afraid that they'd go off – some of them – and form a wild sect and do things against the Torah. Now, I'm not saying my own idea, but in the *sefer Mekor Baruch* he says that. And also in a famous *sefer* called *Zichron Yaakov* he says the same thing. He says at the beginning there were some groups that were doing wild things and they had to be stopped. And the *machlokes* that the Gra made against them caused the *gedolei hachassidim* to call a halt to these groups. They reacted and stopped it. And from then on there's no *machlokes* anymore.

Would you say there's a *machlokes* between the Syrians and the Egyptians and the Hungarian Jews because they have different customs? It's not a *machlokes.* Today there are different customs, that's all. They're all minor things.

All the Jews who are loyal to the Torah believe in one Chumash, one Tanach, one Gemara, and in one *Shulchan*

Mean people look for excuses to fight.

Aruch. The Rema adds certain things, but in general, it's all the same. And therefore, I would say there's no unfriendliness.

If a person wants to exercise his meanness of character and he wants to be mean against *misnagdim* because he's a *chassid,* or mean against *chassidim* because he's a *misnaged,* he'll be mean against fellow *misnagdim* too and against fellow *chassidim* too.

You find that the same person is mean even among his own. Don't you find *chassidim* who fight with *chassidim?* You don't find that? I don't want to talk about that, but you'll find it. And even in the same sect people fight. Mean people look for excuses to fight. If his nose is longer or shorter than your nose, it's also an excuse to fight.

November 1980

Friendly Opponents 2

Q/ Why do we sometimes see that different groups of *chassidim*, let's say Satmar and Lubavitch, are fighting with each other?

A/ Now if you're a *chassid,* then you're going to have to bear with me for a moment because I'm going to have to hurt your feelings.

There is a basic weakness in all *chassidim*, and that basic weakness is "My Rebbe!" Now, "My Rebbe" is a wonderful thing and it accomplishes a lot of good things – but it causes a lot of trouble too.

Before *chassidus*, all Jews said, "My Hakadosh Baruch Hu!" and that's all. However, when the Baal Shem Tov saw that a lot of Jews had stopped saying that, he said that it's better to say "My Rebbe" than to not say anything at all. And if you say "My Rebbe" long enough, then in the course of time you'll say "My Hakadosh Baruch Hu" too.

But there have been very many plain people who never graduated past the "My Rebbe" stage. And therefore it becomes "My Rebbe" vs. "Your Rebbe," and they scratch out the eyes of each other. That's a weakness.

Look, if you advance beyond that stage, then all *rebbes* become "My Rebbe." All Rebbes! The Satmarer Rebbe! Ahh! *Zol ehr lang leiben!* He's a wonderful man. A big warrior; and he accomplished so much for us. The Lubavitcher Rebbe, *zol ehr lang leiben!* He accomplished so much and he is accomplishing so much. They should both be our *rebbes*.

But when someone says "only this one," and the other person says "only this one," then trouble comes.

But when someone says "only this one," and the other person says "only this one," then trouble comes. And that's the basic weakness.

It doesn't have to be that way because people are supposed to graduate. Your *rebbe* is only a ladder. You climb up on your ladder to Hakadosh Baruch Hu. The *rebbe* is only there to make it easier to climb up to Hakadosh Baruch Hu. But if a man just stands on the ladder and never reaches the shelf, then we tell him, "What are you standing there for?!" There are a lot of people standing on ladders and they're all yelling at each other. This one says, "My ladder is better," and this one says, "My ladder is better than yours." So we tell them, "Get going already. Go higher!" But they're busy with the ladders. And that causes trouble.

April 1976

Litvishe Rabbanim

Q/ **You said that sometimes *chassidim* are so attached to their *rebbe* and it leads to fighting with other *chassidim***

The attitude comes from a lot of love, a lot of commitment. A chassid is committed to his rebbe.

instead of being a ladder to climb closer to Hashem. But isn't it true that even among the *misnagdim* they also look up to and emulate the *roshei yeshiva*?

A/ Isn't it true even among *misnagdim*, that the followers look up to their *rav* and they emulate him? Yes, but they don't have this attitude that he's everything.

Now, I said before that there's a loss in this and there's a benefit. The benefit is that people who are influenced by a *chassidishe rebbe* will do more than other people would ever do for an *adam gadol* who's their *rebbe*. It's a fact. Because there's less independence with a *rebbe*. With a *chassidishe rebbe*, it's a *gezeiras hakasuv*. If the *rebbe* says something, he's always right. And therefore, people are more eager to live up to his requirements. Whereas in the case of an *adam gadol* – a *rosh yeshiva* or anybody else – there still is a certain amount of free will and criticism. People use their own judgment too, and they're not always as eager to fulfill his words.

However, we don't find people fighting over "My *rosh yeshiva*, your *rosh yeshiva*." That much you don't find. They're not that committed. As I said before, the attitude comes from a lot of love, a lot of commitment. A *chassid* is committed to his *rebbe*. But it has a certain weakness too, because if people remain just with that and they don't go further, it becomes only a cause of fighting.

There was fighting in Europe too, but in Europe you didn't have newspapers to publicize it. Here you have the Algemeiner Journal and they're making a very bad mistake in writing it up. They shouldn't write about it in the newspapers. These things shouldn't be spoken about at all! It's bad enough on its own but you don't have to spread it; especially among the irreligious Jews and the *goyim*.

Now certainly, עֲשֵׂה לְךָ רַב is a very great principle for success. And עֲשֵׂה לְךָ רַב doesn't come to exclude a *rebbe*. A *rebbe* is also a *rav*. So whether the *rav* is a *rosh yeshiva* or the Chofetz Chaim, *zichrono livracha,* or Rav Aharon Kotler, *zichrono livracha;* whether it's one of these great men or if the *rav* was Rav Yosef Yitzchak, the old Lubavitcher Rebbe, *zichrono livracha,* or it was the old Gerrer Rebbe, *zichrono livracha,* all of them can cause a person to be led on the way to success.

All of them can cause a person to be led on the way to success.

Only that he should make sure that it shouldn't be the cause of his undoing. Sometimes by blinding allegiance – it means being swept away by your emotions without thinking – people can use them just for *machlokes* and that's not the purpose of a *rav* and a *rebbe*.

April 1977

A Rebbe's Advice

Q/ Should someone who is not *chassidish* go to a *chassidish rebbe* for advice?

A/ And the answer is, a *chassidishe rebbe* – it depends on who he is. The mere fact that his father died and the *chassidim* chose him as a successor is not enough.

But if he's an old experienced *rebbe*, by all means! Because he's a counselor to whom thousands have come. Any old *rebbe* – it doesn't have to be a famous *rebbe;* even a local *rebbe* – if he's old and experienced, then he's a fine counselor.

The only trouble is, he doesn't have time. But if you can pay him – of course he doesn't want to take money because he doesn't want to sell his time – but if you could get him

Whatever it is you can get from these great men, by all means.

to listen to your troubles and get him to hear all the details of your life, he could be the very best guide and mentor and advisor there is.

I'm not saying only a *chassidishe rebbe. Roshei yeshiva* are also very fine counselors. But they're busy. The question is how you get them to listen to your problems. You can speak a little bit to them, but at length, they don't have time.

Whatever it is you can get from these great men, by all means.

January 1984

A Rebbe's Blessings

Q/ Why are the *misnagdim* so violently opposed to *rebbishe brachos*?

A/ Which *misnagdim* are opposed to *rebbishe brachos*? Tell me one.

Q/ I went to a *rosh yeshiva* once and told him that I asked a *rebbe* for a *bracha,* and he responded sarcastically.

A/ He's asking, "Why are the non-*chassidim* opposed to a blessing given by a *chassidish* rabbi?" And the answer is that the only time they are opposed is when they think that he is not a rabbi – when they think that he's only a man who dresses like a rabbi, or who has put up a sign on his door. But when they really consider him a *talmid chacham*, a learned man, then nobody is opposed to his *brachos*.

If it's an ignorant man, then what good will it be? How can one expect to avail himself of such a *bracha* without the merit of Torah? So therefore, he has to be, first of all, a *talmid chacham*. אֵין בּוּר יְרֵא חֵטְא וְלֹא עַם הָאָרֶץ חָסִיד (*Pirkei Avos* 2:5). To be a *chassid,* you can't be an *am ha'aretz*. And if you want to be a *rebbe* of *chassidim,* you have to be more than a non-*am ha'aretz;* you have to be a big *talmid chacham*.

If it's an ignorant man, then what good will it be? How can one expect to avail himself of such a bracha without the merit of Torah?

Q/ But Reb Moshe would be opposed to the Lubavitcher Rebbe.

A/ The Lubavitcher Rebbe is a big *talmid chacham*!

Q/ Reb Moshe Feinstein wouldn't be opposed if someone wants to go to the Lubavitcher Rebbe?

A/ No, he would not. He respects him, he has a high regard for him! They have high regard for each other! No question about it. The Lubavitcher Rebbe is a big *talmid chacham*! He's a thinker and a *talmid chacham*. Not only the Lubavitcher Rebbe; there are plenty of *rebbes* I can enumerate, but this is not a subject that I would like to delve into right now.

June 1972

Remaining Silent

Q/ I read a strong statement that was put out from Rav Shach with regard to Lubavitch. How should we treat this subject?

Is there one main leader of Klal Yisroel today?

A/ The question of Rav Shach and Lubavitch is a question that I am not going to talk about.

I'll explain something to you. I'm not a Lubavitcher, but when I was a boy, there was a Lubavitcher rabbi who taught me *Maseches Kesubos* in his home every day; the whole *masechta* we learned and he didn't take a nickel from me.

He never attempted to convert me. He never taught me Tanya. He just taught me straight Gemara. He was the *rav* of the *nusach Ari* shul in that town.

And therefore, I am friendly toward Lubavitch. I have other friends in Lubavitch too. It's difficult for me to look askance at Lubavitch.

Now, I am not a Lubavitcher and I have a certain background where I feel that I don't need Lubavitch. However, to intervene in a dispute between a great man and between Lubavitch? *Tacharishu* – the best thing is to remain quiet.

March 1975

Many Tzaddikim

Is there one main leader of Klal Yisroel today?

A/ That's not for me to say. But what I can say is that we do have leaders today. *Baruch Hashem*, we have leaders.

But I must tell you that I disagree with the attitude of being *mevatel,* of putting down someone else's *gadol*. No; I disagree with that attitude. *Gedolim* can be here and *gedolim* can be there, and we have to appreciate all of them. Your *gadol* doesn't have to be the only *gadol*.

And even though there might be *machlokes,* a disagreement, between them; yes, there may be *machlokes* between them, but we should stay out of it. It's fire! Worse than fire! We shouldn't say a word. Not a word! So if Rav Shach, let's say, and the Lubavitcher Rebbe may have *sichsuchim,* some arguments – I don't know if they have, but if they have some *sichsuchim,* it's none of our business. It's the fire of Gehinom to open up your mouth. Keep your mouth closed. It's a tragic mistake to mix in.

The wisest way is to say nothing at all and to have the greatest derech eretz, the greatest respect, for all those gedolim who are recog-nized.

And the wisest way is to say nothing at all and to have the greatest *derech eretz,* the greatest respect, for all those *gedolim* who are recognized. After all, the Lubavitcher Rebbe is recognized by many people. And Rav Shach is recognized by many people. So we should keep our mouths closed and recognize both of them. That's the way we should follow.

Why did the earth open its big mouth to swallow Korach? Because Korach opened his big mouth to speak against Moshe. So don't open your mouth! Because even today, the earth opens its mouth to bury men. Many are swallowed in an early grave because they opened their mouths. And what's even worse, many are swallowed into Gehinom just like Korach was. So don't open your mouth. You're only going to bring trouble upon yourself.

January 1993

Superior Jews

Q/ Why do Lubavitcher *chassidim* consider themselves superior to *litvishe* Jews?

All idealists who follow certain systems, they do it because they think it's the best system

A/ First of all, Lubavitcher *chassidim* are mostly *litvishe* Jews, you have to know. They are *litvishe* Jews. And if they consider themselves superior, so we can ask the same question: Why is it that most non-Lubavitcher *chassidim* consider themselves superior to Lubavitcher *chassidim*? Why do Breslover *chassidim* consider themselves superior to Lubavitcher *chassidim*? And why do Satmarer *chassidim* consider themselves superior to Breslover *chassidim*? And the answer is that all idealists who follow certain systems, they do it because they think it's the best system – otherwise they'd follow a different system. It's common sense! What should a man be a Lubavitcher if he thinks something else is better? Why should a non-Lubavitcher be non-Lubavitcher unless he thinks that it's better? All idealists follow the system they follow because they think it's the best.

Now, who is going to be the arbiter and say who is the best? Mashiach will come, and in order to keep peace between everybody, he'll say, "You're all the best!" And the truth is that they *are* all the best. But right now, it's not really a question if the Lubavitchers feel superior, because if you ask a *litvishe* yeshiva *bochur* – he feels *he's* superior. Ask a Satmarer and he feels *he's* superior. And go into a Sefardi yeshiva in Eretz Yisroel, go into Porat Yosef, and he knows that he's superior too. Everyone is superior.

And the answer is, that's how idealists have to be. No idealist will do something that he thinks is not superior.

July 1979

Good Choices

Q/ What does Hakadosh Baruch Hu want us to be, *chassidish* or *litvish* or what?

A/ Now that's some big order. He wants me to make enemies, the one asking this question.

Hashem wants you to be the best that you can be. Some people can be their best if they're *chassidish*. Some people can be their best if they're *litvish*. Other people can be their best if they're Sefardi. You have to figure out for yourself what will help you be the best. And you have to really think about it.

The best type of diet depends on each individual person. People are different.

And therefore it's like asking: "What is the best diet for all of mankind?" The best type of diet depends on each individual person. People are different. Some people are so different that their diets are radically different.

So whatever it is that you choose, you should make it a principle in your life to always choose whatever it is that will give you the most success in life – and success in this world means preparing for the next world.

July 1979

QUESTIONS
On Any
SUBJECT

Chapter 5

Voting Jewish

In honor of our parents

Cynthia and Charles Haddad

Ellen and Isaac Jemal

Sponsored by Monique and David Haddad

Contents

Chapter 5

Voting Jewish

Political Involvement

Should Jews get involved in politics?

It depends what you mean by 'involved in politics.' Jews have to be involved only in *avodas Hashem.* In politics, *per se,* we have no interest.

However, when we see an issue that involves morality, we should always vote and it's a mitzvah. You have to know that Hakadosh Baruch Hu expects Jews to participate in improving the moral environment. If your vote can help out, it's your job to vote for morality.

Now, whom to vote for, that's something that depends on the circumstances. But in general, voting is not an act of secular activity. It's not *chullin;* voting is *kodesh.*

The Gemara tells a story. A *chacham* of the Gemara was walking in a certain marketplace and he encountered Eliyahu Hanavi.

He said to Eliyahu Hanavi, "Is there anybody in this marketplace who is a *ben Olam Haba*?

Eliyahu said, "Yes."

That's what Eliyahu Hanavi said caused that man to be a ben Olam Haba.

The *chacham* said, "Show him to me."

Eliyahu led him to a clown who was dancing in the corner of the market. He said, "This clown is a *ben Olam Haba.*"

So the *chacham* approached the clown and said, "Tell me what good things you do."

So the man said, "Well, I'm a clown by profession. But when I hear of somebody who is discouraged, who is in a depression, I visit him and I clown before him to make him laugh and cheer him up."

That's what Eliyahu Hanavi said caused that man to be a *ben Olam Haba.*

Now where does it say that clowning is one of the ways of serving Hashem?

The answer is, when it's necessary to serve Hashem, you do it in any way that's necessary. If you have to be a clown and go to the polls to vote, Hakadosh Baruch Hu will give you a reward for it. Don't say "I'm only *oved Hashem* by putting on tefillin, by davening, by doing the mitzvos that everybody else does." Sometimes, *avodas Hashem* requires you to do queer things.

And therefore, if you can help out in the great battle against gays, against pornography, against any form of wickedness by putting your vote in the right place, then you surely are *oved Hashem* by doing it.

January 1990

Religious Involvement

What do you say about this subject of mixing religion into politics? It's an accusation lately brought up against

Reagan that he's mixing religion and politics too much.

We need your vote; it's a great mitzvah to vote.

A/ And our answer is that we *want* mixing of religion and politics. Because everybody is doing it. If Governor Cuomo went and attended a gay banquet to raise money for the Gays for Political Action, isn't that mixing religion and politics?! Of course it is. That's his religion. What else is it if not religion? Is it public welfare? Is it a benefit for the youth? Is it to make more money for the government? No; it's a religion.

So just as the liberals have their religion of atheism, a religion of hedonism, a religion of corruption and pornography and breaking down all the values of civilization, so why shouldn't the president also have a religion?

On the contrary, if we see the president speaking about religion, we might suspect that he's trying to get the votes of religious people. And if that's the case, then he's getting our votes. Everybody should vote for President Reagan, there's no question about it. If you didn't register yet, then this coming Tuesday, the ninth of October, is registration day. So go and register, from nine in the morning until nine at night. Find out where in your neighborhood. In this neighborhood, it's on East 8th Street, at the public school. Go register and make it your business to vote.

We need your vote; it's a great mitzvah to vote. That's also one of the things that I say will rise up against a man on the Day of Judgment. You mean to say you're going to be lax in this great battle against the forces of evil that are trying to overthrow our civilization? Everybody should vote. I registered already. Everybody should register. It's your business to register.

We want religion in politics! We want presidents who believe in a Creator! We want presidents who believe in values of morality and decency! That's the only foundation of our society. And therefore, our answer is, if a president speaks about religion and makes public pronouncements about it, then he is the man we're going to vote for.

October 1984

Ask the Elders

How should we decide for whom to vote, especially if we cut ourselves off from the news-papers

Q/ How should we decide for whom to vote, especially if we cut ourselves off from the newspapers?

A/ The truth is that the newspapers are not going to tell you who to vote for. If they do tell you, they're the wrong ones. You have to ask people who know. There are people who know.

Someone asked me a question this week. "Should I vote for Marc Mishan because he's Jewish?" The truth is, I didn't even know he was a Jew. I thought he was an Irishman. But this person told me that he's a Jew and he's *shomer Shabbos.* A Jew who is *shomer Shabbos*? What's the question? Everybody should vote for Marc Mishan. He didn't pay me for that, by the way. Sure we should vote for him. But not because he's a *shomer Shabbos*. It's because he's going to support our values.

Now I mention Marc Mishan for a reason. I have a reason for mentioning him. He is a *shomer Shabbos* – but it's more than that. That's not the important part – we vote for good *goyim* too, no question about it. But I say Marc Mishan because he is the kind of fellow who wouldn't vote to give civil rights to what they call the gays. The gays is another name for reptiles; the filthy abomination, the *mishkav zacharniks,* the homosexualists; they're the ones who deserve to be put to death. By the law of the Torah, it's one of the worst capital crimes. And there are some people who are running – I don't want to say their names; it's not my policy now – who are running for office who voted to give them recognition. Marc Mishan is not that kind. You understand?

So if you don't know, ask. There are people who do know. There are a lot of people who are knowledgeable in these things.

"Jail, Not Bail." Jail, not bail! That's the man for us!

And by the way, I want to bring up a shining hero. I never saw him before and never heard of him before, but I say vote for him. I don't even know if he's a *shomer Shabbos* at all, but he deserves our vote. Seymour Kravitz! He publicized his name, his picture, with the slogan, "Jail, Not Bail." Jail, not bail! That's the man for us! Maybe he doesn't even mean it, but still, if he's bold enough to put up that slogan, we're all for him.

And so, if you don't know, ask. People who know can tell you.

October 1977

Voting For Yourselves

Q/ What can we learn from the election of Elizabeth Holtzman?

A/ We can learn a great deal. And we can learn that the public is not aware of the necessity of protecting their interests. I won't go into that now; next time when there is an election we have to talk about it more. But it is important for the Orthodox public – the other public are *beheimos;* we can't talk about them because they don't understand the issues at all; they read the newspapers, they listen to the radio, and they are prisoners of television; they swallow all the propaganda that is fed to them. And if a Democrat chairman tells them, vote straight

It is very important to be aware of the issues,

Democrats, so that is what they do, and therefore they elect somebody who is harmful for their interests, and many of the public benefits that could have been gained by different candidates go lost.

People who want to protect their interests have to take action, and it is already a little late in the season – the Orthodox Jews have to wake up and they have to realize they have to vote not for what somebody promises to give them, some benefit, some handout, some small program or some privilege; they have to vote for the overall benefits to the general public because what the public benefits from, the Orthodox Jew is also going to benefit from. It is very important to be aware of the issues, and if you yourself are not fully competent, then you should consult the Torah leaders who know what is what.

November 1981

Voting Registration

Should a yeshiva *bochur* register to vote?

Should a yeshiva man register to vote?

It depends. If he knows how to vote, he should. If he doesn't, he shouldn't.

Now sometimes, it's a question between this crook and that crook and so, it's a waste of time. But if you have a special intention by voting, then by all means, because we should put our weight in the right direction.

Today, it's important, if possible, to throw our weight against the liberals. Whatever you can do against liberals. It's a great tragedy that the Jews are not apprised of the danger.

The liberals are endangering our safety. Jewish liberals are undermining the country.

The liberals are endangering our safety.

And whatever you can do to vote against a man who is against capital punishment, do it. If a man is against capital punishment, vote against him! If a man is for homosexuals, vote against him! If a man is for E.R.A., vote against him! Vote only for those who want to uphold the standards that the country lived by until now. Vote for those who want to make America strong. Armaments! Not disarmaments.

Vote against those who want to spend more money for welfare. It's a very wicked thing President Carter did; he made a national cabinet for education and he put a woman at the head of it. Up until now, anybody who wanted to contaminate the education system did so through state and city channels. Now it's going to be done on a national scale. Carter is a liberal and he started something new. It'll cost a pile of money; millions, billions it will cost, and all those billions will go towards corrupting America.

Whatever we can do to unseat the liberals, by all means.

November 1979

Voting Conservative 1

Q/ **Who should we vote for for president?**

A/ We should vote for the one who appears to us to be the most conservative.

Now, I can't tell you who that is. But there's no question that the conservatives of today are extremely more liberal than the liberals of thirty years ago. We have already advanced so far beyond the borders of liberalism, that today

You know, Cuomo is an Italian and the Jews owe a debt of gratitude to Italy.

we can afford to retreat many miles behind these boundaries and still remain at the forefront of liberalism. And therefore, today there's no such thing as too much conservatism. You have to vote for conservative candidates on every level – on national, state, and city levels.

That's my opinion. By the way, nobody here has to agree with me – on anything. Only, I don't have to agree with you either.

August 1976

Voting Conservative 2

Q/ How should we view the endorsement given to Cuomo by Jewish personalities?

A/ When you see Jewish personalities who endorse Cuomo – even some Orthodox personalities – they have their reasons; but we have our reasons. And our reasons for not endorsing Cuomo are because of Jewish self interests. Our Jewish interests require the preservation of Jewish lives. And in order to save Jewish lives that are being destroyed constantly by wanton murderers, it's important to restore the death penalty – at least in the books. I will explain something to you before I go on because there's another question here that someone passed up on a piece of paper. It says, "Is Lehrman's intermarriage any reason not to vote for him and to vote instead for Cuomo?" [*Ed: Republican Lewis Lehrman ran against Democrat Mario Cuomo in the 1982 New York State Gubernatorial race.*] Now, pay attention to what I'm going to tell you.

You know, Cuomo is an Italian and the Jews owe a debt of gratitude to Italy. First of all, Italy is the oldest continuous civilization in Europe; it means that Italy is the most civilized country in Europe. The Jews in Italy lived most happily, more than in any other country. Even under the shadow of the Pope, the Jews were more protected than anywhere else. When they personally appealed to the Pope, they got results. When Mussolini took over Italy, the Jews had nothing to fear. And even when Hitler became the master of Italy – there's a book called The Destruction of the European Jews by Hilberg, and he brings statistics that show how the Italians were most active in defying Hitler's demands for handing over Jews. More than any other country that was under Hitler's domination, the Italians resisted and saved Jews. And therefore, we Jews should have a certain affection for Italians.

But besides being good neighbors, the Italians are excellent for public office.

But besides being good neighbors, the Italians are excellent for public office. And since Cuomo is an Italian, actually, we ought to vote for him just because of that. Italians are the very best people when it comes to public office. Our Italian councilmen are the best people; they're the most reliable. But that's only as long as they remain Italians! The problem is that Cuomo is not an Italian anymore. He went to college!

Now, there are some who survive college and still remain Italians. Some don't go to college altogether. There are still a lot of normal, hardworking Italians around. That's why even today I say that if we would take the justices of our state supreme courts and from the United States Supreme Court and we would put them to work pouring concrete on sidewalks, and instead we would take the Italian construction workers and put them on the supreme courts, they would do an excellent job and the country would be much better off. Why? Because they have common sense. They wouldn't make society so disturbed with the laws defending criminals and making it impossible to apprehend violators of laws. Today a policeman has to be, first of all, a lawyer, and he has to be a judge too; he has to know the whole book before he can even arrest somebody. So he thinks, "Why should I bother?"

If we took, let's say, the construction workers and the ones who sell bananas on the street, and put them onto the supreme court, they'd restore society!

And even after he arrests the criminal, the lawyers and the judges are on the side of the criminals. But if we had Italians there – if we took, let's say, the construction workers and the ones who sell bananas on the street, and put them onto the supreme court, they'd restore society! I mean it seriously! They'd restore society to a normal kind of existence.

However, when an Italian like Cuomo is against the death penalty, he's not an Italian anymore. I think Lehrman is the real Italian! He married a gentile woman and he supports the death penalty; he's the real Italian*). And I think that all the Italians should vote for him, besides the Jews. He's for the death penalty so he deserves our vote because every person today is in danger of his life. It's terrible what's happening in the streets today. Wanton murder just for the fun of killing people. They're poisoning candies today. It's fun to murder people, to shoot into a crowd of people, to drive your car into people. Nothing will happen to you anyway. Even if you get a tough judge, you'll be sentenced to, let's say, ten years in a hotel at the state's expense. You'll get color television, you'll get good food – nutritionists take care of your food; they plan out your meals. You'll get free medical and dental care. So why shouldn't you? And after a while, you'll get out anyway.

So if you vote for Lehrman, it's a vote for your own safety, for your own self-preservation.

So you'll ask me, but Lehrman has a non-Jewish wife. Imagine a murderer is coming at you with a knife. What are you going to do?! You're in terrible danger! Suddenly, a Jewish policeman is rushing towards you to save your life.

---

*) **Q: Will Lew Lehrman's conversion to Catholicism help or hurt him politically?**

A: I don't know but I wish him the worst. He's a *shoteh!* What can I do? I can't wish him anything better than the worst.

April 1985

"Stop! You're a Jewish policeman? I have to know first who you are married to." Would anybody say that? If he's going to save your life you have no *kashas* to ask. And therefore, the man who is for the death penalty, that's the man we want to elect! And Lehrman is for the death penalty.

The man who is for the death penalty, that's the man we want to elect!

There's another thing that's also a very serious matter. Cuomo has committed himself that when he becomes governor he's going to issue an executive order for the entire state of New York in favor of gays. It means the gays are going to have special rights; it's going to flood the state with the most terrible immorality. And don't think that New York is just one state. New York is a keystone for the union. All over America it's going to have a tremendous effect. And therefore, in the best Jewish interests, I think that everybody should try to try their best to help Lehrman become elected. All the Italians should feel that he's their man. He is the closest to their hearts because he's more Italian than Cuomo! And the Jews? Of course; why not? All the Jews should also vote for him.

October 1982

Lomdus in Voting 1

Q/ Should a person refrain from voting for a candidate simply on the grounds that he's Jewish, because that would mean that if he's elected, it would cause him to be *mechalel Shabbos* and things like that?

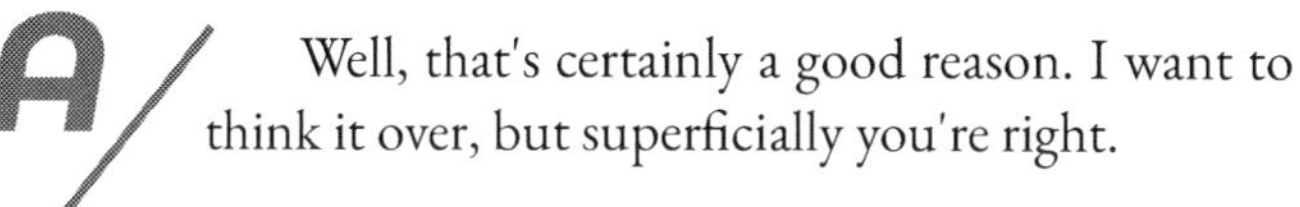

A/ Well, that's certainly a good reason. I want to think it over, but superficially you're right.

October 1972

Your question is a difficult question and I'll have to think it over. And it's a question in a field in which I am not an expert.

Lomdus in Voting 2

Q/ **If there are two big candidates like a Democrat and a Republican running against each other, and a small candidate who follows the Torah viewpoint is also running, but he has no chance of winning, is it permissible or desirable to vote for the third party candidate?**

A/ I'll tell you, your question is a difficult question and I'll have to think it over. And it's a question in a field in which I am not an expert; it's a field of politics. Maybe I can discuss it with you privately if you give me a chance to think it over. But at the moment I don't want to say a snap decision.

October 1982

Saving the Environment

Q/ **What do you say about not voting altogether?**

A/ If you're able to vote, I think you should because it's a good thing. Anything that improves the environment is good for us.

October 1972

Voting on Israel

A lot of crooks are running for office who drag in the word 'Israel' just to get votes.

Q/ Is it of considerable importance to look at a candidate's voting record on issues involving Israel?

A/ I want to tell you something. A lot of crooks are running for office who drag in the word 'Israel' just to get votes. One crook is Hart. Gary Hart is a low character. Up until recently, you couldn't hear a squeak from him about Israel. All of a sudden, he's a lover of Israel. The same is Mondale. The same is Jesse Jackson – Jackson! There's a lot more to be said about him.

We have to know that there are issues that are more serious to us, because these people, once they get in, they won't do a thing for Israel. They're absolute crooks.

Suddenly they brought up a new issue. Transferring the American Embassy from Tel Aviv to Yerushalayim. Now, people, know that that's just crooked politics. Reagan is in office now and he cannot promise it because it will cause a lot of trouble. These fellows who are running can promise anything right now. Once they get in, they'll forget all about it. They won't carry out their promise.

Let's have a candidate that tells us he runs on the ticket of arming America. America must be armed! Ah, arming America; people think it's unimportant. It's popular today to protest against nuclear rearmament. We don't realize that that's a vital issue.

What about saving the budget? You know, America is getting into debt in such a perilous manner that in a few years it will be impossible to manage the government. But nobody is worried about that. The politicians are promising more and more money for handouts in order to buy votes.

So therefore, we shouldn't be deceived by these liars who send us newsletters and give press releases about their love for Israel. They love Israel as much as they love Nicaragua and they will never do a thing for Israel.

May 1984

An Easy Choice

Q/ **Which candidate for president should we vote for? Bill Clinton or Bob Dole?**

A/ I'll say don't be *meshuga.* That's my answer. Don't be crazy.

October 1996

A Not-So-Easy Choice

Q/ **Who should we vote for in the upcoming election, Carter or Ford?**

A/ How one should vote, I won't spend time answering now. But I can tell you only what I told a young man today. If it's a question of whom to elect for president, take a nickel and throw it up and see how it lands. And that's how you should decide your vote.

October 1976

If it's a question of whom to elect for president, take a nickel and throw it up and see how it lands. And that's how you should decide your vote.

Voting for Jews

What they want is that the Russians should take over all the surrounding countries.

Q/ Should a person become a registered Democrat in order to vote for Noach Dear?

A/ Absolutely. Of course, in the final elections you can vote for Republicans too; you don't have to vote for the Democrat ticket. But to help Noach Dear, I think it's a very big thing today because the gays are after him.

Besides the fact that he's a *shomer mitzvos,* it's a *chiyuv* to help out a fellow Jew.

September 1989

Not Voting for Jews

Q/ What do we learn from the American invasion of Grenada?

A/ We learn that there are a lot of traitors in the United States. The United States is swarming with traitors – all the liberals are traitors. What they want is that the Russians should take over all the surrounding countries. And finally, they'll move into southern Florida too; they'll move into southern California and parts of northern California. And then the liberals will say, "It can't be helped. For the sake of peace, we'll keep quiet about it." That's what they want.

And therefore, everybody should know that it's time to put a stop to this. I was talking to an important politician; he was a Democrat, but he had some sense in him. And he said,

We must go out and work and wake up the people and tell them it's a sakanah

"What's it our fault? The Jews all vote for liberal people. It's their fault."

And now, Reagan is up for reelection. Everybody must know it's an ideal to vote for Reagan. Not because we love Reagan so much – I have nothing against him but we love him because of his opponents. He has such rotten opponents that we have no choice. Every one of them is *mamash* a dead rat! A dead rat! They smell like dead rats – every one of them! They're terrible, his opponents! We have no choice! And we must go out and work and wake up the people and tell them it's a *sakanah* – even more than the first time. We have to work hard so that Reagan should be reelected! Not because of Reagan; just to keep those other fellows out of office!

A tramp like Cranston; he's one of the worst and lowest fellows! Or the others, all of them! Mondale? Mondale is a piece of garbage.

And I'm being kindhearted by saying these words! I'm pulling punches – I'm not telling the truth!

February 1984

Rav Miller's Endorsement

Q/ Whom do you endorse as the Democratic mayoral candidate: Bellamy, Farrell, or Koch?

I endorse all three to go to Gehinom.

June 1985

Voting for the Death Penalty 1

You have to know there's a wind of liberalism blowing and it's all lies.

Q/ What lesson should be learned from the killing of a police officer this past week?

A/ And so, we have to repeat an old lesson. You have to know there's a wind of liberalism blowing and it's all lies. They tell you statistics that are lies. Their statements are all lies. People will never refrain from crime unless they're afraid of punishment! And murder has to have the death penalty. Otherwise they'll never stop it! But these liars say, "There's no proof that the death penalty is a deterrent."

You know, the Italian construction man has more intelligence than the editors of New York Times! No question about it! Because these are artificial people; they don't think straight. It would be the very best thing if the editor of New York Times once took a walk in Central Park and he'd get a drubbing from some bums who would flash a knife at him. Then he'd stop being a liberal.

Because in the ivory towers, it's all affectation, showing off – it's all showing off. "I'm against taking human life," they say, "Oh, it's terrible. We're horrified!" So what do they do? They're killing millions of babies every year. They're for abortion, that's alright. But taking human life? Oh no! Whose human life? A murderer. "Oh, no! We don't repay murder with murder. Society itself becomes the murderer. That's the very worst example, to murder a man who killed a policeman. It means we are the murderers."

It's all garbage. They are fools. They have no intelligence at all, but they're doing it for a purpose, an affectation of showing off to make an impression on the world that they

There's only one way to deal with crime; that there should be strict, stern punishments.

are higher people. The truth is, they're the lowest of the low because they're the ones who advocate every form of perversion, every form of wickedness there is.

And as long as we listen to these fools, we are the fools. And so, how long, how long, fellow Jews, will you be blind, and you'll vote for such people like Governor Carey? You don't even think twice. Such a *rasha m'rushe.* Carey is the one whose hands shed the blood of all those innocent victims when he vetoed the bill for the death penalty! Carey is the arch-murderer!

And all those people – I won't say the names of those Orthodox Jews – who make deals with Carey; if Carey will see to it that they get certain funds from the state, so those Orthodox *askanim* will get the Jewish votes for him; they're all shedding blood – innocent blood and Jewish blood.

There's only one way to deal with crime; that there should be strict, stern punishments. For stealing, there has to be stern punishment! For every kind of crime!

And therefore, the world will never be safe when the liberals are in charge of the attitudes of the public. We have to free ourselves from these attitudes.

And so, what do we learn from a murder of a policeman? We learn that we must go back to what was years ago when they didn't murder policemen. They were afraid to murder a policeman because they knew it meant sure death. If they would murder somebody else, there was also a pretty good chance that they'd end up in an electric chair. But with a policeman, they knew for certain that that was their sure destination!

But today, you see the results. That's what it caused. And we are the ones who are to blame. And our own lives, *chas v'shalom,* are in danger because we're stupid enough to be swayed by these winds that sway the *resha'im.*

February 1980

Voting for the Death Penalty 2

Your own votes are killing you actually killing you! It's not a mashal!

Q/ What is your opinion of the death sentence that was carried out in Florida with the consent of the governor there?

A/ I say everybody here ought to write a letter congratulating the governor of Florida for carrying out the death sentence. Everybody!

I know there are a lot of fools right here today. I'm telling you to your face. There are a lot of damn fools who read the New York Times and sympathize with the murderer who was executed. So you're sympathizing with potential murderers of yourselves, *chas v'shalom*. You're fools! You're being led astray because you're sleeping. If you'd wake up, you'd write letters to the governor in Florida saying, "We're with you. We wish you were the president." That's what you should do. That people should be so crazy in this country to do such things as to let murderers out for nothing! It shows they're lunatics. What do lunatics do? They continue voting for the liberals.

So you dumb Jews, you *shotim*, your own votes are killing you – actually killing you! It's not a *mashal*! They're shooting you down. Your votes! Your votes are raising wicked judges who let off criminals. It's time for Jews to wake up and say, "We see what's happening. Our lives are in danger. The liberals are ruining the country."

And so, it's time to throw our weight behind ousting the liberals. Whatever we can do to undermine them, by all means.

June 1979

If you want your children to grow up in a sane world, you have to do something about it now.

Democrats or Republicans

Q/ What do you think is better for the Jewish people, Democrats or Republicans?

A/ That's a good question. It depends on who the candidate is.

And I'm going to take this opportunity, I don't care what you think about me. I say people vote for Nixon! And spread the word. Spread the word! There are a lot of muddle-headed Jews still today living in a time that's long passed by.

If you want your children to grow up in a sane world, you have to do something about it now. *B'ezras Hashem*, that's what you're expected to do. Vote for Nixon.

And let me tell you, Agnew is a very good man. People are making a big mistake about Agnew. The truth is that – I heard someone say this – if Nixon would be shot and Agnew would be president, it would be a good thing. The second half! The second half! May Nixon live long as far as I'm concerned. But Agnew is a good man.

I want to explain something to you. Agnew is an immigrant. He's a son of immigrants, Greek immigrants. He worked his way through college. He's a self-made fellow. He's a decent man and he's a smart man. He was governor of Maryland. He was a successful governor of Maryland.

Only what made the so-called liberals hate him? When they were burning stores in New York and in Los Angeles, some African American in Baltimore got the idea of following suit. So Agnew did what nobody else did. He called in the heads of the African-American community and he told them off. He said, "I want you to be responsible to see that this stops!" He gave them a whole lecture. It had a good effect.

But when the liberals heard about that, oh ho! In permissible America?! And therefore he gained a bad name. But if after Nixon's term is over – let him live long – after his term is over, if Agnew is elected, America is not going to do anything but gain thereby. And so, you should vote and spread the word. Tell people it's their duty to vote for Nixon. Other candidates – I'm not able to tell you right now.

October 1972

You should vote and spread the word. Tell people it's their duty to vote for Nixon.

QUESTIONS *On Any* SUBJECT

Chapter 6

All About Food

Chapter Sponsor

לזכר נשמת

ר׳ **חיים ברוך** בן **בנימין** ז״ל

מרת **אסתר הינדא** בת **מיכאל** ע״ה

From their grandchildren,
Carolyn, Barry, Rachel, Noam, Binyamin Stein

Contents

Chapter 6

All About Food

Eating for Success

Q/ How would you describe the picture of a Jew who is eating successfully? What foods should he eat?

A/ Now, which foods a person should eat or not eat depends on the individual, but how a Jew should eat, that we can say.

Whenever he eats, he should think two thoughts. Number one, "I'm doing it to have the *koach* to serve Hashem." Let's say when he's sitting down to eat supper; "I'm eating supper now in order to have *koach* to serve Hashem."

And secondly, "I'm eating it in order to see the *chesed* of Hashem." בְּחֵן בְּחֶסֶד וּבְרַחֲמִים, Hashem feeds us not with bland, tasteless foods; He feeds us tasty, delicious foods, and by eating and enjoying it, we're learning the *chesed* of Hashem.

Now, learning the *chesed* of Hashem by means of eating is a practical and very important thing. You see that when Yitzchak Avinu had to give a *bracha* to his son Eisav, he said "וַעֲשֵׂה לִי מַטְעַמִּים – *Prepare for me a meat dish and make it tasty;* כַּאֲשֶׁר אָהַבְתִּי וְאָכְלָה – *Prepare it the way you know that I like, and I will eat it;* בַּעֲבוּר תְּבָרֶכְךָ נַפְשִׁי – *in order I should give you a bracha*" (*Bereishis*

You have to use that opportunity to become an oheiv Hashem from the food. That's a very important purpose of food!

27:4). Yitzchak, in order to give his son Eisav a better *bracha*, wanted to enjoy the venison that Eisav would roast for him.

Isn't that remarkable? Yitzchak needed to enjoy the food? "The way that I like it"?! The answer is yes. No matter how great your mental idealism is, when it's supported by physical motivations – you're now enjoying the food he brought for you – that makes it more powerful, much more powerful. And therefore, in order to make the *bracha* have more effect, Yitzchok needed to eat what Eisav prepared for him.

And so, when you eat Hakadosh Baruch Hu's bounty, you have to use that opportunity to become an *oheiv Hashem* from the food. That's a very important purpose of food, to appreciate Hakadosh Baruch Hu and to love Him.

It's very important, these two ideals. Number one, *l'sheim Shamayim* and number two, *ahavas Hashem.*

And so, what exactly to eat I'm not going to tell you, but when you do eat, if you can add these *kavanos* – "I'm eating in order to have *koach* to serve Hashem, and I'm eating in order to discern the *chasdei Hashem* – these two *kavanos* are ways of being successful when it comes to eating.

August 1999

Eating in Uniform

Q/ **Should a yeshiva *bochur* wear his hat while eating in the yeshiva dining room?**

A/ This depends on the *minhag hamedinah;* it depends on the accepted custom.

I want to explain something. My *shver, zichrono livracha,* never ate without a hat in his house. Always with a hat. Lunch, breakfast, supper, whatever; it was always with a hat. Because he was a Slabodka *talmid,* and he learned the dignity of being a Jew.

A Jew is like a Kohen Gadol, and it says by the Kohen Gadol, וְעָשִׂיתָ בִגְדֵי קֹדֶשׁ לְאַהֲרֹן אָחִיךָ לְכָבוֹד וּלְתִפְאָרֶת – Aharon must be dressed with honor and with beauty. And so, a Jew is a Kohen Gadol, and the table is not a feeding trough where horses are led to feed on oats. A table is a *mizbei'ach* and it's a place of *avodas Hashem*. That's how Jews who learn Torah understand it.

When you approach a table, there is salt on the table. עַל כָּל קָרְבָּנְךָ תַּקְרִיב מֶלַח – *On all your offerings there should be salt.* Even if you don't like salt, put a little bit of salt. Dip your bread three times in salt. One, two, three, just to show that you're doing it for a purpose, not just for taste. One, two, three. That's a *korban* to Hashem.

And also, it's not a bad idea that you should think, like it says in *Shulchan Aruch*, in *Chayei Adam*, שֶׁכָּל כַּוָּנוֹתָיו יִהְיֶה לְשֵׁם שָׁמַיִם. You should think, "I'm eating this meal now to serve You, Hashem." Isn't that a beautiful way to eat?

It won't detract from your gusto, from your appetite. You can eat with appetite. You can relish your food, but say it beforehand; eat with this thought in mind, "I'm approaching the table to serve You, Hashem. I want to get strength in order to fulfill Your commandments."

It won't detract from your gusto, from your appetite. You can eat with appetite. You can relish your food.

And also, when you approach the table, you realize that Hakadosh Baruch Hu is your host and you're only a little orphaned boy or orphaned girl being fed at Hashem's table. תַּעֲרֹךְ לְפָנַי שֻׁלְחָן – *You set the table before me, Hashem.* And therefore, when you approach the table, you approach it with the greatest *derech eretz.*

A man once told me that he had an old European mother. When he was a little boy, he used to run and play and sometimes he would sit on the table, and his mother

It's always a sign of nobility when you approach a Jewish table with a head covering.

drove him off the table. "*Ah Yiddishe tish is kadosh!* A Jewish table is holy," she said. An old European mother. "You can't sit on the table!" You hear that? She drove him off the table. He became a professor later in life; a very cultured, successful man. He never forgot his mother's teaching, "You can't sit on a table." A Jewish table is *kadosh.*

And so when you approach the table to eat in the yeshiva dining room, if you want to wear a hat with this *kavanah*, because you're serving Hakadosh Baruch Hu, just like you wear a hat for *Shemoneh Esrei* – you shouldn't stand *Shemoneh Esrei* with just a yarmulke; a yarmulke is too informal when you're standing before a king. If you have no hat, well, it can't be helped. If you have a hat, it's better to wear a hat during *Shemoneh Esrei*. So if you want to sit at the table in the yeshiva dining room with a hat, why not?

However, I said this with a modification at the beginning. If nobody wears a hat in your dining room, maybe you shouldn't be different from the *minhag*. But if you have a choice, it's always a sign of nobility when you approach a Jewish table with a head covering.

Even in the hottest weather, my father-in-law, *alav hashalom,* never took off his jacket at the table. He always sat with a jacket and a hat at the table. It was a principle. He learned it from Slabodka, you have to be a man who exemplifies the teachings of the Torah. Be dignified! A Jew has to be dignified.

בָּנִים אַתֶּם לַה' אֱלֹקֵיכֶם – *You are My children, says Hashem,* לֹא תִתְגֹּדְדוּ – *you shouldn't cut yourself,* וְלֹא תָשִׂימוּ קָרְחָה בֵּין עֵינֵיכֶם לָמֵת – *you shouldn't pluck out your hair.* You shouldn't pluck out your hair because of a dead body, *chalilah.* In mourning, you shouldn't pluck your hair.

So Rashi brings, "You're My children, וּצְרִיכִים אַתֶּם לִהְיוֹת נָאִים – *and you have to be beautiful at all times,* even not at the table, וְלֹא גְדוּדִים וּמְקֻרָחִים – *you shouldn't look tattered.* A Jew must look dignified. A Jew must be well dressed and dignified. And therefore, there is something in the principle of approaching the table wearing a hat.

March 1989

To Enjoy or Not Enjoy

Q/ Many times, we find that *gedolim* avoided eating something that they enjoyed immensely. How would that fit in with this idea of eating to recognize the *chesed* of Hashem?

A/ Many times, we find great men who avoided things that they enjoyed very much. The Alter of Slabodka once was served some delicatessen and he felt a special interest in it, so he made it a principle all of his life not to touch it anymore. That's a matter of self-discipline and it's perfectly correct.

But we're not talking now about pursuing pleasures. Let's not deceive ourselves. You are sitting down now to a chicken supper. Your wife has worked two hours tonight and she has made an excellent chicken supper for you.

But we're not talking now about pursuing pleasures. Let's not deceive ourselves.

So if you're going to sit down and do an exercise in abstinence, you're going to look at it and not eat – that's your business! But we're talking about the fact that you're going to eat it up! So why should we be hypocrites and say, "Look, I'm going to eat it up and I'm not going to enjoy it because there are great men..." But they *didn't* eat it! Since you *are* eating it, look at what you're eating and thank Hakadosh Baruch Hu for it. And in the midst of the bite, between one bite and another, stop and reflect about the things we spoke about here.

February 1973

Say Yes to Sugar

Add the sugar and the flavors, and do it l'sheim Shamayim.

Q/ **The *Shulchan Aruch* (see *Orach Chaim* 231) says that when you eat, it must be *l'sheim Shamayim,* for the purpose of serving Hashem. Does that mean we shouldn't make our food more tasty by adding sugar or other flavors?**

A/ And the answer is, no. Add the sugar and the flavors, and do it *l'sheim Shamayim*.

Now how could you do that? If you're enjoying it, what's the *l'sheim Shamayim* there?

The answer is, even when you're eating plain bread without any flavors, without any spreads, how is it *l'sheim Shamayim*? You're hungry; that's why you're eating.

The answer is that even if it's not entirely *l'sheim Shamayim,* but you're saying that you want to do it *l'sheim Shamayim*, so Hakadosh Baruch Hu says הַבָּא לְטַהֵר מְסַיְּיעִין לוֹ, I'm going to help you. If you want to get *l'sheim Shamayim,* then הַחִיצוֹנִיּוֹת מְעוֹרֶרֶת אֶת הַפְּנִימִיּוֹת, because of your outward act of saying it's *l'sheim Shamayim*, Hakadosh Baruch Hu will help you eventually do it *l'sheim Shamayim*.

So you start out eating the chocolate cake *l'sheim Shamayim*. "I'm eating, Hashem, to have *koach* to serve You." It could be that the chocolate cake is not such a good thing for you, but say it anyhow. Say it anyhow! And after a while you start convincing yourself, and you'll be doing it *l'sheim Shamayim*.

So when you sit down on Yom Tov or Shabbos for a good *seudah*, you should eat *l'sheim Shamayim*. How can you do it? When you sit down to eat a piece of hard bread and a glass of water – it's easier, but now you're sitting down to a good *seudah* of delicious foods, how can you do it *l'sheim Shamayim*?

The answer is, the *tziruf*; just add the *kavanah* of *l'sheim Shamayim* to your own *kavanos* of wanting to eat, and it's considered *l'sheim Shamayim*.

Hakadosh Baruch Hu doesn't want you to suffer; He wants you to enjoy the food and still add *l'sheim Shamayim*. And it is accepted by Him and it's considered an achievement.

June 1994

Sometimes a candy or a piece of cake is important to give you a lift; sometimes it's not wrong.

Say No to Sugar

Q/ Is there anything wrong with eating candies, cakes, doughnuts, and things like that?

A/ The Rambam in *Hilchos Deios* (3:2) states that a man who is wise will eat what's healthy for him, what's beneficial. He says, לֹא יֹאכַל כָּל שֶׁהַחֵךְ מִתְאַוֶּה כְּמוֹ הַכֶּלֶב וְהַחֲמוֹר – *Don't eat only things that your palate desires, like the dog and the donkey do.* You're not an animal that eats only what it thinks is delicious to eat. אֶלָּא יֹאכַל דְּבָרִים הַמּוֹעִילִים לוֹ – *You should eat only the things that are beneficial for you*. So we see that following your desires means that you lack sense, like a donkey or a dog.

Now, will we specify for you that candies and cakes are wrong to eat? It would be foolish for anybody to make such a rule. Sometimes a candy or a piece of cake is important to give you a lift; sometimes it's not wrong. Many times people are down and they need a lift, and then it's recommended that they take a nosh and enjoy life a little bit more than the regular routine.

The wiser man is the one who chooses a diet that is healthy and nourishing.

Yes, sometimes you can do things that are not wrong to do, only that they're not recommended, but you do it in order to raise your spirits. And for happy occasions too, sometimes people can be stimulated to a little more joy because of these things. Therefore, it requires discretion.

But ordinarily, things that are full of sugar will cause your teeth to rot unless you brush your teeth after eating them. And sometimes they take the place of the nourishing foods that you should be eating, and therefore, it's not sensible for a person to waste his efforts on *nosherei.*

And therefore, the wiser man is the one who chooses a diet that is healthy and nourishing. Not organic and special health foods; I don't know about that. But foods that are healthful and nourishing and that people can get the most benefit from, that's how a wise man should eat. You don't need me to tell you; you know that yourself.

January 1987

Sweetening Your Spirits

Q/ Is it permitted to eat superfluous sweets even if I'm not hungry, just for the sake of getting some enjoyment?

A/ There's a *sefer* called *Shevet Mussar,* a very strict *sefer*. He talks about *onshim,* punishments. It's a very severe sefer, the *Shevet Mussar*. And yet, the *Shevet Mussar* makes a statement as follows. In case a person needs *yishuv haleiv,* to gain some calmness of the mind, it's *muttar* to take walks in parks and in gardens. That's what he says there. He gives his permission to take walks in parks and gardens to gain *yishuv halev*.

And therefore, we'll say the same thing over here. If people are down, and they take a nosh just to pick up their spirits, they're justified. But when you're not depressed, and you're just doing it for nothing at all, then it's no mitzvah because you're becoming enslaved to the habits of passion. So it depends what the *kavanah* is.

December 1995

I am sure that if the foods are free of pesticides and free of additives, I'm sure they are more healthful

Eating Healthy

Q/ In order to better take care of our bodies, should we eat natural health foods?

A/ Should we eat natural health foods in order to preserve our health? Now, this is a subject which I am not competent to speak about. I would be happy to give information, but I'm not the competent one.

I am sure that if the foods are free of pesticides and free of additives, I'm sure they are more healthful, because there's no question that Hakadosh Baruch Hu can concoct better things than mankind can. But more than that I cannot say.

If you have whole wheat bread, for instance, we understand that you have all the elements that Hakadosh Baruch Hu intended you to have; whereas if you mill out certain parts, you're losing out. Like everybody knows the story of rice. There was a time when white rice was considered the only way of eating rice; they used to mill off the brown covering of the rice kernel and eat only the kernel. The brown covering, the husk, was considered garbage; they threw it into the backyard for the chickens. And that is when they started suffering from beriberi. And they didn't understand the cause.

There is no question that human beings have made great errors in matters of food.

But they saw the chickens were thriving; the chickens who were fed the husks were thriving, but the human beings were declining. And then a Dutch physician discovered that they were giving the best part to the chickens! The husks have thiamine, the vitamin B1. And so we understand Hakadosh Baruch Hu put the husks on not merely to protect the kernel inside; the husks are there to be eaten because they add certain things.

So there is no question that human beings have made great errors in matters of food. But I cannot tell you anything because I know nothing about the subject at all.

October 1976

Vitamins and Supplements

Q/ Is it worthwhile to take vitamin supplements in order to prolong your life?

A/ And the answer is, is it worthwhile to live longer? That's the answer. Is it worth living longer? Then you should do anything that will help you live longer.

Of course, I'm not saying that it *will* help you live longer, but if it will, if it is something that *al pi teva* is supposed to help you live longer, it's a big mitzvah to live longer.

We say that חַיִּים בִּרְצוֹנוֹ – *Hashem wants us to live* (*Tehillim* 30:6). Hashem wants us to live. חַיִּים בִּרְצוֹנוֹ. He wants us to live. Certainly, He wants all frum Jews to live, no question about it. And therefore, you have to be very careful with your health.

June 1994

Eating to Serve

The only recommendation I'm able to give: Eat what's healthful for you, and it will be included in your service of Hashem

Q/ Should a person eat meat every day?

A/ Now, that's not my line – I'm not in the nutrition business. But I'll merely say this: In addition to having a varied diet of all kinds of food, not only one kind, in addition to that, everyone should learn not to be a slave to the dinner table. We eat for the purpose of being healthy. The Rambam says that you should eat what's good for your health. He says, *lo k'kelev u'kechamor,* not like the dog or the donkey who eat only what's sweet for them. Animals eat what's sweet to them but we have to eat what's good for us.

And therefore, that's the only recommendation I'm able to give: Eat what's healthful for you, and it will be included in your service of Hashem if you'll add the thought of why you're doing it. Like it says in the *Shulchan Aruch*; the *Shulchan Aruch* says you should eat with the intention, *kedai she'uchal la'avod es Hashem,* so that I should have the strength, the energy, to be able to serve Hashem (*Shulchan Aruch O.C.* 231). Always think that. I would recommend that you should say it too when you start eating. It's not a bad idea, only that your wife shouldn't hear it – she'll laugh at you. Or your husband will laugh at you. But you should say it anyhow: "I'm going to eat now *kedai she'uchal la'avod es Hashem.*" That's what the *Shulchan Aruch* says. You're eating in order to serve Hashem.

September 1989

Can a frum person be a vegetarian if he wishes?

Meat Eaters

Q/ **The Gemara (*Pesachim* 49b) says, מִי שֶׁעוֹסֵק בַּתּוֹרָה יֹאכַל בְּשַׂר בְּהֵמָה וְעוֹף, that only someone who learns Torah should eat meat. What does that mean?**

A/ It means this: In principle, anyone can eat meat. But to enjoy meat, to enjoy it as a frequent part of his diet, he has to do something to earn it. He has to use his time for spiritual purposes.

If he's a man who is sordid, crude, he doesn't live spiritually, so Hakadosh Baruch Hu says, "You have a right to live, but for that you can eat spinach. If you want luxuries, then you have to make use of them to serve Me."

But meat, per se, is not forbidden to anybody.

Q/ **But it says עַם הָאָרֶץ לֹא יֹאכַל בָּשָׂר – an *am ha'aretz* shouldn't eat meat?**

A/ It doesn't mean it's forbidden as something that's *assur*. It means he has no right to use it as a luxury. But if he sometimes takes a taste, it's not like eating *chazir*. It's not like eating *chazir*! Only he can't use it as part of his diet, that's all.

December 1995

On Being a Vegetarian

Can a frum person be a vegetarian if he wishes?

A/ It depends. If a person is a vegetarian because on principle he thinks that it's wrong to slaughter animals, then he's an *apikores* and he doesn't belong to the Jewish people. Anybody who goes overboard for animals shows that he doesn't have Torah in his mind. He's lacking a Torah mind.

Some people are enamored with birds. Birds! The Audubon Society, ah! It's a sign of an aristocrat; you're an intellectual, you're a liberal, if you belong to the Audubon Society. Love birds, and write letters to the New York Times protesting about the mistreatment of pigeons, and so on. All this artificial baloney is a sign that a person's mind has become corrupted by garbage.

We also love birds. We love birds when they're served, let's say, as roasted chicken. We love those kinds of birds.

We also love birds. We love birds when they're served, let's say, as roasted chicken. We love those kinds of birds. We want chickens to increase and multiply; why not? We want the number of pigeons to increase. Pigeons are also delectable to eat. Did you ever eat a roasted pigeon? It tastes good too. It's a kosher bird; why not?

But just to be interested in birds for the sake of birds, because of an artificial interest in something that's far away from Torah attitudes, that's nothing. I'm not saying it's a big sin, but it's silly as can be, and it's certainly not a Torah attitude. When a person has pity on animals because he thinks it's wrong to slaughter them for human consumption, then of course, that person is against the Torah.

Now, if a person feels that it's better for his health to be a vegetarian, that's something else. We have no quarrel with him. It doesn't mean that he's right, but still, we're not interested in quarreling with him about that.

January 1987

There are better ways of enjoying life than eating out. What's so great about eating out?

Eating Out

Q/ Does Hakadosh Baruch Hu really mind if we enjoy ourselves once in a while by eating out in a restaurant?

A/ First of all, not only does Hashem not mind if you enjoy yourself once in a while, but He doesn't mind if you enjoy yourself all the time. And not only does He not mind, but He *wants* you to enjoy yourself all the time. And you must get that into your head. If you would frequent these lectures regularly you would know that Hakadosh Baruch Hu wants us to be happy all the time, and whatever we do, we should do with happiness.

But the question really becomes – what is happiness? Now, if you eat out, for the moment it might seem like fun, but when you come home at night and at 3:00 in the morning, you have to start running because you don't know what they served you in the restaurant, it's not fun anymore. Look, it's certainly not as wholesome as what you could eat at home. I told you once, a man once told me that he was in a restaurant and he peeked through the swinging doors into the kitchen. He saw a waiter spit onto a plate and wipe it clean with his apron – a true story!

There are better ways of enjoying life than eating out. What's so great about eating out? It costs less to eat at home. What it is really is only imagination. Because people have put a premium on eating out so they think it's fun. However, we're not going to go into details now about this foolishness.

But there is no question that Hashem is happy when His children are happy – of course, if it's all done in a good way, in a virtuous and kosher way.

July 1979

Eating McDonalds

Q/ **Is there anything wrong with patronizing a kosher branch of a *treife* fast food chain? Let's say a *glatt* kosher McDonalds or something like that?**

A/ Go someplace else; the name already smells bad.

December 1998

Eating Chinese

Q/ **What should be the attitude of an Orthodox Jew regarding *glatt* kosher Chinese restaurants?**

A/ I think it's superfluous to even speak about this. We're definitely happy that they are *glatt* kosher. And if they would close down entirely it would be even better.

December 1973

Pizza and Restaurants

Is it befitting for a ben Torah to eat in a pizza place?

Q/ **Is it befitting for a *ben Torah* to eat in a pizza place or a restaurant?**

A/ Let me explain something to you. If you're a yeshiva *bochur*, a *kollel* man, or a working man who wants to do what's right, make yourself a sandwich before you leave the house in the morning. Take the

The best thing is, take along something from the house, a lunch box, and eat it where you're able to sit by yourself

sandwich along with you and eat the sandwich for lunch. Why waste money on a restaurant? I don't understand it! For years and years, I ate sandwiches that I took with me to the yeshiva every day. Why not? It costs a load of money to eat in a restaurant. You're not חָס עַל מָמוֹן יִשְׂרָאֵל? You need that money for yourself. For more important things than pizza or restaurant food.

Secondly, if you're eating in a place where *leitzim* come together, there's no excuse for that. It's a *moshav leitzim* and there's no excuse for you to sit in such a place! וּבְמוֹשַׁב לֵצִים לֹא יָשָׁב. You can't sit down over there! Especially in some restaurants and pizza places where girls – frum girls – come. Frum girls at this table and yeshiva boys at another table. Not good at all. Not good at all!

And therefore, the best thing is, take along something from the house, a lunch box, and eat it where you're able to sit by yourself, in the office or some other place. And you don't have to spend any money. And you don't have to associate with the wrong people either.

December 1998

The Miracle of Desire

Q/ **How can someone break a desire for eating?**

A/ *Chas v'shalom!* We should never break that desire. The desire for eating is a *nes*. Does your car have a desire for gasoline? You go out in your car. It stops in the middle of the street. No gasoline. If your car had a desire, it would slowly go to the side, to the curb, when it sees a gas station. It's hungry for gasoline so it walks over to the curb. It doesn't do that.

The desire for food is a miracle. It's a *nes* that you have a desire for food. And you should never lose the desire for food.

The desire for eating what you're not supposed to eat, that's a different story. There are many things you're better off if you don't eat.

How can you do it? I'll tell you privately. I have an *eitzah*. If a person has a *taivah* for *nosherei* that are harmful, then I have an *eitzah* for you. I'll tell you what to do, not publicly though. Privately I'll tell you an *eitzah*, a very good *eitzah* I've told many people.

The desire for food is a miracle. It's a nes that you have a desire for food.

March 2000

Overeating Solution

Q/ Is there a cure *al pi Torah* for excessive eating?

A/ Now I'm not an expert in this subject, but I'll give a little suggestion. First of all, a person should learn the *dinim* of *nedarim*. If you're not able to learn the Gemara, learn it in *Shulchan Aruch* or learn it at least in *Kitzur Shulchan Aruch*. Learn how severe a *neder* is. A *neder* is very severe. To make a vow is very severe. First learn that.

Then take out of your house all tempting things. No chocolate cake. No candy in your house. See that it doesn't come into your house. And the people of your family have to cooperate with you.

So the first thing is לְהַגְדִּיל אֶת הַיִּרְאָה, to increase the fear of Hashem by learning the severity of a *neder*, and the second is לְהַקְטִין אֶת הַנִּסָּיוֹן, to minimize the test by getting the *nosherei* out of the house.

How can one with a craving for food control himself from overeating?

And then, let's say, when you finish eating, make a *neder* that all food is *assur* to eat until the next meal. Now that's four hours, let's say. So for four hours, you can keep a *neder*. Don't make a *neder* for ten days. No. For four hours you can make a *neder*.

At the end of the four hours, if you want to let go and eat a lot, it's not so terrible. But after supper, say the same thing again: "I won't eat anything until tomorrow's breakfast." And say it with a *neder*.

However, don't start this until you first make the *hakdamah* and learn the severity of *nedarim*. As it states, נְדָרִים סְיָג לִפְרִישׁוּת – *Nedarim are a fence for abstinence* (*Avos* 3:13). It helps people.

There was a man who told me he's going to a place where a certain woman was flirting with him, and that day he had to be there. He was very much disturbed. Very much disturbed. So I told him, "Swear right now that you won't talk to her that day." And he swore. And the day passed by successfully. That's the purpose of *nedarim* and *shevuos*. Otherwise don't do it.

May 1992

More on Overeating

Q/ **How can one with a craving for food control himself from overeating?**

A/ Number one is, don't have it in the house.

After you stuffed yourself to excess on one thing, then make a *bedikas chometz* and throw everything you have in the garbage can. It's not *baal tashchis;* בַּל תַּשְׁחִית דְּגוּפָא עֲדִיף – *Your body is more important* (*Shabbos* 129a, 140b). Don't have anything in the house except the barest necessities.

The question arises, suppose there is a husband and a wife in the house and she wants to reduce and he doesn't; what to do? That is a problem.

And she says, "How can I have all these things in the house that you like, I can't resist them."

Unless he has a separate refrigerator or a closet with a lock on it and he has the key.

You must drink enough water, and most people aren't.

September 1986

The Very Best Drink 1

Q/ Is there anything wrong with drinking beer?

A/ For *havdalah* you can drink beer. Otherwise, I suggest H^2O. Water is the best drink. You're surprised? Many people are not drinking enough water. And that's one reason why they have constipation and trouble with their stomach.

You should drink enough water every day. Sixty years ago I suffered from constipation. One day I was walking home from yeshiva, and a young man told me to drink a glass of water every day before davening. I started doing it. Only that I did it twice – two glasses of water every morning. *Baruch Hashem*, it was an עֵצָה נִפְלָאָה, a wonderful piece of advice.

You need water to loosen up. When you eat, drink some water. It won't be so hard anymore. Dilute it with water. Make a soft mass inside of your body. That soft mass inside of you is digested more regularly. You must drink enough water, and most people aren't. I'm not saying it's *assur* to drink beer, but what's the benefit of it? It's just dirty water.

January 2000

It's good to teach children to forget about juice. Sink juice, that's all you should drink.

The Very Best Drink 2

Q/ Is it healthy to drink a punch drink?

A/ I see that tonight we're getting scientific questions.

When you invite guests to your table, those people who are not schooled in proper behavior get busy on the apple juice and the orange juice and they drink one glass after another. The host himself sometimes drinks a glass of juice during the meal, but these people, they're guzzling it by the gallon. It looks like they came just to take juice.

Same thing, you invite your children and grandchildren to your table, the first thing is the juice. So it's good to teach children to forget about juice. Sink juice, that's all you should drink. Forget about juice. It's *nosherei.* It's just yielding to the desire for taste sensation. Get accustomed to drinking clear water, tap water.

You can say this to the child: "If you'll drink three glasses of tap water, then I'll let you drink all the juice you want."

And we ourselves should train ourselves not to yield. It's just a temptation of color and taste, that's all it is. It's expensive too. It's a pity to waste all that for nothing. You can drink good water just as well. Of course, sometimes juices will give you nourishment, but when people sit down to a meal and they pour and pour, it shows they are victims of the *yetzer hara* of *nosherei.* That's all it is.

So what kind of drink should you drink at the meal? Punch drink or not punch drink, I don't know. But first of all, get accustomed to drinking good healthy water.

August 1987

QUESTIONS *On Any* SUBJECT

Chapter 7

Dressing Jewish

Chapter Sponsor

Dedicated in honor of my wife,

Leslie Ann

who by example encouraged hundreds of women to dress Jewishly

Chuck Lowenstein

Contents

Chapter 7

Dressing Jewish

Dressing With Derech Eretz

Q/ Why is it so important to be a part of the *tzibbur* in matters of dress?

A/ He's asking why a person should be conventional in how he dresses.

There is such a thing called *derech eretz* and I'll explain it briefly because our time is up. *Derech eretz* means good manners. But good manners in Hebrew means 'the way of the world.'

Good manners stand on three foundations. There are three *yesodos* of *derech eretz.*

One, the one that is most commonly understood, is that you have to realize that other people have feelings. So therefore, if you sit down at the table to enjoy a delicious soup and you're going to slurp and to gargle that soup, it's going to nauseate somebody.

So you can say, "Well, am I harming anybody?"

Of course, I don't say you should wear an overcoat in August, but you should wear something.

Certainly you're harming people. It's annoying! You don't do annoying things.

So the first is *gemilas chasadim*. You have to be kind to other people, and don't do things that annoy them.

Another principle of *derech eretz* is *gadlus ha'adam*, the awareness of the greatness of mankind. We dress the way we do because we wish to demonstrate that we're not animals. People walk out in the street dressed like horses – you see women do that. Men, by the way, are fully clothed; most men are fully clothed. But women...

Why is it that so many women are dressed like horses? The answer is, because that's what they are. They think that by displaying the horse in them, they're going to become more admired. But that shows a lack of understanding of this important principle: *We dress to demonstrate that a human being is not an animal.* Notwithstanding all the scientists, we say what the Torah says: A man was formed in the image of Hashem. His mind, his soul, and his character are sublime. And to demonstrate his immortality – that he lives forever – he puts on clothing. Even when it's uncomfortable!

Of course, I don't say you should wear an overcoat in August, but you should wear something. You should demonstrate that you're not an animal; that you believe in the greatness of mankind that Hakadosh Baruch Hu has declared.

Now, there's another principle included in *derech eretz;* the third principle is to be like other people. If somebody disregards the ways of other people, it shows arrogance. It's not good to despise the opinion of mankind.

Now if everybody in the world wore long hair flowing down over their buttocks, then we would too. In the ancient times, Jews wore long hair because that was the way. They didn't go to the barber every month or every three weeks or every two weeks. They wore long hair. You shouldn't be different from other people; that's also included in *derech eretz,* the way of the world.

Which world? What is the way of the world? We're talking about a decent world. We should have a decent consideration for the ways of other people in the decent world. And anyone who tries to be an exception is demonstrating that he is superior; he doesn't care for others. He is going it alone. And that's a wickedness. Mankind doesn't go it alone. We go together; we go side by side with all men.

Jews also. Of course, we have our peculiar particular Jewish ways, but in general, we go side by side with all the decent people of mankind. And when somebody tries to step out of line, he is demonstrating that he despises the rest of mankind, and such a man is already too arrogant to be allowed to continue. There's no place in the world for him, because then he's capable of anything. It's nothing but a decent regard for the opinions of mankind that keeps people on the right path. And therefore, to dress the way that's considered proper, that's *derech eretz.*

It's nothing but a decent regard for the opinions of mankind that keeps people on the right path.

Now if you'll ask me, since so many women go undressed in the street, is it therefore decent in regard to their opinions to wear the same kind of un-clothing that they do?

And the answer is, there are two things in this. One is a regard for the opinions of mankind, but another is a regard for mankind itself. And women go with so much of the body exposed for the purpose of arousing an interest in males – that's all it is; that's the only reason women wear those garments, because you see that their own men don't wear such garments. He wears sleeves. He wears pants. So why does she wear such garments? It's because she's a female and she thinks she can arouse all the horses on the street. And therefore, that's already an insult to mankind. You're making dogs out of all the men.

Such a thing is contrary to the foundations of civilization. No civilization ever sanctioned that. In America, it's all a passing mode because the time will come when they'll see that civilization cannot endure in such a way.

A blessing on our Jewish women. You see Orthodox Jewish women, Orthodox Jewish girls, blessings on their heads!

And therefore, a blessing on our Jewish women. You see Orthodox Jewish women, Orthodox Jewish girls, blessings on their heads! Whenever one passes you, you should think in your mind that Hakadosh Baruch Hu should give all of them great happiness because they are the ones who are upholding the standards; not only of our nation but the standards of mankind.

August 1975

Dressing With Nobility

Q/ Why do all religious people dress like they're in mourning? Why should they all dress in black?

A/ And the answer is, black is not a sign of mourning. Black is a sign of nobility. They dress like important people. Don't you know many senators wear black Homburg hats? They used to anyway; senators used to wear black Homburg hats. It was a sign of importance.

And so, when Jews wear a black hat, it's a sign that they belong to a *mamleches kohanim.* They're a nation of important, dignified people. And this dignified clothing reminds them that their behavior should be dignified.

Now, if you wear a white straw hat, it doesn't mean that you're permitted to be undignified. Nevertheless, when people choose dignity in their garments, it has a very big effect, an unfailing effect on their character.

Here is a tough bum, and he is admitted to the police force because now they lowered all the requirements. You don't have to be six feet tall anymore; you can be a runt. You don't even have to pass the police academy test; he failed all the tests but there's affirmative action so he's a policeman now.

So he puts on a uniform and now he stands on the street and he's determined to enforce the law. And as he's twirling his baton, his club, he's looking for troublemakers. The truth is, some of these are better law enforcers than the white fellows.

When you dress in a dignified way, you become dignified.

Now, what makes the change? The uniform! Clothes make the man. *Sartor Resartus!* There's a book on that subject. The clothes make the man! The uniform he wears affects his behavior. He lives up to his uniform – he tries at least.

And so, when you dress in a dignified way, you become dignified. That's why it's always important for men and women to remember dignity in clothing, to be dignified in how we dress. That's what Hakadosh Baruch Hu wants at all times, and that's going to change a man's inner behavior; because his mind is attuned to his externality.

September 1984

Colorful Attire

Q/ What is your opinion of colored shirts with white collars?

A/ What is my opinion of a pink shirt with a white collar or a blue shirt with a white collar? I have to think it over.

May 1986

Today, if you wear the clothing that the frumme wear, that's how you identify with the shevet of Hashem.

Ancient Dressing

Q/ How come we don't dress like the *chachamim* of old did?

A/ First of all, we don't know how they dressed.

Secondly, they didn't always dress the same way. There were generations when they dressed one way and there were generations when they dressed differently.

I'll explain something to you. There were twelve *shevatim*. Each *shevet* was entirely different. They lived by themselves; they didn't intermarry. They had their own *minhagim,* they had their own *malbushim,* ways of dressing. Even the way they spoke *lashon hakodesh* was different. So today, we don't know whom to emulate. So therefore, we are not breaking the tradition of the past – we have no way of knowing the tradition.

So, if a Jew maintains the traditions that the frum Jews of the last century have done, then that's wonderful. It's very good; that's enough. Because all these generations of *shomrei mitzvos* are also a *shevet Hashem* – a tribe of Hashem. So that much we know, and therefore we follow their *minhag* as much as we can.

But since we don't know what the ancient *chachamim* really wore, we don't know exactly what it was, we can't follow their *minhagim.* Today, if you wear the clothing that the *frumme* wear, that's how you identify with the *shevet* of Hashem, and that's what Hashem wants.

November 1996

Black Hats and Tefillin

It's so important to demonstrate that you identify with the bnei Torah, with the frumme.

Q/ Why do we wear a black hat more than any other type of hat?

A/ Very good question. And the answer is that if all the *bnei Torah* would wear yellow hats, then we should all wear yellow hats. Color is not important. The main thing is to identify. A black hat is a tremendous *zechus.*

You know that when a boy approaches his bar mitzvah, he gets a pair of tefillin that costs five, six, seven hundred dollars, and he also gets a black hat. To me, the black hat is no less than the tefillin. The black hat shows that וְשִׂים חֶלְקֵנוּ עִמָּהֶם – "I want my portion, my lot in life, to be together with them, with the *tzaddikim.*" וְשִׂים חֶלְקֵנוּ עִמָּהֶם! I want to be together with them! It's so important to demonstrate that you identify with the *bnei Torah,* with the *frumme.*

And therefore, wearing a black hat is an extremely great achievement. When a boy in our shul puts on a black hat, I give him a *mazel tov* as if he's putting on tefillin. That's how important it is.

November 1998

Separated By Dress

Q/ How can one convince a Modern Orthodox woman not to wear pants?

A/ I don't know.

But this we can say: Anyone who wears pants is not identified with the Jewish nation. That's a flat statement.

You can complain all you want but Hashem does not owe anything to anybody.

The Jewish people are interested in demonstrating the *kedusha* of their nation. Our nation is a holy nation. And one of the elements of *kedusha* is decency. Women who wear pants are identifying with the other side of the fence.

Right now, I'm not going to go into the question of what's wrong with pants. But it's certain that those who don't wear pants are more easily identified with the Klal Yisroel than those who do.

Therefore, anyone who raises a flag of the enemy does not belong to us. The flag of Torah Judaism, the flag of the historic Am Yisroel, is those people who demonstrate that they like to be with us. When a woman puts on pants, she demonstrates that she is going after the other part of the world and she is lost to us. It doesn't make any difference how Orthodox she's going to be in practice. Her heart is in the camp of the enemy.

Now, no matter what you're going to say, you have to realize that the person who does things that the Jewish nation does not approve of in its historic appraisal – it does not approve of women dressing like men; I won't go into the *halacha*, but it's certainly disapproved by the real Jews – then that person has put herself on the wrong side of the fence and she has lost her rights to the privilege of כָּל יִשְׂרָאֵל יֵשׁ לָהֶם חֵלֶק לָעוֹלָם הַבָּא.

Let me explain something. Olam Haba is not something that Hashem gives to everybody. You can be a pretty decent person, but if you're not a member of the Jewish people, you are not promised the afterlife. Now, you can complain all you want but Hashem does not owe anything to anybody. He gave you a life. He gave you a gift of a body and you enjoyed it for many years; you had plenty to eat, you had clothing to wear. Don't complain. When the time comes, leave the world in good grace and be happy that you're not going to Gehinom. Nobody has a claim on Hashem.

יֵשׁ לָהֶם חֵלֶק כָּל יִשְׂרָאֵל – *But if you identify with Yisroel,* לָעוֹלָם הַבָּא – *then you have a special claim.* It's a gift. It's not your due. You didn't earn it. It's a privilege. And if you throw away the privilege, if you discard the privilege, that's your hard luck. But if you hold onto the privilege, you are a privileged person in the World to Come.

Now, who is privileged? Those who want to belong to that class of Olam Haba people. If you're ashamed of being a Jew, if you're ashamed of Jewish ways, if you're ashamed of living among Jews, if you try your best to look like a *goy*, if you try your best to get lost among *goyim*, then you have already forfeited your right to Olam Haba.

And therefore, only those Jews who try their best to identify – to identify with the Jewish people – these are the ones who are going to live forever. Hakadosh Baruch Hu says, "עַמִּי – *My people.*" And 'My people' means those who are עִמִּי – *with Me.* If you're not with Me then you do not have any claim on Me in the World to Come.

February 1988

Separated and Proud

Should I put up my peyos and hide my tzitzis when I go to work?

Q/ **Should I put up my *peyos* and hide my tzitzis when I go to work?**

A/ It depends. Sometimes I would say yes; it depends. After all, *parnassah* is very important.

But many times, people are unnecessarily embarrassed. Look; here's a Hindu, *l'havdil.* A Hindu is coming in with big pants, a mile too big for him, and a big shirt, also a mile too big for him. And he's wearing a turban too. He's not embarrassed!

I wouldn't tell you a general rule because parnassah is very important.

And how many Hindus are there around here? But *l'havdil,* the Jews, there are plenty of them, so we have less reason to be embarrassed.

And so, in most cases it won't harm you. However I would say that in your individual case you should consult your local *rav* or *rebbe*. I wouldn't tell you a general rule because *parnassah* is very important. Consult your local *rav* and *rebbe* if you want to know how far you should go.

April 1996

Thanking for Clothes

Q/ How should a frum Jew get an appreciation of his clothing?

A/ By thinking, מַלְבִּישׁ עֲרוּמִּים! He clothes the naked! A frum man is saying the words – he's saying it with *kavanah,* but he's not thinking a thing about his *begadim*! Did you ever think about buttonholes? Buttonholes! There's a seam around the buttonholes. Without the seam, the hole would get bigger every day. Do you ever thank Hashem for the seam? Let me see *you* make a seam. That's serious!

A *rosh yeshiva* told me this many years ago, over sixty years ago. "Could you make this?" he said.

"No," I said. "I can't."

So I'm telling other people the same thing; I'm telling you what I heard from my *rebbe*. *Malbish arumim*! A seam around the buttonhole!

And the buttons! Buttons are a luxury. They didn't have buttons in the time of the Shas. They had a stone. You put in a stone here and you pushed the stone through a hole here.

It was difficult. When you went to sleep, you put the stone down. Sometimes it fell on the floor. You had to climb on the floor to look for the stone. But now there are buttons. They're sewn to your suit. You don't have to look for them.

Zippers! I remember when zippers first came out. A big chiddush.

And coated fabrics. Once upon a time, they didn't have slippery fabrics. When you were putting on your sleeve, your fingernail got caught, and it used to tear the sleeve all the way through. Now clothing feels like it was lubricated. Slippery fabric – it slides in! Coated fabrics – I remember there were no coated fabrics once upon a time!

Zippers! I remember when zippers first came out. A big *chiddush*. Most of the zippers didn't work – they used to get caught. Today the zippers work; nothing is hard. It goes smoothly like it's lubricated.

Are you thanking Hashem for your garments? It's a serious subject! We're fast asleep!

January 2001

Dressing With Thought

Q/ **What should we think about when we get dressed in the morning?**

A/ When you put on your clothing, don't just put it on without the slightest thought. *Baruch atah Hashem malbish arumim.* You're clothing me. Get accustomed to the idea. You're putting on a shirt? Hashem is giving you that shirt.

Where did it come from? Where did the material of the shirt come from? Do you know that it comes from miracles and miracles? It grows out of the earth. A shirt grows out of

That's why Hashem made everything, for the purpose that it should be a reminder of Him.

the earth? Yes, a shirt grows out of the earth. Fundamentally, it's nothing but material that grew out of the earth.

You put on your jacket? You're thinking, "It's unbelievable that this jacket of wool grew out of the back of a sheep." Imagine a sheep that has on its back a nice black jacket with buttons and buttonholes and pockets – and he produced it from himself. On the back of every sheep. All you have to do is peel off the coat from his back and put it on yourself. That's exactly what happens. And therefore, your clothing has to remind you of Hashem.

Now that's why Hashem made everything, for the purpose that it should be a reminder of Him. Like it states in *Ashrei,* יוֹדוּךָ ה' כָּל מַעֲשֶׂיךָ – *Hashem, all of Your acts, Your deeds, praise You* (*Tehillim* 145:10). They speak about You.

And you have to thank Hashem for your clothing! מַלְבִּישׁ עֲרוּמִּים. Clothing! What a *nes* it is! What a *chesed* it is! It keeps you warm.

We have to bang home this nail; we have to hammer it in, because people are not aware of their responsibilities of saying to Hashem, "Thank You, Hashem, for what You have done for us."

But not only does it keep us warm – it keeps us dignified. Hashem said, "I'm not satisfied that Adam and his wife made girdles to cover their nakedness. I'm not satisfied with that. I want them to have full tunics for the purpose of demonstrating that they are not animals."

You see a policeman's horse in the street? It doesn't wear any pants. It has no coat. You see everything. That's a horse. A human being has to wear clothing for the purpose of demonstrating that he has a *neshama* in him. Clothes are the dignity of mankind. The Gemara says that. רַבִּי יוֹחָנָן קָרֵי לְהוּ לְמָאנֵי מְכַבְּדוּתַי – *Rabbi Yochanan used to call his clothing 'my dignity'* (*Bava Kama* 91b).

Clothes are our dignity. That's our greatness! It's very important to understand that! I'm saying it most superficially. I should spend the whole hour only on clothes, and maybe more than an hour.

January 2001

Clothes are our dignity. That's our great-ness! It's very important to un-derstand that!

Dressing With Seder

Q/ Why does the *halacha* recommend that a person give preference to his right hand and right foot over his left when getting dressed? When we put on a shirt, we do the right sleeve first, and with shoes, we put on the right shoe first. But then we're supposed to tie the left shoe first. What's this about?

A/ The answer is, we have to train ourselves for greater ideals, even when getting dressed.

For example, we know that we have to give precedence to someone who is older. An older person must walk in first. That's the Jewish way. Don't look at the fools in the street. Here is a boy and his father going to shul; the boy walks through the door first, a yeshiva boy walks through first. He's an *am ha'aretz,* he's a boor, an ignoramus. The father must walk first! A boy has to learn that a father goes first. A boy has to learn that an older boy goes first. An older man goes first. That's how we have to train ourselves.

Now in order to learn this lesson, we give our right arm precedence. The right arm does more mitzvos than the left arm. The right arm is the arm that puts on tefillin for you; the left arm can't put on tefillin. The right is the arm that points in the *siddur* and in the *sefer* where you're reading. The right arm does a lot of good things! The right arm gives *tzedakah.* You don't give with your left arm, you give with your right.

Anyone who learned a little knows that among Jews, the proper way when dressing or undressing is to remain covered.

So with your right arm, you do so many good deeds, you have to honor the right arm. The right foot also is more dexterous than the left.

Therefore, when you wash, when you're in the bathtub, you have to wash your head first, you have to learn that the head is important. The head of the family, the head of the nation, is very important. You wash your head first, then your torso, then your right arm, then your left arm. Then your right foot, then your left foot.

Now don't think this is a meaningless ceremony. It's good practice. It's good practice in being a *mentch*. It's good practice in *derech eretz*.

That's why you put on your right shoe first. It's practice. And then your left shoe. And you tie your left shoe first, because your left shoe resembles your left arm, where you tie your tefillin, so you tie the left shoe first to remind yourself that when it comes to tying, the left side has a preference.

Now all these things are training. You're only getting dressed, but at the same time you're reminding yourself of even bigger ideals. All these forms of behavior in Jewish life are really a training for greater things, for bigger ideals.

November 1975

Modesty in Dressing and Undressing

Why are we required to get dressed and undressed under a blanket?

A/ Anyone who learned a little knows that among Jews, the proper way when dressing or undressing is to remain covered (*Shulchan Aruch O.C.* 2). When a frum Jew is disrobing he should try to cover up as much as possible. He shouldn't expose.

Now remember, this Jew doesn't have any audience watching him. He's not on the stage. He's in his private room. The door is locked and there's nobody present and the light is out – it's dark too. And yet, the scrupulous Jew tries his best when he's taking off his clothing – it's not easy – or when he's putting on his clothing, he tries his best not to expose himself. He dresses and undresses in such a manner that his body is never revealed.

Now that's very surprising. The room is closed. The shades are down. It's dark. Nobody sees me. Who's looking? The *Tur* (ibid.) asks that question. He says a person will ask מִי יִרְאֵנִי – "Who sees me? The shades are down!"

So the *Tur* answers, it's a *pasuk* in *Yirmiyahu*: אִם יִסָּתֵר אִישׁ בַּמִּסְתָּרִים וַאֲנִי לֹא אֶרְאֶנּוּ נְאֻם ה' – *"Can a man hide in secret places where I shouldn't see him?" Hashem says,* הֲלֹא אֶת הַשָּׁמַיִם וְאֶת הָאָרֶץ אֲנִי מָלֵא – *"But I fill the Heavens and the Earth."* (*Yirmiyahu* 23:24). So the answer is that Somebody is there; Somebody with a capital S. Hakadosh Baruch Hu is there. He's looking.

But that's a queer thing to say because the question is, what does covering help? If Hakadosh Baruch Hu is everywhere and that's why you have to cover up, what's the purpose, then, of covering up? If Hakadosh Baruch Hu is looking, He can see through fabric. He has X-ray vision. He can see through walls too. So what will you accomplish by covering up? He can look through garments too. What does it help to cover yourself up? And if garments will help cover you up, why shouldn't darkness help to cover you up? Or the four walls of your room should cover you up.

The answer is that it's for ourselves. By covering ourselves up every morning and every night, we remind ourselves always of this great truth that Hashem is looking at us.

By covering ourselves up every morning and every night, we remind ourselves always of this great truth that Hashem is looking at us.

Always see that you're covered up as much as possible.

Isn't it a pity? We can live our whole lives without attaining an awareness that ה' מִשָּׁמַיִם הִשְׁקִיף – *Hakadosh Baruch Hu is looking* (*Tehillim* 14:2).

And so this *din,* this *halacha,* is a valuable exercise; it develops the muscles of the mind. Little by little, it enters our consciousness that Hakadosh Baruch Hu is looking at us. Every time you undress or you dress, you don't make yourself naked. You make sure to be covered up with something while you're undressing. Unless you go into the shower, the bathtub, you can't help being naked. Otherwise, when you undress, try to have something over you. Always see that you're covered up as much as possible.

Now, not always is it possible. But as much as possible, always be covered up to remind yourself that Someone is looking. It's a drill to remind yourself that Someone is looking. The covering up is not in itself the purpose. The covering up is to create in your mind an awareness that Hashem is looking. Even though it makes no difference to Hashem, still, the fact that we cover ourselves up indoctrinates us. It trains us to be aware that Hashem is looking. That's the great lesson of how a Jew dresses and undresses.

July 1982

Dressing Elegantly

Is it wrong for a man to dress fancy?

A/ To dress fancy, I don't know what that means. You have to show me the man before I can pass judgment on him. But to dress silly – it certainly is wrong. He shouldn't be ostentatious.

To dress correctly? That's all right, certainly. But if a person does things in imitation of a gentile fop, a gentile dandy, it's a shame. What are you? A monkey that imitates low people? So you should dress decently in a conservative, decent way.

What are you? A monkey that imitates low people?

I'll tell you a story. I was walking in the street and a man stopped me. How he was dressed! I was frightened. A real bum. As he spoke a few words, I realized he was a college professor whom I knew. I knew him. A college professor, an Orthodox Jew. But he was a real bum – the way he looked.

So the word 'fancy,' I don't know what that means. But absolutely you should dress decently, conservatively.

January 1986

Shoe Shines and Hat Brushes

Q/ How clean should men be in the way they dress?

A/ There's no question that it's a valid question; it's very important. It's a matter of *kavod Shamayim,* especially for *bnei Torah.* Everybody should make the most favorable impression.

Now whether 'clean' means beyond the boundaries of cleanliness, of being a fop, a dandy, and squirting perfume over your body – this, of course, is out of the question. But otherwise, there's no question that everyone, especially the Orthodox, especially *bnei Torah,* should make it a principle to defend the honor of the Torah at all times.

Your shoes must be shined always. So take a look right now and criticize yourselves. It's not right. You shouldn't have dusty shoes.

If you wear a black hat, it must be dusted. Otherwise switch to a gray one.

If you wear a black hat, it must be dusted. Otherwise switch to a gray one. A black hat signifies either a *chassid* or an Orthodox Jew or something. A black hat has to be spotless.

One foolish fellow once told me, when I criticized him that he has dust on his hat, "וְאָנֹכִי עָפָר וָאֵפֶר – I am dust and ashes" (*Bereishis* 18:27). That's how you should be in your *character* – you should feel like you're dust and ashes. You should be humble. But not on your hat.

February 1974

Head Covering

Q/ The Gemara says that covering our heads helps us gain *yiras Shamayim*. How does that work?

A/ Oh, that's important! How do we gain *yiras Shamayim* by covering our heads?

Now pay attention. By the *kohanim* it states that they had four *bigdei kehunah*. They had *mitznefes*, a head covering, an *avnet*, a belt, and a *kesones* and *michnesayim*, a robe and pants.

Now the Torah, when it talks about the head covering of the *kohanim*, it calls it פַּאֲרֵי הַמִּגְבָּעֹת. *Migbaos* means 'hats' from the word *givah*. It makes your head taller, like a hill. A hat makes you look taller.

But *pa'arei* means the glory, the glory of the hat. It's from the word *pe'er*. What's the glory?

And the answer is, the glory of the hat of the *kohen* was that it showed he was an *eved Hashem*. He was a servant of Hashem.

But Hashem says that we are all *kohanim*. We are a מַמְלֶכֶת כֹּהֲנִים – *a nation of priests* (*Shemos* 19:6). We're all servants of Hashem. Even if you're a storekeeper or a tailor, no; your main business in life is you're a servant of Hashem, a *kohen Hashem.*

If that's the case, when you put something on your head, you're showing that you are a member of *mamleches kohanim*, of the nation of *kohanim*. In a small way, we're imitating the *kohanim.* The fact that you wear something on your head, whether it's a silk top hat, a *shtreimel*, a yarmulke, a straw hat, whatever it is a Jew puts over his head, a tarboush, whatever it is, it's a demonstration that you recognize your purpose in the world. We show it by covering our heads.

When you put something on your head, you're showing that you are a member of the nation of kohanim.

And what is the glory of being a member of the *mamleches kohanim*? כַּסִּי רֵישָׁךְ – *Cover your head,* כִּי הֵיכִי – *in order,* דְּתִיהֱוֵי עֲלָךְ אֵימְתָא דִשְׁמַיָּא – *you should have fear of Shamayim* (*Shabbos* 156b). That's our glory. The glory of the Am Yisroel is that they are aware of and afraid of Hashem. שִׁמְעוּ דְּבַר ה' הַחֲרֵדִים אֶל דְּבָרוֹ – *Those who tremble at his words* (*Yeshayahu* 66:5). We're excited. We fear. That's the greatness of the Am Yisroel.

That's our glory! *Yiras Hashem*, awareness of Hashem, that's the greatest *kavod* there is. The more *yiras Hashem* you have, the more you're a *kohen Hashem* and the more you are *nichbad*. And so, when you put on a hat in the morning, think of the great privilege, עוֹטֵר יִשְׂרָאֵל – *You're crowning us,* בְּתִפְאָרָה – *with glory!* What happiness it is! What an honor it is!

And if it's a black hat, even better. You're identifying not only with the Klal Yisroel, but with the best of the Klal Yisroel. And it's a crown of glory.

Now pay attention. That's only the beginning. Because you're also getting a greater awareness of Hashem when you cover your head with these ideas. You're getting *daas*

The more you think of Hashem, the more you're getting daas Hashem.

Hashem. The more you think of Hashem, the more you're getting *daas Hashem*. Of course you should think when you're saying that *bracha*. Each time you put on your hat, think about that.

Now, the Rambam (*Hilchos Teshuvah* 8:2) says when you come to the next world after a hundred and twenty years, there is no eating and drinking; it's only צַדִּיקִים יוֹשְׁבִים וְעַטְרוֹתֵיהֶם בְּרָאשֵׁיהֶם – *The righteous are sitting and their crowns are on their heads.* Does that sound familiar – the crowns on their heads? וְנֶהֱנִים מִזִּיו הַשְּׁכִינָה – *and they are enjoying the ziv, the splendor of the Shechinah* (*Brachos* 17a).

So the Rambam says as follows. They'll enjoy the splendor of the Shechinah according to the kind of crown they're wearing. And the crown, he says, is *daas haniknes*, that's the knowledge, the awareness of Hashem, that they acquired in this life. So in this world while you're alive, you acquire knowledge of Hashem, *yiras Hashem*, and when you come to the next world, you'll have a bigger crown on your head, and you'll have therefore more *ziv*, more glory of the Shechinah to enjoy. The more you have a crown on your head, the greater is your happiness in the World to Come.

So עוֹטֵר יִשְׂרָאֵל בְּתִפְאָרָה, when you put on a hat, you're crowning yourself with glory. You're crowning yourself in the next world with a crown of *daas Hashem,* and that's going to be your real happiness. So how great is the *simcha* when you cover your head.

But not only are you happy for the glory in this world, that you're from the *mamleches kohanim.* It's a happiness forever and ever in the World to Come. That's what you should think when you put on your hat or your yarmulke.

October 1998

A Woman's Glory

We're all queens because our husbands wear crowns. We're queens!

Q/ Why do the women in *birchas hashachar* say עוֹטֵר יִשְׂרָאֵל בְּתִפְאָרָה if they're not obligated to cover their hair with a hat?

A/ Women, why do they say עוֹטֵר יִשְׂרָאֵל בְּתִפְאָרָה – *You crown Yisroel with glory*?

When women look at men, and they see they have a crown. They look at their sons and see that they're wearing yarmulkes, their husbands are wearing black hats – so they say, "You crowned our husbands; you crowned our sons. We're all queens because our husbands wear crowns. We're queens! We're the mothers of princes; our sons wear black hats."

So therefore, it's an honor for the women that their men are crowned. When a woman sees her son wearing tzitzis, it's an honor for her! When she sees her son wearing tefillin, it's an honor for her! Her husband learns Torah, it's an honor for her.

And they get a one-hundred percent share in all the good things that they cause the men to do. They train their children to be frum, to learn Torah. נָשִׁים בְּמַאי זַכְאִין – They get a merit, a one-hundred percent partnership. And therefore, they have to make a big, loud *bracha* of happiness when they see their sons covering their heads and learning Torah and putting on tefillin and wearing tzitzis.

March 2000

Baseball Caps

Q/ There's a fashion in society now to wear baseball caps. I was wondering if you think someone should be allowed

You shouldn't wear a baseball cap in the street either.

into the *beis hamedrash* wearing a baseball cap and davening in a baseball cap?

A/ Should you be allowed into a *beis hamedrash* with a baseball cap? I'm not gonna say anything. It depends on the *beis hamedrash.*

But I'll say this. You shouldn't wear a baseball cap in the street either. A baseball cap with a team on it, the Yanks or the Mets, means you identify yourself with people who have no heads, people who underneath such a cap have empty minds; you're identifying with people who go to baseball because they want to see a fellow with a bat, and he slams the ball, and everybody goes wild on this *tzaddik.* A home run! Such *meshuga'im!* It's an empty world. You want to identify with that world?

And therefore, you should never wear a team's baseball cap, even outdoors, no matter what.

July 1999

Chapter 8

Sleeping Jewish

Chapter Sponsor

In honor of our dear daughter

Rivky **תחי'**

you are a constant source
of nachas to us!

We love you and are so proud of you,
Tatty and Mommy Drezdner

Contents

Chapter 8

Sleeping Jewish

Sleeping to Thank

Q/ **Why did Hashem create sleep? Isn't it such a waste of time?**

A/ Why did He create hunger? It's a waste of time to eat.

Why did He create the necessity to go to the bathroom? It's a waste of time to sit in the toilet.

It's a good question but I'll tell you why. Hakadosh Baruch Hu made this world for the purpose of recognizing Him. Now, how can people recognize Hashem? They're busy in this world. They're thinking of their own affairs. They forget about Hashem. So Hashem said, "I want to remind you of Me."

So therefore, if you have to eat, you need food. You need food to eat. And then, when you get a piece of bread, "Oh, I thank You Hashem! What would I do without the bread? I can't live without bread. בָּרוּךְ אַתָּה ה' – *I thank You.* And so, the bread causes you to be grateful and to love Hashem.

Now, let's say a person gets tired. You get tired, don't you? The body gets worn out. So you want a miracle to make you rested? Hashem says, "No. I'm

Sleep is a blessing. You have to thank Hashem for the sleep. That's why He gave it to you.

going to create a process, a system, for you to be rejuvenated. It's called sleep. And now you'll be reminded of Me."

Now if you go to sleep, you have to thank Hashem for that. Some people can't sleep. Some people are sick and can't sleep. Sleep is a blessing. You have to thank Hashem for the sleep. That's why He gave it to you.

Ah geshmake, pleasant night's sleep! It's better than eating the most delicious food. When you get up, you're refreshed; you're a new person and you have a new opportunity to be grateful to Hashem. מוֹדֶה אֲנִי לְפָנֶיךָ – *I thank You, Hashem.*

So sleep is for the purpose of causing people to be grateful, more and more grateful to Hashem. You lie down on the pillow and you fall asleep, and while you're asleep, all good things are happening. You were unconscious and then, *baruch Hashem,* you got up in the morning! You're a new man. הַנּוֹתֵן לַיָּעֵף כֹּחַ – We have to thank Hashem for sleep.

That's only one of the benefits. The other benefits of sleep I'll tell you some other time, but this is one of the benefits included in the great program of making people more perfect in this world, of helping people achieve more *shleimus* in this world.

April 2000

Eight Hours of Rewinding

Q/ We are put in this world in order to accomplish. Why did Hashem make it necessary to sleep so long? Eight hours? The time could have been better spent.

A/ Now, I want to tell you something about that. The last remark is not necessarily true. The Gemara (*Sanhedrin* 71b) says: שֵׁנָה לָרְשָׁעִים טוֹב לָהֶם וְטוֹב לָעוֹלָם

– Sleep for the unworthy is a very good thing for them and for the world. While you're asleep, you're not a bother anymore to other people and therefore, Hakadosh Baruch Hu has a great benefit when you're out of circulation for those eight hours.

However, to ask a question why the body needs eight hours or so to rejuvenate its ability, that's a question of lack of understanding. You have to understand that the body is the most complicated piece of machinery in the universe. And therefore, it must be rewound in thousands of ways; nerves, all the cells, every part of the body requires rewinding. It takes a long time in order to do a proper job. Exactly why it's eight hours instead of seven hours or instead of ten hours, we'll ask Hakadosh Baruch Hu when we see Him, why He did it that way. But there's no question that eight hours is a bargain.

Nobody should neglect the sleeping hours, because many people have courted disaster by not sleeping sufficiently.

By the way, I want to say that nobody should neglect the sleeping hours, because many people have courted disaster by not sleeping sufficiently. And once they become nervous and they upset their metabolism and their nervous system, sometimes years pass by before they recover.

So an ounce of prevention is better than a pound of cure. Better to sleep every night properly and utilize your waking hours to the best of your ability rather than allow yourself to go to sleep late and wear out your nerves, *chas v'shalom*.

I have seen instances where people didn't sleep well and they regretted it subsequently. It should never happen to you. So make sure that you sleep on time, eat your meals on time, and you do all the things you're required to do in your waking hours.

February 1995

Eight Hours of Medication

Why do we sleep for eight hours?

Sleeping is better than eating. It's a medicine; it heals many illnesses.

A/ And the answer is, it's a *nes*. What takes place during these eight hours is something that no medicine can do.

Sleep is better than food. Sleep cures the mind. People who don't sleep enough all have disturbance in their mind. Thousands of things take place, processes whereby the body heals itself during sleep. Sleep is such a *nes*. You can never finish thanking Hashem for it.

A great deal has been written about sleep. They still didn't discover all the benefits, but there's no question that sleep is the *yeshuah* and the *refuah* and one of the great benefits we have to thank Hashem for. It's wondrous, the fact that you're able to sleep. Sleeping is better than eating. It's a medicine; it heals many illnesses. While you're sleeping, your nerves that were frayed are coming together again. Many things are healed by sleep.

Now, why eight hours? What are you surprised about? For sixteen hours of activity, you need eight hours to recover, to rebuild. You're tearing down cells, using up your viscera, your muscles, your mind.

And therefore, after sixteen hours of activity, you must have at least eight hours to recuperate.

November 1999

Sleep is Necessary

Q/ What do you say to someone who has trouble getting to sleep on time?

A/ Briefly, the *seforim* say that a man has to be a *zariz*. *Zariz* means he has to have alacrity to serve Hashem. הֱוֵי גִּבּוֹר כָּאֲרִי – *Be strong as a lion,* לַעֲשׂוֹת רְצוֹן אָבִיךָ שֶׁבַּשָּׁמַיִם – *to do the will of your Father in*

Heaven (*Avos* 5:23). Sometimes it takes the strength of a lion to do the will of Hashem.

And the *seforim* say that among the things included in being strong like a lion, is to force yourself to go to sleep on time. If you just dawdle around after bedtime, you'll get up in the morning without energy and you'll waste the next day. Your davening will be without much energy and surely your learning will suffer. And so, you must force yourself to hit the hay on time. You have to be a *zariz*, and strong like a lion, to get to sleep on time. That's the way to prepare for the next day of achievement.

January 1985

If you just dawdle around after bedtime, you'll get up in the morning without energy and you'll waste the next day.

Sleep is Important

Q/ If one has low spirits because he's not getting enough sleep and he's exhausted, is that feeling of unhappiness also considered a sin that he's accountable for?

A/ Every individual is responsible for his own body – for his or her own health. And therefore, everyone must make it their business to get enough sleep. In most cases, you can plan your schedule to allow for a program of a proper amount of sleep. Even if your child is up at night, you can plan ahead and get the sleep you need. And don't waste time at night doing nothing, just fiddling around.

And if you can get someone to take over for a little while every day, you can sleep by day for a half-hour. A half-hour sleep by day is a *yeshuah!* Sometime you can sneak in even more than a half-hour. But either way, it's up to you to preserve your health and to remain in good spirits by getting enough sleep. That's your responsibility.

June 2000

Sleep and Temptation

Make sure you go to sleep every night on time. Sleep eight hours every night.

Q/ What would the Rav give as some advice for conquering the temptation to sleep?

A/ The answer is, don't conquer it. Make sure you go to sleep every night on time. Sleep eight hours every night. The trouble is that people don't sleep enough. And then they start to break down, and they go to psychologists and they get medicines and *es toigt oif kapparos.* It's not worth it. It's counterproductive to not get enough sleep.

Sleep is very important. It's more important than food. It's more important than vitamins. It's so important to sleep. I can tell you from experience. I know so many people, so many fine people, young people, who ruined their careers of serving Hashem by not sleeping.

Now, some *tzaddikim* are very strong. And they can get along with less sleep. But don't begin to suspect that you're the one. Don't think that you're the one.

March 2000

Sleep Blessings 1

Q/ At night, right before we go to sleep, we recite the *Hamapil* blessing thanking Hashem for sleep. Can you explain to us the purpose of that blessing?

A/ Sleep is one of the biggest benefits that we enjoy in our lives. Sweet sleep is more important than medicines, because at nighttime, your worn-out nerves become mended. Everything in the body is restored by sleep. That's why it's good, if you're not well, *chalilah,* to sleep all you can. Even in the daytime. Sleep and sleep and sleep.

Sleep is a miracle. Why do you fall asleep? All of a sudden, you lie on the pillow and you fall asleep. It's a *nes*. And therefore, when you make that blessing you should appreciate that gift because some people unfortunately cannot sleep. It's a tragedy.

Sleep is a miracle. Why do you fall asleep? All of a sudden, you lie on the pillow and you fall asleep.

You know, many people can't sleep. A man told me once – an old man – "*Ich hob farloyren dem shlof* – I lost my sleep." It's a tragedy. You're able to sleep! You're a young man; you put your head on the pillow, immediately you fall asleep.

Did you ever think of thanking Hashem? Yes, you make a *bracha*, but you're not thinking about what you're saying. בָּרוּךְ אַתָּה ה'... הַמַּפִּיל חֶבְלֵי שֵׁנָה – *I thank You, Hashem, that You caused me to fall asleep.* What a blessing sleep is! You didn't thank Him? Some people never thank Hashem all their lives. They could be saying the *bracha* every night and not once thinking about what they're saying.

December 1995

Sleep Blessings 2

Q/ Why does *Hamapil* end with הַמֵּאִיר לָעוֹלָם כֻּלּוֹ בִּכְבוֹדוֹ? Why are we thanking Hashem for light when it's nighttime?

A/ At the end of that blessing we thank Hashem "who illuminates the world with light," which means: We are going to sleep with one hope – that Hakadosh Baruch Hu should once more give us a chance tomorrow. "Hashem, we're going to sleep and we look like we are dead. We beg You, revive us tomorrow morning and once more let us see the light of day."

Now, why mention the light of day? Because the light of day is the glory that bespeaks the presence of Hashem.

The light of day that spreads over the face of the earth when the sun rises, that's the kavod Hashem.

This needs to be explained. The light of day that spreads over the face of the earth when the sun rises, that's the *kavod Hashem.* The *malachim* say, "בָּרוּךְ כְּבוֹד ה' מִמְּקוֹמוֹ" when they see it coming it out. And we hope to see the light of day tomorrow. We say to Hashem, "Please Hashem, we thank You for giving us the gift of sleep, but please, please, please, revive us tomorrow morning! We should once more see the light of day!" הַמֵּאִיר לָעוֹלָם כֻּלּוֹ בִּכְבוֹדוֹ.

Now, suppose it happens! Suppose you open your eyes and you see the light of day! Oh, is that a *simcha!* You should be excited! מוֹדֶה אֲנִי לְפָנֶיךָ – *I thank You,* מֶלֶךְ חַי וְקַיָּם – *O' King who lives forever and endures,* שֶׁהֶחֱזַרְתָּ בִּי נִשְׁמָתִי בְּחֶמְלָה – *You returned my life to me with compassion,* רַבָּה אֱמוּנָתֶךָ – *how great is Your steadfastness!*

How great our happiness should be every morning! Another day! You mean to say I get to wake up again?! I remember once there was a member in my synagogue who went to sleep. In the morning, his wife came and said, "Mordechai, wake up!" Mordechai didn't move. "Mordechai! Wake up!" He didn't move. It was all over.

And therefore, if you can move in the morning, how happy you should be! הַמַּחֲזִיר נְשָׁמוֹת לִפְגָרִים מֵתִים – *He restores the souls to the dead bodies!* How happy we are in the morning! Once more we have a chance to look at the sunlight and say, בָּרוּךְ אַתָּה ה' יוֹצֵר הַמְּאוֹרוֹת – *We thank You, Hashem, for the sunlight.*

And therefore, when we go to sleep at night, keep in mind that you have to pray to Hashem for tomorrow. Don't take it for granted! This happened to a young man, by the way. Mordechai was a young man. Don't take it for granted!

So pray for tomorrow. And when tomorrow comes, be enthusiastic in expressing your gratitude.

December 1995

Going to Sleep 1

What should a person think about while he's waiting to fall asleep?

Q/ What should a person think about while he's waiting to fall asleep?

A/ When you're waiting to fall asleep, you should think there's going to be a day when you'll fall asleep permanently. That's not a sad thought, by the way.

The Gemara (*Brachos* 57b) says that שֵׁנָה אֶחָד מִשִּׁשִּׁים עִם מָוֶת – *Sleep is one sixtieth of the experience of death.* So when you go to sleep, it's an opportunity to practice up your trust in *techiyas hameisim.*

Because you have great trust in Hashem that tomorrow morning you'll wake up and you'll say, בָּרוּךְ אַתָּה ה' הַמַּחֲזִיר נְשָׁמוֹת לִפְגָרִים מֵתִים. You'll thank Hashem for giving you back your life again. You trust in Hashem, don't you? Certainly you trust Him. And in the morning when you wake up, "Oh, Hashem! You made me live again!"

But there will come a time when you'll close your eyes forever. Eventually, that's what will happen.

Not forever, however. The time will come when you will once more arise from the ground. יִחְיוּ מֵתֶיךָ – *Your dead will live again,* נְבֵלָתִי יְקוּמוּן – *the carcasses will arise from the ground,* הָקִיצוּ וְרַנְּנוּ שֹׁכְנֵי עָפָר – *all of you who dwell in the dust, arise and sing* (*Yeshayahu* 26:19). You will all sing.

So when you go to sleep, it's a rehearsal for *techiyas hameisim*. You can think about how you're going to sleep

You should utilize that opportunity of going to sleep and waking up.

now but you're going to wake up again. And every morning when you say, מוֹדֶה אֲנִי לְפָנֶיךָ, think, "Last night I closed my eyes and I said פֶּן אִישַׁן הַמָּוֶת – *maybe I'll sleep the sleep of death.* And now You allowed me to wake up once more." That's a rehearsal for the great experience of *techiyas hameisim*.

So don't miss that glorious opportunity. Every night and every morning you're practicing for that great experience!

That's why every day when you say בָּרוּךְ אַתָּה ה' מְחַיֵּה הַמֵּתִים in *Shemoneh Esrei*, think about *techiyas hameisim*. Don't be happy that you said מַשִּׁיב הָרוּחַ וּמוֹרִיד הַגָּשֶׁם, and now you're *yotzei*. Once you pass מַשִּׁיב הָרוּחַ, you're happy, you didn't forget to say מוֹרִיד הַגָּשֶׁם. No! You're not happy yet. You haven't passed *techiyas hameisim* yet. Will you think about *techiyas hameisim*? Don't miss that opportunity! בָּרוּךְ אַתָּה ה' מְחַיֵּה הַמֵּתִים! What happiness we'll have then!

And so, you should utilize that opportunity of going to sleep and waking up.

December 1994

Going to Sleep 2

Q/ It was once recommended here to think about death as you go to sleep. And you said it's not a sad thought. But it seems quite morbid to me. Can you explain your statement?

A/ Have you ever seen a dead man? It looks exactly as if he was sleeping. And the Gemara says שֵׁנָה אֶחָד מִשִּׁשִּׁים מִמִּיתָה – *Sleep is one sixtieth of death* (*Brachos* 57b). So the question is, what are the *chachamim* telling us this for? What's the purpose of this information that sleep resembles death?

There are a number of lessons there, but one lesson is that someday we'll fall asleep and we won't wake up. It's very important to hear this because most people don't know about it. It's a big *chiddush* that it will happen to them. They don't believe it. Let's say when you'll be 120 years old, your great-grandson will come over to visit and he'll say, "*Zeide? Elter Zeide?* Wake up!" And you won't wake up.

The thought of death makes us want to enjoy life more and accomplish more.

And so, the *chachamim* want us to think about death in order that we shouldn't waste our lives. Time is running out! The thought of death makes us want to enjoy life more and accomplish more. That's why the *chachamim* want us to be aware that life comes to an end.

And so, every night, when you lie down and surrender your consciousness, it is supposed to remind you that the end will come and you should get busy. Every night we practice it. Every night as you lie in bed, you're rehearsing for that great event where you're going to say farewell to everybody. So tonight, when you go to sleep, lie down with the thought that that's a *mashal* to rehearse to prepare you for the great idea that someday, 120 years from now, you're going to be asleep and you won't wake up anymore.

Does that make you sad? No. On the contrary, it makes you realize how important the days are.

And in the morning when you open up your eyes and you see it didn't happen to you, ooh! The next morning you do wake up, oh, thank You Hashem. Good news! מוֹדֶה אֲנִי לְפָנֶיךָ – *I give thanks to Hashem,* שֶׁהֶחֱזַרְתָּ בִּי נִשְׁמָתִי – *that You returned my life to me.*

So now you see how grateful you are. Every morning you're getting a new gift. Life is so much sweeter if you regain it every day. You're enjoying life if you know that it's a new gift that you didn't deserve. Who deserves to live? Hakadosh Baruch Hu every day is giving you again the opportunity.

December 1994

It's a good business. If you forgive others, Hashem will forgive you. It pays.

Business Before Sleep

Q/ Is one obligated to say the *tefillah* in the siddur before going to sleep, הֲרֵינִי מוֹחֵל לְכָל מִי שֶׁחָטָא כְּנֶגְדִּי – *I forgive those who sinned against me*?

A/ You're not *mechuyav*. But if you want to say it, it's good business. Because the Torah says, לְמִי נוֹשֵׂא עָוֹן – *Who does Hashem forgive?* לְמִי שֶׁעוֹבֵר עַל פֶּשַׁע – *Someone who himself forgives what others did to him* (*Rosh Hashanah* 17a). So it pays. If you don't want to, you don't want to. But it's a good business. If you forgive others, Hashem will forgive you. It pays, it pays to say it. But do you have to say it? No.

February 2000

The Meaning of Dreams

Q/ Is there anybody alive today who can interpret dreams as far as the future is concerned?

A/ I don't know. But I'll tell you one thing, though; an *eitzah*, an *eitzah tovah*. Go to a person who will be *poser chalom* for you in a good way. He'll take your dream and interpret it for good. If he interprets your dream to have a good meaning – whether it's right or not, it makes no difference; וַיְהִי כַּאֲשֶׁר פָּתַר כֵּן הָיָה – *The way a person interprets it, that's how it will turn out* (*Bereishis* 41:13, *Brachos* 55b). If he interprets your dream for good, then it means Hakadosh Baruch Hu will listen to that to some extent, and it will turn out that way.

September 2000

Meaningless Dreams

What significance do dreams play in our lives?

Q/ What significance do dreams play in our lives?

A/ It depends when, today or years ago or in the days of the Tanach.

Today it means almost nothing. אֵין מַרְאִין לוֹ לְאָדָם אֶלָּא מֵהִרְהוּרֵי לִבּוֹ – *Today dreams only show you what you were thinking about during the day* (*Brachos* 55b). And therefore, many times it's quite embarrassing to have dreams.

Sometimes, sometimes, Hakadosh Baruch Hu sends a dream as a warning. Sometimes He sends a dream as a warning, and therefore, the Gemara says that it's a good idea to go to a *chacham* and ask him to interpret your dream.

Let's say, the *chacham* will say, "What was your dream?" and you'll say, "I'm so sorry I have to tell you that, but I dreamed that my son was drowning."

"Oh," he'll say, "That's a wonderful dream. It means your son will be so full of learning in the *yam haTalmud,* he'll be immersed in Gemara all his life; he'll be drowning in Gemara all his life." So וַיְהִי כַּאֲשֶׁר פָּתַר לָנוּ כֵּן הָיָה – *Like he interprets the dream, so it will turn out.* So you can go to a *chacham,* and he's *poser chalom.* But in general, most dreams are meaningless.

But in the times of old, in times of the Gemara, dreams meant something because they still had *ruach hakodesh,* and therefore dreams were very serious then. And in the times of Tanach, even more so! And therefore, dreams have a place in our history.

The truth is, in the times of the Gemara, not only dreams meant something. If you would ask a little boy, "Tell me, what *pasuk* did you learn today in the *cheder?*" and the boy told you a *pasuk* that they learned that day, so that *pasuk* was something of a *nevuah* for you. That's how it was in the days of the Gemara. In those great days, Hakadosh Baruch Hu still allowed us to have certain visitations of information.

But today, it's usually meaningless; things have changed because we're not great enough. Once upon a time, they were *malachim.* Then the *malachim* stopped! But there were still *sheidim*. Then the *sheidim* stopped, and today we are left 'down to earth,' with nothing – because we *are* nothing.

February 1995

Meaningful Dreams

Q/ **What is the purpose of dreams nowadays?**

A/ One purpose of dreams today is to make us aware of our faults. I'll give you an example. Did you ever dream that you were sitting in a bathtub full of money? You never dreamed that? I remember years ago, I once dreamed I was sitting in a bathtub full of money. It was a dry bathtub packed with money. It was a pleasant dream but then I asked myself, "Why is it that I don't dream about Hashem?" A very big *kasha!* Why don't I dream about Hashem?! Maybe that Hashem spoke to me, something else maybe. It never happened! Years and years pass by. I talk about it all the time but I never dreamed about it.

I once dreamed I was sitting in a bathtub full of money. It was a dry bathtub packed with money. It was a pleasant dream

The answer is, now I see what a hypocrite I am. אֵין מַרְאִין לוֹ לְאָדָם אֶלָּא מֵהִרְהוּרֵי לִבּוֹ – *A man is shown in a dream what he really thinks about* (*Brachos* 55b). It shows what I was thinking about; it shows. It tells you the truth about yourself. You understand that? A dream sometimes reveals to you important things about yourself. There are other purposes in a dream, but that's very important. There are some people who have the wrong kind of dreams.

You could dream about learning. Now, many times people dream about Gemara. They have nightmares that they can't answer a *kasha,* a difficult question, they have in the Gemara. All night, they're rolling in bed, they can't figure it out. Then, when they wake up in the morning, they see there's no *kasha* at all. It happens many times. That's also a good dream. It shows you that you'd better start learning better; otherwise you'll have these half *kashas* left in your mind. So dreams have a purpose, yes.

November 1991

You need hundreds of people to ruin their health just because you want to make a wedding?

Late-Night Weddings

Q/ **What do you say about weddings that go until late at night?**

A/ Why should weddings take so long? You need hundreds of people to ruin their health just because you want to make a wedding? People should go home early – it's a crime to keep two-hundred people up until very late at night! The next day two-hundred people will be walking around looking like ghosts because of you. It's a strain on the heart and a strain on the kidneys. It's too much!

The truth is that it's too much to expect, even of a good friend. Even a good friend should sneak out! Don't bother to go over and excuse yourself. Because then he'll start importuning you. Just sneak out and forget about it. He'll be angry? Your body will also be angry at you if you stay, and it's more important to be friends with your body.

August 1975

Reb Yisroel said that if you steal sleep, you're just as bad a thief as anybody else.

Stealing Sleep

Q/ The Torah says אַל תְּהְיֶה עֵר בֵּין הַיְשֵׁנִים, that you shouldn't remain awake among the sleeping. Since this is so, why did Dovid Hamelech stay up at night and learn?

A/ There's a statement someplace, not in the Torah, but it's a statement, that you shouldn't be awake among the sleeping (*Derech Eretz Zuta* 5:5). It means that when people are sleeping at night, and you are walking in the streets, don't make any noise. Don't show that you're awake. It's very bad manners; some people get up early in the morning, and they stand on the street corners, and they yell across the street, "Hello, Jerry!" And a lot of people who couldn't sleep at night, and just before morning they doze off a little bit – it would save their lives if they could sleep that one hour – and all of a sudden, this roughneck is standing on the corner, and he disregards everybody's feelings and he wakes them up.

Now there are a lot of gentiles – and Jews who are like gentiles – who stand on the street in the morning and shout and make noise. But even the frum Jews; even the frum Jews sometimes make errors like that. I was once walking with an elderly rabbi down a sleeping street. He was talking loudly. I said "Shhh!" I said it once. He didn't catch on. I said it again, "Shhh!" But he didn't catch on. He never learned in those yeshivos where they spoke about it. Where I went, they spoke about that. Reb Yisroel said that if you steal sleep, you're just as bad a thief as anybody else. But there's a big difference, because when you steal sleep, you can't be *mekayem* the mitzvah of *hashava*. You can't return it.

Here are two *tzaddikim,* they're walking early in the morning to *selichos*; it's still dark and they're talking in learning in a loud voice and they're waking up people who are sleeping. They are stealing people's sleep. It's no excuse that they're talking in learning. Or one time, two *tzaddikim* were going to the *mikveh* very early in the morning; it was still dark. Hakadosh Baruch Hu should bless them. Excellent people. But they were talking in a loud voice in the street and they woke up the people. Now that's a form of stealing for which you can never make restitution. You can't pay back.

Should one sleep on Shabbos after-noon?

You yeshiva men, when you walk in the street late at night, you have to be careful. If you're walking down a sleeping street with someone, and you want to talk *divrei Torah,* then you must talk in a whisper. There are people who are very tired, sometimes they're not well, either, and they finally fall asleep for a little while, and then you come and rob them of their precious rest. Certainly you're held strictly accountable. And there's no way that you can make restitution. What to do, that's a problem.

The truth is, it doesn't enter your mind that you did anything wrong. But you're held responsible, שֶׁהָיָה לוֹ לִלְמֹד – why didn't you learn? After all, it's in the *seforim*. Why didn't you come to places where they speak about these things?

And so, when people are asleep, don't be awake among them, אַל תִּהְיֶה עֵר בֵּין הַיְשֵׁנִים. If you are awake, you don't have to display it. Dovid Hamelech was awake when everyone else was asleep, but he didn't make any noise. He sat in his room and he studied Torah and he said songs to Hakadosh Baruch Hu with his harp all night. And he didn't cause anyone any discomfort.

June 1977

Shabbos Sleep

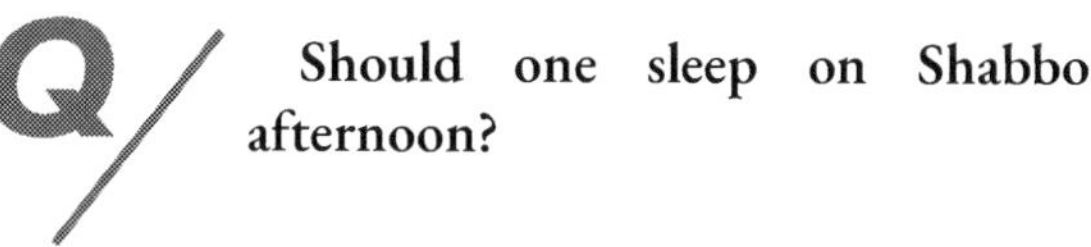

Should one sleep on Shabbos afternoon?

Shabbos is a wonderful opportunity for much better things than sleep.

A/ Absolutely. Absolutely! However, that doesn't mean that you should climb into your pajamas and remain there all Shabbos. Because Shabbos is a wonderful opportunity for much better things than sleep. There's so much thinking you have to do; about *brias ha'olam yesh mei'ayin,* about *olam chesed yibaneh,* about *beini u'vein bnei Yisroel.* There's so much to accomplish on Shabbos.

But you must understand that sleep is extremely important for our health. It's extremely important for our mental health, and it's being neglected by very many people. Shabbos is a good opportunity to catch up on your sleep. Because of Shabbos, many people are able to survive the week – otherwise, they would collapse for lack of sleep. So certainly, you should utilize Shabbos for sleep. But of course, don't overdo it.

And by the way, since you mentioned the subject, I will tell you that you must be careful to go to sleep on time every night. And make sure that you get enough sleep, because due to lack of sleep, many, many people have ruined their lives.

June 1999

QUESTIONS *On Any* SUBJECT

Chapter 9

Dying Jewish

Chapter Sponsor

Contents

Chapter 9

Dying Jewish

Entertainment for the Elderly

Q/ **Would watching television be permitted for old people in nursing homes who have no other interests?**

A/ The answer is, old people in nursing homes – would it be right for them to drink poison if they have nothing else to do?

You have to realize that drinking poison is much more beneficial than watching television – especially for old people. A young person who watches television, so it ruins his mind, it ruins his *neshamah*. But still, there's some hope left that maybe, before he dies, he'll repent, and maybe he'll learn a lot of *Mesilas Yesharim* and erase part of what he listened to or what he saw from his mind. But old people, just before they die? They have to purify themselves most! And if they're going to pollute their minds in their last days, that's how they'll go to the next world. They'll take all the *arayos,* all the wickedness, with them to the next world. Not because they'll practice it. They're too old to practice immorality. But they have it in their heads! Immorality in the head of an old man is the very worst thing.

Here's an old man. He can't go out in the street. You go to visit him in his house. He's sitting and looking at the television. *Gevald, gevald!* His

Television for old people in nursing homes is the very worst thing you could do for them.

children are murdering him. He should say Tehillim in his last days. He should speak to Hashem in his last days. He should prepare himself. He's reading something that's dirty or looking at dirty magazines meant for the old folks to enjoy before they die, so he's taking all that garbage with him into the next world. Old people especially have to prepare! And that's why television for old people in nursing homes is the very worst thing you could do for them.

December 1983

Reciting Vidui

Q/ How important is the *Vidui* that we say at the end, before we die?

A/ To finish life properly is more important than anything else. It's so important that in your last moments you should say, "Hakadosh Baruch Hu, I'm sorry. I regret all my sins. Forgive me! And let my death be a *kapparah* to atone for them." That's *Vidui shechiv mera,* the last confession of a Jew.

It's good that you came tonight just to hear this; it's so valuable, so priceless, to know this, to be prepared. It's so important that I cannot talk about it enough. If I got up and screamed, if I shouted to the ceiling, I wouldn't be overdoing it.

You know, it's very difficult to tell an ignorant man, when he's about to die, when he's very ill, to say *Vidui.* Go to a sick old *am ha'aretz,* an ignoramus, a man or a woman, and tell them, "Say *Vidui.*"

"What's *Vidui*?"

"*Vidui* is the confession of a dying man."

"I'm dying?!"

The man is on the verge of death. He has more than one foot in the grave. And still, he's holding onto life with the biggest hope. He hopes to live for the next ten million years. To take an *am ha'aretz* and to unclasp his fingers from this precious commodity of life – you can't do it.

He has never heard such a thing before. Tell an *am ha'aretz* to say *Vidui,* he thinks you're crazy. Of course, you have to tell him, you have to try, but he never heard of such a thing. He's ignorant; he never heard this.

But if he would have been here tonight, at least he would know that there's such a thing. Because when you say *Vidui,* at least you leave the world on the right note. You leave the world as one who has been cleansed and purified. You did *teshuvah* at the last moment. There are no words to describe the importance of that! טוֹב אַחֲרִית דָּבָר מֵרֵאשִׁיתוֹ – *The way you end something is more important than the way you began it* (*Koheles* 7:8).

You leave the world as one who has been cleansed and purified. You did teshuvah at the last moment.

That's why, in some congregations in Europe, there was a custom that if a man lay ill for three days, no matter what it was, even a cold, it was a custom that the *gabbaim* and the *chevrah kadisha*, the burial society, came in. They came into him even if it was nothing.

He said, "What are you coming for? It's just a cold. I'm getting up tomorrow."

So they said, "It's a rule; it's a *minhag.* We can't help it."

And he accepted it. What could he do? It was custom in the congregation that if a man was sick for three days, they had to come in and tell him to say *Vidui.* That was a *takanah gedolah.* That way, all those who were on the verge of death would also say it.

It is a very big *gemilas chesed*, a very big favor, to let people know this, the importance of *Vidui.*

He had accomplished in those few minutes a tremendous achievement. He'll never know until the next world, what he did for this man.

Once, across the driveway from me, an elderly *mechalel Shabbos* was very unwell. Suddenly, he began to die. Now, I'm a *kohen* and I cannot go into a house where a man is dying, but my son-in-law was present, so I told him, "Run in and say *Vidui* with this man!"

So he ran; he dashed across, went upstairs, and he took the dying man by the hand and he said to him, "Say, 'Ribono Shel Olam, Master of the world, I am sorry for all my sins. Forgive me!'"

And the man said yes, and he repeated the words after my son-in-law, and then he died.

I told my son-in-law that he had accomplished in those few minutes a tremendous achievement. He'll never know until the next world, what he did for this man.

That's the benefit, by the way, of living next door to somebody who knows something.

February 1973

Spiritual Wills

Q/ What are the benefits of making a *tzava'ah,* and at what age should a person make a *tzava'ah* if he doesn't know when his day will come?

A/ At what age should a person make a *tzava'ah*?

You have to use your own judgment. If you're a robust person and you think you'll live a long time, you can wait a little longer.

It depends what kind of *tzava'ah* you want. If it's a *tzava'ah* of money, that's not so important; a money *tzava'ah* is not so important.

But there's a spiritual *tzava'ah*. There's a *tzava'ah* where people leave over instructions: "Children, I want you to know..."

I remember once in Baltimore, there was a family, and on his deathbed, the father called all the children together and said, "I want you to promise me that you'll keep Shabbos forever." In those days, keeping Shabbos was a rarity. "I want you to promise to keep Shabbos forever," he said. And the children promised. Soon after that, he died.

And the children kept Shabbos all their lives. They weren't *frum!* But they kept Shabbos. They promised their father on his deathbed and they kept Shabbos.

There are some people on their deathbed who tell their children, "I want you to be careful to go in the *derech Hashem*, to always to be loyal to the *talmidei chachamim*, to always support the yeshivos, to always try to make yourself perfect in behavior." He tells them what to do.

By the way, that's something that's recommended in the *seforim*. Because what a man says on his deathbed makes a tremendous impression on his children! The spiritual *tzava'ah!*

Many people have utilized that opportunity, and their last words ring in their children's ears forever and ever.

November 2000

Fear of Death 1

Should one be frightened at the prospect of death?

Q/ **Should one be frightened at the prospect of death?**

A/ The answer is, it depends what you mean by 'frightened.' Does it mean he's depressed? Then no, by no means. We don't dwell on the subject of death. We don't try to emphasize morbidity. That's why the Torah starts with a *beis*. A *beis* is closed on all three sides. It's open only in the front, ahead. Look ahead, to life. Don't look sideways or at the cemetery; keep focused on life. You live for this world; try to achieve whatever you can in this world.

Get married; try to live happily and joyfully. Shabbos should be joyful. Mitzvos should be joyful. Torah, the *simcha* of Torah!

Do everything with zest and live happily. Don't worry; don't be sad and morbid.

Do everything with zest and live happily. Don't worry; don't be sad and morbid.

But in the back of your mind, there should always be the idea that life is not forever. Yes. Life is not forever. We spoke about that before. But the Torah does not want anybody to fall into a depression because of the prospect of death.

February 1979

Fear of Death 2

Q/ You said tonight that death is just a change, moving from one place to another. If so, why does everybody fear death?

A/ Why should we fear death? We have to fear death because that's what we learn from Moshe Rabbeinu. When Moshe Rabbeinu was told that he would soon leave this world, it says: וָאֶתְחַנַּן אֶל ה' בָּעֵת הַהִוא – *At that time, Moshe prayed to Hashem* (*Devarim* 3:23). Moshe put up a fight, a big fight, begging Hashem that he shouldn't die. He fought more than anybody else. Do you know why? Because more than anybody else, he knew what life meant.

When you tell a person he's going to die, if he wants to show he's a hero, he doesn't get excited. He acts stoic – he's willing to accept it like a hero. No, he's not a hero – he's a *shoteh!*

The Vilna Gaon passed away on Chol Hamoed Sukkos. So when they brought the esrog and the lulav to him for the last time on his deathbed where he was lying sick, he started weeping, "It's the last time – the last time I'll be able to *bentch* lulav and esrog." He burst out crying because he lived his life only to serve Hakadosh Baruch Hu and to do mitzvos! That was the whole wealth of his life, and now it was coming to an end.

People who understand the opportunity of life, they know that death is a great tragedy.

That's why Moshe Rabbeinu put up a fight – he didn't want to pass away! "Look at all that I can still do!"

I remember that when Reb Aharon Kotler, *zichrono livracha,* was on his deathbed, he was weeping. "Ribono Shel Olam, let me live! I can do so much in this world!" he wept.

People who understand the opportunity of life, they know that death is a great tragedy. וְאַחֲרִיתָהּ כְּיוֹם מָר – *The bitter day of death, a very bitter day* (*Amos* 8:10). It's not bitter because you won't eat supper anymore, or because you won't make money anymore. People who understand the true wealth of life know that death is the greatest tragedy of all tragedies.

Now, as soon as the time comes, as soon as one passes into the next world, he's so busy seeing the *ziv ha'Shechinah,* the splendor of the Shechinah, that he forgets it all. אֶשְׂבְּעָה בְהָקִיץ תְּמוּנָתֶךָ – *He gazes into the Face of Hashem* (*Tehillim* 17:15) and he forgets everything; he forgets it all in the happiness of Olam Haba. But while we're still alive, we should keep in mind that this is the time of the greatest happiness. יָפָה שָׁעָה אַחַת – *Every moment in this world is precious* (*Avos* 4:17).

June 1991

Sometimes, a person wants to yield to his yetzer hara, but he reminds himself that there will be a day of reckoning, a day of judgment.

Death as Motivation

Q/ **Can the prospect of death be utilized in a proper manner?**

A/ The answer is, certainly. No question about it. If people realize that life comes to an end – now many people don't realize that; they think they'll get out of it in some way, but if they'll realize there will be an end, that's a spur to try to achieve more.

Also, if a person is arrogant, if he's wealthy and powerful and arrogant, the prospect of death is a spur and a stimulus to become humble. Or sometimes, a person wants to yield to his *yetzer hara,* but he reminds himself that there will be a day of reckoning, a day of judgment. So, there's no question about it; thinking about the *yom hamisah* will make you more successful.

You have to keep two kinds of bookkeeping. On one side of the ledger, try to get the benefits of remembering the day of death. But on the other side, beware of the harmful effects of morbid thoughts of death.

December 1992

Dying with Mesiras Nefesh

Q/ **How does the ideal of dying with *mesiras nefesh* apply to us, who live in a generation where, *baruch Hashem*, it's not like the days of the Crusades and times like that?**

A/ The *pasuk* says that you should love Hashem בְּכָל נַפְשְׁךָ – *with all of your soul* (*Devarim* 6:5). And the Gemara says that it means אֲפִלּוּ בְּשָׁעָה שֶׁנּוֹטֵל

אֶת נַפְשְׁךָ – *Even when He's taking away your soul* (*Brachos* 54a). Even then, at that last moment, you have to love Hashem.

And therefore, *rabbosai*, you have to make up your mind now, that when you're 119 years and 11 months and 29 days old – when you have one more day left to live, and you'll think, "The time is up already? Is this fair? I should live another thousand years." That's how you'll think at the end. You won't be happy to leave. "To go away from this world? I never promised to go away from this world. I never signed up for the *chevrah shtarbers*. So why should I have to leave the world?

You're lucky you came tonight just to hear that, to get ready for your last moment.

And at that moment, think, "Hashem, I love You anyhow. I love You anyhow."

Now keep this in mind, *rabbosai*. At your last moment, think this thought. "You're taking my life away, Hashem. I love you anyhow." בְּכָל נַפְשְׁךָ אֲפִלּוּ בְּשָׁעָה שֶׁנּוֹטֵל אֶת נַפְשׁוֹ – *Even when he's taking away your life*, say, "I love you anyhow."

Oh, it's a very great *zechus*, if you'll think that way. You're lucky you came tonight just to hear that, to get ready for your last moment.

Pray to Hashem that you shouldn't be in a coma at the last moment. You should have full awareness in your last moments; just before you breathe your last breath, say, "I love You Hashem."

But don't wait! Don't wait. Practice it beforehand. It's not so easy when a man's about to die, to love Hashem.

So while you're healthy, you're walking in the street and breathing the air and you're full of food and your blood is pulsing through your veins, you can learn to love Hashem. The mitzvah of loving Hashem – that mitzvah is one of the most neglected of all mitzvos; to love Hashem!

You never had a broken bone in your life? Then you have to love Hashem.

And so, start on it right away without any delay, while you're young and healthy. Start thinking of all the things that happened to other people. There are so many things that happened to other people and that didn't happen to you.

Love Hashem that you never had an eye operation. That's enough – to love Hashem that you never had an eye operation. An eye operation – you'd have to wear a bandage on your eyes for weeks and weeks. *Baruch Hashem*, you never had an eye operation.

Some people never had a bone broken. You have to love Hashem for that! שׁוֹמֵר כָּל עַצְמוֹתָיו – *He guarded all of your bones,* אַחַת מֵהֵנָּה לֹא נִשְׁבָּרָה – *even one was never broken* (*Tehillim* 34:21). Have you ever thought about that? You never had a broken bone in your life? Yes, there are some people who never broke a bone. Then you have to love Hashem.

Get busy now. Don't waste any more time. This mitzvah requires everything you have, to learn to love Hashem בְּכָל לְבָבְךָ וּבְכָל נַפְשְׁךָ וּבְכָל מְאֹדֶךָ, with everything. But at least a little bit, you should love Hashem, and that's not too difficult. On a small scale, it's certainly possible. Of course, if you keep on practicing, you'll become more and more expert.

And if you practice, then in your last minute it's easier. In that last minute, you'll acquire a *zechus gedolah ad l'Shamayim*. And that's called dying with *mesiras nefesh*, with a love of Hashem.

April 1995

Loving Him at the End

How can a person make use of the suffering that he has on his last day in order to serve Hashem?

A/ Here a *tzaddik* is lying on his deathbed. He's suffering; he's suffering very much. But he has prepared himself. All his life, he was saying *Krias Shema,* anticipating this moment; every day he was saying, "And you should love Hashem *bechol nafshecha,* with all of your soul." And our sages (*Brachos* 54a) tell us that it means, אֲפִלּוּ בְּשָׁעָה שֶׁנּוֹטֵל אֶת נַפְשְׁךָ – *Even when He's taking away your life, you still have to love Him.*

And so, he's lying on his deathbed and he says, "Yes, Hashem. I love You. I cannot forget what You did for me, Hashem, all my days; how happy I was all my days. I sang to You all my days because of all the good You did for me. You gave me health all my days. So just because of what's happening now, I'm going to forget that? No; I won't be so ungrateful like that. Now is an opportunity to love You *despite* my pangs. I'm going to sing to You. I'm going to die with gratitude to You, with the greatest love to You."

That's how the *tzaddik* passes away. Ah! That's called loving Hashem אֲפִלּוּ בְּשָׁעָה שֶׁנּוֹטֵל אֶת נַפְשְׁךָ – *even while He's taking away your soul.*

Not everybody is prepared to utilize such a privilege. You have to train yourself. It's not easy to love when you're hurting all over. Have you ever seen a dying man? I once visited a dying man. He was lying in a bed that had walls around it so that he shouldn't fall out; like a baby bed with walls, like a crib. He was rolling in the bed with *yissurim*. It's not pleasant to die. It's very difficult to prepare for that moment properly.

But suppose a man had studied this all his life; like the Gemara (*Brachos* 61b) says: כָּל יָמַי הָיִיתִי מִצְטַעֵר עַל מִקְרָא זֶה – *All my life I was working on this pasuk,* מָתַי יָבוֹא לְיָדִי – *thinking, "When will it come to my hand, that I should be able to fulfill it?"* You have to practice that every day when you say *Krias Shema.* In the midst of your happiness think, "I love You Hashem for giving me food every day, for giving me

It's not pleasant to die. It's very difficult to prepare for that moment properly.

It's never time to die, no matter how old you are.

parnassah, for giving me a roof over my head, for keeping my family well. I love You Hashem, for all You're doing for me."

You're thinking about that constantly. And little by little, the love becomes part of your entire personality, and eventually, when the last day comes – like it must for everybody – you're thinking about how Hashem is going to bring you into the next world, the world of happiness, and you love Him even more and more, and that love overcomes all of your suffering.

September 1989

End-of-Life Illness

Q/ Is there any benefit to the physical infirmities and sicknesses that come with old age?

A/ The infirmities that people have in their old age; there's a special purpose to them, because nobody wants to let go of life. Everybody likes to hold onto it for the next million years. It's never time to die, no matter how old you are. You could be sure that in the olden days, at the age of 990 when they were dying, they regretted that they had to leave the world so early.

And therefore, Hakadosh Baruch Hu makes it easy. He sends infirmities, he sends sickness, and people start getting disgusted when they're very old. They say they'll never get well, and they give up and look forward now; they'll die soon anyhow and they'll be relieved. They're eased out of the world, and therefore, when their time comes, they don't mind it so much.

Besides, they're becoming such a big nuisance to their relatives; they're senile and it costs a pile of money to support a senile mother. And the son has to hire an aide to take care of her day and night, and that aide is eating up all the inheritance that he hoped to get. His mother's savings that he's hoping to get someday are being consumed by this aide. And so, when the day finally comes, nobody is too sorry. Both parties have resigned. That's why the infirmities of old age have beneficial purposes.

And so, when the day finally comes, nobody is too sorry.

Another reason is, it gives you the final preparation for the next world. We're so conceited that everything that happens to us in the world is like water off a duck's back. We get bumps and knocks. We're not humbled. So Hakadosh Baruch Hu tries to humble us once and for all, for good, just before we leave. He gives us a big kick and we leave the world with the most ungraceful exit. You don't leave the world romantically. You get kicked out of the world. Either you're lying on a table and the surgeon is cutting into you when the end comes, or a man collapses in the street, or some other unromantic way. And all this is for the purpose of giving you one last massive dose of humility. If you didn't acquire humility before, here's your last chance.

May 1974

Fading Away; A Blessing

Q/ If a person is senile or close to senile at the end of his life and he dies without the ability to do *teshuvah* in his last years, or to review, let's say, his learning or some other *avodas Hashem*, is this a form of punishment from Hakadosh Baruch Hu?

A/ When a person passes away in senility and he's not able to think thoughts of repentance or other important meditation, is that a punishment from Hashem?

When a person is willing to accept the atonement, it wipes out many sins.

I wouldn't say it's a punishment. It could be that Hakadosh Baruch Hu wants to make it easier for him to leave the world.

Let's say he's an important man; he has a very big business. Now, suppose he would die with all his faculties. It would hurt him to no end to give up such a great career that he has. So what does Hakadosh Baruch Hu do? He makes him senile. Little by little, this person withdraws from public life. He doesn't feel the loss so much now, and as he dies, he doesn't suffer so much. Whereas a man who dies in the midst of his career, he's thinking, "How can I give up all my money for somebody else? I worked all my life. How can I give up my fame, my great name?" But now, this way, he retires little by little. He doesn't walk in the streets anymore. People don't visit him anymore. There's not much there to talk to. He doesn't understand anymore. Little by little, he retires from active life, and he fades away in a peaceful way; so it's a good thing for him.

February 1973

An Atonement for his Sins

What's the purpose of *yissurim* at the end of life?

A/ Now, the sufferings of death have two purposes among others. One purpose is, it's an atonement. When a person is willing to accept the atonement, it wipes out many sins. Another purpose of suffering and death is, it makes him happy to say goodbye to this world. Otherwise, nobody wants to go out of this world. But when he's suffering, he's glad to get rid of his sufferings, and therefore death is a gift to him. When a man understands that and he is grateful to Hashem, then he passes out of this world with gratitude, with service to Hashem; that man is dying for a purpose.

September 1989

If a person is in a coma before he passes out of this world, isn't he losing a great opportunity?

Repent Every Day

Q/ **If *yissurim,* particularly at the end of one's life, are a blessing, a gift from Hakadosh Baruch Hu, what happens if a person ends his life in a coma or with Alzheimer's disease? What is it then?**

A/ If a person is in a coma before he passes out of this world, isn't he losing a great opportunity?

The answer is yes. He's losing a great opportunity. And that's why we're told שוּב יוֹם אֶחָד לִפְנֵי מִיתָתְךָ – *Repent one day before you die* (*Shabbos* 153a). So the Gemara says, do you know when that day is? No. Therefore, every day you should do *teshuvah.* If a person tries to always do his best, so *chas v'shalom* if he goes into a coma before he passes out, at least he had the period beforehand in which he could have achieved.

November 1993

Dying With Awareness of Hashem

Q/ **A very old person who is very close to death, is there really any purpose in him davening to Hashem to be saved? Isn't it a waste of time and energy?**

He achieved maybe in his last minutes more than he did all of his life.

A/ Let's say a man is on his deathbed. He's an old man, 119 years old. Look, he can't expect to live much longer. But he cries out anyway on his deathbed; he wants to live. And finally he passes away. Did he waste his time? No! He achieved maybe in his last minutes more than he did all of his life. Because he's thinking about Hashem.

He's crying out on his deathbed, "Hashem, heal me!"

"Oh, that's so silly!" you say. The bystanders think it's ridiculous. "He wants to be healed?! How long do you want to hang around here? Was 119 years not enough?"

And the answer is, it's not enough. He wants to live a thousand years. Why shouldn't he? He had a grandfather who lived a thousand years. Mesushelach lived almost a thousand years, so why shouldn't he? So he's crying out; he's allowed to cry out.

And when he finally passes away, don't say that he didn't accomplish what he wanted. He did accomplish! The crying out is the *purpose* of the deathbed – it's so that he should cry out to Hashem and become more and more aware of Him. That's the biggest achievement there is. So nobody should ever be frustrated in crying out, because he is achieving. He is gaining more awareness of Hashem.

May 1985

Clinical Life Extension

Q/ Today's medical technology can virtually keep one organ alive while the rest of the body shuts down. What instructions should we give when assigning a healthcare proxy for a healthcare agent who will speak for us in the event we are,

to take an extreme case, are being given artificial nutrition, artificial hydration, are on a respirator, or are maybe even brain-dead? What's the Jewish view?

We cannot easily abandon the efforts to maintain a person's life

A/ Now I cannot speak for the *chachmei ha Torah.* Let them tell you.

But I'll speak for myself, and I shall say that whatever was done for our forefathers should be done for us too. Anything additional is not necessary. But to do everything necessary that our forefathers did, that should be done, by all means.

And if feeding and giving oxygen and other means are feasible, by all means, you should continue.

Now, more than that I'm not going to say. We have *poskim, gedolei Yisroel*; let them decide what to do. But the minimum should always be done, and never should a person despair. There have been cases, very few, where people who were entirely brain-dead recovered part of their capabilities.

A person who regains a little consciousness for a little while and he can say a few words – "Ribono shel Olam, heal me. And if it is decided that I have to pass away תְּהֵא מִיתָתִי כַּפָּרָה עַל כָּל חֲטָאתַי – *Let my death be an atonement,*" then it was worth that effort of keeping him alive for a long time. Even that brief moment of consciousness is such a tremendous achievement.

So therefore, we cannot easily abandon the efforts to maintain a person's life even though it seems for the moment that there is no achievement in the efforts.

June 1994

The Jewish body is not your possession. The Jewish body is sacred.

Organ Donation

Q/ Can I make plans to donate my organs after my death for the purpose of medical research and the advancement of medicine?

A/ The answer is that the Jewish body is not your possession. The Jewish body is sacred. Now, just like a Jew cannot commit suicide because it's not his body and it's not his life – it's only entrusted to him, and so, it's like murdering somebody who is entrusted to him – so too, you can't give away your organs. They're not yours. They belong to Hashem.

Therefore, if in your bequest you tell the physicians that you're giving away this or that, you are really stealing from Hakadosh Baruch Hu. The Jewish body is so sacred that it has to be interred.

If the doctors are interested in experiments, let them order bodies from India like everybody else does. You can buy a body for fifty dollars. India exports them in big quantities! So it'll cost the hospitals a little money – that's no reason for you to allow them to do their experiments on your sacred body that doesn't even belong to you; let them experiment on others!

July 1977

Chapter 10

On the Israeli Army

Chapter Sponsor

Sponsored by

The Scheiner family

Contents

Chapter 10

On the Israeli Army

Appreciating the Military

Q/ Is having a Jewish army in the State of Israel before Mashiach comes considered a *meridah b'umos,* a rebellion against the nations of the world (*Kesuvos* 111a)?

A/ Whatever it is, it's like I said many times before. Suppose a dog is chasing you; a mad dog is running after you. And along comes an *apikores* holding a club and he gives the dog a blow with his club and drives it away. Do you want this *apikores* to drop dead? This *apikores* is running after the dog with his club, and he is trying to save you from this dangerous dog. Do you want the *apikores* to drop dead or not? He's saving you from the dog! At least let him live until he finishes the job of saving you from the wild dog.

So therefore, as long as the army is fighting to protect the Jews in the *yishuv hayashan,* okay. The Jews need protection against the Arabs. If the Arabs would come in – *chas v'shalom, chas v'shalom!*

Naturally, an army is a protection, so we want the army to be successful. Whether the army is kosher or not kosher is something else.

Now, it could very well be that they are to blame. It could very well be that the Zionists are to blame for creating the atmosphere of hostility against the frum Jews. Yes, yes; but right now, that's the story. The army is a protection.

Of course, Hakadosh Baruch Hu could protect us in other ways too, but we have to look at the natural things. And naturally, an army is a protection, so we want the army to be successful. Whether the army is kosher or not kosher is something else. When the *apikores* is coming to rescue you from the mad dog, what can you do? The *apikores* should succeed at that. That's all. It's not a matter of appreciating his *kashrus* or his *tzidkus.*

December 2000

The Necessity of the IDF

Q/ The Rav has mentioned many times that the Israeli army is *chotei u'machti*. If there was a choice right now between only two, what would be better for Klal Yisroel, no Israeli army or yes an Israeli army? You can only pick one out of two.

A/ That's not a question at all. If you said the question is, should you join the Israeli army, I'd say, "No."

Should it continue to function? Absolutely. It should continue. It should have victory, overcome enemies. No question about it. What enters your mind at all? Certainly it should conquer; otherwise the Arabs will overrun Eretz Yisroel. Who knows what'll happen if the Arabs win this war? It's a *sakanah* for us.

Not only them. Suppose a bandit is chasing after you, and along comes a *goy* and wants to hit the bandit.

Do you want the *goy* to succeed or not? What's the question?

December 2000

IDF Martyrs

Q/ Are all Israeli soldiers who die in battle considered martyrs for *kiddush Hashem*?

A/ I would say no. If they died defending the Jewish people, they are rewarded to a certain extent, no question about it. But a martyr for *kiddush Hashem* is something different. They can have the reward of suffering for a good cause – for defending Jewish people from the attack of an enemy. But a martyr for *kiddush Hashem* is somebody who voluntarily chooses that role. Like Rabbi Akiva; he volunteered to teach Torah in public knowing that it meant death.

They can have the reward of suffering for a good cause – for defending Jewish people from the attack of an enemy.

So you can't just bandy around words; you can't throw around titles like "*kiddush Hashem*," and "martyr for *kiddush Hashem*." If someone went to fight the enemy voluntarily – nobody forced him – only his conscience told him to go out and protect the Jews from an enemy, then perhaps you could say that. But if a man is drafted into the Israeli army without any intention except to do his stint and then get out, you can't call him a martyr for *kiddush Hashem* if he falls in battle.

October 1978

Atheist Soldiers

Q/ You said before that an atheist will absolutely not get Olam Haba. But if we have a principle that Hakadosh

Baruch Hu does not deny the reward of any creature, shouldn't even atheists get a reward?

An atheist will not get Olam Haba. He gets some reward in this world, but not Olam Haba.

A/ That's true. But we're talking now about Olam Haba. An atheist will not get Olam Haba. He gets some reward in this world, but not Olam Haba.

Q/ **But what about an atheist soldier in the Israeli army who is killed? He's going to be dying the next minute. So there's no Olam Hazeh for him.**

A/ If he's dying the next moment? So in Gehinom he will have some reduction; that's all, but he will not be *zocheh* to Olam Haba. Because that's a *klal.* An atheist will not get Olam Haba. Nothing will help.

You have to understand this. We live in this world not to do good deeds alone. We live in this world only for Hashem. It's the greatest misconception to think that you can work for ideals and turn your back on Hakadosh Baruch Hu. And this big misconception has been fostered by an atheistic society. But anybody who knows a little Torah knows that it is entirely false. There's no question about it.

So therefore, let's take Motzei Yom Kippur when Golda Meir and Dayan were broadcasting to the Jewish nation to summon their courage. Let's say Golda Meir; I don't know if she fasted, but she doesn't eat kosher. Dayan does not eat kosher. So with their unclean mouths from a *treife* meal, they got up, and they spoke to the Jewish nation on the radio.

They didn't mention a word about Hakadosh Baruch Hu. Here is what they said: "We trust in our army." That's the only trust they expressed.

It's a nation headed by atheists. And the fact that they are fighting for the State of Israel does not mitigate this at all, because the State of Israel without Hakadosh Baruch Hu is exactly the same as the State of Albania. Nothing will help.

What kind of a Jew is that, and what kind of s'char in Olam Haba could there be?

You see, all the rabbis who talk in the opposite vein are talking because they want to please the people. The newspapers that write in this vein want to please the people. You know why? Because it's money. Everybody speaks for the purpose of getting something out of the people; therefore, they say what the people want them to say.

But the truth is that it's as simple as could be – there is no such thing as a Jew who doesn't believe in Hakadosh Baruch Hu. If he doesn't believe, he's not a Jew. And *al pi din,* he's *chayav* to be put to death. An atheist is *moridin velo ma'alin.* I won't translate that because there might be some hotheads who hear this, but that's the *din* of an atheist. So what kind of a Jew is that, and what kind of *s'char* in Olam Haba could there be?

And these ridiculous rabbis and these ridiculous radio broadcasts that are making *kedoshim* out of them, it's only because they're appealing to the public. They're lowering themselves to the level of the ignorant multitude.

So for old ladies in Florida who are sitting now and discussing our tapes and saying that our tapes are against Israel; those poor *beheimos,* they just don't understand. Anybody who is against Hakadosh Baruch Hu is not Israel, is not a Jew, is nothing at all.

And we won't budge. We shouldn't budge from that because it's the ABCs. It's elementary. There cannot be any Olam Haba! Olam Haba means to live forever with Hakadosh Baruch Hu. The only ones who live with Him are the ones who believe in Him.

It could be that if a man, an atheist, in his last moment did some very heroic deed of kindliness, it could be that in

It's enough that they lived. He owes them nothing.

our charity toward him, we'll credit him, maybe in his last moment, when he was losing his life for a good deed, that maybe he was thinking about Hakadosh Baruch Hu. That's the only condition that we could allow.

But suppose we would ask him when he's dying, "You don't believe?" and he says, "I don't believe," then there's nothing to talk about. Then he's exactly like an Eskimo who did good deeds. He won't get Olam Haba if he doesn't believe in a Creator.

Q/ **But it's not their fault. They don't know. They're *tinokos shenishbah.***

A/ But this you already heard. If a person is an atheist, even though it's not his fault that he is an atheist, he isn't worthy. He has lost this opportunity.

It's not a question of blame here. We have to have *emunah.* Does Hakadosh Baruch Hu owe any man Olam Haba? Hakadosh Baruch Hu doesn't owe it to anybody. He doesn't owe it. It's just a gift. It's a gift given in the virtue of our forefathers.

Does Hakadosh Baruch Hu owe Olam Haba to virtuous birds or virtuous horses? No. And men, also not. It's enough that they lived. He owes them nothing. When a man's time is up, he has no claims on Hakadosh Baruch Hu. Olam Haba is just a gift. Nobody can demand Olam Haba.

Just for the piece of bread we eat every day and for the glass of water we drink, we have to work and do mitzvos, because we have to pay for it. Nobody can claim he deserves the next world. The only ones who get it are those who are identified with our forefathers, and our forefathers had only one ideal, and that was to serve Hakadosh Baruch Hu. And therefore there's no such thing as a *kofer* getting Olam Haba.

October 1973

Olam Haba for Soldiers

Q/ I'd like quote to the Rav an anecdote from some of the greatest *roshei yeshiva* and thinkers such as Rav Chaim Shmuelevitz, *zt"l,* and the previous Vizhnitzer Rebbe, *zt"l,* that the irreligious Israeli soldiers have one of the most honored places in the World to Come. And, *yibadeil l'chaim tovim,* Rav Moshe Feinstein, said that most of the irreligious world, *ruba d'ruba,* are considered *tinokos shenishbah,* and only a small amount are considered *resha'im.* In light of this, would you perhaps reconsider your strong statements that you made against the irreligious Jews who died in the wars in Israel?

A/ As far as irreligious soldiers who died in the wars, I don't recall any statements that I made. If I did, so they're like any other irreligious Jews. Irreligious Jews, you have to know, are better than most gentiles. And we don't need any authorities to back that up; it's common sense. Even American irreligious Jews are generally better than gentiles – certainly the irreligious Jews whose parents came from Russia or from Hitler's crematoria are; usually they're not yet homosexuals and adulterers, and they don't yet have as much malice as the *umos ha'olam.* There's no question about that – you don't have to quote anybody about that. You can quote me because I said it in my very first book – that the worst Jews are better than most of the good gentiles.

You can quote me because I said it in my very first book – that the worst Jews are better than most of the good gentiles.

Q/ But you specifically mentioned in one of the Thursday night lectures that they have no share in the World to Come?

It's not a question of blame. To merit Olam Haba you have to be maamin in Olam Haba.

A/ The share in the World to Come is something that Hakadosh Baruch Hu alone can know, that's what I said then. Only, why should they be given a share just as a gift? Hakadosh Baruch Hu will give them if He wants, but we go by certain rules. And one of the rules is if a person is a *kofer*, if he's an atheist, so he's not going to have a share in the World to Come. If a person doesn't believe in Olam Haba, he won't have a share in the World to Come. The Gemara says in *Sanhedrin* (46b) that if a man says, "Don't bury me because I don't want a *kapparah*" – when a person is buried, it's a *kapparah* for him – he won't have a *kapparah*. If he doesn't want a *kapparah,* he won't have it! If a person doesn't believe in Olam Haba, then there's no Olam Haba for him. That's one of the fundamentals: הָאוֹמֵר אֵין תְּחִיַּת הַמֵּתִים מִן הַתּוֹרָה – *If one says that there's no next world and resurrection of the dead,* the Gemara in *Sanhedrin* (90b) says that he won't merit the next world.

So what will it help if a *gadol* will give him a paper, a certificate? The question is: Does he believe in Olam Haba?

You say he's a *tinok shenishbah?* So I'll quote Rav Chaim Brisker. Reb Chaim Brisker said, "*Nebach* an *apikores* is still an *apikores.*" It doesn't excuse it! We're not talking about blaming him, it's not a question of blame. To merit Olam Haba you have to be *maamin* in Olam Haba. And if a person is not a *maamin* – it's not a question of whose fault it is – he won't get Olam Haba!

All you can say in the name of Reb Moshe is not that he's a *ben Olam Haba;* you can say maybe that he's better than the *umos ha'olam.* But the *umos ha'olam* also have no *chelek* in Olam Haba, so there's no need to say that this irreligious Jew should get any Olam Haba.

Rav Chaim Brisker is also an authority, and he speaks clearly on this subject. And he's not talking merely whether they're better than the gentiles. And he said that – he said that they won't get any Olam Haba!

Q/ **But Rav Aryeh Finkel of Mir quoted Rav Chaim Shmuelevitz as saying that all people killed in the wars are on the highest level?**

So now we're becoming ridiculous! We're saying ridiculous things!

A/ Highest level? Where? In Gan Eden? Where does he say that? Highest level? He means the highest level of the gentiles. Read to me the words aloud about Olam Haba. Not other words – just about Olam Haba. What does he say about Olam Haba?

Q/ **In the *sefer Pirkei Geula* from Rav Shachna Zohn that has *haskamos* from Rav Elya Lopian and Rav Yechezkel Levenstein and all the great –**

A/ I'll tell you what you should do. Instead of telling me something from a translation that's just a few words that are clipped from here and there, show it to me inside that one of these authorities say that he's on the highest level in Olam Haba. To be on the highest level in Olam Haba, you have to be not like the Chofetz Chaim – you have to be like Rabbi Akiva! Rabbi Akiva is higher than the Chofetz Chaim. So when you say this irreligious soldier is on the highest level, you're saying he's higher than the Chofetz Chaim. Or you're saying he's higher than Rav Chaim Brisker. I'm not measuring who is higher, Reb Chaim Brisker or the Chofetz Chaim, but let's say Rav Velvel Brisker. Rav Velvel will tell you he's less than Reb Chaim, his father. So if you say the highest level, then he's at least with Reb Velvel. And if not with Reb Velvel, at least, let's say, he's with Reb Yosef Chaim Sonnenfeld.

So now we're becoming ridiculous! We're saying ridiculous things! We're talking about the people who were drafted into the army – they had no alternative; if it was up to them, they'd be eating on Yom Kippur in a Tel Aviv café. But now they're drafted into the army, and they get killed against their will! It's ridiculous to put that soldier next door

Should a man serve in the Israeli army?

to the Chofetz Chaim in the next world. Unless a person doesn't believe in the next world, then he can pretend that true *tzaddikim* can sit up there next to anybody off the street. But the next world doesn't come that cheap.

So you have to show me some authority who says that they're sitting – not on the highest level in the next world; show me that they're sitting in Olam Haba at all. That's what I want to see! Bring me proof that they're in Olam Haba at all!

You have to understand that when you speak to the public, sometimes you have to say words that can be construed with double meanings. So "the highest level" means compared, let's say, to Idi Amin [*Ed: President of Uganda 1971–1979, known as the Butcher of Uganda due of his torture and murder of thousands of civilians*]. Idi Amin is on the lowest level; he's going to be on the lowest level in Gehinom, so these soldiers will be a little higher than he is.

March 1979

To Serve or Not to Serve 1

Q/ **Should a man serve in the Israeli army?**

A/ And the answer is no. By no means should one serve in the army. Because it doesn't pay to get killed for nothing! When you go out in a *milchama*, a battle where the *chachmei ha Torah* command you to go out and fight, then you're sacrificing your life for *kavod Shamayim.* But if you're going out in a war because of what others tell you, *baal habatim* – even Orthodox *baal habatim,* but they're *baal habatim* – so it means you're giving the greatest donation that you have, for something that might be nothing at all. It's too much to donate. Your life is too precious.

By no means should you serve in the Israeli army. I say, stay away!

So you'll ask me, "Well, what about helping out our fellow Jews?" Let me explain something to you. Suppose a fellow says, "I'm going to go pick a fight with the colored people in Brownsville." He gets on his bike, and he wears, let's say, a black hat and a beard, and he cycles into Bedford Stuyvesant, and he starts calling people names. You know what's going to happen to him.

Now, you happen to be passing by on a bus – there's a bus that goes through Bedford Stuyvesant – and you're looking through the window and you see this hero surrounded by all of these menacing people. So you'll ask me, maybe you should get off the bus and help this fellow in his fight?

Look, if you want to be safe, you'd better just keep on riding until you get to Williamsburg. Because what are you going to do already? Is it your fault? Who told people to put themselves in such a situation? Did the *gedolei Yisroel* say it?

Now, there's a lot to say on this subject, but I can't speak anymore now because the time is brief. But if you're asking me for my opinion, then I'll tell you: By no means should you serve in the Israeli army. I say, stay away! If you have to go there, make sure not to renounce your American citizenship. And don't allow yourself to be drafted.

October 1977

To Serve or Not to Serve 2

Q/ Is there any problem with frum Jews in Eretz Yisroel going into the army?

It's almost impossible for a person to remain decent in the army.

A/ The answer is that if they would go to the army, then there wouldn't be any frum Jews left in Eretz Yisroel. Because the army is meant for the purpose of intentionally ruining the character of the Jewish youth. Now pay attention to me, because they say it themselves. They say that they have girls in the army for that purpose – in order to break down the restrictions against immoral behavior.

They say as follows: "The Jewish *z'nus* is a special type of *z'nus.*" We never heard of such a thing, Jewish *z'nus.*

Therefore, the army is made to break down the morality of the Am Yisroel. It's almost impossible for a person to remain decent in the army. Of course, some are *omed b'nisayon,* some withstand the test, but it's extremely difficult. There cannot be a frum population if the boys go to the army. It's out of the question.

Hashem yeracheim! Hashem should be מֵפִיר עֲצַת רְשָׁעִים, and they shouldn't be able to do anything against the frum boys.

It might be necessary that all the frum Jews leave Eretz Yisroel, *chas v'shalom*. But that the boys should go into the army?! *Chas v'shalom!* It would be impossible for us to exist. And the *resha'im* know that. They want to take our boys into the army and they want to do whatever they want with them in order to turn out new products – Israelis. And we don't want to become Israelis. We want to be frum Jews who remain loyal to the Torah and Hakadosh Baruch Hu.

June 1999

Nachal Chareidi

Q/ There has been talk in Eretz Yisroel about the *frumme* agreeing to join the IDF in separate regiments called

Nachal Chareidi. What does the Rav think about this?

We have to maintain our privilege that all the countries give, that rabbinical students are exempt from the draft.

A/ Some people are proposing to take frum boys into the army in frum regiments. You should know that it's a *shtus*. The army is made *l'chatchilah* for the purpose of changing the minds of the boys in the army. It's a statement that was made long ago. It's well known. And it's only a trick that they're using now to deceive the *frumme* into entering the army.

The truth is that Am Yisroel has to keep out of the army. We have to maintain our privilege that all the countries give, that rabbinical students are *patur* from the draft, exempt from the draft. We must continue to fight for it and not to yield and not to listen to the sinners who are talking about frum regiments for frum boys.

November 2000

The True Defense

Q/ **What's more important for defending the Am Yisroel: soldiers who are at the front stopping terrorists, or yeshiva men who are learning Torah?**

A/ גְּדוֹלָה תַּלְמוּד תּוֹרָה יוֹתֵר מֵהַצָּלַת נְפָשׁוֹת – *Learning Torah is greater than saving lives* (*Megillah* 16b). It's a greater thing, a more meritorious thing to learn Torah than to go out and save lives.

Now, that doesn't mean that you're allowed to choose learning if you're the only one available to save someone's life, but still you have to know that it actually is a greater thing. And that is a *limud,* a lesson forever.

They entered a town and asked, "Who are the neturei karta? Who are the guardians who guard this town?"

Now in every specific case, I can't tell you what your responsibility would be – it depends on you and the situation and many factors – but we follow the *psak* that we pray to Hakadosh Baruch Hu, "Ribono Shel Olam, don't give us opportunities to save anybody's life. Give us opportunities to pursue our studies, to become closer to You, to love You more, and to understand You more."

If *chas v'shalom,* something comes up and we have to close our Gemaras and go out and do battle to save Jewish lives, we will have to do it. Maybe we will be saved that way, but we prefer the other way, because גְּדוֹלָה תַּלְמוּד תּוֹרָה יוֹתֵר מֵהַצָּלַת נְפָשׁוֹת – *Studying Torah is the biggest way you can achieve perfection for yourself* (ibid).

And by the way, it is the biggest way you can save the Jewish people. תַּלְמִידֵי חֲכָמִים מַרְבִּים שָׁלוֹם בָּעוֹלָם, the *talmidei chachamim,* they are the armies of Hashem (*Brachos* 64a).

Rebbe Chiya sent his sons around in the cities of Eretz Yisroel – it was after the war of Beitar when the cities had been demolished; in many places there was no Hebrew school for children, so he sent his sons to inquire what could be done for Torah education.

They entered a town and asked, "Who are the *neturei karta*? Who are the guardians who guard this town?"

So the elders of the town summoned the guardians, and there came two men on horses with big clubs, big burly men, and they said, "These are the guardians, the watchmen who guard our town."

So Rebbe Chiya's son said, "They're not the *neturei karta*. They're not the ones who guard the town. They are *charuvei karta*. These two people, these fellows, are ruining the town." They were rough fellows, those two. After all, you don't take guardians from the spiritual aristocracy. You take them out from someplace, from a saloon, from a wine café.

"These fellows are ruining the town," he said, "they're not guarding the town."

So the people asked, "So who is guarding the town?"

So he said, "A Hebrew teacher. Get a *melamed* to teach your children Torah. He is going to guard the town."

Now, does that mean if you have a *melamed* who teaches the children Torah, you don't have to have locks on the doors? Does it mean that you don't have to have a guard who will guard you? Of course not. You need everything, but the guard will be effective only when the *melamed* is sitting and teaching Torah, because Hakadosh Baruch Hu is the One Who will make the guard effective.

The fools in Israel, they think their little toy army, that's what's going to keep them?!

What will it help you if you have a self-defense corp, if you have weapons and you have military precision, and you are perfect in self-defense, if Hakadosh Baruch Hu is not pleased with you? The fools in Israel, they think their little toy army, that's what's going to keep them?! Of course we have to try to protect ourselves. But to put your trust in that? And to be atheists? I hope they'll never discover their error in a tragic way.

So the very first thing is, we have to win Hashem on our side, and then we have to take all necessary precautions, too. But the ones who truly guard the city are the ones who teach Torah to the Jewish people.

I know it is a difficult thing to hear. Years ago, I said this in public – I said that the students of the yeshivos, they're our army, that's our artillery, they're our navy, they're our tanks – and Jews were incensed. It was many years ago and they were incensed when they heard that. But they looked away from the experience of generations.

Look, we didn't have any army in the Middle Ages. And yet, there was no Hitler who destroyed us. They tried again and again, but we survived.

In case you're a Zionist, keep your blood pressure down, because I'm not going to spare you anything.

When did Hitler come? When the Jews were at their best. We had Jewish scientists. We had Jewish generals too. We had everything. Colleges were crammed with Jews. And still, nothing helped when the time came, because Hakadosh Baruch Hu was no longer on our side.

So, the number one requirement is to win the victory with Hakadosh Baruch Hu, and then, of course, we take all proper precautions, all necessary measures, and Hashem will give them success.

August 1982

Fighting Without Weapons

Q/ How could you say that Jews should avoid doing military service in Israel if there are millions of Jews who need to be protected?

A/ Oh, this is a harking back to an old discussion. So in case you're a Zionist, keep your blood pressure down, because I'm not going to spare you anything. Now, you don't have to accept what I'm telling you – but I'm not going to accept what you're saying.

So, I'll ask this gentleman here, the questioner, what's he doing here? Why is he a slacker?! There are millions of Jews who have to be protected – let him go and sign up.

The answer is, you have your reasons. You think, maybe, that right now you want to study here and become a physician and eventually you'll go there and you'll help them out in that way. So, you have an idea to help the people there in a different way; not by putting on a uniform right now. That's your idea of helping them. It sounds reasonable.

So, we also have ideas of how to help the people in Eretz Yisroel. And one idea is to send a lot of money to the yeshivos, to poor *talmidei chachamim.* That money goes into the economy. Any money you send is going to be spent there; it's spent at the butcher shops and in the grocery shops. It's spent on products, and you're therefore supporting the people who work in the factories. Whatever money you send to *talmidei chachamim* living there goes straight into the economy. It's very important. Believe me, if you asked the people at the head of the State, "Would you excuse about twenty or fifty or a hundred or a thousand people from the army to go to the United States and raise big sums for your economy?" they'd gladly agree, because money is the blood of a nation. You can't fight a war without money.

The Arabs in Israel are increasing more than the Arabs in any other place in the world.

So, if you really want to help out, I'll give you a list. I have a list of blue-ribbon poor families who are doing a big job for Eretz Yisroel. They're raising a lot of children. You know, there are other Jews who are not raising children. Eretz Yisroel is a country with a great deal of abortions. Authorities have said that at least a million Jewish children were aborted from the beginning of the State until a few years ago. That was years back; now it's much more. And all the while, the Arabs are having children like nobody's business; they've never had so many children before. Because the Arabs in Eretz Yisroel are getting the best medical treatment. The Arabs in Israel are increasing more than the Arabs in any other place in the world.

So how long will it take before the Jews will be outnumbered? It's only a matter of time. Even right now, there's a big problem – the Jews are dwindling and the Arabs are snowballing. So here you have some Jews who are busy trying to equalize the population; they are the hope of the future – the *apikorsim* in Tel Aviv are not doing their part – so you should send money to them, and that money goes into the lifeblood of the nation. That's one way of helping to

Hashem is the One making the wars against the State of Israel. Now, of course they wouldn't believe that, but we do!

defend the Am Yisroel. It's a beautiful way of supporting the people there.

And if you want another way to help the Jews there, pay attention. You have to know, הַשֵּׁם אִישׁ מִלְחָמָה – Hashem is the One making the wars against the State of Israel. Now, of course they wouldn't believe that, but we do! Hakadosh Baruch Hu is the Man of War. בַּעַל מִלְחָמוֹת – *He makes the wars.* And there are reasons why He makes wars. Do you know why He makes wars on Israel? Listen to me; but keep your blood pressure down. A man told me today that he was in Israel in 1966. He went to a movie. This is the kind of a man who's not a *shomer mitzvos.* He went to a movie and he saw – now, I'll have to wash my mouth out after I get through telling this to you – he saw movies where a certain form of *toeivah* was being practiced in the movie, on the screen. Now, what that means – it's enough, I can't tell you anymore. And it was supposed to be only for adults. It means past sixteen. Sixteen and up, that's adults over there. But he was in places, he was in various theaters there, and this is what he told me. He told me that he saw children of five and six years old at these movies. Which means that the youth in Eretz Yisroel are being conditioned for a life of degeneracy.

The gays are planning next year an international world conference for gays in Yerushalayim. And he said that they have two synagogues of gays in Eretz Yisroel. He said three, but I want to make it within the bounds of surety. And in Tel Aviv you have anything that you can find in Times Square – they're not behind one bit.

Now, we want to save הָעָם הַיּוֹשֵׁב בְּצִיּוֹן, we want to help out the Jews who live in Eretz Yisroel. We want to stop the wars; and therefore, if we're going to fight against the adverse influences there, if we're going to exert pressure on the government that they should remedy these evils, maybe we can have a hand in protecting the Jews in Eretz Yisroel. We want them to wipe out pornography.

We want them to stop drafting girls into the army. Because girls in the army means only one thing. That Israeli general who wrote a book about the Israeli army – we can trust what he tells us. And he states openly that for most girls, their induction into the army is their first experience in *z'nus.* For most Israeli girls, the army is a house of harlotry. So now you have an institution, the Israeli army, which is one big house of prostitution, and the girls are forced into it. Now, that's not *my* statement. It's a statement by a general who wrote a history of the Israel Defense Forces, and he makes that statement openly. He doesn't make it in a clandestine, secret way that you have to read between the lines. He says it openly. They're not ashamed.

It's a statement by a general who wrote a history of the Israel Defense Forces, and he makes that statement openly.

So we have to exert pressure because we don't want that. Because it says that הַשֵּׁם אֱלֹקֶיךָ מִתְהַלֵּךְ בְּקֶרֶב מַחֲנֶךָ לְהַצִּילְךָ וְלָתֵת אֹיְבֶיךָ לְפָנֶיךָ – *Hashem walks in your midst to help you against your enemy.* But it says also וְלֹא יִרְאֶה בְךָ עֶרְוַת דָּבָר וְשָׁב מֵאַחֲרֶיךָ – *If He'll see immorality among you, so the Shechinah will depart* (*Devarim* 23:15). It means He'll let you be defeated. So if we want to help the people in Eretz Yisroel be protected from the enemies, it's our job to speak up and fight against all of the wickedness in the State of Israel.

So, just like this young man who doesn't go right now, and he puts on a uniform because he wants to help them eventually by becoming a physician, we're also helping in our own way. It's a very big help if you write letters and protest against what's going on there. Of course, now there's a better regime. Up until now there was a Marxist regime, but now there's a better regime, and let's hope that these things are going to change.

February 1978

QUESTIONS *On Any* SUBJECT

Chapter 11

The Yeshiva Bachur

Chapter Sponsor

In memory of

הרה"ג ר' **יצחק אהרן** בן הרה"ג ר' **אליהו זינגער** זצ"ל
וזוגתו הרבנית **רייזל** בת הרה"ח ר' **יששכר דוב** ע"ה
הרה"צ ר' **ישראל אריה ליב האלפערן**
בן הרה"צ ר' **ברוך** מסאקאליווקא זצ"ל
וזוגתו הרבנית **שבע** בת הרה"ג ר' **אריה ליבוש** ע"ה

And in memory of our mother
Rebbetzin Bluma Singer ע"ה

Contents

Chapter 11

The Yeshiva Bachur

A Difficult Rebbi

Q/ **What should a *bochur* do if he's not in a good *shiur* and his *rebbi* doesn't answer his questions?**

A/ Now, I don't know if it's not a good *shiur*. It could be that it's a very good *shiur;* that I can't tell you. But if your *rebbi* doesn't answer your questions, there are plenty of other people to answer your questions. So make sure to learn what you can from your *rebbi*. He needs *parnassah* so make sure not to discourage him. Honor him and make him feel good. And after the *shiur,* walk over to him and say, "Rebbi, I enjoyed your *shiur,*" even though you didn't. It's a mitzvah to be *mi'odeid anavim* so make sure to encourage him.

And your questions you can mark off in the Gemara as you get stuck, and then take your Gemara down to the *beis hamedrash* and ask an older *bochur.* He'll tell you the answers. You'll find someone to tell you the answers.

November 1999

If he comes late because he goes to sleep late and he gets up late, the first suggestion would be to go to sleep early.

Simple Advice

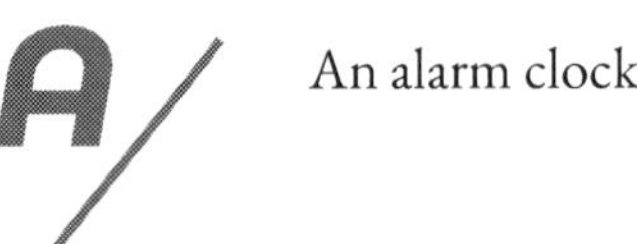

What is good advice for a *bochur* who doesn't get up on time for davening?

An alarm clock.

June 1998

Not-So-Simple Advice

Someone who has a nature to come late; what would be an *eitzah* to improve himself?

First of all, if he comes late because he goes to sleep late and he gets up late, the first suggestion would be to go to sleep early. He must get enough sleep. You must get sleep! And after a good night's sleep, have an alarm clock to wake you up.

Now, in case it doesn't help, make a *neder.* Listen to me; make a *neder* that the first time you'll come late, it will cost you fifty dollars for a yeshiva that you don't like. Just one time. Not forever. Just that the first time you come late, you'll have to make a fifty-dollar donation to the yeshiva. You'll keep on putting off the first time. You're getting up in the morning for fifty dollars. If *chas v'shalom* you are *oiver,* it costs you fifty dollars that week.

Then make another *neder.* The first time it happens again, another fifty dollars. I guarantee, little by little, you'll stop coming late.

May 2000

The Good Yeshiva People

Q/ What does one do in a yeshiva where you have wicked people who ridicule you if you did a good thing?

A/ The answer is, there is no such thing. It's like the man who joined the army, and he said to the sergeant who was scolding him, "Why is everybody out of step with me?"

So, if a person joins a yeshiva and he discovers that there are wicked people there, he'd better discover what is wrong with him! And I mean that seriously. In a yeshiva, there aren't wicked people. Of course, there are all kinds of people there; there are some people who need training, there are some people who are raw, some people who are contentious, but wicked people don't go to a yeshiva.

I happen to know about yeshivos. I have fought with yeshiva men for many years; I fought with them! Not with all of them; with some of them. But there aren't any wicked ones in the yeshiva. I have been forty years in the American yeshiva world and there are no wicked ones in the yeshiva.

I have been forty years in the American yeshiva world and there are no wicked ones in the yeshiva.

June 1979

Respecting the Rosh Yeshiva

Q/ If I find myself in a yeshiva where they're not standing up for the *rosh yeshiva,* how should I conduct myself?

A/ Nobody gets up for the *rosh yeshiva* and you do get up? אַשְׁרֶיךָ יִשְׂרָאֵל מִי כָמוֹךָ! You're a lucky fellow. If you were in a yeshiva where everybody got up, your *s'char* would be very small compared to that. But now, *baruch Hashem*.

When a person gets up for good things when other people don't, he's chosen by Hashem. Like it says וַיָּקָם פִּינְחָס מִתּוֹךְ הָעֵדָה – *Pinchas got up* (*Bamidbar* 25:7). Everybody was sitting. Pinchas got up. Ah! Hashem says "הִנְנִי נֹתֵן לוֹ אֶת בְּרִיתִי שָׁלוֹם – I'm making a special covenant with him" (ibid. 12). The man who gets up, he's the one Hashem chooses.

When a person gets up for good things when other people don't, he's chosen by Hashem.

December 1996

Warming Up to the Rosh Yeshiva

Q/ **How should one come close to a *rosh yeshiva* who is cold?**

A/ You expect *him* to be hot? *You* supply the warmth. You be a warm *talmid* to the *rosh yeshiva*; if you'll be a warm *talmid*, he'll respond to you. A *rosh yeshiva* has to teach, doesn't he? You expect him to be hot when he's teaching, let's say, a *shiur* in *palginan dibura*? He has to be practical. It's a mathematical question there.

However, if you come over to him sometimes and speak to him, you'd be surprised. He's not cold at all. Sometimes, he can become a good friend of yours.

I've spoken to people who have problems. I said, "You come from Boro Park and you're calling me up about a problem? What about your *rav* in Boro Park?"

"Well," he says, "I have no business with a *rav*."

You have no business with a *rav*? What kind of business is that? You should go over to the *rav* and say "Good Shabbos!" And sometimes talk to him. You'd be surprised. *Rabbanim* have something to say to you. They can be your guide, your mentor in life. So many people are at fault *not* because their *rav* or the *rosh yeshiva* is cold.

You should go over to the rav and say "Good Shabbos!" And sometimes talk to him. You'd be surprised.

I remember in Europe, I was in a small town, and somebody told me that the *rav* is a cold *rav.* I happened to know the *rav.* He was a very warm-hearted *rav,* a man who went out of his way to do favors for people. But the people were cold. They were looking for faults.

Come closer to him! Warm up to him. You'll discover that this man was a great *baal chesed,* a man who would spend days doing favors for people.

And people had the audacity to say he was a coldhearted man.

And so, who says the *rosh yeshiva* is cold? Maybe you're cold.

May 1986

Finding a Chavrusa

Q/ **What should I do if I have a hard time finding a *chavrusa* in yeshiva?**

A/ The first thing is to ask the *mashgiach* to give you a *chavrusa*. He might find someone for you. Another *eitzah* is to learn well by yourself. I want to tell you – some people have succeeded very well without a *chavrusa*. And when your *chaveirim* see you learning well, people will come over to you asking you to be their *chavrusa*.

Today he is maggid shiur for one of the highest shiurim in a mesivta.

Now, you have to know how to learn properly if you want to succeed. While you're learning, don't just say the Gemara and keep on going. Stop, and talk it over in your own words – talk over the *shakla v'tarya,* the discussion in the Gemara, and you'll succeed. First of all, it will help you understand that which you didn't understand yet, and secondly, you'll remember it better.

I remember once there was a man – I saw him in the yeshiva for years and years just sitting and talking over every little piece of the Gemara again and again and again and again. At that time, he was a *beinoni,* an average fellow – and today he is *maggid shiur* for one of the highest *shiurim* in a *mesivta*. I see him walking in the streets talking *divrei Torah* with his boys, his *talmidim*. Because when he was sitting and learning by himself without a *chavrusa,* he utilized the opportunity to talk it over with himself.

When a person does that, he becomes an *amkan*, he understands well and can reach into the depths of the words of the Gemara, and he remembers it well too.

Now, that's in place of a *chavrusa*; but if you do this, then eventually, you'll get a *chavrusa* too.

September 1996

Using English Seforim

Q/ Should a yeshiva *bochur* use an English-language Chumash or Gemara?

A/ And the answer is, use anything that will help you. As long as it's not written by *apikorsim*.

There are plenty of English translations by frum Jews today. Why not? Didn't the Rambam write the *Moreh*

Nevuchim in Arabic? Wasn't the *Chovos Halevavos* written in Arabic? Nothing wrong! Excellent *seforim*. So if it's for the purpose of *avodas Hashem,* why not? If you don't need it, you don't need it.

December 1995

Wasn't the Chovos Halvavos written in Arabic? Nothing wrong!

Changing Yeshivos

Q/ When should a yeshiva man decide that it's time for him to change yeshivos?

A/ That's a question that is up to the *bochur* himself, and to people who know him well. It's impossible to give a general idea.

Sometimes, it states in the Gemara likes this: דְּבִישׁ לֵיהּ בְּהַאי מָתָא – *If it's bad for him in this town,* לֵיזַל לְמָתָא אַחֲרִיתָא – *let him go to another town* (*Bava Metzia* 75b). So it means, if it's bad for him he should leave, but if it's good for him in a certain town, let him remain in the town.

The only reason to leave the town is if it's no good. If you're succeeding in the yeshiva, then keep on succeeding. It's only if you feel that you're not succeeding enough.

Now, sometimes, you're succeeding, only you feel that you're not utilizing your capacity. You might succeed much more elsewhere. Then that's a delicate question, and I certainly couldn't give an opinion in a general way. And that's why I said it's up to you to take counsel from people who know you well before a decision is made.

April 1993

Every yeshiva has a lower class. And therefore, it's up to you to gravitate towards the better ones.

Learning in Eretz Yisroel

Q/ **Should a *bochur* go to Eretz Yisroel to learn?**

A/ I don't know if it's always justified. You have good yeshivos here in America, and you could become a *gadol b'Yisroel* in these yeshivos here.

I'm not saying you shouldn't go, but I don't think it's a big necessity. I know *talmidei chachamim* who never left this country. They grew great, and today they are *roshei yeshiva* who head the biggest yeshivos in America. They never went to anyplace else except to America.

March 1999

Bad Influences in Yeshiva

Q/ **What should I do if I'm in a yeshiva where not everyone is exerting a good influence, and I have to stay in that yeshiva for now?**

A/ I want to tell you something. In every yeshiva there's an underworld. Not the underworld, let's say, of New York City, but relatively speaking, it's an underworld. Every yeshiva has a lower class. And therefore, it's up to you to gravitate towards the better ones. You have to make sure you associate with the best.

It's always that way. It's not only in the yeshivos. In every *kehillah*, in every congregation, there's an underworld. There are always a few lower people, grumblers, dissatisfied people who like to make trouble. So if you're a low fellow, you'll gravitate to them. And you'll ruin yourself.

Wherever you go, you'll have a choice of who to gravitate towards. If you have any sense, you'll seek out the idealists wherever you are. And therefore, it makes no difference. Wherever you may be, you must always utilize your discretion to choose the very best people with whom to associate. If you want to be the best, make sure to associate with the best.

If you want to be the best, make sure to associate with the best.

January 1987

Sleeping Well

Q/ What should a yeshiva *bochur* do if he is annoyed by depression and sadness, and he doesn't know what the reason is?

A/ I want to tell you one thing I do know from experience. Many times boys in the yeshiva cause an upset in their nervous system because of a lack of sleep. In the dormitories, you can't go to sleep early. Even if he gets into bed, somebody comes in at 1:00 and doesn't let him sleep.

I once told a man about this problem and he went and took his son out and put him in a separate room. He was a wealthy man and he paid money to the dormitory for a separate room so his son should be able to sleep.

It's very important to sleep. I myself know two cases of boys who didn't go to sleep on time and they went insane, *nit eingedacht*. Yes, it happened. They ruined their lives. Without sleeping sufficiently, your nervous system is upset.

Now, once a person gets into a depression, it's not so easy to get out of it. And therefore, an ounce of prevention is worth a pound of cure. So try with all your efforts not to upset your system and get your sleep every night.

He told the boys to go to sleep. "You can learn tomorrow," he said.

Now, some people say, "Well, I'm a *porush*. I want to be a *masmid*." We'll, I'll tell you what the Chofetz Chaim said. Once, the Chofetz Chaim came into the yeshiva in Radin at night, and he saw boys learning late so he said to them, "*Gei shlufen. Morgen is oich a tug*." He told the boys to go to sleep. "You can learn tomorrow," he said.

And that's the sensible way. That's saving the lives of people by advising them, "Learn by day and sleep at night."

Now, sometimes there are other factors, but one of the most general factors that I know from my experience is this one of not sleeping sufficiently.

June 1995

Dormitory Life 1

Q/ **What should a *bochur* do if his *chaveirim* in his dormitory room are speaking *lashon hara*?**

A/ He should walk out of the room until the people go to sleep. Let him sit in a *beis hamedrash* until his *chaveirim* go to sleep. And in case they don't go to sleep until late, he should tell them, "*Chaveirim*, please excuse me. I have to go to sleep. When you talk, I can't sleep. Do me a favor!" Ask *rachamim* of them and go to sleep so you shouldn't hear their *lashon hara* and you should be able to get up to *daven* the next morning on time.

The Rabbeinu Yona gives an *eitzah*. When you hear *lashon hara* and you're not able to reprove, to rebuke the people, if for some reason, you can't tell them, "It's *lashon hara*," at least don't show any interest. Show a sad face, he says, an uninterested, bored face, and that will discourage them. He brings a *pasuk,* וּפָנִים נִזְעָמִים לְשׁוֹן סָתֶר – *An unhappy face will dispel the false tongue* (*Mishlei* 25:23).

But if you show an interested face – he's talking to you and you show an interested face, a lively face – it means you're encouraging him, "Keep on. Keep on." And he'll keep on pouring *lashon hara* into your ear. But if he sees that you're discouraging, that you're not interested, that will stop him from talking *lashon hara*.

April 1993

A yeshiva man should always be presentable because he has the responsibility of the Torah on his shoulders.

Dormitory Life 2

Q/ Should yeshiva men at the dormitories be taught to shower, etcetera, in addition to learning?

A/ Absolutely. Everyone should be taught that, especially *bnei Torah.*

February 1974

Dress Code

Q/ Should a yeshiva boy wear nice clothing even during the week? What about a tie?

A/ Now, this question is in order. A yeshiva man should always be presentable because he has the responsibility of the Torah on his shoulders. He represents the Torah and therefore it's a heavy responsibility. Like the Gemara (*Shabbos* 114a) says on the *pasuk,* כָּל מְשַׂנְאַי אָהֲבוּ מָוֶת – *All those who hate Me, love death*

(*Mishlei* 8:36). Hashem says, "Those who hate Me, love death." But our Sages add another layer of meaning to this *pasuk:* אַל תִּקְרֵי מְשַׂנְאַי אֶלָּא מַשְׂנִיאַי – *Don't read it as "those who hate Me," but "those who* make others *hate Me."* If you're known, if you're recognized as a yeshiva man, if you wear a black hat for instance, then the hat has to be dusted, not dusty. Otherwise, wear a gray hat. Certainly people who represent the Torah, people with beards and so on, must make a good impression.

People who represent the Torah, people with beards and so on, must make a good impression.

What about a tie? It depends on which group you belong to. Some groups don't wear neckties.

March 1974

Leitzanus in Yeshiva

Q/ In some yeshivos and in some *batei midrash,* there is sometimes an atmosphere of sarcasm and *leitzanus* about the outside world. Is that a good thing?

A/ It depends what they are making *leitzanus* about. If it's about evil things, then we're all for it! That's what a *beis hamedrash* is for, to learn how to belittle the evils of the outside world.

But if they're making *leitzanus* of good people, let's say a *misnagdishe* boy is making fun of *chassidishe rebbes,* that's a big error, a big mistake. You have to be careful who you are talking about. And if *chassidim* make *leitzanus* about *misnagdishe gedolim,* that's also a big error. Those are fatal mistakes to make. Nobody should ever make *leitzanus* about anything unless he knows that it's absolutely wicked.

March 1984

Following Sports 1

Q/ May a yeshiva *bochur* listen to sports?

A/ I'll add to it another question. May a yeshiva *bochur* stand on his head? He can if he wants to, but he's a *meshugene* if he does.

What's it our business if the Yanks and the Mets hit the baseball? It's so meshuga.

What are sports? It's so silly. What's it our business if the Yanks and the Mets hit the baseball? It's so *meshuga. A goyishe meshugene velt.* The headlines, Yanks! It's so silly. It shows how empty the gentile world is.

And therefore, we have to take a lesson from that and say, are they any example for us? בָּרוּךְ אֱלֹקֵינוּ שֶׁהִבְדִּילָנוּ מִן הַתּוֹעִים – *He separated us from these lost neshamos.*

December 1999

Following Sports 2

Q/ Is there anything wrong if a frum yeshiva *bochur* goes to sports games once in a while if he's careful to watch himself?

A/ I don't know what that means, "careful to watch himself."

And the answer is that it certainly is wrong for a yeshiva *bochur* to go to sports games. A yeshiva *bochur* – not only a yeshiva *bochur*, I think every frum Jew – should disassociate himself from public amusements. Some people are so Americanized that they identify with the American scene. You must know that all these places are places where

We should disassociate ourselves from the mob of non thinkers. Even the Orthodox mob.

people are victimized. What a stupidity to come and watch other people getting exercise! And you pay money for it! Isn't it stupid to be enthusiastic as people are skating or playing lacrosse or basketball or soccer, whatever it is, and you are paying to watch it?

If you could get on the field yourself and kick the ball around – at least you get exercise. But you're sitting on a chair, and all you're doing is getting hemorrhoids from sitting on a hard chair. And they're getting money from you. So you've been victimized. Don't be a fool to just join in the herd that's being led to the slaughter.

In general, even though there's nothing wrong with a game – it's stupid, it's meaningless; who cares who wins, yet there's nothing wrong – but the mere fact that you identify with the herd, that fact that you're being stampeded by the herd, is a tragedy. You lose your identity – you're the *am hanivchar,* the Chosen Nation; you have different things. You're not interested in that garbage.

And therefore, when you go to a rock 'n' roll gathering or a gathering of other music – even to kosher places – it's so silly to be part of a big crowd sitting and listening to syncopations, to noise, to banging on the drum and blowing on the flute. What is it? It's music that means nothing. There's no ideal to it.

And so, we should disassociate ourselves from the mob of non-thinkers. Even from the Orthodox mob. We are expected to be הֶן עָם לְבָדָד יִשְׁכֹּן – *Behold the nation that dwells alone,* וּבַגּוֹיִם לֹא יִתְחַשָּׁב – *and we're not counted among the goyim* (*Bamidbar* 23:9).

Stay away from the *goyim* and just do what the Am Yisroel does. If you want to go to a place where there's singing, then go to a *rebbe*; go to a big *melaveh malka* where a *rebbe* is sitting at a table and five hundred Jews are sitting there and they're singing together. That's something you could do if you want. I myself prefer to sit and learn Motzei

Shabbos. But if you like a *melaveh malka*, go to a *melaveh malka*; there's plenty of places to go. Go to places where Jews are sitting and hearing Torah or learning Torah. Identify with Klal Yisroel! Don't identify with anybody else.

Go to places where Jews are sitting and hearing Torah or learning Torah.

Therefore, a yeshiva *bochur* who's going to the sports game, and even though he's "watching himself," – he doesn't talk to anybody, he just sits and enjoys – but that man is making himself into a zero. And it's a tragedy when you can become a million, and instead you become a zero.

November 1984

Immoral Teachers

Q/ What should a *bochur* in a *mesivta* do if he has a teacher in the English department who wishes to discuss immorality with the students?

A/ And the answer is, he should go to the *rosh yeshiva*. He should go complain to the *rosh yeshiva*.

Now, that's a very painful question; it's not so simple because I know from experience that the people in charge do this. The *rosh yeshiva* will tell you, "Talk to the principal." So you go to the principal, but he wants to keep his teachers; he doesn't want to cause too much opposition, so he tries to soften the problem. "The teacher didn't mean it," he says to the boy. "He didn't intend it."

So now the boy is stymied. He can't go back to the *rosh yeshiva*, and the principal has already put him off; so the boy now has to find other ways.

Now, I'll tell you the other ways; I have other ways, but I won't say them in public because you might be the high

Forget about it. It's wickedness. It's corruption. It's a corrosion of the neshama

school principal yourself. So if you want, when you see me in private, I'll tell you what to do.

November 1982

Cheating in School

Q/ Is it permitted for yeshiva people to cheat in school or to steal the Regents exam?

A/ And the answer is no and no and no. It's *assur* to steal. It's *assur* to cheat.

Don't forget, you're not cheating the Regents. You're cheating your teacher. You have a teacher there, and the teacher is giving you the exams, or the principal is, and they're kosher Jews. The principal is a kosher Jew. You're *gonev daas habrios.* So what's the *heter* for cheating the principal?

And therefore, forget about it. It's wickedness. It's corruption. It's a corrosion of the *neshamah* and a person like that will someday be *mechalel shem Shamayim b'farhesia.* He'll end up in jail and his family will go around collecting money for him and he'll suffer physical illness as a result. And the rest of his life, he'll be a failure, all because he tried to be a wise guy and cheat on the Regents. It doesn't pay to be a crook.

May 1979

Shmiras Einayaim

How does a *bochur* counter the effects of *pritzus* in the street?

A/ You must know that Hakadosh Baruch Hu has created cement on the sidewalk for a purpose; not only to make it comfortable and clean to walk. The purpose of cement is that you should gaze at it when you walk in the street. Study the cement on the sidewalk as you walk. That's a very important admonition and it's very beneficial. So as you walk in the street, keep your eyes on the cement.

Now, you know what cement is for? Cement is a wonderful product. No animals use cement. Birds don't need cement. Lions don't need cement. Only we need cement. Now you know why we need cement? *That's* the purpose of it.

August 1994

Cement is a wonderful product. No animals use cement. Birds don't need cement.

Toras Chesed

Q/ How much *chesed* should a full-time yeshiva *bochur* be involved in?

A/ And the answer is that a yeshiva *bochur* should never allow anything to interfere with his learning. Now, if it's possible for him to do *chesed* when he's not learning, why not? But don't go away from the *beis hamedrash* for *chesed. Talmud Torah k'neged kulam.* And even if it's a mitzvah, as long as it's *efshar la'asos al yedei acheirim* – as long as other people can do it – then let them do it.

It's essential to know that our entire career is in learning Torah. *Ki heim chayeinu*. It is so important! For a yeshiva man, the number one thing on the agenda is to succeed in learning. If you can do it together with *shleimus*, with *daas*, with *mussar*, with *yiras Shamayim* – absolutely, those are also

If you'd learn mussar, you wouldn't smoke. If you'd learn mussar, you'd take care of your health.

important. But it's necessary to know that you must succeed in learning Gemara. You must be successful in your learning.

After all, that is the bread of our lives. The Gemara is the bread of our lives. And even though other things are like butter on the bread and like jelly on the bread – that's all very good, but the bread comes first. And that's why I say to all yeshiva men – never neglect your learning for anything else.

November 1999

Bochurim and Smoking

Q/ What do you think of a yeshiva *bochur* who smokes?

A/ Now, if a person reads on the package of cigarettes that the surgeon general of the United States – he knows something about medicine – is telling him that smoking could cause lung cancer and this yeshiva *bochur* disregards it, then I'd say he is a *beheima*! That's what I think of him. That's all he is; a *beheima*!

I walked into a yeshiva once. I saw a boy sitting at the table smoking. And the floor under the table was littered with cigarette stubs. At least pick it up and put it in the garbage can. He's a double *beheima*.

And so, you need a great deal of *yiras Shamayim* to be taught in the yeshivas today. And *yiras Shamayim* means knowing how to save yourself in this world. *Mussar* and *yiras Shamayim* is for happiness in this world. If you'd learn *mussar*, you wouldn't smoke. If you'd learn *mussar*, you'd take care of your health. If you'd learn *mussar*, you'd be a *mentch*. You wouldn't drop cigarettes on the floor.

And therefore, we follow the advice of *Mishlei*, הַחֲזֵק בַּמּוּסָר – *Hold on tight to mussar,* אַל תֶּרֶף – *don't let go,* נִצְּרֶהָ כִּי הִיא חַיֶּיךָ – *guard it because it's your life* (*Mishlei* 4:13). *Mussar* is your life. When people don't learn *mussar*, they don't know how to live. And therefore, you have to learn *mussar* in order to know that smoking cigarettes is a very big sin equivalent to committing suicide. That's what it is. No two ways about it.

September 1991

Everybody needs some physical exercise.

Physical Fitness

Q/ **Should a yeshiva man spend time on exercising?**

A/ Everybody needs some physical exercise. Exactly how much time each one should use depends on his circumstances. I wouldn't give any general advice. But I would say everybody should do some walking. It's a very great benefit. People cannot live a sedentary life always and allow themselves to deteriorate physically. Exactly what to do – each person has to be taught to do according to his necessities.

November 1982

Bein Hazmanim 1

Q/ **Is it preferable for a yeshiva man to learn in the yeshiva during summertime, or take a job in a children's camp?**

Every yeshiva man should spend the entire year only in learning Torah.

A/ What's the question? If you don't need the money, why should you be a waiter or a counselor? Learning is, after all, our career. A yeshiva man should learn twelve months in the year. Why should July and August be different?

It's really a ruination of one's career to stop learning during the summertime. And therefore, every yeshiva man should spend the entire year only in learning Torah. He should never sell his time for money unless he is forced to do so.

May 1985

Bein Hazmanim 2

Q/ **Is it wrong for a yeshiva *bochur* to do manual labor during *bein hazmanim?***

A/ It's very wrong because he has other, better things to do. It's as foolish as could be. He spent months and months learning Gemara, and now it's going to evaporate. All that labor will be lost.

A wise yeshiva *bochur* spends *bein hazmanim* reviewing all that he has learned. Even if it's only in a superficial way. Over and over and over, he should review the Gemara and lock it in. הַלּוֹמֵד תּוֹרָה וְאֵינוֹ חוֹזֵר עָלֶיהָ דּוֹמֶה לְאָדָם שֶׁזּוֹרֵעַ וְאֵינוֹ קוֹצֵר – *If you learn and don't review, it's like a man who plants things to grow, a whole crop, and then, when the time comes to reap the crop, he doesn't bother coming* (*Sanhedrin* 99a). So what worth is the work that you put in during the *z'man;* what's going to happen to all that work if you don't review?

So here this fool goes, and he becomes a *shlepper* during *bein hazmanim,* he *shleps* bottles, he works hard making some money. For what? What's the purpose? If he needs the money to support himself, it can't be helped. But if he can sit and learn and review what he learned, that's his job during *bein hazmanim.* Save yourself! All your learning is going to get lost; it's going to get lost entirely! It's a tragedy! You have to sit and review and review. The investment you made during the *z'man* in yeshiva; you can't let that investment go lost!

Even kosher pizza shops are frequented by low people.

Therefore, I say that *bein hazmanim,* every yeshiva *bochur* should be busy all day long learning and making sure that he's consolidating all that he has labored for during the yeshiva *z'man.*

August 1990

Yeshivamen at the Pizza Shop

Q/ What's wrong with a yeshiva man who eats in a pizza shop?

A/ Nothing's wrong. Except that he has to watch out for bad company. Even kosher pizza shops are frequented by low people. You have to know that among the Orthodox there also is an underworld. There's an underworld. They wear yarmulkes, they eat kosher. There's an underworld, however. When I was in Slabodka they said that in the yeshiva in Slabodka there was an underworld. Of course, each place has a different type of underworld. They all learned well. Everybody learned in the yeshiva. Everybody kept everything, but compared to the others, they were considered inferior. And therefore you were expected to choose to associate not with the underworld, but with the better ones.

I don't want anything. All I want is to sit in the yeshiva and learn for some more years.

The Orthodox bum is better than the outside bum, but keep away from him too. He's a loafer and he doesn't work – what's he doing in the pizza shop in the middle of the day? You're a yeshiva man, you're taking a rest, a break, between the *sedorim*, but what's he doing there, this other fellow? It's bad company. And therefore, that's why it's better to avoid these places. הַרְחֵק מִשָּׁכֵן רָע – *Keep away from bad company* (*Avos* 1:7). You don't know how great the consequences are! Even talking to them sometimes can start a train of evil results. So stay away from places unless they're where the very best people go – like the yeshiva dining room.

December 1988

Secular Education

Q/ What advice would you give to a twenty-year-old yeshiva man regarding his parents' wish that he embark on secular education?

A/ It depends. He could say, "Look, suppose I was just an American boy like all American boys, and I wanted to go out and smoke pot. Would you be able to stop me?" Don't all the American boys do what they want, and they become bums, and their parents give them money even to buy narcotics? And here you have a nice, decent son who wants to sit in the yeshiva and learn; shouldn't he have his way too? Just like the bums in America are favored by their parents – girls and boys bum around and their parents give them cars to do all kinds of wicked things; they give them plenty of money, too. "And I don't want anything. All I want is to sit in the yeshiva and learn for some more years." So some parents will listen to that. "That's my way of being a spoiled child. I want to sit and learn."

In case the parents are adamant, so the yeshiva man should tell them, "Look, I'm only twenty years old. There is plenty of time in life yet, so let me learn a couple more years, and then we'll discuss it again." Two years later the parents will say, "Nu?" so he'll say, "Look, I'm only twenty-two. Let's discuss it in a couple of years." By that time, they'll already get disgusted and they'll give up. It happens again and again, by the way. It works again and again. I saw it. The parents finally gave up. They saw that the boy meant business in learning, so they gave up and he became a *gadol b'Torah.* I know stories like that – I can tell you stories.

It happens again and again, by the way. It works again and again. I saw it.

May 1988

QUESTIONS *On Any* SUBJECT

Chapter 12

The College Boy

Chapter Sponsor

Sponsored by

Anonymous

Contents

Chapter 12

The College Boy

The College vs. Yeshiva Dilemma

Q/ I have a question, a problem. I would like to go to college. But I'm in a dilemma trying to decide what to do. Because I know that I could accomplish tremendously in college; I could do something that would help Jews. But on the other hand, I could also try and make it in yeshiva and be successful there. What should I do?

A/ This young man is faced with a question: Should he go to college where he thinks that he could thereby become equipped to do great things, important things?

So I must tell you, my friend, that I am not competent to give you any answer. It's a question that you have to go to your own rabbis or people who know you well and discuss it at length. This is a question that's too important for me to say anything publicly.

However, this I *can* tell you: One of the biggest achievements in life – not only for yourself, but for the entire Jewish people and for the world – is when a young man makes out of himself a *talmid chacham.*

Taxes are going up and up and accounting is going to become more and more lucrative

Now, don't think it's selfish. If you can transform yourself from a lump of meat – that's what human beings are; an ordinary nobody, but if you can transform yourself in the course of years – and don't be in a hurry; if by the age of sixty you'll become a *talmid chacham*, then you're conferring upon the world an inestimable benefit.

We have plenty of accountants. Of course, taxes are going up and up and accounting is going to become more and more lucrative, but the Jewish nation is not benefiting from accountants. Of course, we like to have fine accountants around, but you'll do more for the Jewish people if you'll become a *talmid chacham*.

You remember the story when Hillel was being tested? Two men made a wager once if they could make him angry. And they waged at 400 *zuz*. One said to the other, "I'll bet you 400 *zuz* that you can't make Hillel angry."

So he went – you know the story. It was Erev Shabbos and Hillel was sitting in his bathtub and this man banged on the door and said, "Where is Hillel?"

Hillel got out of his bath. A man was knocking on the door after all; he couldn't ignore him. So he went out and he wrapped himself around with a dignified garment and he said to the man, "What is it I can do for you?" And the man asked him foolish questions. So Hillel answered him and went back into the bath.

The man knocked again on the door. More foolish questions. And the story kept repeating itself.

Finally, the man said to Hillel, "If you are Hillel, then there shouldn't be many like you."

And Hillel said, "Why, my son?"

And the man said, "Because I lost 400 *zuz* because of you."

So Hillel responded: "My son." Listen to what Hillel said. "My son," he said, "It's worth it that you should lose 400 *zuz* and 400 *zuz* more, and Hillel shouldn't become angry."

What did he mean? Hillel was saying like this: "My son, it's worth 800 *zuz* for you that there should be a man among the Jewish people who doesn't get angry."

It doesn't mean only for you. The entire Jewish nation is 800 dollars a head richer when we have somebody good in our people. One good man is the wealth of the nation! It's riches for us, and that one good man is supplying the riches.

So if you learn Torah and *yiras Shamayim,* if you learn character and good manners, if you learn mitzvos, if you learn how to daven with heart, if you learn to do all the things that make you a perfect example of a man, then you are doing for your people the greatest that you can do. Much greater than being an accountant or a lawyer.

March 1975

All colleges have a terrible odor. They smell bad. You really need a gas mask when you go into a college.

The Truth About College

Q/ **Is it okay to go to Brooklyn College in order to make a *parnassah?***

A/ I'm not going to *pasken* any *shailah,* but I'll tell you this. I had to go to Brooklyn College recently. I went there to help protest against making this homeless shelter in our neighborhood. It was a community protest meeting and it was held at Brooklyn College. And as I walked in, I smelled a terrible odor. The place *poshut* had a *rei'ach ra.* It stank! All colleges have a terrible odor. They smell bad. You really need a gas mask when you go into a college.

You want to be dunked in their toilet for parnassah?

There's no place in America that smells as bad as a college! If you go to the place of the mafia, a mafia den, the mafia den is perfume compared to a college. I mean it. It's not an exaggeration.

And therefore, if a person has to go to a college; let's say he's a plumber, and he's going to a college to fix the plumbing there, he has to walk in and hold his nose. He can't help himself; it's his *parnassah;* he has to go there.

But to go there and allow yourself to be dunked in their toilet, that's a different story altogether. You want to be dunked in their toilet for *parnassah?* I'm not telling you what to do. Go to your *rebbi* – he knows you better. Let him *pasken* for you. I wouldn't *pasken* that. I should *pasken* that you should dunk your head in a full toilet for *parnassah?* It's too much that I should be able to tell you that.

November 1991

College vs. Mafia

How are the colleges worse than the dens of the underworld?

A/ If you ever attended a meeting of the underworld, of the mafia, let's say, so you'd go to Bensonhurst, in a basement. Over there, they're serving beer and lobster and discussing ways and means, let's say, of taking over a garbage collection service from another group of Italians.

How do they do it? Well, at first they try persuasion. They try to bribe them. And if not, there are other methods.

But they're not indecent. They're not gays. They go to church. They give charity. They dress like human beings.

They have families. They must behave. Their sons and daughters are married. Absolutely they are. They live an ordinary, more or less, decent gentile life.

Many of them are themselves busy collecting garbage. Only when it comes to some sort of crisis, do they come together in the basement to decide what to do. But otherwise, they're living normal lives.

But when you talk about the colleges – a college is a place that is worse than a house of ill-fame. Boys and girls get together in dormitories – I don't want to say anything more.

The colleges are the places where everything good has been broken down.

The colleges are the places where everything good has been broken down.

Marriage is considered a myth. "The myth of marriage," they call it. "The myth of marriage." All wickedness prevails on the college campuses. And therefore, the colleges today are the very worst places in the nation.

September 1998

University: Slavery of the Mind

Q/ You said once that going to college means you're becoming a slave. Is it really that bad?

A/ It's worse than that, because you're going to be a slave to slaves. Let me explain it to you. If you go to college because you have to get a diploma to make a living – I'm not giving any *psak halacha* here, but you have to know that you're becoming a slave of slaves because the teachers in college have no minds at all. They're enslaved to what their foolish teachers told them. They don't see the truth at all. They believe in things only because of their '*emunah.*'

The theory of evolution doesn't have a foot to stand on.

You have to know, the colleges have more religion than anybody else. *Halevai* the frum Jews should have as much religion as the colleges. It's nothing but *emunah*. All their teachings are based on bias, and they twist every fact in order to conform to their theories.

I'll give you an example. The theory of evolution doesn't have a foot to stand on. Evolution doesn't have a single set of fossils that show a development from the lowest form to the highest form. And today, that has caused such a consternation that there is a very big school of evolutionists who have broken away from the old system of gradual development. They say they must because the fossils disprove it.

So what are they saying? Not that it gradually happened; that was the old religion; that, let's say, a rat finally began to grow wings because of gradual development. It wanted to be safe from the cats that were pursuing it, and therefore, the rat decided that it would be better if it could climb up into the trees. So at first, it attempted to jump, and little by little, it learned how to jump better and better, and as it jumped, its hair began to turn into feathers, and its forelimbs began to turn into wings. And finally, the rat succeeded in flying into the tree and it became a rat bird.

Now, we always ridicule such nonsense, but that's what was taught in all the universities, and if you go to university your mind becomes a slave to these false ideas.

Today, it's already ridiculed by the Sudden Mutation Theorists who already comprise a very large part of the academic community. They declare that there are just no fossils to back up the Gradual Development Theory. We don't find rats who have incipient wings. We don't have rats whose bones demonstrate that they gradually turned from rats into rat birds.

So what is their theory? They substitute The Hopeful Monster Theory – that rats were living an ordinary career as rats do today, but there was an accident once; by some confusion in the genes, a pregnant female rat, instead of giving birth to a little rat, gave birth to an egg, and lo and behold, when the egg hatched, out came a new creature, a rat bird. That's the Hopeful Monster Theory.

There is nothing of human wisdom that can approximate even remotely the process of reproduction.

They say there's no other way that we could explain the lack of fossils. Gradual Development is a false basis to explain the appearance of new species.

Now the gradual evolutionists ridicule this new school of the sudden appearance of Hopeful Monsters, but the Sudden Mutation theorists are working overtime to try and explain how it could be.

And we say that each one is right in saying that the other ones are false. We accept their testimony, because together they comprise a mass of blind and misguided persons.

Anyone who is fair-minded cannot help but recognize the miraculous arrangement of plan and purpose, of bottomless wisdom in the process of reproduction. Can you imagine two computers that are left in the room for a few million years, and eventually you would come and find a generation of progeny that they reproduced?

Just as this is insanity, so is it insane to think that any kind of inorganic matter could gain the ability to reproduce itself in such a complicated form as living things represent. That two rats should produce a baby rat is the most infinitely complicated designed and planned process. There is nothing of human wisdom that can approximate even remotely the process of reproduction. Every step must be precise; every chemical change, every organic change. And there are hundreds of thousands of steps and changes, and each one must be perfectly exact in order to produce an offspring.

So how could it be that so many people believe such nonsense? It's because they're miseducated. They go to the universities and they become enslaved to these false ways of

If you pour hot water into cold water, it won't remain hot.

thinking. And therefore, absolutely, going to college is a form of slavery. It's the worst form, slavery of the mind.

June 1989

Collateral Damage 1

Q/ This young man asks: If a person has good *hashkafos,* how can college harm him?

A/ So I'll answer that quickly. Suppose a person is in good health but he goes into a place where there are contagious diseases. So you say if he has good health, what does he have to be afraid of? The answer is, he'll lose his good health, right? And he'll lose his good *hashkafos*. That's all.

A man can have the best *hashkafos,* but if he goes to a place where he constantly hears the opposite, so the *hashkafos* are bound to change. Nobody is the same.

Now it doesn't mean he'll become a *kofer, chalilah,* but there is no question that he is weakened. The Chofetz Chaim says a *mashal,* that if you pour hot water into cold water, it won't remain hot. A hot Jew who sits in college and the teacher is a *letz* – they're all *leitzim* – and he can't reply because he doesn't want to fail the course, he listens and he's silent. When he leaves that evening, he's not the same man he was when he came in. No question about that.

Whether you should go to college or not, I leave that to the *gedolim* to *pasken*, to your *rebbis* to *pasken*. But if you go to college, you have to know it's going to cost you a great price! There's no question, it's a costly experience. It takes away a great deal of your *hashkafos*.

June 1974

Every boy should get advice from his rebbi on what to do.

Collateral Damage 2

Q/ Why do you disparage a boy who goes to college?

A/ Now I didn't say – it's not up to me to say that a boy shouldn't go to college if he wants *parnassah*. I always say when they ask me: "Go to your *rebbi*. It depends on your circumstances. Let your *rebbi* talk to you and let him *pasken* for you."

So I didn't speak disparagingly at all. I did say that you have to pay a price for it, though. There's no question that some innocence is rubbed off of you.

The truth is that the same applies even when you're not going to college. Let's say you'll get a job as an electrician. Some innocence will rub off of you because you're going to hobnob with some tough fellows in the profession. Some of them speak obscene words; they're pretty rough, some of them.

But what can you do? Even if you're a *chassidishe* Jew, you're a Satmarer who drives a truck, so you have to deal with business people and with other truckers; so something rubs off.

So I wasn't speaking disparagingly of boys who want to go to college because of *parnassah*. But I do make this

A person cannot go through college without a scar on his neshama

condition: Every boy should get advice from his *rebbi* on what to do.

June 1978

Automatic Effects

Q/ Is a boy who went to university for *parnassah* reasons automatically less eligible than a boy who never went out at all?

A/ And the answer is yes. Now it doesn't mean that because he went to college, he cannot be a person of good character, but there's no question that he has to battle against certain tendencies that he acquired in that company. Because when you sit and listen to atheism...

Let's say you're in a biology class or history college; you're listening to atheists and to *leitzanim*. So you must fortify yourself against them.

Now sometimes, the result is beneficial; he becomes more aware of the *emunah* as a result. But it needs work. Otherwise a person cannot go through college without a scar on his *neshamah*. It's impossible to be in company without being affected in some way by that company.

May 1978

Parnassah Without College

Q/ How can a young man find a *parnassah* to support his wife and family if he doesn't go to college?

A/ And the answer is, there are so many fields of endeavor where people can make money, not less than with a college degree. Today, a college degree doesn't bring as much return as it used to.

When a person has normal abilities, he can make a good living if he's properly trained.

There are so many different fields which people can enter, only you have to make up your mind and choose one. Because there's a lot of money today for computer technicians; certainly you can earn a respectable living.

And therefore, take counsel from those who are qualified to give you guidance, vocational guidance. And if you are willing to work, certainly you'll succeed.

If one doesn't have any head, then even if he has a college degree he'll remain a failure, but when a person has normal abilities, he can make a good living if he's properly trained. And training is available, especially in America.

January 1984

College and Careers 1

Q/ How does a person become a professional without going through the system?

A/ How can you become a professional without losing your mind?

Now this needs private guidance. It's possible to be done, but it needs special instruction.

In public I can't say it, but it's possible. I won't say it in public for a reason, because I don't think everybody should go to college. But those individuals whose role it will be to go,

We should appreciate the frum professionals we have today.

have to be trained and prepared for their career. And it has to be said in private.

June 1981

College and Careers 2

Q/ Is it *muttar* to go to college *l'sheim Shamayim,* in order to become a doctor?

A/ And the answer is, it depends where you're going, and it depends what alternatives you have.

If a person is going to go, let's say, into a regular college like Anne Arbor Michigan, it means he's walking into a toilet, an old-time toilet, where after he goes out his garments will have an odor forever and ever. His *neshamah* will never be able to air itself out anymore from the bad odor. So it doesn't pay. Nothing pays. You don't ruin yourself *l'sheim Shamayim*.

Now, most of the places are like that today. You want to go to Touro or to some other place like that, then it depends.

Now, *l'sheim Shamayim* is not such a simple thing to analyze, but if a person would want to make out of himself a *talmid chacham l'sheim Shamayim*, there's no question, we could say yes. But to sacrifice a career – where he has a good head and is capable of becoming a *talmid chacham* – in order to become a physician? A physician, after all, is like a plumber. It's a good plumber; it's very important to have a good plumber. A good plumber serves the public, and he could do it *l'sheim Shamayim* too. No question about it. But the question is: Do I want to sacrifice my one visit to this world – I'll never come again – in order to be a plumber for people? I'll have to think that over.

The same is to be a physician. It makes no difference.

If he's a lawyer already, he might as well try to be a judge.

But I want to say one word, although I'm going to dodge this question: We should appreciate the frum professionals we have today. The frum professionals are a *kiddush Hashem*. Whether we'll tell their children to do the same, that's a different question. But we should honor our frum professionals. It's real *kavod Shamayim*.

You look elsewhere, you see professionals who disdain the Torah; they have *ga'avah*, they think they know it all. And here, our professionals are loyal to the Torah. And although they're certainly not less capable than anybody else, they're fully Torah-observant. You have doctors with their tzitzis out, dentists with their tzitzis out; it's a pleasure to look at them. It's a *kavod Shamayim*. We have to respect them. I honor them.

When I was a boy, there wasn't a single professional who was a *shomer Shabbos*. That's why today I still can't get over the excitement when I see a frum professional. It's a *chiddush* to me.

"What's the *chiddush*?" The doctor says, "What's the *chiddush*? There are so many of us!"

Baruch Hashem! *Kein yirbu, kein yigdelu*. A wonderful thing to see frum professionals. We honor them.

I see a frum judge – we have frum judges today too. What is a judge? It's nothing today, because the judges are bums today. Judges are criminals today, low characters. That's what they are. *Chavrei ganavim*; that's what they are, *chavrei ganavim*. But when you have a frum judge, it's a pleasure to look at him. We honor him.

And so, should a person become a judge or seek to aspire to it? If he's a lawyer already, he might as well try to be a judge.

But should you give up your career where you could become a *gadol b'Torah?* I'm not going to tell you that.

When a girl enrolls in college, she is lessening her marriage chances to the better ones by at least seventy percent.

However, *b'dieved,* since you studied already and you already have a degree and you're practicing, I say you deserve to be honored. Yes.

April 1993

Kosher College

Q/ **What if I want to go to a frum college where men and women are separate?**

A/ Talk to your *rav*. If you're in a yeshiva, talk to the *rosh yeshiva* and he'll give you advice on what to do. It depends on who the person is.

August 1995

Girls in College 1

Q/ **Can you please give us some general guidelines to help us to decide whether or not to pursue a college career?**

A/ If this is asked by a young lady, then I urge you by all means to forget it. And there are practical reasons.

You know, there are a big number of fine yeshiva men who refuse to marry a college girl, even a Bais Yaakov girl who goes to college.

There are a big number of yeshiva men who *go* to college and prefer a girl who didn't.

There are a big number of Orthodox Jewish college men who don't object to a girl who didn't go to college.

And then there are a small number of yeshiva men who are ill informed and prefer a college girl.

And therefore, when a girl enrolls in college, she is lessening her marriage chances to the better ones by at least seventy percent. Now, it's not easy to get married to a good prospect. And therefore, it makes sense for a girl to shoot at matrimony with a double-barreled gun. The college girl is limited in the number of prospects.

I'll tell you a remarkable thing. You won't agree with me, but I'll tell you anyway.

Now there are better reasons than that, but for the time being, that's a good enough reason. For girls, I urge you to get married as soon as you graduate from high school and forget about a career. Careers for girls lead up a blind alley, and it makes it all the more difficult later to find a *shidduch.*

March 1974

Girls in College 2

Q/ What are the dangers of a girl going off to college?

A/ If it's a dormitory college, then you don't need me to tell you the dangers. She might as well look for a job in a house of prostitution, because a house of prostitution at least pays a salary. And it's not a joke at all – I'm completely serious. A dormitory college is for girls nothing but a house of ill fame. It's not a *mashal,* it's not merely a comparison; that's exactly what it is. Don't deceive yourself.

If a girl has to go to college – and I don't know why she has to go, because a girl should be planning for marriage – but

A girl dedicated to a career; you have to know that it's going to be a big conflict with her chosen career of being a mother and a wife.

she shouldn't go to an out-of-town college. She shouldn't go to a college where she has to be away from home. She must come home every day and she must be under supervision constantly. Every girl.

I'll tell you a remarkable thing. You won't agree with me, but I'll tell you anyway. In the letter of the Vilna Gaon that he wrote to his family when he was going to Eretz Yisroel – he never made it there, but when he left and was on his way, he wrote a letter of instructions to his family. And he said there that his daughters shouldn't, *chas v'shalom,* walk out the door of the house. Now, he didn't say that to his wife. To his wife he said, "Don't go shopping. If you have to go to the grocery, send somebody. Even though you might have to pay four times as much," he said, "it's better to send somebody. You might have to send somebody else, a boy, a child, and you'll pay four times as much because of that – but it's worth it. Because when you come to the store, you'll meet others and you'll exchange gossip, and that's the very worst thing you could do – *lashon hara*." For his wife, he didn't tell her not to go at all, only not to the store where people congregate, but to his daughters, he said, *chas v'shalom,* that they should go out *mipesach habayis.*

Now that was in the Gra's times, when the streets were kosher. The Jewish streets were innocent. And still, a girl had to be watched. A girl has to watch herself too!

Now, on the general question of a girl going to college and becoming a career girl, a girl dedicated to a career; you have to know that it's going to be a big conflict with her chosen career of being a mother and a wife. Because she'll be ambitious. She'll want to practice whatever she studied. She'll want to use her degree, and that's going to take her mind off of her real function in life. And therefore, as I said here many times, any young man who is looking for a mate, the choicest one is somebody who never went to college. Sometimes, there are good ones who went to college and then they regretted it, but ordinarily it's going to be a big barrier to happiness and success in life.

July 1983

Girls in College 3

She says she's not sorry she went because it had no effect on her.

Q/ How do I answer my cousin who says she went to an Ivy League college and wasn't affected? She says she's not sorry she went because it had no effect on her.

A/ There was a man who ridiculed the speed laws; he was always speeding in his car, and he was warned that he'll be sorry someday. And now he's in the morgue. He ended up against a lamppost and now he's dead.

Now this man is not sorry for speeding. He can't be sorry because he's dead. Now, if he wouldn't die, if he'd just be crippled, then he would be sorry, but when he's dead he can't be sorry.

That girl who went to college is not sorry because she's dead. She lost her mind. She became educated, which is equivalent to having an operation – your brain is removed from you. Now, it could be that your cousin never had any brain in the first place. That's also possible. Whatever she had, however, was replaced by an artificial set of ideas. And today, it's a dangerous set of ideas that they teach in college today. Marxism and humanism. They teach them to be blind to the wonders of nature. When you learn biology, it's especially planned that you should not see the plan and purpose.

So first of all, if you're a woman, forget about it. Be merachek him, not mekarev him.

And therefore, if your cousin tells you she went to college and wasn't affected, you can tell her it's because she's already in the morgue.

November 1983

College Kiruv

Q/ **How can I be *mekarev* a sincere college professor who is my physics teacher?**

A/ So first of all, if you're a woman, forget about it. Be *merachek* him, not *mekarev* him.

But if you're a male, give him a book called Scientific Creationism. You can buy it here for five dollars. And tell him to read it through, twice. Buy the public school edition; that's the kind that doesn't have any religious propaganda at the back. That's the one we sell here. Tell him to read it twice. If he has any questions, tell him to call me up – not you, because you won't be able to answer him.

Last week, a man was here and I saw that he wasn't understanding a very simple matter. When we were talking about the wonders that you see in creation that demonstrate the presence of the Creator, this man said, "Who created the Creator?"

Now, that question has no bearing on the subject. Let's say a man built a house. Now you come and see the house years later. You see walls, you see doors, you see windows. That house didn't happen by itself. It wasn't a result of hurricanes that blew down trees and blew off the bark and split them into boards and blew plastic materials together and finally it all became a house after millions of years of storms and hurricanes. Nobody will say such a stupid thing. Somebody made that house! It's basic intelligence!

Now here comes a *chacham* and says, "Who made the maker of the house?"

Who cares who made him?! Our point is: Somebody made a house. Who made the builder of the house?! Go ask his father and mother who made him. That's not our point. It's a question that's entirely irrelevant.

If you would say a house was made by somebody and that's all you said, then this fellow could say, "Who made the maker?" But we're not talking about who made the house. We're saying that the presence of a house demonstrates intelligence. Without intelligence it couldn't be, that's all. Once we prove there was intelligence, then asking who made the intelligence doesn't interest us anymore. If there's an intelligence that can make a tree, so now go look for that intelligence. It's someplace. But who made that intelligence? That's a question that's an idle question. It has nothing to do with our subject.

Give him "Rejoice O Youth," and tell him to read it three times.

So this college professor – he should read the book Scientific Creationism. If it's a *goy*, let it stop at that. He has questions? Let him speak to somebody who knows the subject. Don't answer it yourself unless you're very competent.

But if he's a Jew, give him "Rejoice O Youth," and tell him to read it three times. If he has any questions, he should call me up.

And that's how to be *mekarev* a college professor who is sincere.

Now it may be that he is not sincere. It may be that he puts up a good face. It could be that he is a sincere evolutionist, which means he's a stubborn liar. No matter what, he's going to stick to his theories even though you show him *b'osos uvemofsim*. So for most of them, it's a lost case, but if there is somebody, and it pays to try, then this is what's suggested.

September 1982

QUESTIONS *On Any* SUBJECT

Chapter 13
World of Music

Chapter Sponsor

This chapter is dedicated to the memory
of my great-grandfather, חיים בן מנחם נחום,
a remarkably talented musician whose legacy lives on in me.

Through the gift of music that I have inherited,
I am privileged to serve Hashem
and use my talents for Chinuch and Chesed.

May this work be an Aliya for his Neshama and inspire others
to channel their gifts toward holy and meaningful endeavors.

Contents

Chapter 13

World of Music

Music in Yiddishkeit

Q/ **What place does music have in the life of a frum Jew?**

A/ And the answer is, no place at all.

Now, let's understand this. Once and for all, let's get rid of the American *meshugas.* It's all assimilation.

The Chofetz Chaim, *zichrono livracha,* if you look in his *seforim* – that's a pretty good picture of the life of a frum Jew – you won't find the word music once. The word *niggunim* – you never find it once. It's not there at all.

If you look in the Gemara, you'll find the *levi'im b'shiram,* but if you look in the Chofetz Chaim's *seforim* – after all, we're living in his age and he wrote *seforim* that covered the whole spectrum of Jewish life – nothing is mentioned about music at all.

Now, to say music is *assur,* it's not for me to say. I'm not a *posek* to say such things. But what *place* does it occupy? No place at all.

If you want to be *mesame'ach,* if you want to use some music to be *mesame'ach,* singing a *zemer* on Yom Tov, *zemiros* on Shabbos, go ahead. Why not? It has a place. But music, recorded music that comes from musicians? Unless you're talking about music at a *chasunah* – otherwise, it has no place at all. If you need it for a *chasunah,* hire musicians and get it over with, and that's all. You sing *zemiros* on Shabbos, that also. And we wait for the Beis Hamikdash to be rebuilt, and then we'll have kosher music as *avodas Hashem.*

He's dancing all by himself in front of a music store. It's as disgusting as could be.

But the ideas that American people have today all come from the outside world. There's nothing noble in music. Intrinsically, it's nothing at all. Somebody is tickling a piece of catgut that was dried and became a fiddle string, and it causes sound waves that tickle your eardrums and excite your nerves, and that's all there is to music.

Now, I know it's going to sound harsh to people who were brought up with American ideas, but I have already been conditioned to seeing what music is.

I walk in the street. Here is a music store. Outside there is a middle-aged man. I'm sure he's a Jew. A gentile wouldn't be so silly. He's a Jew and he's dancing a jig to the music on the street. What's he doing it for? If nobody was around, he wouldn't bother doing it. He wants to demonstrate that he's a lover of music. Now, an Italian wouldn't be that dumb to do such a thing. You can be sure he's a Jew, a liberal, a *shoteh,* and he wants to show off that he's a music lover, so he's dancing all by himself in front of a music store. It's as disgusting as could be.

And all the people who crowd the music stores to buy tapes and records are people whose heads have become vacant. The worst place in the world for intelligence is a music store. The world used to say a *chazan* is a *naar.* They used to say that a *chazan* is a *naar.* What does that mean? Because a *chazan* likes music, and you cannot have in your head two things, intelligence and music. So if you have music in your head, then you don't have any *seichel* in your head. The space it takes to put in music cannot be occupied by something else.

Now it's an important point. Think it over. Maybe someday you'll realize how true it is.

I know that I'm going to get a bad name by talking about this, but I'd like to do it anyway.

Q/ But what about classical music? Isn't it true that *chashuve* people listen to classical music?

A/ Now this is an affectation. It's a bluff. There's no such thing as classical music. Classical music was written by people who in their times were *hefkeryungen, mufkarim,* low people. The fact that it was a hundred years ago doesn't make it classical. All music – you can quote me as saying this – is garbage.

September 1982

The Falsity of Music

Q/ You said a few weeks ago, if I quote you right, that you despise music, or what's being done with music. So I'm wondering if you're denying the good effects that music can have on a person like *teshuvah* and *hisorerus* to *ahavas Hashem*?

A/ It's good you brought this up. I like to talk about this subject.

But first of all, you have to know that arrayed against us is a tremendous amount of propaganda. Affectation! Music for music's sake! Art for art's sake! And therefore, I

Do you study eating appreci-ation? If you enjoy it, you enjoy it; that's all.

know that I'm going to get a bad name by talking about this, but I'd like to do it anyway.

One of the false idols – not ideals; false *idols* – of modern civilization, is art. Anything that is officially included in "art," you're expected to say, "Ooh" and "Ahh." Ooh and ahh! The truth is if they would put baseball under "the arts," you would also have to say, "Ooh and ahh." Don't you see today the fools who don't know what they're talking about? The Met and The Mets or The Mets and The Met. The Met means the Metropolitan Museum of Arts and the Mets means the baseball team, but today, anything can be art. Once upon a time baseball was just for roughnecks, but since they put the Mets together with the Met, baseball can be included in art too.

It's only a question of what's officially recognized. So you go to school and you study music appreciation. The question is, do you study eating appreciation? If you enjoy it, you enjoy it; that's all. Are you going to go to a school and study how to enjoy it?

What music appreciation actually means is: affectation, showing off. That's all it is. The whole opera is nothing but showing off. It's for rich people to come and show that they're cultured – aside from showing off their diamonds.

And even the Orthodox world has been bamboozled. People sit on Motzei Shabbos and listen to records. What is there? The same droning silliness over and over again. I don't want to say which records, the same word, ten times the same word, over and over. It's sickening. It's meaningless. It's only for people who live with emotions and don't live with thoughts.

The Jewish world used to say, "A *chazan* is a *naar* – a cantor is a fool." And the reason was because he's a man who lives with emotion; he doesn't live with thought.

That's why you walk into some modern synagogue and you hear them singing, "*Yehei ra'ava ...*" I don't want to sing the words the way they sing it. *"May it be Your will that You open up my heart in the Torah."* People who never opened up anything more than a *siddur*; and they sing it so pathetically, יְהֵא רַעֲוָא קֳדָמָךְ דְּתִפְתַּח לִבָּאִי בְּאוֹרַיְתָא. But it's the tune! Ahh, the tune! So you see that the words have nothing to do with the tune. It's just music by itself. There's no thinking in it.

Life is wonderful! There are secrets in life! There is splendor in life!

And what is music after all? It's nothing but the excitement of the nerves caused by sound waves. That's all it is. And the sound waves come from a piece of dried catgut.

However – and this was mentioned here – we have to know that it's *not* false. There is a great truth in it. Because if music inspires us, it's for the purpose of letting us know that there is within us a great world of nobility. It's only the excitement that makes us aware of what we are, of what we can be. Life is wonderful! There are secrets in life! There is splendor in life! That we don't see it is only because our eyes are fleshy eyes of materialism. But there's no question that life itself, this world as long as we're here, is full of the most splendid things to learn and to understand and to do.

And we become aware of that, faintly aware, when we hear music. Music stirs in us tremendous ambition. But what do the fools do? So they take these wonderful feelings, the tune, and they put in worthless words: "I love you." "I want to be close with you." "Forever and always and eternally." And that's a tragedy. It's taking the sublime emotions of our soul – our souls have depth, sublime depth – and it's expending it on nothing.

And therefore, it's true! We have sublimity within us – music tells us what's true about ourselves; it inspires us. Only that, just as we're ready to receive the great secret, all of a sudden, this low character comes and gives the steering wheel a turn, and we go off the track. We bump against a wall.

I know beforehand that people have ingrained attitudes toward it; people have their ideas.

So therefore, music certainly has a place, but only when it's in the hands of righteous people. And that's what the *Kuzari* says. What I'm telling you now is what the *Kuzari* says. The *Kuzari* – it was written 900 years ago – here's his statement: He says that music was once "the servant of Hashem." It was used in the Sanctuary by our greatest prophets. They had these noble ideas, and they expressed them with a lyre and with a harp. And once you have the nobility of spirit, then the music coupled with that gives you the ability to raise your feet from the earth. It's like an airplane. An airplane is able to fly if you fuel it. You put in the high-octane fuel; then it soars. It goes to the clouds, above the clouds. And the man who has greatness of spirit, together with music – he becomes much bigger than he was before.

But the *Kuzari* adds that today, music has become the plaything of *avodim u'shfachos,* servants and servant girls. Music has become, he says, the accessory for immorality. What is most music? Most music is love songs. And if it's military songs, it's not much better. So it's martial music and love music. And that's why music has been prostituted from its great place that it once had as a servant of Hashem.

Q/ You're not including symphonic music in that, are you?

A/ The truth is, I'm not including anything because I know beforehand that people have their ideas and –

Q/ But I know that you've mentioned in the past certain types of music, like pop music or rock 'n' roll.

A/ The truth is, I don't want to bring it down to anything specifically because I know beforehand that people have ingrained attitudes toward it; people have their ideas. And I want you to leave this place with your good opinion of me. So that's why I'm speaking only generally.

January 1971

Caviar doesn't taste good. It's only if you train yourself.

Music Appreciation 101

Q/ **What's wrong with a course in music appreciation?**

A/ I told you once. If there was a course in playing the trombone, or in banging a drum, I understand that. It's fun to bang it. It's fun to blow. It's fun even to bang a tom-tom.

But do I have to go to take a course to learn how much fun it is to bang a tom-tom? *Mimanafshach;* if I enjoy it, I'll do it. If I don't enjoy it, I won't.

Do I need a course to teach me how to eat Limburger cheese if I don't like it? A course in appreciation of Limburger cheese?

It's like caviar. Caviar doesn't taste good. It's only if you train yourself. If you have, let's say, the attitude of being an upstart, you want to be a person who affects culture, so you force yourself, at the beginning, to eat caviar. The first few weeks you retch; it's disgusting. But after a while you get a taste for caviar. It's an expensive taste. Does it pay to acquire that taste?

And therefore, what's music appreciation? It pays to acquire that taste? Music is nothing but irritation of the nerves; sound waves that irritate the nerves. So if it irritates

Music has absolutely no value, unless it's accompanied by noble thoughts.

you pleasantly, good. But do you have to learn how it should irritate you? If it doesn't, it doesn't.

May 1973

The Truth About Music

Q/ I saw in a *sefer* that music is the highest form of spirituality, right underneath the level of Torah. Is that true?

A/ That's *sheker v'chazav.* It's totally false. Music is *lo klum* – it's nothing at all. Sometimes you have a man who sings well, and he wants to sell you his merchandise, so he tells you, music is this and music is that. No, no. It's nothing at all.

The Chofetz Chaim didn't have any music in his place. There was no music in the Chofetz Chaim's house. No kind of music. He sang *zemiros* at the table, but it was mostly pensive, thoughtful things that he sang, nothing fancy.

Rabbi Yisroel Salanter didn't have any music. The *gedolei Yisroel* didn't have any music. Music is for the *hamon am,* for the commonfolk. You have a lot of *amei ha'aretz,* a lot of common folk, and you want to attract them to your table, so you sing. No harm. It's better than going out in the street on Motzei Shabbos. So they gather around the *rebbe's* table and they sing *zemiros* – very good. No harm done.

There was a man who told me that when he came to America as a boy, he would have gone lost – but the *melaveh malka* saved him. They sang there and that saved him. But it doesn't mean that it's the best way to do it. When people get together and they speak דִּבְרֵי אֱלוֹקִים חַיִּים, when they speak words of Torah, that's the very best music.

So music has absolutely no value, unless it's accompanied by noble thoughts. And the *levi'im* didn't just sing *bim-bum-bim-bum-biddy-bum-bum* in the Beis Hamikdash. They sang words. שִׁירוּ לוֹ זַמְּרוּ לוֹ שִׂיחוּ בְּכָל נִפְלְאוֹתָיו – *Sing to Him; make music to Him* (*Tehillim* 105:2). שִׁירוּ and שִׂיחוּ means *words.* Words, yes. Words of music are inspiring. Words that help create Torah thoughts in your mind. But music without words is just tickling your nerves, and it's a waste of time.

September 1986

It's a mitzvah to show our happiness and gratitude to Hashem with music as well. It's a mitzvah.

Music Lessons

Q/ When I asked you once about music lessons for children, you said it's a waste of time. But tonight you said that Dovid Hamelech reached greatness because of his constant singing of praises to Hashem. Can you explain that?

A/ Yes, I'll explain. שִׁירוּ לוֹ זַמְּרוּ לוֹ – *Say poetry to Him; sing to Him* (*Tehillim* 105:2). What does that mean? *Shiru lo* means to say poetry to Hashem. Not singing, but poetry. To talk with enthusiasm, to speak in an enthusiastic manner. That's poetry. And then it says *zamru lo,* sing with music to Hashem. Not only to say poetry to Hashem, but to sing with music as well. So we see that it's a mitzvah to show our happiness and gratitude to Hashem with music as well. It's a mitzvah.

Now, if we teach our children to be grateful to Hakadosh Baruch Hu, that's the first step. Parents have to teach their children to appreciate all the things that Hakadosh Baruch Hu gives us in this world. And it's a very big task, believe me. But to teach your son how to sing with music before that first step is like telling a person to blow into a horn. But he doesn't know what to blow. He has no notes. And so, his blowing

Just to arouse your nerves by the excitement of music without having the noble thoughts to accompany the music is nothing.

the horn is nothing. And therefore, the first thing is to train your children in the art of thanking Hashem. Most people play music and they don't thank Hashem. They don't think about Hashem at all. And that's why it's a waste of time.

When you pass a music store, you should know that it's a place for *meshuga'im.* Only wild people frequent such a place. No decent people go into a music store today. Because all it is, is a wildness of the nerves. Music excites the nerves for nothing. But if you have a *tzaddik,* an *eved Hashem* who learned how to talk about Hashem and how to thank Hashem, and now he wants to express himself with song, that's different. That's the שִׁירוּ לוֹ זַמְּרוּ לוֹ that Dovid Hamelech was speaking about.

I once went into a certain *shtiebel* and a *rebbe* was sitting there singing. I can't forget it. He was singing אֲנָא אֲנָא אֲנָא עַבְדָּא דְקוּדְשָׁא בְּרִיךְ הוּא. It went into my blood and I'll never forget it. That's already something else. A man who has *yiras Shamayim,* and he's singing, and he's putting all of his *yiras Shamayim* into the song, that's something else entirely! I was listening to him and it had a tremendous influence on me.

But some people want to play music and sing, but their minds are empty. That's a one-hundred percent waste of time. Just to arouse your nerves by the excitement of music without having the noble thoughts to accompany the music is nothing.

And that's why it's so important to teach our children to sing to Hakadosh Baruch Hu about everything in our lives that we mentioned tonight. *Shiru lo. Lo!* To Him! That's the first step. And after they accomplish that, if they are already perfect in the *shiru lo* – in the *avodah* of speaking with enthusiasm about Hashem – then you can move on to *zamru lo,* and teach your child music so that he'll be able to sing and thank Hashem with music.

December 1999

Singing in Avodas Hashem

So the first thing is to realize that this is a happy world.

Q/ **Is singing songs and *zemiros* called *avodas Hashem?***

A/ Now, this question I happen to like. It's a very important subject. It says in the *pasuk*, שִׁירוּ לוֹ זַמְּרוּ לוֹ – *Sing to Him and make music to Him* (*Tehillim* 105:2).

Now, many people fulfill the *lo,* to Him, but they lack the *shirah,* the singing, the enthusiasm. They say, "Hashem, we thank You," but they're not *singing* to Him. They're not really grateful. They're not happy.

So the first thing is to realize that this is a happy world. I don't care what you'll bring me, even proofs from *tzaddikim,* what I'm telling you is the truth – it's in the Chumash: וַיַּרְא אֱלֹקִים אֶת כָּל אֲשֶׁר עָשָׂה וְהִנֵּה טוֹב מְאֹד – *Hashem saw everything He made and it's a very good world* (*Bereishis* 1:31). And Dovid Hamelech said, אָנִי אָמַרְתִּי – *I said;* it means *"I came to the conclusion,"* עוֹלָם חֶסֶד יִבָּנֶה – *that the world was built for kindliness* (*Tehillim* 89:3).

Now, when a person begins to realize that this is a very good world – what a pleasure it is to be alive! Even just to sit here without money, without a penny in your pocket, is a pleasure! Just to be alive! It's happiness! When a person comes to that realization, then that person can start singing.

And you have to take singing lessons until you learn to sing all day long to Hashem. לְהַגִּיד בַּבֹּקֶר חַסְדֶּךָ – *To start in the morning,* וֶאֱמוּנָתְךָ בַּלֵּילוֹת – *and to sing all day long down to the nighttime when you go to sleep* (ibid. 92:3). And therefore, singing is certainly *avodas Hashem.*

Now, if you're going to sing things that are meaningless, if you're going to sing without thinking anything, that's

Singing is a very great form of service of Hashem. A very great form.

worse than a waste of time. It's insanity. If you want to find a place that looks most like a lunatic asylum, pass by a music store. That's the craziest place. They're singing for nothing. What are you happy about? Not the slightest *machshavah*, not the slightest understanding.

And the fools who sing about love? That's the most stupid thing. What is love? Love is just a delusion. What is love? Of course, a husband and wife have to develop a relationship of respect and affection; certainly. A husband and wife are the closest relatives. Certainly, there is a loyalty to each other and they're happy with each other, but it's not an ideal about which you have to sing all your life. There are certain things in life that Hakadosh Baruch Hu wants us to always sing about, and the most important one is He Himself. Sing about Hashem! הוֹדוּ לַה' – *Sing to Him.*

And therefore, singing is a very great form of service of Hashem. A very great form. If you sing on Shabbos at the table, do it with *machshavah*. Think about what you're saying. The beautiful songs of Shabbos express great ideals! But to go to places to hear singing, or to go let's say to Brooklyn College to concerts, it's a one-hundred percent waste of time and money, because what you'll hear there when a lot of hippies and bums gather together is garbage; the atmosphere is *tumah sh'betumah.* It's the worst; you're not singing to Hashem.

If you walk in the streets, however, and there's a big din of traffic – nobody can hear you – so you open up your mouth and you sing to Hashem on the street, you're a wise man. Practice it up. You never did it before? Try it. Walk under the El [*the elevated train tracks*] as the trains are thundering overhead, and open up a big mouth and sing to Hashem. For what? Sing to Hashem that you have no colostomy. "Ahh! *Baruch Atah Hashem!* I have a normal aperture where it belongs! Am I not happy? Oh, it's such a big happiness! *Baruch Hashem*!"

Sing to Hashem that you're able to hear. Hearing is a very great gift. You put two ears on the side of my head in the right place where I need them. It's a wonderful arrangement. Sound is a miracle. Those who didn't study physics don't understand what a wondrous phenomenon sound is.

You should sing to Hashem that you can hear. There's so much to sing for, we'll never get through it.

You don't hear with your ears. You hear with your brain. There are sound waves that travel in a marvelous fashion. One wave pushes the other and jumps back again. It pushes the next wave and jumps back again, and the waves finally reach your eardrum. It's very sensitive, your eardrum, very sensitive. Then there are three bones attached to the eardrum and they magnify the sound, and then it goes to nerves and it goes through to your brain. By that time, it becomes something that we call sound.

The question is, suppose there's nobody to listen and the music is playing. Will there be sound? There's no sound if nobody is hearing it. Sound is right here [*the Rav pointed at his head*], not in the musical instrument. Sound is only in your brain. That's where the *nissim v'niflaos* happen. So you should sing to Hashem that you can hear.

There's so much to sing for, we'll never get through it. But you have to learn how to sing. And let me tell you, if you do that, you'll be rewarded in this world with great happiness and you'll be rewarded in the World to Come too. Like you always hear in this place: כָּל הָאוֹמֵר שִׁירָה בָּעוֹלָם הַזֶּה זוֹכֶה וְאוֹמְרוֹ לָעוֹלָם הַבָּא – *If you say a song in this world, you'll be rewarded to sing to Hashem forever in the World to Come.*

February 1989

Music in Mussar

Q/ Some people say that there's a certain power in music. Is that the case?

A/ And the answer is that it's absolutely true. Although music per se, music by itself, is nothing at all, but if it's utilized for an ideal it becomes a powerful motor to help you arrive at your destination. Now, suppose a man has a motor, an excellent motor. It turns over, let's say, so many and so many revolutions per second – its performance is the smoothest there is. Only that the motor doesn't have any belt that connects it to the wheels! So it accomplishes nothing! The spinning is useless; it's a complete waste of energy.

Music is only important if it's connected to an ideal. When Reb Yisroel Salanter started the study of *mussar,* he introduced the practice of saying: יְסוֹד הַחֲסִידוּת וְשֹׁרֶשׁ הָעֲבוֹדָה הַתְּמִימָה הוּא שֶׁיִּתְבָּרֵר וְיִתְאַמֵּת אֵצֶל הָאָדָם מַה חוֹבָתוֹ בְּעוֹלָמוֹ – *The foundation of all piety and the root of the perfect service of Hashem is that one should recognize what is his duty here in this world, what is his duty here in this world.* Then they started off singing to themselves, "מַה חוֹבָתוֹ בְּעוֹלָמוֹ, מַה חוֹבָתוֹ בְּעוֹלָמוֹ – *What is my duty in this world? What is my duty in this world?*" That's what they did in the old yeshivos at the instigation of Reb Yisroel Salanter. They learned *mussar* with a *niggun* – it was a sad, pensive, meditative *niggun*; that was a way of using music, and it began to enter their hearts. מַה חוֹבָתוֹ בְּעוֹלָמוֹ – "What is your duty in this world?" And they said it about fifteen times, over and over again, and they said it with a tune. If you do it that way, then it pierces the shell of your heart, your hard-armored heart, and it comes into the softness of the heart, and you begin to think, "Actually, what is my duty in this world?"

So music, when it's utilized for *mussar*, when it's utilized for *avodas Hashem,* absolutely, it's an excellent expedient. And that's why Dovid Hamelech, when his spirit moved him and the *ruach hakodesh* came upon him and he said בָּרְכִי נַפְשִׁי אֶת הַשֵּׁם, he took out his harp, and the harp helped him begin to ascend on the wings of music to the heights of perfection of the soul.

The harp helped him begin to ascend on the wings of music to the heights of perfection of the soul.

But when music is used for "your eyes," and "your lips," and your this and your that and "how I miss you," and all the rest of the garbage, the *Kuzari* says that means that the music which once was used for the service of Hakadosh Baruch Hu has now become the plaything of the maidservants and the boys in the street. The *Kuzari* said that almost a thousand years ago. And it has deteriorated since then. Originally, however, there's no question that music was intended to assist in the elevation of the spirit.

March 1978

Unholy Musicians

I'll quote from Plato in order to preface my question: "At the sight of beauty, wings grow on the human soul."

Q/ I'll quote from Plato in order to preface my question: "At the sight of beauty, wings grow on the human soul." So what is your real reason for knocking the great musicians and artists of this world, artists who were able to rise above themselves and create such beautiful works?

A/ He's asking for a reason for my knocking of Stokowski or my knocking of Leonard Bernstein.

Leonard Bernstein gave ten thousand dollars as a contribution for Mirrer Yeshiva – oh excuse me! It was for the Black Panthers, I meant. He contributed ten thousand dollars to the Black Panthers. Now the Black Panthers is a very noble organization dedicated to the uplifting of society, to helping the poor, and to making peace on the streets and making it safe in this world. And Leonard Bernstein took ten thousand of his dollars – of course, it doesn't mean much to him. But if it doesn't mean much, then why didn't he give ten thousand dollars to Mirrer Yeshiva?

The answer is, Leonard Bernstein is a *chanuf;* he's a false soul. He doesn't care about true values at all, and he wanted

Now, if people have noble ideals and they're able to convey them to us on the wings of music, certainly!

to flatter the enemies. Just like that fellow Lear, what's his name? Norman Lear. Also a great artist, and he received a citation, a prize given by the Jewish Federation of Los Angeles for outstanding service. Do you know what his service was?

Norman Lear gave fifty thousand dollars to the ACLU with the express purpose that it's earmarked to see that the Nazis win their court case to be permitted to march with their banners and slogans. Norman Lear took fifty thousand dollars out of his pocket for that. Now fifty thousand, even to him, means something. And he said, "It's only for the purpose – and nothing else – of helping the Nazis win in the courts for the right to parade with their banners."

You know what the Nazis are saying in America? They want to send the Jews to the gas ovens.

And Stokowski, as I mentioned before, may his soul rest in pieces, Stokowski was asked – somebody asked him, "Is it decent that you take away the wives of the members of your orchestra?" He dallied with the wives of the members of his orchestra. "Is it honest?" he was asked.

"Whatever it is, it's fun," he said.

That's Stokowski.

Mendelssohn, the great composer, was a *meshumed.* He forsook his people, and for the sake of buying glory from the gentiles, he bowed down to strange gods. And he was an adulterer too, like so many others.

The list is endless.

Now, if people have noble ideals and they're able to convey them to us on the wings of music, certainly! That's what Dovid Hamelech did, *l'havdil elef alfei alafim* of *havdalos.* And that's what the *levi'im* in the Beis Hamikdash did. But when they convey to us empty lies, falsehood – it's just music, nothing attached to the music, just music – it's nothing. Music in itself is nothing but a tickling of the nerves.

So if you tickle my nerves – let's say I'm sound asleep and you give me a tickle at about 3:00 in the morning. I get up. "What's it all about?" I ask. And you say, "It's tickling *l'sheim* tickling." So I give you a kick and go back to bed.

Now if you tickle me at 3:00 in the morning so that I should get up to *avodas haBorei,* I might also give you a kick, but at least then you'd be justified. But to awaken my nerves, to arouse my nerves, for nothing at all? It's one-hundred percent a waste of time.

But to awaken my nerves, to arouse my nerves, for nothing at all?

Now if you'll say "art for art's sake," well, I'll give you an example of art for art's sake. Here is a big institution with a great building, and the building is belching fire. The fire has a queer smell, however. You get closer and you might discover that it's the odor of burning human bodies. A very big institution. Around it is a big courtyard, and naked people are being marched to the gas chambers in preparation to be burned. That's the Nazi gas chambers. Men, women and children are being marched naked. It's freezing cold and they have to march for four blocks, but they take off their clothes before they start the march, because that's part of the Nazi plan of making death as difficult as possible.

These people can barely walk. They're weary, emaciated. And as they're staggering to the gas chamber, they pass by a platform, and on the platform there's an orchestra, and they're playing music. All this is happening under music! And they're playing German music. They're playing Beethoven and Wagner and whatever garbage there is in the German pantheon of musicians.

So you say, "Well, they're misusing their music."

They're using the music as music was created – for no purpose at all.

Had they set words to their music, words of kindliness, words of tolerance, words of love of mankind, of noble idealism, we would give them credit. No question! We

Is it permitted to change a rock 'n' roll song into a Jewish song?

give credit to Wordsworth. I give credit to Wordsworth. Wordsworth said beautiful words, words of nobility. Even a *goy* who says good things deserves credit.

But the musician doesn't say anything. He's just banging it out on the instruments. And therefore, since he's not saying anything, he's nothing.

And the question is, what is he personally? If personally he's a *mufkar,* if he's a lewd, salacious low character, what is there to praise? The fact that he can make noise?

November 1979

Converting Music

Q/ **Is it permitted to change a rock 'n' roll song into a Jewish song?**

A/ As far as adapting these melodies to Torah themes, it depends. If no one recognizes these melodies any longer, there's nothing wrong in using them for Torah themes. You can sing Shabbos *zemiros* with them. But if they're still recognized, then you should wait until Purim. On Purim you can do that.

February 1974

Non-Jewish-Inspired Songs

Should we avoid Jewish songs that have a gentile flavor?

Is it forbidden to listen to rock 'n' roll music?

A/ It depends. If people still remember the source of the tune, then it's certainly better not to sing it, even with holy words. But if the source of the tune has long been forgotten, it's like being *megayer*. We convert the *niggun* and make it a Jewish *niggun*.

Q/ **But I saw in a *sefer* an idea that if you take one of their tunes and you apply it to worship of Hashem, you're doing something that's virtuous.**

A/ Now it could be. I'm not going to argue with a *sefer* whose author I don't know, but there are two sides to that question. It could be that it's best to avoid it. But I'll leave this over to greater people than myself.

August 1975

Napoleon's March

Q/ **Haven't many *tzaddikim* taken songs like Napoleon's march and other songs and made them into *niggunim* for special purposes?**

A/ Look. When Napoleon is long dead and people have forgotten what his march sounded like, you can resurrect it and make it anything you want. But when people take local, current *niggunim* that are recognized as gentile *niggunim,* it's best to let them rot away in the grave for a long time before you resurrect them.

March 1984

It's not forbidden. Only that you're a meshugene if you do it.

Rock 'n' Roll Music

Q/ **Is it forbidden to listen to rock 'n' roll music?**

A/ The answer is no, it's not forbidden.

Isn't that surprising, for me to say that? It's also not forbidden to walk out onto Ocean Parkway, take off your shoes, and dance a jig. It's not forbidden. Only that you're a *meshugene* if you do it. And you might very well get a tack in your foot.

And if you listen to rock 'n' roll, you'll get some tacks in your brain. There's no question, it's not going to make you any smarter. But if you're asking if it's forbidden, I can't tell you it's forbidden.

November 1975

QUESTIONS *On Any* SUBJECT

Chapter 14

World of Mussar

Chapter Sponsor

Leilui nishmas
our beloved parents and grandparents

ר' **שמחה** בן ר' **זרח** ע"ה

מרת **נחמה רבקה** בת ר' **דוב בער** ע"ה

Ari and Chana Shapiro
Aliyah, Gabriella, Carmela and Dov Ber

Mishlei 17:6 - עֲטֶרֶת זְקֵנִים בְּנֵי בָנִים וְתִפְאֶרֶת בָּנִים אֲבוֹתָם

Grandchildren are the crown of their elders,
and the glory of children is their parents.

Contents

Chapter 14

World of Mussar

The Opposition

Q/ Why was it that when the *mussar* movement started, it faced such fierce opposition?

A/ Why was there opposition to the *mussar* movement?

There are two reasons: One was that some people were afraid that it was a movement to break down Jewish attitudes. And the truth is that it was. It was a new attitude that people should get together – not that they looked into a *Mesilas Yesharim* on their own – they got together in the *batei midrashim,* many *balebatim,* to learn *mussar*. Not the yeshivos; in the beginning it was all *balebatim* – they gathered together and began learning *mussar.*

And they learned it in a very enthusiastic way. They were shouting! That was the *mussar* system – to shout over and over again *maamarim* of Chazal that applied to you personally in order that you should hear. They said, "It's not enough to hear, you have to *derher. Herren*, that's not enough. No;

"Yes, it's a meshuga'im house. You come in meshuga, and you go out sane."

derherren – you have to internalize it. And until they could *hear* it, they had to repeat it many times – many, many times.

Now, if you walked in there, it looked like a madhouse. Once a man from Germany, a frum Jew, walked in, and he said, "What's this? A *meshuga'im* house?!"

Rav Yisroel Salanter was there and he said, "Yes, it's a *meshuga'im* house. You come in *meshuga,* and you go out sane."

Now, some people were afraid; they were afraid. I must tell you, I'm sure that some important *talmidei chachamim* were jealous, too. Because it reflected upon others – why don't you do it? So they felt a certain amount of personal animosity. There's always jealousy.

And Reb Yisroel Salanter said, "Any good thing that you start doing, you have to expect that there's going to be a big opposition to it." That's a *klal gadol.* There isn't a single good thing that you'll start doing that opposition won't arise against it. It's a *klal gadol!* And sometimes the opposition is led by people who are big *lamdanim* too.

So the first *machlokes* was the same *machlokes* that was against *chassidim* in the beginning. When the *chassidim* started doing things that the people in Europe were not accustomed to doing, they suspected that a new sect was coming up, like *chalilah* the *Frankistim* and the *Shabtai Tzvi* people. And they were afraid – who knew what could happen?

That's why they opposed them at the beginning. That was also the first *machlokes* against the *mussar* movement.

The second *machlokes* was later, when they introduced *mussar* into the yeshivos. That raised another storm. "A yeshiva," many said, "is a place where the youth should be trained in the *lomdus* of Torah – and *only* that. You don't take time for other subjects. You want to learn some Chumash with them in the yeshiva? Now, there's nothing wrong with

Chumash, but a yeshiva is not a place for Chumash. You're going to learn with them *Pirkei Avos* or *Mesilas Yesharim*? That's not the place for it. Because if you start bringing *mussar* into the yeshivos, it might dilute the quality of the enthusiasm for learning. That's what they thought. A yeshiva should only be a place of learning *halacha*, *pilpulim*, mental exercises. But moral instruction, that's something that should be taught outside, voluntarily or individually.

There was a big clamor that they're spoiling the nature of the yeshivos.

And so, that was a new battle, and it was a very big *chiddush* when they finally did win and they introduced *mussar* in the yeshivos.

So it was two things. First of all, they suspected at the beginning that it was a movement that might make a schism, it might make a new sect; who knows what could happen, *chalilah*. Like when you suspect any good thing as long as it's new. And the second was when it came into the yeshivos, there was a big clamor that they're spoiling the nature of the yeshivos.

The truth is that the *mussar* yeshivos were yeshivos of learning like all the yeshivos; like all the yeshivos. In Slabodka, it was like a battlefield; all day long it was a *milchemes ha Torah* – all day long they were talking in learning; it was roaring in the *beis hamedrash*. And still, when it came time for *mussar* at night, they all stopped immediately. They knew they had to learn *mussar*.

And then they started learning *mussar b'kol,* and a new voice arose. A loud voice, people were shouting *mussar* – shouting! There were some people who specialized in shouting in *mussar!* Shouting in *mussar* loudly, and the *beis hamedrash* was full of the *kol* of *Mesilas Yesharim* and *Chovos Halevavos* and *Shaarei Teshuvah* for half an hour.

In addition, three times during the week, the heads of the yeshiva spoke – for an hour and a half each time.

Our nation had the practice of good conduct as a tradition. We always were endowed with good middos,

And so, the youth were inspired with the examples that they heard. There's no question that after so much indoctrination, people were different; they were not the same when they left the yeshiva.

So the fact that there was opposition does not have any bearing on the nature of the thing. It only shows that it was a good thing, and all good things, at the beginning, are opposed by a strong opposition.

May 1995

Avodas Hamiddos vs. Mussar

Q/ An important part of *mussar* is the training of good *middos*, good traits of character. But didn't the Jews of two-hundred years ago, before Rav Yisroel Salanter, also practice the laws of *middos tovos*?

A/ You must know that our nation had the practice of good conduct as a tradition. We *always* were endowed with good *middos,* because you don't learn good *middos* only from *seforim*. It was handed down from father to son, from mother to daughter. From the beginning, from Avraham Avinu, it was an unbroken tradition of proper conduct.

However, in the course of time, people tend to become habit-ridden. They begin doing things without idealism. And not only in *middos*. Anybody, you should know, who lacks in good *middos,* is at the same time lacking in *avodas Hashem.* Because all of *avodas Hashem* requires the practice of certain ways in *bein adam l'chaveiro. Bein adam l'chaveiro* also is a form of *avodas Hashem.*

Now when people congregate, let's say, in a *mikveh* when they're getting ready for Shabbos and it's a *moshav leitzim* or they talk *lashon hara* there, actually, their *tevilas hamikveh* is a superficiality. It's a *mitzvas anashim melumadah* and the *avodas Hashem* is a pretty cold form of *avodah*.

On all levels of national life, Rav Yisroel breathed in a new spirit

And therefore, when Rav Yisroel Salanter came along, it was not a case merely of being weak in *middos* that he had noticed in the people. He saw there was a general coolness, a weakening of enthusiasm for everything. And when he began teaching the *toras hayirah*, it was not only in *bein adam l'chaveiro*. Certainly he spoke about *bein adam l'chaveiro*; you can't teach *yiras Shamayim* if you don't teach the importance of *gezel* and business matters. You have to teach *shemiras halashon* – you shouldn't slander and you shouldn't ridicule people. You have to teach you shouldn't be a *baal ga'avah* – you shouldn't look down and scorn people. Naturally he taught good *middos*. But good *middos* are only one part of the general picture of *avodas Hashem*.

And therefore, certainly when Rav Yisroel came, it was necessary to reawaken the people to the importance of good character, *bein adam l'chaveiro*. But it was just as necessary to reawaken them to the importance of *ahavas Hashem*, *chovos halevavos*, *emunah*, *bitachon,* and all the other qualities that a man has to have to be a true *oved Hashem*.

It was not merely in one area that the people needed regeneration. And therefore on all levels of national life, Rav Yisroel breathed in a new spirit – *bein adam l'chaveiro* and *bein adam l'Makom*.

And therefore, certainly people, no matter how good they are, must have from time to time a spiritual recharging of their batteries. Everybody needs to be told when he's weakening and he needs a reinforcement of his spiritual energies.

You listen again and again, and each time, the impression becomes more and more realistic.

And so, it's not a criticism. It's a natural process that from time to time, people must be made aware of the necessity for new efforts in their service of Hashem.

January 1985

Enthusiastic Mussar

Q/ What's the benefit of the shouting, the *limud mussar b'hispailus*, learning *mussar* with excitement or enthusiasm?

A/ Any ideal, if it is merely thought in your mind, has much less effect than if you express it in words. And if you express it loudly and enthusiastically to yourself then it goes through your ears and into your mind more readily. By repetition, especially enthusiastic repetition, you listen again and again, and each time, the impression becomes more and more realistic.

May 1995

Mussar vs. Chassidus 1

Q/ What's the difference between the study of *mussar* and the study of *chassidus*?

A/ The answer is, *b'etzem* there is no difference at all. Only that the material is somewhat different.

I'll give a *mashal*. There's one group of *chassidim* – I won't say their name – that they learn *Mesilas Yesharim*. They believe in *Mesilas Yesharim*. There's another group that won't look into *Mesilas Yesharim*. They have their own *seforim*. But *hatzad hashaveh shebahem* is, you're laboring to change your *machshavos* into true thoughts of Hakadosh Baruch Hu. Each one follows his *derech*. So *sifrei mussar* and *sifrei chassidus* are both, you can say, *hashkafah*. It's a world outlook that they're creating in different ways.

You have to talk to yourself and urge yourself

Now, *mussar* utilizes all standard *seforim* like the *Chovos Halevavos* and the *Shaarei Teshuvah*. It uses the Rambam's *Hilchos Teshuvah* and *Hilchos Dei'os* and the *mussar shmuessen* from the yeshivos, the *mussar* yeshivos. That's one *shitah*.

Rav Yisroel Salanter's *shitah* in learning *mussar* was to sit down and to say a *maamar Chazal* over and over to yourself many many times. He used to call people together in a *mussar shtiebel*, the *balebatim;* in the evening they sat down and each one would start learning *mussar*. He picked a *maamar Chazal* and said it again and again aloud, aloud, aloud and in the end they were shouting. They became so excited; they were shouting. People, when they left that place that evening, they were different people. They were changed by that.

They spoke to themselves. אִם אָדָם לֹא יְיַסֵּר אֶת עַצְמוֹ מַה יּוֹעִיל לוֹ הַמּוּסָרִים – If a person won't *mussar* himself, what will the *mussar* that he learns help (*Shaarei Teshuvah* 2:26). You have to talk to yourself constantly. Like Dovid Hamelech said, הַלְלִי נַפְשִׁי אֶת ה' – *My soul, praise Hashem* (*Tehillim* 146:1). He's talking to himself.

You have to talk to yourself and urge yourself, and after a while, the self that's concealed within you, that's hidden within you, starts coming out. Your *yecholes,* your potential greatness, starts coming out to the surface.

So both actually, *chassidus* and *mussar,* are working on the same idea of creating a *machshavah* of Torah attitudes.

February 2000

They used to gather in their little shtiebel, and he used to sit with them around the table at various times and on special occasions

Mussar vs. Chassidus 2

Q/ What is the difference between the *chassidus* movement and the *mussar* movement?

A/ *Chassidim* have built their ideology mostly on the presence and the influence of a *rebbe*. The *rebbe* is a man who has a lot of authority, and therefore he influences them, either by direct personal contact or indirect contact by means of the chief *chassidim*.

I don't know how it is today, but in the olden days, the chief *chassidim* used to go out from the *rebbe's* place and they used to travel back to their hometowns, and every town had somebody who was considered the main authority of his *rebbe's chassidus*. And they used to gather in their little *shtiebel,* and he used to sit with them around the table at various times and on special occasions; sometimes there was a little whiskey and cake on the table too, and he told them stories about the *rebbe* and words from the *rebbe* and thus inspired people.

Some of them used to travel too; some *rebbes* traveled, but some were stationary, each one in his town. And so, the *rebbe* spread his influence by means of these *shluchim*. And many times people came to him in the thousands for Yom Tov or even for a Shabbos, and they were influenced.

Mussar was an entirely different movement. *Mussar* was a movement where people took the statements of Chazal or statements from *mussar seforim,* and they studied them and they began saying them over to themselves in a way that little by little, it penetrated.

That's one of the tenets of *mussar*, to repeat certain statements over and over, gradually letting them enter your mind more and more.

Sometimes in one evening, let's say in the yeshiva, in a half-hour, you might say the same thing, the same *pasuk* or *maamar Chazal,* over and over a hundred times; but with a *niggun,* a melancholic and meditative *niggun.* And sometimes, people became quite excited over that.

On Motzei Shabbos, they sat in the dark for an hour and they repeated *maamarei Chazal* to themselves aloud. And at the end, before the hour was over, some people were in ecstasy.

I myself recall certain things I said to myself that I had always known before, but I repeated them so many times that they became illuminated in my mind, and thereafter, I could never forget them anymore. And so, *mussar* is a system of training the thoughts and also training the qualities of character by various exercises.

Mussar is a system of training the thoughts and also training the qualities of character by various exercises.

August 1983

The Spirit of Mussar

Q/ Why was *mussar* chosen as the way to rejuvenate the Am Yisroel rather than the art of talking with Hashem?

A/ And the answer is, talking to Hashem is only one part of the subject of *yiras Hashem.* And *mussar* actually includes it, because when people commune with themselves, what are they doing? They're talking with Hashem.

And when they learn *mussar* properly – then when they *daven,* when they talk to Hashem, it's not merely a formality that they have to discharge their duty. It becomes a form of talking to Hashem.

And so, people who are imbued with the spirit of *mussar,* when they stand in *tefillah,* that's an opportunity.

Mussar tells you how to do things in a way that you'll be most successful in life.

Baruch Atah! "You," they say. If you don't learn *mussar,* then it could be that you don't mean anything. So it's a wasted opportunity to say "You" to Hakadosh Baruch Hu.

Certainly, you more readily and more sincerely commune with Hashem if you're inspired to understand what you're doing.

January 1985

Time Spent on Mussar 1

Q/ How much time should a yeshiva man spend on learning *mussar*?

A/ Before I answer you, I'll say this. Rav Simcha Zissel, *zichrono livracha,* once asked Rav Yisroel Salanter this question for himself.

So Rav Yisroel said, "Not too much. Only three hours a day is enough."

Rav Simcha Zissel was a big *lamdan* already. We need time to learn Gemara. Gemara is not easy. So we cannot afford three hours a day. But it's good to put in time on *mussar*. I'll tell you why.

Mussar is not just *yiras Shamayim. Mussar* is how to live happily, and Hashem wants you to be successful in living happily. *Mussar* tells you how to do things in a way that you'll be most successful in life. You'll learn to talk to people with *nachas*, gently. People will listen to you. You'll get a good name. *Mussar* is full of things that are practical in this world.

I had a *rebbe, zichrono livracha,* and he said to me, "Learn *mussar*. You'll go to America, you'll make money on speaking *mussar*." He said that; I remember it like yesterday. He said,

"You'll go to America and you'll make money from teaching *mussar*."

You'll make more than money. You make a life out of *mussar*. That's why it's a good thing to learn *Chovos Halevavos*, *Mesilas Yesharim*, *Shaarei Teshuvah*, *Hilchos Teshuvah*. You should know that it's our lives. It's our lives.

Of course you must learn Gemara. Gemara takes up most of our time and it's very full of practical, useful instruction. However, *mussar* is the spirit, the *ruach hachaim* in everything. No question, you must have *mussar*. How much? Utilize it according to your abilities.

May 2000

Whatever his yeshiva prescribes for him, that's what he should follow. His teachers know better than him what is good for him.

Time Spent on Mussar 2

Q/ How much time should a yeshiva man allot to the study of *mussar*?

A/ By *mussar*, this questioner probably means *mussar seforim* such as *Chovos Halevavos*, *Shaarei Teshuvah*, *Mesilas Yesharim* and the like.

Now this is not a simple question. If you would ask the author of *Mesilas Yesharim* or the author of *Chovos Halevavos*, the answer might surprise you.

Once, Rav Simcha Zissel was counselled by his *rebbi*, Rav Yisroel Salanter, that he should not learn so much *mussar*. Rav Simcha Zissel was taken aback. He was surprised to hear this from Rav Yisroel. Rav Yisroel said as follows: "It's not necessary to learn so much *mussar*." But he then added, "Three hours a day is sufficient."

Everyone has to know what his kochos are, and we need a lot of mussar.

Nowadays, if a yeshiva man would spend three hours a day on *mussar*, he wouldn't have enough time for Gemara. Gemara is a big and difficult subject, and that claims most of our time. And I'm not saying that a young man should give even two hours for *mussar*. The true answer is, whatever his yeshiva prescribes for him, that's what he should follow. His teachers know better than him what is good for him.

If he is succeeding in his studies and he has an inclination to go a little further, why not? But that depends on the individual. There may be individuals who could take much more, who *need* much more, whose souls yearn for the insight, for the illumination that comes from meditation, from contact with these great *seforim*. And therefore, it's best for a young man to be in contact with some advisor who could tell him what is good for him individually.

November 1970

Time Spent on Mussar 3

Q/ **How much *mussar* does a person need to learn every day? Rav Chaim Volozhiner said ten minutes is enough, but you're saying more.**

A/ Look. How much sleep does a person need? Since the Gra slept two hours a night, are you going to sleep two hours tonight?

So people are different. Everyone has to know what his *kochos* are, and we need a lot of *mussar*. Ten minutes of *mussar* is wonderful. But we need more.

November 1984

The Way to Learn Mussar

When I came to Slobodka, I discovered that they learned one line for a half-hour every night. The same line! For a half-hour!

Q/ When one learns a *mussar sefer*, should he learn one line over and over again like I heard the Rav mention once, or should he keep moving and finish the whole *sefer*?

A/ Let me tell you, that's a good question. A very good question. And the only answer is that you have to do both things. You should learn the entire *sefer*, because you need *yedios*; there are so many important ideas that we don't know. The *Mesilas Yesharim*, for instance, is a chest full of diamonds. Every line is full of important *yedios*. So you must learn it all.

And yet, when you skim through the lines superficially, you'll soon discover that you have missed out. You'll never get the real meaning unless you think about a single idea again and again and again. And later in life, sometime, you'll go back to it again and you'll say, "Why didn't I understand that when I was a boy? Why did I miss out on such an important idea?" And the answer is that you learned it too rapidly.

And therefore, you need both things. You have to learn it all, so that your mind will be filled with Torah ideals. But you also have to learn one line many times, again and again, like they do in some yeshivos, until it finally sinks in.

When I came to Slobodka, I discovered that they learned one line for a half-hour every night. That was *mussar seder*. The same line! For a half-hour!

And on Motzei Shabbos, they didn't have any lights in the yeshiva; it was dark. It was after *seudas shlishis* and we all sat in the dark. And each one of us was saying a line by himself, aloud. Louder and louder. And louder and louder. At the end, everyone was shouting. The whole yeshiva was

Do the local yeshivos place enough emphasis on mussar?

shouting! All their *kochos*, all their strength, went into that one line. And then there was a *klop* on the *bimah*; וְהוּא רַחוּם יְכַפֵּר עָוֹן, and we davened *Ma'ariv*.

I must tell you that it was a tremendous experience. It was like going through a *mikveh*, a *mikveh* of fire, of *kedusha*. One line for an hour! It was electrifying! A full hour in the darkness! And you concentrate on it. And you begin to feel what the words are saying. What are the words telling me? You begin to feel it. And you should know that you still don't understand it fully. But it's still a tremendous achievement!

Our great men were able to contain in a few short words a whole world of wisdom. The Gra said about the *Mesilas Yesharim*, "I read the first eleven *perakim,* and I didn't find one superfluous word." And so, it's to your greatest benefit that you spend time on each line, and that's besides for going through the *sefer* and gaining *yedios*.

November 1998

Mussar in Slabodka

Q/ Do the local yeshivos place enough emphasis on *mussar*?

A/ I cannot tell you what the local yeshivos are doing, but I can tell you what they *should* do. There is no question that *mussar* is essential. It's impossible to bring up idealistic *bnei Torah* unless there's *mussar* at the same time.

I want to tell you something about my old place where I was in Slabodka. In the *mizrach* in Slabodka, there were two people standing. One was Rav Bentzel Birzher, *zichrono livracha,* and one was Rav Zalman Serevnika. They were two older *bochurim,* and they were considered the biggest *lamdanim* in the yeshiva. They were ideals of *lomdus* in the yeshiva. They were in the *mizrach* right near the *aron kodesh*. Anybody who had questions came over to them and asked them questions.

At 8:30, the old *mashgiach* used to pull out the drawer with the *mussar seforim*. That was the signal to learn *mussar*. Everybody in the yeshiva, including these two giants of Torah, stopped talking in learning immediately. It was *mussar* time. They all realized that there's a time for *mussar*.

Now these two great men, they were the *metzuyanim* of the yeshiva, and they were busy talking in learning with other people who came to ask them questions. And so, I would think that they disdained it when the old *mashgiach* pulled out the drawer at 8:30, and they would continue for one or two more minutes. No. Immediately they stopped, *toch k'dai dibbur*.

It was self-understood. A yeshiva without *mussar* is not a yeshiva. When people learn *mussar*, it transforms their *Bava Kama*. It's a different *Yevamos*. Everything is different if it's done with the spirit of *mussar*.

A yeshiva without mussar is not a yeshiva. When people learn mussar, it transforms their Bava Kama.

January 1995

The Seder Halimud of Mussar

Q/ The *Mesilas Yesharim* is written in *madreigos*, first how to achieve *zehirus*, then how to achieve *zerizus*, then *nekiyus*, etc. Should one learn the whole *sefer* straight or rather stay on *zehirus* until he gets it, and only then go to *zerizus* and stay on that until he gets it, and then go on to *nekiyus* and so on?

Say it out loud and slowly and think about the words until they sink into your mind.

A/ When you're learning *Mesilas Yesharim*, learn it slowly, like you learn a *Tosafos.* But you have to finish it. Then go back and learn it again. And then learn it again. Each time as you review it, it will sink in more. It's important to know the last *perakim* in order to understand the first *perakim.* You'll see that.

Mesilas Yesharim is like a *Shulchan Aruch* of *shleimus*, and *shleimus* is what Hakadosh Baruch Hu wants of us. We should make something out of ourselves. We're not merely doing mitzvos; we're transforming ourselves. *Asher kideshanu bemitzvosav* – He makes us holy through the mitzvos. And holy means *shalem, shleimus.* The more you do it, the more *shalem* you become.

And the *Mesilas Yesharim* teaches how to do it in the best way. So by all means, keep on learning the whole *sefer* again and again.

March 2000

On Mesilas Yesharim

Q/ How many times in one *z'man* should a *bochur* finish *Mesilas Yesharim*?

A/ Go slowly with the *Mesilas Yesharim*. It's a very deep *sefer*. The right way to do it is to say the words over and over again, every line over and over again out loud. Say it out loud and slowly and think about the words until they sink into your mind. Just reading it fast is not a waste of time, but the real effect is only when you say it slowly; it penetrates your mind and becomes part of your personality. And therefore, if you want to do it right, you can't do it so many times in one *z'man*.

June 2000

Sifrei Mussar vs. Mussar Shmuessen

Q/ **If a person learns *sifrei mussar* inside, does he also have to listen to *mussar shmuessen*?**

A/ The question is, the subject of *mussar* instruction, should it be in the form of learning *seforim* or also listening to *shmuessen*?

And the answer is, it should be everything. You can never have enough. There's so much to know; nobody will tell you *baal peh* all you have to know. The Gra, *zichrono livracha,* when he read the first eleven chapters, he said that there is not one unnecessary word. And still, he said that if the *Mesilas Yesharim* were alive he would walk from Vilna to Italy to be *meshamesh* him.

And so, the *Mesilas Yesharim* is all diamonds. But you need *peirush,* no question about it. He's not able to tell you all the examples. And therefore, טוֹב לִשְׁמֹעַ – *It's good to hear* (*Koheles* 7:5). *Tov lishmoa;* it's good to hear as much as you can. When a boy is a little child, or a girl, and their mother and father tell them things, they should listen to them. שְׁמַע בְּנִי מוּסַר אָבִיךָ – *Listen to the mussar of your father* (*Mishlei* 1:8). And your mother too. A tremendous amount of experience can be gained if they'll listen.

Of course, children don't know – they merely obey, but they don't take it as a lesson. No. Listen. Listen. Absorb it.

Listen. Listen. Absorb it. Because that teaching is going to remain with you; it will become part of your wisdom.

Because that teaching is going to remain with you; it will become part of your wisdom.

When you get older and you hear older people telling you advice, listen. Listen. שׁוֹמֵעַ לְעֵצָה חָכָם – *A wise man listens to counsel* (ibid. 12:15).

February 1998

How much mussar is a person required to learn every day? And what kind of mussar is best to learn?

Learning More Mussar

Q/ **Should a yeshiva *bochur* learn additional *mussar* if the yeshiva *sedorim* of *mussar* are not enough?**

A/ *Mussar* can never hurt you, and the more the better. A man once complained to me, "I learn *mussar* but it doesn't have any effect." So I said, "I'll tell you what the doctor says. Increase the dose!"

January 1996

What to Learn

Q/ **How much *mussar* is a person required to learn every day? And what kind of *mussar* is best to learn?**

A/ How much *mussar* depends on who you are. If you are a *talmid* in a yeshiva, then you have to keep the *sedorim* of the yeshiva. You cannot go off someplace by yourself and be a failure in what the yeshiva requires of you. However, there is time. There is enough time to learn *mussar*. There's time *bein hasedorim*. There's time Friday afternoon. When the yeshiva disperses you can still sit and learn *mussar*; there is time.

Now, how much time you should allot in your spare time also depends on who you are. But this I *can* tell you. That if you invest time in *mussar*, you're investing in your future. You're not giving away time, you're gaining greatness! *Mussar* means to develop your mind in the model of the great truths of the Torah in an abstract form – in the form that's most useful for people who like to think.

The Shlah says that in Sefer Devarim you have all the mussar found in all the mussar seforim.

Now what kind of *mussar*? I would say that at the beginning, you should spend more time on *Mesilas Yesharim*, and also on the Rambam's *Hilchos Yesodei HaTorah*, *Hilchos Teshuvah,* and *Hilchos Dei'os*. Also focus on Rabbeinu Yonah's *Shaarei Teshuvah* and on *Chovos Halevavos*. Other *seforim* can come later. But the ones that I just mentioned, I think should be the fundamental *seforim* to study.

April 1982

The Original Mussar Seforim

Q/ How did people learn *mussar* before we had the *Mesilas Yesharim* and the *Chovos Halevavos*?

A/ Before we had these *seforim,* people learned *mussar* from the Gemara and from *Mishlei* and from *Sefer Devarim*. The Shlah says that in *Sefer Devarim* you have all the *mussar* found in all the *mussar seforim*. The difference is this: When we learn Chumash, so if it's simple, if it's not difficult, we run through it. When they learned Chumash, even the most simple statements, they used to think into them. They went more and more deeply into them, and they learned the *mussar* from *Sefer Devarim*. *Sefer Devarim* is a treasure house of *mussar*. That's a very important lesson.

Ladies can achieve greatness if they learn Mesilas Yesharim. The Gra told his daughters to learn mussar seforim.

And then of course, there's *Mishlei*. *Mishlei* has tremendous lessons! All the *divrei Nevi'im* are also full of *mussar*. Our forefathers studied the Nevi'im in a way that was superior to anything that the *Chovos Halevavos* or *Mesilas Yesharim* or *Shaarei Teshuvah* can teach you. It's only because people lost the ability to understand properly, to properly utilize the words of the *kadmonim*, that it became necessary to have *mussar seforim*.

It's like in the olden days, when they wanted to train a baby to eat food. The child didn't have teeth yet, so how did the mother prepare him for eating food when she wanted to wean him from the mother's milk? So the mother used to chew the food and put it into the child's mouth. That's how they used to do it; the mother used to chew the food in her own mouth and then put it into the child's mouth. That's how the child learned to eat. It was pre-chewed by the mother. That's how it was in the olden days.

And so, when we lost the ability to chew over and taste the real meaning of the *pesukim* in *Mishlei* and Chumash and so on, we had to have the *Chovos Halevavos,* who pre-chewed it and predigested it for us. But actually, the *kadmonim* understood *mussar* much better than we do, even without the benefit of these later *seforim*.

July 1994

The S'char for Learning Mussar

Is there a reward for learning *mussar seforim*?

A/ I don't understand the question. For learning *mussar seforim*, there's a *tremendous* reward. There's Torah, there's *yiras Shamayim*. And therefore, by all means.

Mussar has to be the means of bringing you closer to Torah.

By the way, I want to tell you that ladies can achieve greatness if they learn *Mesilas Yesharim*. The Gra told his daughters to learn *mussar seforim*. Women who learn *Mesilas Yesharim* can become very great in *daas Torah*, and they can teach in seminaries as a result.

April 2000

Mussar over Gemara?

Q/ **What should a person do if he enjoys learning *mussar* and *hashkafah* more than Gemara?**

A/ So we say it's an excuse for laziness.

If you enjoy learning *mussar* more than putting on tefillin, is that an excuse not to wear tefillin? If you enjoy learning *mussar* more than going into the sukkah, is it an excuse not to go into the sukkah?

And learning Torah is more than the mitzvah of tefillin and the mitzvah of sukkah; it's *kineged kulam.* That's part of a Jew's obligation; he has to put Torah into his mind.

And he has to know, by the way, that it's a very selfish thing to do. And Hakadosh Baruch Hu praises that selfishness. It's *kineged kulam.* Fill your mind with Torah. And the more you have Gemara in your mind and the more you have *halachos* in your mind, you should know that you're going to have a greater happiness in the World to Come. Don't deceive yourself. *Mussar* has to be the means of bringing you closer

Without mussar, whatever you learn has no taste. Don't deceive yourself.

to Torah. If *mussar* takes you away from learning, then you should know that you're not succeeding.

Now, if one is *mehalech baderech,* walking on the road, and he sees an *ilan na'eh,* and he says *mah na'eh ilan zeh,* so it depends. If he was learning and he stopped learning because he wanted to take a rest from learning – it's easier for him to look at the tree and admire it, so it's an excuse not to learn. But suppose he does it because he says, "I cannot miss this opportunity. I don't have this every day, such a beautiful tree. I'm looking at the *niflaos haBorei!*"

So that's a good *mashal* for a person who's learning a *sugya* in Gemara and suddenly sees a *mussar sefer* that he long wanted to get but he couldn't find lying right in front of him. So he stops learning and he looks in the *mussar sefer*. Like the yeshivos, they stop learning to learn the *mussar seder*. That's not considered forsaking his learning.

I don't believe that there is such a person, a person who learns *mussar* all day long and avoids learning Gemara. No, there's no such thing.

If you have an hour extra, what do you do? Listen to me. A man told Reb Yisroel Salanter, a businessman; he said, "I only have one hour a day, what should I do?

So Reb Yisroel said, "Learn *mussar* for that one hour."

So the man said, "What about learning Gemara?"

Reb Yisroel said, "If you learn that one hour of *mussar*, you'll discover that you have a lot of hours to learn Gemara too." The *mussar* will teach you. *Mussar* opens your eyes.

Once, a *bochur* who learned in Slabodka said, "I became a *baal ga'avah* in Slabodka."

So his *rebbe* said, "You didn't *become* a *baal ga'avah*. You *discovered* in Slabodka that you were a *baal ga'avah*."

So learn *mussar*, and you'll discover that learning Gemara is a pleasure too.

May 1995

The spirit of mussar is waiting. It's needed in America more than ever before

Gemara Without Mussar

Q/ How would you answer a person who wants to learn only Chumash and *parsha* but no *mussar*?

A/ You can say Chumash and *parsha* and Gemara also, but no *mussar*.

So tell that person that if you're eating a good piece of meat – it's expensive and it's kosher and it's fresh and it's cooked – but it's only cooked in water, then the meat has no taste. You need a little bit of salt, a little bit of garlic, maybe a little bit of onion. You need something of a condiment. Without *mussar*, whatever you learn has no taste. Don't deceive yourself.

Now, by *mussar* we don't mean that you must learn *Mesilas Yesharim* – no. If you have somebody who'll teach you the Chumash in the way that *mussar* utilizes, then that's *mussar*. If somebody will teach you Gemara with the system of the *baalei mussar*, that's *mussar*. If somebody teaches you *chassidus* with the purpose of bringing lessons out that help you utilize your learning in practice, certainly.

But just to learn for the purpose of knowing information, information that won't be translated into ways of thinking and attitudes that produce a different kind of behavior, that's not called learning. כָּל הָאוֹמֵר אֵין לִי אֶלָּא תּוֹרָה, אֲפִלּוּ תּוֹרָה אֵין לוֹ – *If a man says, I have nothing but Torah, he doesn't even have Torah* (*Yevamos* 109b).

September 1984

The spirit of mussar is waiting. It's needed in America more than ever before

Mussar in America

Q/ How could yeshivos nowadays improve their standards in order to match the old standards in Europe?

A/ And the answer you heard already. The spirit of *mussar* is waiting. It's needed in America more than ever before in order to awaken the latent greatness, the dormant greatness in Jewish men. You must know, young men today are thirsting. Not only for Gemara. They want Gemara; they want *lomdus*, but they're thirsting for the message that translates the *lomdus* into thoughts and actions and feelings and emotions. And therefore, it's of the greatest importance today if people will have the foresight to revive the spirit of *mussar* in American yeshivos.

January 1985

Chapter 15
Finding Your Bashert

Chapter Sponsor

Sponsored by

Ari and Faigie Brecher (LA)

לעילוי נשמת

ר׳ **יהושע אליקים** בן

ר׳ **יוסף הכהן ברעכער** ז״ל

And as a Zechus for the הצלחה
of each of our children and grandchild(ren).

May you each find your Bashert בשעה טובה ומוצלחת.

Contents

Chapter 15

Finding Your Bashert

Be Mr. Right

Q/ When does one know that he found his true *zivug*, his true mate?

A/ Now, let me tell you something about this. It's a very great misconception, because it's possible to have 22 mates. You could have twenty wives if you were born before Rabbeinu Gershom made his *takanah,* and if you're wealthy enough to support them. And each one could be your true mate.

Today you can only have one; however, that's only because of the *takanah.* It doesn't mean that this one is your only true mate. So instead of wasting your life and letting the years go by while you're still looking to find "the one," the one who when you see her, a bell will ring within you or a light will go on, and meanwhile, you're getting older and older and you'll have less and less opportunity to raise a family. Because when you're getting older, you're going to get an old girl. If she'll ever have any children, it will be maybe one. Maybe none at all. Isn't it a tragedy to miss the opportunity of raising a family?

A Jew who is raising a family is an oved Hashem. People don't realize; the biggest mitzvah is to raise a family.

I want to tell you something. A Jew who is raising a family is an *oved Hashem.* People don't realize; the biggest mitzvah is to raise a family. You go to work from nine to five or from eight to six working to support your family.

At home at night, the babies are crying and they don't let you sleep. A woman is going crazy from her babies. And you're going mad trying to support all of them.

You have to know, you're serving Hashem. That's the very best service of Hakadosh Baruch Hu: bringing up a family, a Jewish family, sons and daughters who walk in the ways of Hashem. And therefore, you have to start as soon as possible.

We envy these women! You see a woman pushing a baby carriage; two babies inside and six more holding onto the side of the carriage. That woman is a queen! She's a Kohen Gadol! She's serving Hakadosh Baruch Hu; she's doing the greatest thing in the world. There's nothing bigger. לֹא נִבְרָא הָעוֹלָם אֶלָּא בִּשְׁבִיל פְּרִיָּה וּרְבִיָּה – the world was created for that (*Chagigah* 2b). And these people are the true *avdei Hashem.* They're the servants of Hakadosh Baruch Hu.

And therefore, it's a tragedy to wait.

So the only question is, how do you know who is the one you should marry?

I'll give you one piece of advice. After trying your best to ascertain if she is frum, if she is healthy, if she is decent – it means she's not a feminist, she likes the idea of being in the home, she wants a big family, she's not so interested in luxuries – after ascertaining all these things, make up your mind that *you're* going to be the true one. Instead of looking for someone who's better, see to it that you're the one who's better. And you'll succeed that way. Be the best man that could be.

You'll never find a woman who is exactly suited to you. You'll always find something to complain about.

The Chofetz Chaim was a genius; a brilliant man. A very great *talmid chacham,* a *gadol hador.* His wife was so ignorant that she couldn't write. Was she a helpmate for him?

I was once talking to a man – he was a professor in college – and he wanted to marry a certain girl in our *kehillah,* a brilliant girl. And he told me he was so sorry that he couldn't marry her. He wanted to walk hand-in-hand with her through life.

So I said to him, "Don't be foolish. Nobody walks hand-in-hand with his wife through life. It's only a dream."

Do we find Rabbi Akiva walking hand-in-hand with his wife through life? Do you find any *gadol?* They don't walk hand in hand. Each one has his or her function and they succeed, each one in their own realm.

The Chofetz Chaim didn't walk hand in hand with his wife. He wrote his *chibburim* and he lived his life of *zechus harabbim.* She took care of him; she took care of the children. Each one did their function. She's in Gan Eden together with him. She's the queen, the wife of the Chofetz Chaim. But she wasn't made especially to suit him according to his genius abilities.

So don't think you'll find a wife that's exactly going to participate in all your interests. You'll live your life, she'll live hers, and each one has to do the best in his or her sphere.

And therefore, instead of wasting time looking for the best one, look for a good one and then get busy making *yourself* the best one.

August 1987

Don't think you'll find a wife that's exactly going to partici-pate in all your interests.

In order to make sure you married the right one, YOU should be the right one.

Knowing When it's the Right One

Q/ **How does a frum boy or girl know that they married their real *zivug*, the right one?**

A/ Now I won't answer that question entirely. I'll answer it partially however.

In order to make sure you married the right one, *you* should be the right one. You hear that? Make it your business once you're married – you're going to be the right one.

November 1995

Losing Your Intended 1

Q/ **If a girl says the wrong thing on a date and she loses her intended, will she find someone else?**

A/ It's *maasim b'chol yom;* it happens every day that they do.

However, it doesn't mean that the second one is as good as the first. Never console yourself like that.

Of course, the one you marry, he's the one with whom to do the best job that you can to make him the happiest, and to be the happiest you can be with him. Because it's a waste of time bemoaning your fate and thinking you could've gotten better. That's foolishness; it's useless and Hakadosh Baruch Hu wants you to make the very best of your opportunities.

But there's no question that sometimes the person can lose a better opportunity by saying the wrong words.

April 1976

"We gave you a house. Who told you to set fire to the house?"

Losing Your Intended 2

Q/ If Hakadosh Baruch Hu sets up *shidduchim* forty days before the creation of the baby, why do we find so many divorces?

A/ And the answer is, why do you find so many fires? If you sit in your house and you count; how many times a day do you hear the fire engines clanging down the street?

And the answer is, because people misuse opportunities. Matches are not made to light cigarettes while you're lying in bed. Matches are made only to keep in the kitchen. There are a thousand and one things that people do that cause fires and burn down homes, and in most of the cases, it's negligence. So are you going to blame the architect and the builders who made these homes, why didn't they make them in such a way that a fire couldn't happen? They say, "We gave you a house. Who told you to set fire to the house?"

Hakadosh Baruch Hu says to this couple, "I gave you a house. Don't make a fire."

If you set fire to your house, it's your own fault, not the fault of Hakadosh Baruch Hu. A man and a woman are made for each other, to enjoy each other. Like the Gemara (*Kesuvos* 61a) says, לְשִׂמְחָה נְתַתִּיהָ וְלֹא לְצַעַר. It's given for happiness. If you're a fool and you use your wife to cause yourself *tzaar,* or she uses her husband to cause her distress, it's only your fault.

How do you do that? You needle your husband. What do you get back? You get a needle back. So therefore, you're taking the cause of happiness, and you're turning it into a cause of distress. It's your own fault.

Almost every man and every woman can get along happily in life.

Almost every man and every woman can get along happily in life. It's possible for a man to marry almost every one of 100,000 women or vice versa, and still live happily. It's because of the cussedness in human beings who seek out opportunities to be unhappy. And that's their own fault and not the fault of the great Shadchan. He makes expert *shidduchim.* But despite all of His good efforts, people ruin them.

Here is a perfect *shidduch.* But she is careless and willful. She is selfish and she fights with her *chassan;* a nice person, a *ben Torah*. Finally there's a *get.*

And now she married a second-rate fellow. Because she can't marry a first class fellow; she's a secondhand article, so she marries a second grade fellow.

And now she looks back, and she sees what she once had and she regrets it. And that story is repeated over and over again.

And the same is he. He gets a beautiful *kallah,* and he finds faults in her – the faults are all in him, not in her. And afterwards, when the divorce is accomplished, they look back and they see what they missed. Of course, they won't say that; each one says it's the fault of the other one. But that's a tragedy.

July 1979

Hishtadlus for Girls

Should a girl prepare for a date by making herself attractive, or should

she think that the one who's destined to her from Heaven will take her anyway?

Hashem promises you and if you win after all that effort, it's His promise that is being fulfilled.

A/ And the answer is that Hakadosh Baruch promised our Forefathers to give them Eretz Canaan; He promised them Eretz Yisroel. And he didn't give it to them unless they did their best to get it. What did they have to do? First of all, they had to cry out in Mitzrayim. They had to cry out from the bottom of their hearts in various expressions of pain: צְעָקָה נְאָקָה שַׁוְעָה זְעָקָה. They cried out in various ways.

Finally, it says that Hashem said, "I heard their outcries and I'll help them. And also I remembered My covenant with Avraham." All of a sudden, He absentmindedly reminds Himself? He remembers there's a covenant too?

The answer is that it *was* a covenant; and it was *some* covenant, a *bris bein hab'sarim.* It's a covenant! But you have to *activate* the covenant. Hakadosh Baruch Hu wants you to work very hard that the promise should come true. And finally, when He took them out of Mitzrayim and now they came to Eretz Canaan, what happened? Seven years of war. Seven years of war!

What do they have to fight for? It's a promise! The answer is, Hashem promises you and if you win after all that effort, it's His promise that is being fulfilled. Because a lot of people have tried more than seven years of war, and they ended up with failure.

And so here is a *bashert,* a beautiful and wealthy big *lamdan;* a young yeshiva man is waiting for you, and his name is written right next to yours on the invitation printed in Heaven. It says קוֹל שָׂשׂוֹן וְקוֹל שִׂמְחָה on the Heavenly invitation and your name is there and his name is there. But you'd better be energetic about it. Otherwise it will never be delivered to you. The postman will get mixed up on the way.

He's so innocent, he thinks you were born with those curls.

So by all means, in order to get him, you do whatever it takes.

You say, "He's a frum fellow; he doesn't care about hair."

He cares about hair! He's so innocent, he thinks you were born with those curls. He doesn't realize that it takes three hours to make the curls. So get busy and spend the three hours.

And the same is with everything else. Hakadosh Baruch Hu gives us promises but we have to work very hard so that the promises should come true.

December 1979

Divorcing Your Bashert

Q/ Is it possible for one to divorce his *bashert,* the one assigned to him by Hashem? And how would you know if you divorced the right party?

A/ The answer is that in this world, Hakadosh Baruch Hu doesn't reveal any secrets. And everybody has to treat the one that he has as if it's the right party. Sometimes because of ideological differences, let's say if the husband turned to the wrong path, *chas v'shalom,* and became a *rasha,* so certainly she has to go away from him. Or if the wife *chalilah* turns bad, then you have to divorce. But otherwise, everybody should consider his mate as the one that's foreordained, and do his best. If he suspects every now and then that he made an error, let him not let on. And in the next world he'll discover that even if he thought it was the wrong one, it was the right one. Because Hakadosh Baruch Hu tests everybody according to his abilities.

And therefore, when you marry somebody, *that one is the right one!* It's the *yetzer hara* who tells you otherwise. Hakadosh Baruch Hu knows what He's doing. That's your *zivug*, that's your *bashert.*

December 1982

It's up to a man to utilize the opportunities when the opportunities come

The Imperfect Bashert

Q/ Can a person pass up his *bashert*? I mean, is it possible for a person to let go of an opportunity for marriage that was ordained by Hashem?

A/ Now, that's a question that many people are confused about. Let's make it clear that it's up to you to use your free will. Hakadosh Baruch Hu is not going to interfere with the principle of *bechirah* just because He chooses a mate for you. Which means that many times, when a man was young and marriageable, he met a dozen *"basherts"* that he passed up on. Not just one; a dozen! In the olden days, if a man was wealthy enough, he could have married a whole dozen. Surely one you could have married.

But he let the years go by, and now he is much older and he cannot get the same young girls as before. And it's even a big question if he'll get a woman who is capable of childbearing. That man has surely passed up his *bashert.*

Later, he marries an elderly girl – maybe she's a nice girl, but she's too old to have many children. Now the truth is, she is also a *bashert;* it's not just one that is ordained for a man – a man can be ordained by a number of women. And therefore, it's up to a man to utilize the opportunities when the opportunities come; his free will makes him responsible for passing up opportunities.

Even a mean wife or a mean husband is better than no wife or no husband.

And while we are on the subject, I want to tell you that it's a tragedy for people to wait; nobody should postpone marriage even one more year. And in case he's passed the time when he can get a girl who is capable of having children, he should marry an elderly woman. He should marry an elderly woman! Be married! Don't be by yourself. That's why in decent Jewish communities in the olden days, it wasn't permitted. Every man had to have a mate and every woman was expected to be mated.

And any marriage, you should know, is better than no marriage. Even a mean wife or a mean husband is better than no wife or no husband. It's a tragic error to think otherwise; only that people are following the evil examples of the misguided masses and they look for divorce as an alternative. Divorce is not an alternative; the grave is a better alternative. Better to be married to someone you don't like than not to be married at all. I know it doesn't sound good today, but it's the plain truth.

And therefore, when we speak about *bashert*, don't be misled. Like somebody said, it's important to seek the right person in marriage, but it's even more important to *be* the right person. So when you're married, make up your mind, no matter who your mate is, the big question is who *you* are going to be.

When you get married, you have to be married through thick and thin, no matter what. You'll stick by your partner forever. You want to be buried side by side in the cemetery. And you'll go to the next world side by side.

You're not perfect, she's not perfect. She's not perfect, he's not perfect. Nobody is perfect in this world. And it's silly to aspire to perfection, to find the "perfect" mate. Of course, before you're married you can choose – and someday I might give a lecture on what to look for, *bli neder* – but once you're married, it's done, it's final, and you have to be loyal no matter what until the end of your days. Do the best you can. And for that, you'll get Olam Haba.

January 1986

Missing Your Bashert

Q/ If a person's *zivug* is announced *b'Shamayim* forty days before he is born, can a person marry another one who is not his predestined *zivug*? If so, what happens to the other one?

A/ Everybody gets an opportunity to marry his predestined *zivug,* but nobody is forced into it. She crosses his path during the eligible time.

Only, if he is a *feinshmecker,* and he is dreaming of an apparition that will come down from Mars, a princess, and actually his *bashert* has fat legs, so he takes one look at the legs and says, "Nothing doing," he lost her. If he doesn't bother seeing if she is an אִשָּׁה יִרְאַת ה' and that שֶׁקֶר הַחֵן וְהֶבֶל הַיֹּפִי, that it is all foolishness; if she is healthy – a person has to choose by health – then אִשָּׁה יִרְאַת ה' הִיא תִתְהַלָּל. Maybe she is the one.

I remember a case years ago; there was a woman who had a very unsightly face. A true story. And she was a model wife and a model mother. She stands out in my memory as one of the most successful women I ever knew. If her husband would have made the error of passing her up...

December 1983

She stands out in my memory as one of the most successful women I ever knew.

His eyes were poked out by the Plishtim because he followed his eyes.

My Bashert, My Choice

Q/ If a *zivug* is appointed by Hashem, why is it my fault if I married a girl and she's not so *tzanuah,* modest, and not so frum?

A/ The answer is this: The Gemara (*Moed Katan* 18b) says מִן הַתּוֹרָה וּמִן הַנְּבִיאִים וּמִן הַכְּתוּבִים מֵה' אִשָּׁה לְאִישׁ – *We learn from all of Tanach that a woman is destined a man from Hashem.* And the Gemara brings three *pesukim*.

One *pasuk* is in the case of Rivka. It says מֵה' יָצָא הַדָּבָר – the thing comes from Hashem (*Bereishis* 24:50). So we see a *shidduch* comes from Hashem.

In *Kesuvim* it says, בַּיִת וָהוֹן נַחֲלַת אָבוֹת – *Wealth you inherit from your parents,* וּמֵה' אִשָּׁה מַשְׂכָּלֶת – *but a wise woman is a gift from Hashem* (*Mishlei* 19:14).

Now what's the proof from the Nevi'im?

So the Gemara brings a proof that when Shimshon wanted to marry a Plishti woman, his parents remonstrated with him. They tried to stop him. But they didn't know, it says they didn't know כִּי מֵה' הִיא – *That it was from Hashem* (*Shoftim* 14:4). So it means that the *shidduch* with the Plishti woman was from Hashem.

The Plishti woman had converted, the Rambam tells us. She was a *giyores.* But Shimshon is criticized for taking her. That's why he lost his eyes at the end. His eyes were poked out by the Plishtim because he followed his eyes. Whatever that means has to be explained, but he wasn't praised for taking her.

So the question is this: If it is one of the three proofs that a *shidduch* is *me'Hashem,* why is Shimshon blamed for taking her?

And the answer is, sometimes a woman is decreed *min haShamayim* for a man just to test him. It's *me'Hashem* that he should run away from her. She's especially made to be a *michshol,* a test, a *nisayon* for him. Because when he takes a look at her, he should think, "Look, maybe she's not good enough for me; maybe she's not frum enough." When he finds out that there are *chisronos*, he shouldn't think "Just because she has a pretty face, therefore I'll overlook everything." No. That's his *bechirah* not to take it.

So we see, *me'Hashem* sometimes means *me'Hashem not* to take.

April 1983

Why should we blame anybody who marries a girl who is no good, or if a girl marries a boy who is not good?

A Test in Form of a Shidduch

Q/ If Hashem is the Shadchan – He's the Matchmaker and He's *mezaveg zivugim* – why should we blame anybody who marries a girl who is no good, or if a girl marries a boy who is not good?

A/ I'll paraphrase the question. Why do we blame people – let's say if a *kohen* marries a *grushah,* a divorcee – why blame him? Hashem is *mezaveg zivugim!* Or if Shimshon married Delila, why was he blamed?

Now let me explain what was explained here many times already. Hakadosh Baruch Hu is *mezaveg zivugim* for the purpose of man being able to accept or to refuse. He brings

It comes to you, but it doesn't mean you have to take it.

a *zivug* to you. It comes to you, but it doesn't mean you have to take it.

Sometimes, Hashem sends the wrong person to him to test him. Like Shimshon was tested and he said, אוֹתָהּ קַח לִי – *Take her for me,* כִּי הִיא יָשְׁרָה בְעֵינָי – *because she's good in my eyes* (*Shoftim* 14:3). He failed the test. Hashem sent her to test Shimshon. He wasn't supposed to take her.

Sometimes it's the other way around. Sometimes a man turned down the right *zivug* because her nose was just a little bit too long or some other blemish that he thought was a blemish and he lost his great opportunity. Hashem was *mezaveg zivugim* – only that this picky man didn't accept it.

And therefore, *mezaveg zivugim* doesn't mean that Hashem makes shotgun weddings – He doesn't say, "You must marry." He gives you opportunities to marry. Therefore, if people marry correctly, if they obey the instinct that He put into them and they take the opportunity, then they are happy that Hashem gave them the right one.

Now study that, and understand that when a man marries a forbidden woman, they're *chayav malkus*. They have to give a *get* right away because Hashem is *mezaveg* only kosher *zivugim*. And if a person did make a wrong *zivug,* it means he was offered the opportunity to be tested and he failed the test.

September 1987

Heaven and Hishtadlus

Q/ If a person's future wife is ordained in Heaven, then how is it up to us to choose her?

A/ This question was asked many times, the same question: If matches are made in Heaven, how can anybody choose or attempt to choose in this world?

The answer is, matches are made in Heaven on the basis of your good sense. The Gemara is full of advice on how to marry. The Gemara that says matches are made in Heaven – that same Gemara warns you, don't marry this kind of a woman or this kind of a man, find out who her brother is. The Gemara tells you whom to marry, whom not to marry.

The answer is, matches are made in Heaven on the basis of your good sense.

So we see that although marriages are made in Heaven, it means: Once you've married the right one, that's made in Heaven. If you marry the wrong one, it's also made in Heaven; but it's made to persecute you and punish you for your carelessness.

So a fellow who marries because of her perfume, he's going to suffer for years and years up to the divorce court. And his nervous breakdown and all of his *tzaros*, that's made in Heaven.

So what's made in Heaven is made in conjunction with the way we're going to behave with our free will.

August 1981

Made in Heaven, Destroyed on Earth

Q/ We believe that *shidduchim* are made in Heaven; so what's the principle in the Gemara that you have to hurry up to find something good because שֶׁמָּא יְקַדְּמֶנּוּ אַחֵר – maybe somebody else might snatch the opportunity away from you (*Moed Katan* 18b). If it's ordained, it's ordained; what's there to worry about?

He said, "I'm going to divorce you, I want to divorce you." Finally she took the hint and she left him.

A/ This is an old question that is asked here constantly. And the answer is that when it comes to marriage, to a *bashert*, it's ordained that you should have the opportunity. But you could lose the opportunity – in a couple of ways.

One way is if a nice frum girl, a decent girl, comes along, but it just happens that her nose is a fraction of an inch too long and you say no, so you lose the opportunity. Hakadosh Baruch Hu is not going to make a wedding at the point of a gun. He brought the *kallah* to you. You saw her, you rejected her – it's your hard luck. That's one way of losing out on what's *bashert.*

Another way is, if you're already married to the nice girl, but you are so silly that you constantly tell her that you don't like her. If you're a *meshugene*, you tell her that girls in the street are prettier than she is. Or you're crazy enough to bring up the word divorce. Sometimes you'll say, "I want to divorce you."

There was a man – a yeshiva man – who said it constantly to his wife. Constantly, he said, "I'm going to divorce you, I want to divorce you." Finally she took the hint and she left him. She left him.

And he ran around to all the *roshei yeshiva,* all the *rabbanim,* asking them to intercede and to beg his wife to take him back, but she was so accustomed to the idea that he dinned into her ears for years; he'd been telling her for years that he wanted to divorce her, so finally she took it seriously. So he lost out on the girl that was *bashert*.

So now you have two ways. One is not to take the right girl, and second is, once you have her, you lose her.

Now don't say, it's *bashert* that you shouldn't have her. Nobody should say, מִפִּי עֶלְיוֹן לֹא תֵצֵא הָרָעוֹת וְהַטּוֹב (*Eicha* 3:38). Don't say that. Don't say that all those things that happened are only a *gezeiras Hashem.* מִיֶּדְכֶם הָיְתָה זֹּאת לָכֶם

– *It's your own fault* (*Malachi* 1:9). You didn't live properly – you couldn't keep a good wife, so you lost what was ordained in Heaven. Marriages are made in Heaven, but they're destroyed down here on Earth.

September 1984

The boy doesn't know anything about her character. He just sees a nose

Love at First Sight

Q/ Is it true that when the right one comes along, it will be love at first sight?

A/ It's definitely not true. You have to know that Hakadosh Baruch Hu has prepared wrong ones too. And many times, the wrong one comes along first. So you have to make sure it will be love at first sight and second sight and third sight. And the truth is that it shouldn't be your sight you're relying on. The best way to look at your future *kallah* is through the eyes of your mother or your aunt. As your aunt looks at the *kallah*, she sees *her*. You don't see her; you see her hair, all puffed up. But your mother and your aunt see the *kallah*. And that's very important.

And that's why in the olden days, the women used to make the *shidduchim*. They knew this and this girl; that's the right one. They knew her character. But the boy doesn't know anything about her character. He just sees a nose, he sees the painted eyelashes, he sees the paint on the lips, and he is captured! And therefore, the first sight is meaningless.

September 1986

He has to pray that he should find a wife, but it means more than that; he also has to pray to find the right one.

Praying for a Shidduch

Q/ Should I daven to find my *bashert,* or since it's *bashert,* I should just wait?

A/ In *Maseches Brachos* (8a), the Gemara quotes a certain counsel that was given in Tehillim (32:6) as follows: עַל זֹאת יִתְפַּלֵּל כָּל חָסִיד אֵלֶיךָ לְעֵת מְצוֹא – *For this following thing every person who is devoted to Hashem should pray to You,* לְעֵת מְצוֹא – *in their time of finding.*

Now, although he explains that we should pray, he doesn't tell us clearly what to pray for. He only says, רַק לְשֵׁטֶף מַיִם רַבִּים אֵלָיו לֹא יַגִּיעוּ – *he should pray that when there comes a torrent of mighty waters, they should not overtake him.* However, *what* he has to pray about, we're not told. What are the mighty waters?

And on this, the Gemara gives a number of explanations. It doesn't mean that they're conflicting opinions; they're all true. And the first one is אָמַר רַבִּי חֲנִינָא – Rabbi Chanina says, what does it mean you should pray *l'eis metzo,* when it's time to find? לְעֵת מְצוֹא אִשָּׁה – *when it's time to find a wife,* for this he has to pray.

Now we understand that it means, first of all, that he has to pray that he should find a wife, but it means more than that; he also has to pray to find the right one. Any *chassid,* anyone who's devoted to Hashem, should pray to Hashem to find the right one.

And when we say a *chassid* has to pray for that, we also understand that a *chassidah* also has to pray for that. She also has to be *mispallel* to *Hashem* that she should find the right one.

And when it states *al zos,* it means for *this especially.* Because actually, you must pray for everything. Even if you're

Men and women, boys and girls have to pray to Hashem

going out shopping for a pair of shoes, it's proper to pray that she should get the right kind. If they're too small, then you're going to have a great deal of discomfort and then maybe you won't be able to wear them after a while. Sometimes the wrong shoes can bring on headaches. Sometimes the wrong shoes can cause someone to have trouble on his feet, complications that are far removed from the site of the feet.

And so whatever you do, it pays to pray to Hakadosh Baruch Hu to help you. When the time comes to find, which means as soon as he begins to reach the years when you must be serious, then men and women, boys and girls have to pray to Hakadosh Baruch Hu if you are a *chassid;* if you have some connection with *yiras Hashem*, with *bitachon*, with *emunah*, then you shouldn't merely rely on your own efforts.

And it's not only a demonstration that you have *emunah*, that you know that the affairs of this world are in the hands of Hakadosh Baruch Hu, but it helps too. וְהַנְיָא בְעוּתָא – *Tefillah helps* (*Akdamus*, Shavuos). It's important to keep in mind, if you wish to succeed in anything from the biggest to the smallest things, it pays to turn to Hakadosh Baruch Hu for help. But עַל זאת, for this especially you should pray. That's what it means עַל זאת – for this; it means for this *especially*.

So therefore, all of you unmarried men and girls – and of course, if you're married already, you have to pray that it should be the best that it could be; you have to make the best of what you have. But the unmarried ones are urged to turn to Hakadosh Baruch Hu and to put in time; it pays to invest time in *tefillah*.

Before you walk back the three steps in *Shemoneh Esrei,* after you said the יִהְיוּ לְרָצוֹן, put in a request for this. And you could do it in the middle of the day too. And especially when you're going to meet a prospect, certainly put in a *tefillah* that if it's not the right one, she should turn you down.

Ask Hakadosh Baruch Hu to guard your footsteps only towards the one that He chooses for you. They

Don't spare your tefillos; don't be stingy. Put in a lot of words. It's very important,

shouldn't think that things will just happen, merely to say it's preordained, it's *bashert* and whatever will happen, that's what's going to be good for me. The Gemara says, no, you should pray. Because it could be that what's ordained for you, is not for your good. It could be Hakadosh Baruch Hu has prepared a young lady who is going to cause you to have Gan Eden because all of your sins will be atoned in this world! It could be very good for you. But if you mean to have both worlds, you have to get busy and pray to Hakadosh Baruch Hu.

And also you girls. And don't spare your *tefillos;* don't be stingy. Put in a lot of words. It's *very* important, that's why it says *al zos. Zos* is a *miut*, it excludes many other things. It means this more than other things. So put in *koach*, put in a good deal of effort when you're asking for this. And if it's accompanied by some tears, it's still better. Men and women can weep when they pray for their right one. Better weep now than later!

February 1976

QUESTIONS *On Any* SUBJECT

Chapter 16
Inside Marriage

Chapter Sponsor

Dedicated with Love & Honor
to my Eshet Hayil & Matriarch of our family,

Adrienne - Chana Shalom

She has dedicated her life to ensuring we live happily according to the principles of a Jewish Marriage.

May Hashem Bless her with continued energy & exuberance in all her endeavors.

Contents

Chapter 16

Inside Marriage

Her Appearance

Q/ Why should a Jewish woman attempt to look beautiful for her husband?

A/ Now the question is, why did he marry her? Because she is proficient in *Chovos Halevavos*? Because she knows *Choshen Mishpat*? He married her because she's a woman. Never forget that fact.

Of course he wants a frum woman with a good character. Of course he wants a woman who will be a mother to his children. He wants many things. But suppose she decides she stops being a woman; let's say she'll have an operation that will make her something, not a woman. Goodbye! He shows her the door. Marriage is based on the fact that he is a man and she is a woman. And therefore, it's of the utmost importance for a woman to always make it her business to encourage her husband to like her as a woman.

That's why the Gemara says that in the *midbar* when the *mann* used to fall every day, cosmetics fell with the *mann*. It's a remarkable statement! Cosmetics fell with the *mann*. You never heard that before? Cosmetics! The answer is that cosmetics are vital. Forty years in the *midbar* the women won't have an

She has to make it her business to be presentable to her husband.

opportunity to find favor in the eyes of their husbands? It can't be. That's the *midrash* – cosmetics fell with the *mann.*

You know, Ezra Hasofer made great *takanos.* And when he made *takanos,* he didn't deal with small picayune things. He dealt with very great subjects. He was bringing people back to Eretz Yisroel. He was rebuilding a nation. He was busy with big things. Now, among his *takanos*, one that's recorded is a *takanah* that peddlers of cosmetics for women should visit every town once a week. It was a *takanas Ezra!* At least once a week, every Jewish town should be visited by a peddler selling women's cosmetics.

Now, Ezra had no other business than that? Ezra was busy with *muktzeh*. He was busy with *Shemoneh Esrei*, being *mesakein Shemoneh Esrei*. He was busy with all the *takanos* from *Anshei Knesses Hagedolah,* great *takanos* that were forever and ever; he should be busy with a *takanah* about cosmetics?!

Yes! This is also important.

And so, we learn how necessary it is for a woman to always keep in mind, until her last day, as long as she has a husband, that she has to make it her business to be presentable to her husband. I cannot overemphasize this subject. I know there are righteous women who think that with their *tzidkus* alone they deserve to be respected, and they are right. They deserve to be respected and Hakadosh Baruch Hu should give them great reward for all their good deeds. And still they must realize that one of their good deeds is to be *gomel chesed* and to make a great impression on their husbands.

That's why I always say, if you like mopping the floor – some women love to get on their knees and mop the floor; to wash the floor and scrub it – don't do it when your husband is home. When he's away and you're sure he won't come home soon, then you can do these things. When you know he's coming home, put on a *sheitel* and give a dab on each cheek and try to look nice. It's a mitzvah and you get Olam Haba for it, besides all the other benefits in this world.

June 1984

Of course a husband must make himself acceptable, and it's a responsibility of his.

His Appearance

Q/ The Rav has spoken often about the responsibility of a wife to make herself look good and make sure to be presentable in front of her husband. What about the husband's duties towards his wife? Does he have to dress the same way?

A/ The question is: Does the husband have a responsibility to make a favorable impression on his wife? Yes, of course. But there is no question that the wife's responsibility is much bigger. Much bigger. And that is self-understood and it doesn't need any commentaries.

Of course a husband must make himself acceptable, and it's a responsibility of his. The Gemara says that if a woman comes before a *beis din* and says מָאוּס עָלַי – "I can't stand this man," it means something. If she says, "He's disgusting to me," *beis din* takes that into account. מָאוּס עָלַי is a *ta'anah,* it's a claim. So therefore, the husband should make sure that he's not disgusting in her eyes. That's a responsibility of his. No question about it.

However, it's of the utmost importance for a woman to be attractive to her husband at all times. That's one of the most important forms of the marriage bond. A man is not married to a man – he's married to a woman. And therefore, she has to emphasize her womanliness in the role of marriage.

Now, I won't go into details but this is a self-understood axiom and therefore, although everybody should make themselves acceptable – not only husbands and wives – but

"Keep your mouth closed and smell good."

a wife, more than anyone else must feel that obligation at all times and never be negligent. A husband to a certain extent must also be careful. And to a certain extent, everyone must make sure to make himself acceptable to his fellow man.

December 1988

Making an Effort

Q/ What should a wife do if her husband is never happy and satisfied with her?

A/ So, I'll turn back the pages of my old book and I'll repeat some advice. First of all, she should fulfill the sage advice that I said here years ago: "Keep your mouth closed and smell good."

I once met a man – he gave me a lift in his car. He was riding with his wife and he gave me a lift. "You know," he said, "My wife once heard you speak – when you gave that advice – and she's fulfilling fifty percent of that."

Now, if people would only follow the dictates of common sense – women have to know that it's important to put up a good appearance. Women should spend time on their appearance, that's number one. And secondly, they should keep their mouths closed as much as possible.

Now, if a husband is not satisfied despite that, you should know that he is a native crank and nothing will help. And so, you'll have to live out your life and bear it. You'll get Olam Haba for tolerating him.

But I don't believe that this will be the result. I'm sure if one party makes a big effort, then the other party will respond. It's only because two parties engage in the quarrel – it always takes two to make a *machlokes*. And if one makes a real concerted effort, then it's certain that the other party will be influenced.

September 1984

Follow the Leader 1

Q/ When the Torah (*Bereishis* 3:16) says about a wife וְהוּא יִמְשָׁל בָּךְ, that the husband should rule over her, does it mean a woman has to listen to her husband?

A/ The answer is yes, certainly. A woman should listen to her husband.

Let's say you're on a boat on the high seas. You're an officer; you're the first mate. So when the captain gives an order, the first mate can say, "Maybe we should do something else." And the captain pays attention to that because maybe he's wrong. So he must consider the first mate's advice. But suppose the captain listens but then he says, "No, that's my decision." Then the mate can't go against the captain's decision.

So a wife can tell her husband, "Maybe it's not right." But suppose the husband says, "This is my opinion," the wife should go along. You cannot have two captains on one boat. It's out of the question. A family is an organization with a special system. The captain is steering the boat.

A family is an organization with a special system. The captain is steering the boat.

Of course, sometimes the captain has mutinied himself. If he became, let's say, not a *shomer mitzvos,* then the wife takes over. But as long as the captain retains his authority as a captain, as long as he behaves like a captain, then the first mate cannot make a mutiny against the captain.

There has to be one captain. But the captain has to realize that there is a mate also, the first mate.

And so, there's no question about it, that the leadership of the house must be in the hands of the husband.

September 1995di

Follow the Leader 2

Q/ So what do you say about the Orthodox women who disregard this principle of the husband being the "leader"?

A/ And the answer is, it's certainly wrong. אִישָׁה כְּשֵׁרָה עוֹשָׂה רְצוֹן בַּעְלָהּ – *A kosher woman tries to make her husband happy, to do the will of her husband.*

However, you have to know that there are certain conditions for וְהוּא יִמְשָׁל בָּךְ. There are conditions to be a *moshel*. Merely to be born with pants doesn't mean that you're already accredited as a ruler. There have to be certain qualities.

So first of all, you have to bring in the *parnassah*. You have to bring *parnassah* in. If a man sits home and he says, "I'm a writer; I'm a poet. I'm waiting for something to come in," he has no business being at home. He belongs somewhere in a dump in Greenwich Village and he should scratch himself from his lice, and that's all. He's a bum. In addition, he has certain duties towards his wife too besides *parnassah*.

Certainly, if a husband is a Jew who keeps Judaism and a Jew who tries to be decent and make a living, and more or less behaves like a man should behave, it's certainly the obligation of a wife to feel that she is not the boss.

There are no two captains on a ship because then, the only way to get going is to chop the ship in half and to move in different directions. There has to be one captain. But the captain has to realize that there is a mate also, the first mate.

Like it says in the *sefer Shevet Mussar.* The *Shevet Mussar* speaks to the women. He says, "You want to be a queen? Make your husband a king. But if you try to make him a slave, he'll make you a *shifcha*."

I'll repeat that from *Shevet Mussar.* If you want to be a queen, make your husband a king, but if you try to make him a slave, it means you belittle him and say, "I never saw such a low fellow like you; you're the worst fellow there is," then he's going to make you the worst also.

In the good old days, the father used the club to give his son a good beating.

Therefore, there's a certain amount of exchange in this responsibility. He is *moshel* and she is the one who follows, but together they have to respect each other's rights.

December 1978

Following Nature

Q/ How can you so flippantly hand over the leadership of the family to the husband and the father? Doesn't leadership depend on certain abilities?

A/ And the answer is, if you're going to take an entrance examination in every instance to determine who is going to be the leader in the family, then it will never work. Because, first of all, you don't have enough offices and enough examiners.

Secondly, you have to make an institution that agrees with nature; not an artificial thing. And in nature, the father is chosen as the leader. When I say nature, I mean nature with a capital N. I mean Hakadosh Baruch Hu. Because you see, the fact is that all over the world, that has been the case. All over the world – whether it's among the black people or the Eskimos – wherever you go, the case is that the father is the leader.

Hashem set up that system, a system that's ordained for the happiness of mankind.

And it's common sense too, because he has more physical force. Sometimes he has to fight with his son. In the good old days, the father used the club to give his son a good beating. And the father was the one who was best able to do it. The mother has a softer heart, and physically the father is better suited for the job. And therefore, it's impossible to wait until we have an examination to see who is more suited for leadership.

This much I can tell you, however. In those families where the father is not suited for leadership, it automatically is abdicated to the mother. And everybody knows that this is how it was in all Jewish families. Even in Europe, there were women who were *beryos*, women who wore the pants – not literally – no woman wore pants there. But she carried on the business of the house. Because it happened many times that the woman was more capable, and the father quietly allowed it. Sometimes it wasn't so quietly, but whatever it was, nature followed its course.

But in most cases, it's the father who is the leader. Even when the mother was more capable, it paid for her to assign to the father a nominal role as the head of the family. It paid for her.

And she used her abilities to tell the children, "Children, listen to what Father said." Because Hashem set up that system, a system that's ordained for the happiness of mankind. But if you're going to have competition, the end will be a marriage that will go on the rocks.

Don't believe what the magazines, the newspapers, tell you. They quote like this: "I," this businesswoman says, "I am completely liberated, and still, our marriage is successful." *A nechtiger tohg*. It's impossible. It just cannot be! And therefore I would advise any young man who's contemplating marriage to make sure that his prospective bride doesn't have any ideas of feminism. If she thinks of being a careerist, if she dreams of equality, then you should look elsewhere. Because the marriage is certainly going to be ruined.

It need not be slavery. A woman has to be well treated. It's important! אוֹקִירוּ לִנְשַׁיְכוּ – *Give honor to your wives.* And Hakadosh Baruch Hu gives a blessing to a man for that: כִּי הֵיכִי דְּתִתְעַתְּרוּ – *In order that you should become wealthy* (*Bava Metzia* 59a). You'll get rich for that. But it's on the condition that the wife understands her role in the family. And anybody who tries to make an artificial rearrangement is going to discover that the experiment is not going to work.

January 1978

Even among the gentiles up until recently, a woman promised to honor and obey her husband.

Mutual Respect

Q/ When you spoke before about how a man has to honor the wife, you said it's not mentioned in the *seforim* so much about the obligation of a wife to honor her husband. Why not?

A/ We don't speak so much about the obligation of a wife to honor her husband because this was an axiom, it was self-understood. *L'havdil*, even among the gentiles up until recently, a woman promised to honor and obey her husband. Later they became wise alecks and they erased it from the gentile wedding ceremony. So even gentiles understood that a woman must honor and obey her husband.

L'havdil, among Jews there was no question. Every woman considered the husband the leader of the family. She had great awe of her husband. There was no question about that. In ancient times, every husband had a beard and no wife

What does it mean that a man is obligated to love his wife like he loves himself?

had a beard. And therefore, the husbands were recognized by the act of Hashem. That's why the beard grows – to show he is the one who has the authority.

And she has to respect him. He's a leader. He's a leader in Torah. He's the Kohen Gadol of the family; he makes *kiddush* and he leads them in all the *avodas Hashem*. Certainly. It was always understood; it was axiomatic.

But the respect of a husband to a wife could be easily overlooked. He can think, his wife doesn't wear a black hat, she doesn't have a beard, and therefore, he might make the great error of being careless in his responsibility which he undertook at the time of the *kesubah.* And so he has to be reminded constantly.

And it's of the greatest importance always, always, *always,* to work on that because the opportunity for honoring one's wife is something that happens so many times in your daily life that it can add up to the biggest merit or *chalilah,* the biggest demerit.

June 1989

To Love and to Honor

Q/ What does it mean that a man is obligated to אוֹהֵב אֶת אִשְׁתּוֹ כְּגוּפוֹ – *To love his wife like he loves himself* (*Yevamos* 62b)?

A/ He should love his wife like his own body means that since he wants comfort, he should be concerned about his wife's comfort too. A man shouldn't sit in the car, let's say the weather is icy, and send his wife out to do something in the store, on the icy sidewalk. If it's icy, he might as well do it himself.

I knew a man who called his wife from the synagogue one morning shortly after his marriage; she was pregnant already, and it was slippery outside, the sidewalks were icy. He called her up, "Please Sara, bring me my umbrella."

I heard about this and I was amazed at the arrogance! A pregnant wife should go outside on the slippery sidewalks to bring him his umbrella? He's sitting in the synagogue waiting for the umbrella!

I don't like that the husbands sit at the table and shout to the kitchen, "Bring this, bring that." Or "Sara, a little more sugar, please, a little more of this." A monarch sits at the table and gives orders! Get up and bring it yourself! You have two good feet! What are you, a cripple? Get up, you lazy fellow! And do it yourself!

I don't like that the husbands sit at the table and shout to the kitchen, "Bring this, bring that."

So אוֹהֵב אֶת אִשְׁתּוֹ כְּגוּפוֹ means, when it comes to consideration for his body, for his wife he has to have the same consideration. Because there's a tendency in a lot of men to make their wives servants. They give them lowly things to do that they wouldn't do themselves.

And then it says וּמְכַבְּדָהּ יוֹתֵר מִגּוּפוֹ, that he should honor her *more* than his body. When it comes to honor, he should give her more honor than he gives himself. Now that needs a lot of explaining, but the words already say a lot in itself: אוֹהֵב אֶת אִשְׁתּוֹ כְּגוּפוֹ וּמְכַבְּדָהּ יוֹתֵר מִגּוּפוֹ.

January 1977

Affection in Public

Is it proper for a frum couple to hold arms or hands on the street?

And the answer is no and no.

Just like his wife makes supper every day, every week he puts down a minimum sum.

A man should always seek opportunities in private to show his wife that he appreciates her. He shouldn't neglect these opportunities. Let your wife know, even many years after your marriage, that you still feel that you made the right step.

Of course, you should never tell her you made an error. All your life, maintain the impression that you're fortunate. And you are, because the truth is that it's *min haShamayim*. Hakadosh Baruch Hu sent you the right one for you, no matter what you think.

But that's only in private – in public you should avoid any signs of affection. And let me add, even with affectionate words, you have to beware. Of course you have to speak respectfully to your wife always, but beware of special words that signify more than ordinary relations that you have with other people. In the presence of other people, don't show any special affection.

June 1979

Money Matters

Q/ Should a woman submit to her husband's system of doling out money to her as she needs it?

Now the answer to this depends on the circumstances. In general it is not advisable, it is not desirable, that she should have to come to him for every dollar or every five dollars. Because he could use that as a form of pressure and whenever he is in a crabby mood, he could be very oppressive.

The minimum, to my way of thinking at least, is to assign a certain amount agreed on between both parties to be given at the beginning of each week like clockwork. This should not depend on moods. This should not depend on anything. Just like his wife makes supper every day, every week he puts down a minimum sum.

Now, there are a lot of families that operate on the system that the husband brings all his earnings home and puts them in a drawer and it's available for the wife. She puts some in the bank and she takes whatever she needs for the house. In many cases, that is even an encouragement, a stimulus, for her to save money since she knows it's up to her; whereas if she gets a certain allotment every week she might make it her business to spend it entirely.

Whatever it is, I personally disapprove of the system of handing out one-and five-dollar bills and forcing the wife to come as a petitioner for every small thing whenever she needs funds.

December 1973

A Husband's Housework

Q/ What do you say about a husband doing housework chores in the house?

How much should a husband contribute to helping out in the family?

A/ How much should a husband contribute to helping out in the family?

This depends on the circumstances. A token contribution of work he surely must do. It's not a bad idea to show the children an example and wash at least one of your own dishes. Not a bad idea. Now, some husbands will faint when they hear that; they think it's beneath their dignity, so that's why I'm not going to say how much he must do – it depends on the situation. But something should be done to help out in the house.

What should a person do if his wife is busy with the children and doesn't cook, and she tells him to buy food?

There are husbands who wash all their own dishes. There are people like that. Now, I don't say that all wives appreciate that. Some refuse to let their husband do anything, but when a woman is loaded down with housework and the children are bothering, it certainly is a token of *gemilas chasadim* to help out. And there are a lot of ways that a husband can help.

When a husband relegates all the work in the house to his wife, it's not a fair division of labor. He says, "I work all day long and you do all the housework and bother with the children." No, that's wrong.

Now, there are many things he cannot do. She's more capable of dealing with children. She's more capable of dealing with the household things, but at least a token, a sign of encouragement; a little bit the husband should do.

Maybe he should do a lot, but that depends on the circumstances. And in order not to step on anybody's toes, I'm not going to specify what you should do.

April 1977

Takeout Dinners

Q/ What should a person do if his wife is busy with the children and doesn't cook, and she tells him to buy food?

A/ Well, in a certain sense, it's a lucky break. There is so much good food to buy, gourmet things you can buy. So go outside and buy and enjoy life. If you bring it home, then she'll be jealous of you.

Of course, don't eat things that are not clean, that are not sanitary. Find a place where the people can be trusted that they don't put their hands into the food and make sure you choose the right kind of diet. A person can live very happily on outside food.

January 1999

Women are a little wild. And every man is a little meshuga. Men are meshuga.

Fixing Yourself

Q/ How should a husband encourage his wife to change her bad *middos*?

A/ First, he should change his *middos*. That's the first thing. You should know that in most cases, he's the one who has the bad *middos*. In most cases, that is the truth. He has bad *middos*. Otherwise, he would see that his wife is pretty good. She's really pretty good.

Look, every wife is a little wild, you know. Women are a little wild. And every man is a little *meshuga*. Men are *meshuga*. So men and women both have faults. And therefore, don't concentrate on her faults. Concentrate on *your* faults.

I guarantee you that if the husband works on himself and becomes a man of better character, then automatically she'll be better too. Automatically.

April 1999

Fixing Your Spouse

Q/ How does one encourage a husband without becoming just an ordinary nag?

What should a person do if his wife doesn't want him to grow a beard?

A/ And the answer is that חַכְמוֹת נָשִׁים בָּנְתָה בֵיתָהּ – *It is the wisdom of a woman that builds up her house* (*Mishlei* 14:1). Now, that's not an easy answer because you have to learn how to do it. You have to plan what you want to say. Sometimes you feel that you must say something on the spur of the moment. Don't! Wait until you can say it with cunning. And many times, you'll accomplish what you wouldn't have accomplished otherwise.

Sometimes you might want your husband to go out and learn in the *beis hamedrash* at night and he's sitting with his feet up at the table reading a newspaper. That's how he's wasting his evenings. So you have to wait for an opportunity, and then you let pass a remark, "What a nice neighbor, Mr. Cohen next door. I see he's such a fine man; every night he goes out to learn in the *beis hamedrash.*" That's all; don't say any more than that. Just let those words sink in a little bit.

I'll give you another suggestion as well. Sometimes, when your husband does do one good thing, go out of your way to praise him. And that way, you'll give him incentive to do it again.

Whatever it is, you'll have to find tactful ways because the frontal attack usually doesn't succeed and it only causes irritation.

August 1979

Influencing Your Wife

Q/ The Chofetz Chaim wrote a *kuntres* about the prohibition of shaving, and other *gedolim* also wrote about the importance of growing a beard. What should a person do if his wife is not so happy about the idea?

A/ What should a person do if his wife doesn't want him to grow a beard? So, if he can afford a diamond ring, he should invest the money. And if he can't, it's possible little by little, with diplomacy, to convince her that a beard is a good thing. All things need diplomacy, and if you do it with *chachmah,* then I'm sure that in the course of time, you'll be able to win out.

A beard doesn't take away the beauty of the face; on the contrary, a male face is much more attractive when it has a beard.

Now, in the yeshivos in Lithuania before World War Two, nobody had a beard. That's a fact. Only the *kollel* people had beards. But the *bochurim*, even the old *bochurim* – nobody had a beard. Even in the American yeshivos, once upon a time, even the good yeshivos, nobody wore a beard. It was only later on, when the *chassidish* element came to this country more and more, that it had a very big influence and people began growing beards as a result.

Now, you have to understand that *hadras ponim*, the beauty of a Jewish face, is enhanced by a beard. A beard doesn't take away the beauty of the face; on the contrary, a male face is much more attractive when it has a beard. It's like a woman's hair. A woman without hair on her head, a bald-headed woman; she's not attractive. A Jew without a beard on his face is not attractive.

However, not always is it possible to do it. You might have to be patient. And if you're really interested in having a beard, you can consult somebody more capable of giving advice, and little by little, there are ways of winning her over.

Some people, for certain reasons, don't grow their beards. Maybe they think that there are certain places, certain situations, where they'll have more influence without a beard. And therefore, if it's *l'sheim Shamayim*, it could be that it's the proper thing to do.

It's a tragedy of tragedies when people look back after they get divorced and they try to justify their bad behavior to each other.

But anything that you want of your wife, first of all, דְּבַר תּוֹרָה מָעוֹת קוֹנוֹת – *Money and gifts always accomplish Torah results* (see *Eiruvin* 81b). Try it. Maybe you'll succeed.

May 1998

Influencing Your Husband

Q/ What should a wife do if she has some complaints against her husband?

A/ The first thing she should do is write them down on a slip of paper. And then she should take the paper and tear it up. Because in most cases, the complaints are not valid. And the same is for a husband who has complaints. In most cases, it's a transgression against the principle of being שָׂמֵחַ בְּחֶלְקוֹ, of being happy with your portion in life. If you're fortunate enough to be married, then you should appreciate it.

It's a tragedy of tragedies when people look back after they get divorced and they try to justify their bad behavior to each other. He says she was no good and she says he was no good. And really, the truth is that it was a lack of שָׂמֵחַ בְּחֶלְקוֹ.

When you get married, make up your mind that you will get the most happiness out of married life that you can get. Now, the most happiness doesn't mean traveling or doing things. Just being married; that's what we're talking about here! Appreciating the fact that you have a husband. Of course, he has to be a man who works. If he's a loafer you shouldn't have married him. But if he's a man who works and she's a housewife who's willing to do her duties, then you should be very happy with your choice.

Here's a man who is married and he's constantly calling me up, asking me; he wants to reconsider – "Did I do right?" he asks me. What's wrong with his wife? Nothing. Nothing at all! But he's always thinking maybe he could have gotten better. Now, that man is living a very sinful type of life. He should be spending his time considering how fortunate he is! His wife is normal! You know, it happens sometimes that a man marries a woman and then he finds out subsequently that she has a serious illness. I know a man who married, and later he discovered she was an epileptic. Now you can live with an epileptic, but he would have been better without an epileptic.

If your husband goes out to work, if he functions, then it's a great happiness for a wife.

So if your wife is not epileptic, if your wife is not insane, and she functions, then you are a happy man. If she does housework, you should be happy. And if your husband goes out to work, if he functions, then it's a great happiness for a wife. And any complaints, from this one or that one, is nothing but a lack of appreciation – it means that you're lacking in the *middah* of שָׂמֵחַ בְּחֶלְקוֹ.

August 1984

Lifelong Partners

Q/ If Hashem created a passion between a husband and wife for the purpose of them having children, why does that attraction continue even after there is no longer that purpose, like when they're older?

A/ Why does the attraction between husband and wife continue even after they have children?

The answer is Hakadosh Baruch Hu needs that union.

It's never easy to get along with somebody; it always requires a certain exertion of the soul.

First of all, it is of utmost importance that a family should continue even after children grow up and leave the house, because they have to look to their parents for guidance. And it's the two parents together that form the leadership of the family. We cannot estimate the value of an old grandfather and old grandmother. Inestimable value! It's an anchor for the entire family.

The children have to live their own lives and they may do irresponsible things, but always in the back of their mind they think, "What will Abba say? What will Ima say?"

The fact that the father and mother are still around together causes a certain control over the behavior of the children. Very important. Very important!

They give structure and guidance – older children lean on their father and mother for advice – besides for consolation and support. And therefore, because it's so important that the father and mother should remain together, Hakadosh Baruch Hu causes the attraction between husband and wife to continue always down to the end in order to preserve the family.

However, we should not overlook the fact that the union of husband and wife is tremendous *tikkun* for themselves. Every additional day that you live together successfully means that much more perfection of character.

It's never easy to get along with somebody; it always requires a certain exertion of the soul. And therefore, Hakadosh Baruch Hu says, don't think you're finished with the *tikkun* by merely raising a family. The *tikkun* of yourself is extremely important. And therefore, the fact that they're together forces them to continue to adjust to each other down to the last day.

Old people also, each one has his idiosyncrasies. Each one has his foolishness, has his *middos*, his *kaas,* his selfish ideas, and nevertheless, they force themselves to live together. A very great *tikkun*.

And sometimes it's even more important what they accomplish, two old people living together successfully in their last days, more than they ever accomplished in their character all the days of their lives. Like it says טוֹב אַחֲרִית דָּבָר מֵרֵאשִׁיתוֹ – *The way you end your life is more important than the way you begin your life* (*Koheles* 7:8). Sometimes you begin your life with discord, with arguing, constant recrimination. But near the end of your life, you learn how to keep your mouth closed, you learn how to be tolerant to the other person's idiosyncrasies. You learn how to take it. You swing with the punch. In your last days, you can achieve more in perfection of character than you did all of your life. We shouldn't waste those last days.

Living together successfully is a very great achievement.

People think an old man and old woman living together in a house, what are they doing? Their children are out of the house.

They're doing great things. Living together successfully is a very great achievement. Sometimes they were fighting for years and years; fighting, insulting each other. Now they're wiser and more careful. Now they're becoming more perfect in character and they're ending their days in *shleimus hanefesh,* in perfection. That's the very best way to finish off your life.

July 1990

QUESTIONS
On Any
SUBJECT

Chapter 17

The World of In-Laws

Chapter Sponsor

For Beracha and Hatzlacha of our family:

Abud, Nancy, Jonathan David and Alexander

Zury and Fortune Attie
Mexico

Contents

Chapter 17

The World of In-Laws

Your Wife is First 1

Q/ When a husband and wife get married, do their relationships with their parents change?

A/ When people get married, they are still the children of their parents. Only now they have another relationship. That's to yourself. אִשְׁתּוֹ כְּגוּפוֹ – *A wife is like yourself* (*Yevamos* 62b).

And therefore, the wife should come first in matters of respect. Of course, you have to respect your parents too; but suppose your mother or your father would like you to fight with your wife – "Go tell her off, Chaim! Don't let her do that! Tell her off!" Oh no, don't tell your wife off at all! No! Don't listen to your parents! There's no mitzvah in a case like that. Don't make any quarrel with your wife just to please your parents. No.

So you have to honor your father and mother in every respect, only that you have to honor your wife too. And Rava said to the people of Mechuza, אוֹקִירוּ לִנְשַׁיְיכוּ – *Honor your wives!* You hear those words? Honor your wives! כִּי הֵיכִי דְּתִתְעַתְּרוּ – *in order that you should become wealthy* (*Bava Metzia* 59a).

"Mother, we know you don't mean it. You're such a kindly person. We know you love everybody."

Hakadosh Baruch Hu promises to reward you. If you honor your wife, you'll have a reward in this world – in order that you become wealthy.

Now, if you honor your parents, a reward is offered in this world too: לְמַעַן יַאֲרִכוּן יָמֶיךָ – *Your days should become long.* And therefore, after you're married, all these mitzvos are still in place; honoring his father and his mother and honoring his wife.

So let's say your mother is scolding your wife, don't say, "Mother, keep quiet!" No. Start laughing. Say, "Mother, we know you don't mean it. You're such a kindly person. We know you love everybody." And therefore, you'll walk out of the house laughing. Walk out of the house laughing! You don't have to insult your mother to stick up for your wife. And don't say your mother is right and hurt your wife's feelings. Use diplomacy and make everybody happy!

February 1995

Your Wife is First 2

Q/ Should a man say anything to his mother if he knows his mother is saying not nice things to his wife?

A/ Ah! That's an important question! What should a man do when he knows his mother is butting in? She's opening her mouth about subjects she shouldn't be getting involved in or she's saying uncomplimentary things to your wife and it's causing friction.

It says in the Torah, עַל כֵּן יַעֲזָב אִישׁ אֶת אָבִיו וְאֶת אִמּוֹ וְדָבַק בְּאִשְׁתּוֹ – *Therefore a man forsakes his father and his mother and he must stick to his wife* (*Bereishis* 2:24). If he sees that one of his parents is interfering in his family life or is causing distress to his wife, he must make it clear to his mother that she should not do that. He shouldn't hesitate! That's his duty as a husband. He must step in!

That one fight will save a thousand. It must be done, once and for all!

And not just to defend his wife; to argue with his mother and go back and forth. No; he should say like this: "Mother, when this subject comes up, please do not say one word. You cannot say such things to my wife!" And let him say it with a little bit of viciousness. Now, maybe she'll get angry; so there'll be one fight, but that one fight will save a thousand. It must be done, once and for all! The husband must prevent his mother from becoming a source of conflict in the house. Otherwise, there's no end; a box of troubles will open up that has no end.

January 1977

Your Wife is First 3

Q/ How does one bring peace to his family when in-laws are involved in the conflict?

A/ Number one, each partner should tell his or her father and mother, "Pa, Ma, stay out of it. Don't talk to me one word against my husband or against my wife!" Lay down the law and don't be afraid to do it. Your wife comes first. עַל כֵּן יַעֲזָב אִישׁ אֶת אָבִיו וְאֶת אִמּוֹ – *A man should forsake his father and his mother,* וְדָבַק בְּאִשְׁתּוֹ, *and he should be loyal to his spouse* (*Bereishis* 2:24).

It's the most stupid thing for a parent to talk to a child against the child's spouse. And if the parents are so stupid, you have to tell them, "Either you stop talking about that or I won't talk to you anymore." Don't be afraid! "I'll talk about

Of course, don't have your mother-in-law around too much.

everything, but not about my spouse." That's the first thing, to lay down the law.

Secondly, a husband and wife should never criticize each other's parents. Don't criticize your husband's brothers or sisters. Never do that. That's bad manners and it's bad diplomacy. Now, this is elementary and very many people understand it by common sense, but some people must be told.

Now, sometimes it already has commenced – the war is on. What do you do? You must stop it. Of course, it's not easy because they're already angry at you. There's a back and forth, and they want to get revenge for what you did in the past, so you have to find ways and means of making up. Start sending little gifts to your mother-in-law. Little gifts to your sisters-in-law, to your brothers-in-law. Find ways and means of being nice to them. They'll continue to barb you, to needle you. But if you won't react, little by little, it'll die out and after some time, peace will be restored.

Of course, if you start out on the right foot, it's still better. When you get married, start with wisdom. Make up your mind that you're going to be the very best to your husband's family or your wife's family that you're able to be.

Of course, don't have your mother-in-law around too much. A mother-in-law should not settle in her daughter-in-law's house. If she has to live with a child, she has to live with a daughter, but never with a daughter-in-law. Because a mother-in-law would have to be an angel in order to keep her mouth shut. And the daughter-in-law has to be an angel to handle her mother-in-law.

Now there was a case – I had a member here whose mother was a widow and she lived with him. And they lived in tranquility; the mother-in-law and daughter-in-law lived peacefully. It was a remarkable story. Many years passed by and never was there a whisper of dissension. But that's an exception – it's not something that should be the norm.

May 1985

Don't live in the same house with them, by any means.

Living in Close Proximity

Q/ Should a newly-married couple live very close to their parents or in-laws?

A/ Not too close. Don't live in the same house with them, by any means. I know it's not easy. Sometimes you need help with *parnassah* and they give you free rent. Don't do it! Because parents can sometimes, although they're well meaning, see things in the wrong perspective.

Sometimes they hear a fight going on downstairs among their children and they get excited. The fight settles itself by nature – the children, sooner or later, settle down by nature and they make *shalom*. But the parents don't have that nature. They're not husband and wife and they get excited when they see their daughter being insulted. And they mix in, and that's a disaster. Again and again it has happened.

So as much as possible, keep out of the lives of your children. Don't butt into your married children's lives. You want to give money to your son-in-law, yes. Give him all you can. To your daughter-in-law, give all the money you can. Don't give any advice, however. Keep away from mixing into their lives.

And the children should be very careful not to say things against their in-laws or about the in-laws. Don't tell your wife anything against her father and her mother or her brothers or her cousin. Don't let the family come into the area between husband and wife at all.

Now, sometimes a man is fortunate enough, he marries a girl whose parents are dead. The very best thing. Then there's *shalom v'shalva*. And if the parents want to remain alive, let them act like they're not there. They can send checks, they can give money, but otherwise, they're not there. Don't butt into your children's lives at all.

Now if a girl goes, if a woman goes and tells her parents things against her husband, it's *avon plili,* it's a very serious sin. A man should never speak against his wife to his mother. That's dynamite. Never talk against your mate to somebody in your family – or to anybody else for that matter. When you try to unburden yourself to someone in your family, you're only making trouble for yourself because it's going to bounce back.

Never talk against your mate to somebody in your family – or to anybody else for that matter.

And therefore, as far as the question about living with in-laws; try as much as possible to live a life of diplomacy – make it that you see your in-laws only when you're all ready to visit them with a formal visit, but don't be together with them on a day-to-day contact.

August 1992

Making Up

How do I make peace with my mother-in-law?

A/ The first step is to send her a little gift.

A woman was telling me that she was fighting with her mother-in-law for a long time. So I said, "Stop talking against your mother-in-law."

"What can I do?" she said. "She's my enemy."

I said, "The first thing is to send her a little gift."

That's number one. And even if she's going to belittle you again, she'll say, "Such a gift she sends me!" Don't worry. Because she's going to feel, however, a certain warmth, a softness towards you. מַתָּן אָדָם יַרְחִיב לוֹ – *A man's gifts open the doors for him* (*Mishlei* 18:16). It's important to give gifts; small gifts.

A man's gifts open the doors for him. You can make shalom with gifts.

A father-in-law was making trouble for someone here in the *shul*. I said, "Send your father-in-law a seventy-five cent pair of cheap cufflinks. Mail it to him; it's a good beginning. Don't think of it as a small thing."

And therefore, מַתָּן אָדָם יַרְחִיב לוֹ – *A man's gifts open the doors for him.* You can make *shalom* with gifts.

May 1991

Making Peace

Q/ What kind of honor can I give to a mother-in-law who interferes with my life?

A/ Now this is a very big question, what to do with a mother-in-law?

And the answer is – it's not the full answer but it's an important answer – what would you do if you were a mother-in-law? And probably, it wouldn't be much different.

And so, you have to consider the mother-in-law as possessing certain rights, certain privileges, and you have to suffer from her. That's part of the job of living in this world. And if you'll get along with your mother-in-law in this world, you have to know that you're going to get a tremendous reward. That's part of marriage and that's the process of

Learn to be happy! Learn to be pleased with everybody!

smoothing out your character, learning how to live peacefully with everyone – even the difficult ones.

And the truth is that most mothers-in-law are not at peace with themselves and most daughters-in-law are not at peace with themselves. That's an important subject, to learn how to live with yourself. To be happy. Not to be dissatisfied, not to look for faults in life. People who have acquired a happy attitude are going to get along with others much more readily than dissatisfied and complaining people.

Now, more than that I won't say, but to a certain extent, that's the guideline. Learn to be happy! Learn to be pleased with everybody! And then you'll see that your mother-in-law is not such a threatening figure as you imagined.

September 1980

Living Diplomatically

Q/ **How do I deal with my husband's mother who I would consider a difficult mother-in-law?**

A/ The best answer to that is, וְאָהַבְתָּ לְרֵעֲךָ כָּמוֹךָ – *Make sure to love your fellow man like you love yourself* (*Vayikra* 19:18), And you can be sure that if your mother-in-law is difficult right now, part of it is due to difficulties in you. And you love yourself anyhow.

And so, at all times, make your mother-in-law feel that you like her. Because that's what you're going to want your daughter-in-law to do to you. מַה דַּעֲלָךְ סָנֵי לְחַבְרָךְ לָא תַּעֲבֵד – *That which you don't want done to yourself, don't do to others* (*Shabbos* 31a). And remember that someday, you too will be a mother-in-law, and your daughter-in-law will ask the same question about you.

And therefore, get busy now and utilize your mother-in-law. Being a daughter-in-law is a training school for you because you will learn how to be a mother-in-law. If you pay attention, you can prepare yourself by learning about what not to do to your own daughter-in-law.

In general, a mother-in-law must be treated with great diplomacy. You must treat *everybody* diplomatically, but your husband's mother deserves a good deal of thought. Whenever she gives you advice without being asked, don't resent it. Now, I'm not saying you should encourage it; don't go and ask her – even if it's just for politeness's sake – unless there's no risk of her going too far. But if she *does* tell you something, act like you accept it; and then when she hangs up the phone or when she leaves the house, forget all about it.

Always remember her anniversary, and you should do it on other occasions too.

In case she resents the fact that you don't consult her, make it a plan to frequently send her small gifts. Always remember her anniversary, and you should do it on other occasions too. And sometimes you can ask her advice about things that are not important – how to make a certain dish or how to soak a certain object. But don't get her too involved in your affairs.

December 1973

Ignoring Criticism

Q/ How should I react to my mother-in-law who said about my *chasunah* gown, which I made myself, that it's made of junky material?

A/ A man told me, a poor man, that he printed out wedding invitations. He told me that his son-in-law, his future son-in-law, remarked, "It's not raised lettering. It's cheap. It's not raised lettering. It's

There's a great reward for people who keep their mouths shut.

just black ink." And this poor man, it hurt him very much. A nice son-in-law said it to his future father-in-law. The father-in-law called me on the telephone: "How should I react?" he asked me. You know how to react? By not reacting! It's a glorious opportunity. We say it every day in *Shemoneh Esrei*: וְלִמְקַלְלַי – *Those who make light of me,* נַפְשִׁי תִדּוֹם – *let my soul be silent.* וְנַפְשִׁי כֶּעָפָר לַכֹּל תִּהְיֶה – *Let my soul be like dust to everybody.*

You know what a glorious opportunity it is when somebody hurts you and you don't react? You swallow it. Hakadosh Baruch Hu is going to give you such perfection of character. He'll give you happiness in this world. There's a great reward for people who keep their mouths shut.

The Gemara (*Chullin* 89a) says: תּוֹלֶה אֶרֶץ עַל בְּלִימָה – *Hashem hangs the world on the man or woman who keep their mouth closed.* Hashem hangs the world in the merit of the one who is בּוֹלֵם פִּיו בְּשָׁעַת מְרִיבָה, *one who keeps his mouth shut at the time when there's a quarrel.* He doesn't answer back.

It's good for your health too, by the way. Many times you suddenly hear that this and this man passed away. Is that so? Was he sick? Wasn't he healthy? No; people don't realize that he died because of the fight with his wife. That's not in the obituary; it's not mentioned. Most cases of excitement that cause strokes are caused by domestic fights. He said something and his wife couldn't take it. He had a fit and his wife couldn't take it.

I know a man who on purpose used to torment his wife. And she passed away. When she was on her deathbed, he came to her and asked her for forgiveness. She said she can't forgive him. And I don't blame her. He was a devil. A frum devil; an Orthodox devil. And there are women who have killed their husbands; not with a gun, not with weapons – but with their mouths. Of course, when she comes to collect the insurance, nothing is said about that. She's dressed in black, and she's weeping. She killed him; what's she weeping about?! He didn't take out a big enough insurance policy for me! That's why she's weeping.

The people who keep quiet are wise people. I mentioned it last week. A bank manager, even if he's insulted, he keeps quiet. But if you walk outside the manager's office and see the janitor, he gets angry if you even look at him funny. That's why he's a janitor. You have to learn how to take it.

Don't give any advice to your daughter-in-law. Even though you mean well.

And therefore, what should you say to your mother-in-law? Listen to me. Erase it – not only from your mouth, but from your memory! And that's being smart! If you're going to keep on thinking about it, it's *chas v'shalom* a sore – a sore on the lungs, a sore on the liver, a sore on the stomach. *Chas v'shalom*. And someday it could erupt suddenly and make a big tragedy, *chas v'shalom*. And therefore, you are wise, not only spiritually wise, but even in *gashmius* – you are a wise and prudent person if you'll erase it entirely from your mind.

May 1985

Constructive Criticism

Q/ **Many times a mother-in-law might have some constructive criticism for her daughter-in-law. Can she call her son, and the son could take it up with his wife?**

A/ You know my rule already. I've said it a thousand times. Don't give any advice to your daughter-in-law. Even though you mean well.

The question is, can a mother-in-law relay suggestions through her son and the wife won't know where it came from?

Honor your father-in-law and keep your mouth shut.

It's important that the wife shouldn't have even the slightest inkling that it came from her mother-in-law, and wives are usually able to sniff that out. And therefore, mothers who feed suggestions to their sons – that's one of the ways to cause trouble.

The best thing would be to forget about it. Let your daughter-in-law's house be bedlam; let it be confusion. Never mind – don't mix in! It's much better than what you could contribute. All you contribute is hostility. Because every mother-in-law thinks that it's so, that she has just the right advice. She always has suggestions.

And therefore, the best suggestion is to say nothing at all.

January 1977

Honor Your Father-in-Law

Q/ **What's the best way to deal with a father-in-law?**

A/ Don't laugh. That's a very important question. And the answer is that the very best way is to always honor him and to keep quiet. Honor your father-in-law and keep your mouth shut. The less you say, the more he'll like you. He'll think you're a somebody if you keep your mouth closed. Open up your mouth, you'll begin to bray, and he sees that you're a donkey in disguise.

It's very important to know that with your wife's relatives, you always have to smile, no matter what. Smile always and keep quiet. And they'll like you. They'll like you. If you open your mouth however, you're in trouble.

April 1999

Avoiding In-Laws 1

Should I visit my in-laws if they have a TV in their house?

Q/ **Should I visit my in-laws if they have a TV in their house?**

A/ Are they *shomer Shabbos*?

Q/ **Yes.**

A/ Visit them on Shabbos.

May 1974

Avoiding the In-Laws 2

Q/ **What should one do if his mother-in-law dresses immodestly?**

A/ He shouldn't invite his mother-in-law to his house, that's all. If she happens to come along and he wants to make a *bracha,* he should turn around with his back when he says the words. And maybe she will catch on.

August 1998

Avoiding the In-Laws 3

Q/ **What should be done when the in-laws don't let their son-in-law study Torah?**

You have to go to work! You have to support your wife. That's what a man has to do.

A/ What should be done when they don't let him eat kosher? He disregards them.

Now, I don't know what you mean by studying Torah. If it means lying in bed all day long, then the in-laws are right. You have to go to work! You have to support your wife. That's what a man has to do. Unless he has some source of income – then certainly, learning all day is a very good thing.

But if it's just a question of going at night to study Torah or on Sundays or Shabbos, your in-laws have nothing to say about it, just like they have nothing to say about keeping a kosher home. He has to keep a kosher home, no matter how much they disapprove. And learning Torah is part of a kosher home. Like it says וְדִבַּרְתָּ בָּם – *You have to speak in the Torah,* בְּשִׁבְתְּךָ בְּבֵיתֶךָ – *when you sit in your house* (*Devarim* 6:7). And if it's necessary to go to the *beis hamedrash* to learn, you have to do it too.

February 1979

Helping Children-in-Law 1

Q/ **My daughter is getting married soon. Can you give me some advice on how to deal with a son-in-law?**

A/ Always be nice to your son-in-law. Never say anything wrong to your son-in-law. Never. Don't give any *eitzos.* Don't give him your advice. Just give him money and *kavod*. I always tell you my rule: With your son-in-law, keep your wallet open and your mouth shut. Money and honor – that's all you should give him. Otherwise, don't give anything else.

Now, there are many good fathers-in-law, *tzaddikim,* who think that it's their duty to give guidance to their sons-in-law. They take them in hand and they start pushing them. So here's a quiet fellow, it's hard for him to refuse his father-in-law, but it's very bitter for him to have to listen to advice like that. Therefore, in his heart he becomes an enemy of his father-in-law, the *tzaddik.* So even though you're a *tzaddik,* and you want to be *madrich* your son-in-law, get somebody else to do it, not you. Because he's going to resent you, and he'll never forget what you've pressured him into doing.

A husband and wife – every-thing is their own business. They shouldn't tell their parents anything.

Also, your daughter-in-law. Give no advice to your daughter-in-law. No advice to your daughter-in-law! Never mix in.

Your daughter too. Don't ask your daughter how she's getting along with her husband. You shouldn't do that! And she shouldn't tell you anything. It's none of your business. None of your business! A husband and wife – everything is their own business. They shouldn't tell their parents anything.

June 1999

Helping Children-in-Law 2

Q/ **My married son sometimes wants to talk to me about his marriage, his complaints about his *shalom bayis.* Should I get involved?**

A/ If a man complains about his wife to his mother, it's a tremendous sin he's doing. The mother-in-law is waiting for that. Therefore, he should make it his business never to say a word.

Don't talk to your parents about your marital affairs.

And daughters also. They shouldn't say a word of complaint. And if your daughter does ever complain to you about her husband, tell her, "Please, I don't want to listen; your job is to please your husband."

Don't talk to your parents about your marital affairs. When parents mix in, I'll explain what happens. When husbands and wives have a quarrel, nature makes it they get together frequently and they are *mochel* each other to a certain extent; but once one of the *mechutanim* gets angry at the *chassan* or the *kallah,* or the *chassan* gets angry at them, there's no way of being *mevater* anymore. It's forever.

Here's a mother-in-law, an intelligent, educated mother-in-law, she comes in and tells her daughter-in-law, "I'm giving you an ultimatum; you must go to a psychologist!" It's a *meshugene* thing for an educated woman to say. First of all, she should go to a psychologist! And don't say that to a daughter-in-law! An ultimatum! Who are you to give an ultimatum? No one should give an ultimatum! A husband and wife shouldn't give ultimatums either, but a mother-in-law should give ultimatums to her daughter-in-law? Absolutely not!

I'll say something even more. It's a very important point when you're taking an *eidem* or a daughter-in-law. You must make a contract with your wife. You're not going to criticize your son-in-law or daughter-in-law. Even when they're not listening. You won't say anything, ever, to your wife or your husband against your son-in-law or your daughter-in-law.

January 1997

The Mother-in-Law's Bad Rap

Don't mothers-in-law have a bad reputation, when really, they're not as bad as they're made out to be?

A/ If they have a bad reputation, then it's because they don't understand their role as mother-in-law. A mother-in-law must know that she has only one function in life towards her son's wife, and that's to praise. Only to praise. To praise and give gifts. Sometimes to babysit too. And that's all. A mother-in-law must know that nothing but praise is accepted, and since she's not capable of doing it, she should fulfill what it says in *Mishlei* (25:17) הֹקַר רַגְלְךָ מִבֵּית רֵעֶךָ – *Make your foot scarce in your fellow man's house.* Just don't come too frequently.

A mother-in-law must know that she has only one function in life towards her son's wife, and that's to praise.

In-laws should never sleep over at their children unless in an emergency. And their visits, in general, should not be too long because it's hard for a mother-in-law to withstand that test for such a long time, for her to keep quiet. The mother-in-law knows that the daughter-in-law is no good. That she's sloppy. She lets her husband wear rags. She doesn't feed him properly. She overworks him. She spends too much money. Mothers know that their daughters-in-law are ruining their husbands.

It's a big test, and in order that the ordeal shouldn't be overpowering, it's important to make up your mind before you walk into your daughter-in-law's home that you won't see anything but good in that home. While you're holding the doorknob, before you ring the bell, make up your mind that you're not going to see the dirty sink. You won't see the children's shoes thrown all over the place. You'll see nothing but good in that house.

And whatever you do see, the only answer is to put a padlock on your mouth. It's of utmost importance not to say a thing. And the time to start is before the wedding. When your son is already with somebody, keep quiet. Because what you say before the wedding is going to rankle forever in her heart. She'll never forget it. If anything, give nothing but compliments, kind words, and encouragement. It's so important, it cannot be overemphasized. Now it may seem that these are simple words, but many a marriage have gone

Suppose somebody wanted to leave the teivah in the middle of the mabul, what would you say?

on the rocks because his mother did not learn how to speak wisely.

And so, if it's true that mothers-in-law have a bad reputation, they have to put in the hard work to change that. And since someday, you too will be a mother-in-law, the time to work on it is when your children are not yet married. Practice. Learn from your husband's mother's error, like it says מַה דַּעֲלָךְ סָנֵי לְחַבְרָךְ לָא תַּעֲבֵד – *Don't do to others what you don't want done to yourself* (*Shabbos* 31a). That's what they do, however. They say, "My mother-in-law criticized me and now it's my turn." She means it's her turn to eat up her heart. It's her turn to make herself sick. It's her turn to gain enemies. It's her turn to be a failure in life.

January 1977

Sons-in-Law in Kollel

Q/ Should a wealthy father-in-law support his son-in-law in *kollel* even if he's not such a serious learner?

A/ You have to know that today, when you leave the yeshiva, it's like going out of the *teivah* of Noach. Suppose somebody wanted to leave the *teivah* in the middle of the *mabul*, what would you say? Outside, there is a *mabul* today. Not a *mabul* of water, but a *mabul* of filth, of wickedness. And therefore, the longer he is in the *kollel*, the better off he is.

Now, if you can teach him a *parnassah* while he's in the *kollel* so that gradually he can get a decent living, then maybe he'll be able to establish himself in a good, frum neighborhood with a *parnassah* – even better. But whatever it is, as long as he can he should be in the *kollel*. He should get married from the yeshiva and stay in the yeshiva so that the first years are *kollel* years. And his wife gets accustomed to being a *kollel* wife and the children are *kollel* children. What happens later, we'll see. But at first, keep him in the *kollel* as long as you could afford to keep him there.

At first, keep him in the kollel as long as you could afford to keep him there.

March 1996

Divrei Torah at the In-Laws' Table

Q/ When I go to my in-laws for Shabbos, should I say *divrei Torah* at the table?

A/ It depends. If it's something that's brief, all right; but don't say any *maarachos,* any long boring *maarachos.*

June 1998

Marrying a Bas Talmid Chacham

Q/ You said on one of your tapes that when a man marries a girl, he is really marrying her father. If this is so, how could the Avos have married the women they did?

A/ This questioner is holding me down to my statement that if a man marries a girl, he's marrying her father too, so how could our Forefathers have married girls whose fathers weren't worth marrying?

A girl is the beginning of a career of serving Hashem.

The answer is, in those old days they had no choice. They had to marry somebody. And today too, sometimes you marry a girl whose father is not marriageable. Many times it happens that a girl is worth marrying, but not her father.

What we're talking about is, when you're marrying a daughter whose father is somebody, she's a *bas talmid chacham,* let's say, that's the ideal marriage – so then you have to feel that it's not just this little piece of painted flesh that you're getting. Just a girl, that's all you're getting?

A girl is an introduction to Hakadosh Baruch Hu. A girl is the beginning of a career of serving Hashem. So then you might as well include her father also in it, if the father is worth knowing.

So therefore, when somebody married, let's say, the daughter of the Chasam Sofer; let's say a man married the Chasam Sofer's daughter. In those days, you could be sure he wasn't marrying the girl at all. He was marrying nothing but her father because the only way to get close to the father was by taking his daughter. So he took the daughter. If you're lucky enough to get a girl who is an idealist, who has *yiras Hashem*, an *ishah maskeles,* so she herself is something worth marrying and her father also is worth marrying. And her brother also. So marry all of them and that way you'll be even more successful in life.

December 1976

A Bochur Who Misses Seder

Q/ What should I think of a prospective son-in-law who misses the *seder* of the yeshiva to go out on a date with my daughter?

A/ Now it could be that if he didn't go out in the afternoon when it's the second *seder*, he'd have to go out at night, and at night, he has a third *seder*. He doesn't want to miss the third *seder*. Or it could be that at night, it's not safe for him to be out.

And therefore, we must excuse him because of the exigencies of the circumstances. He has to get married. So let's think the best that we can about him.

February 1974

Criteria for a Son-in-Law

Is there anything wrong when parents prefer a profes-sional son-in-law to one who is a laborer or a plain employ-ee?

Q/ I find that when Jewish parents are considering husbands for their daughters, they give great preference to young boys with high professions as opposed to laborers and other people who work with their hands. Is there anything wrong with that?

A/ Is there anything wrong when parents prefer a professional son-in-law to one who is a laborer or a plain employee?

Nothing wrong. Only there's another criterion which supersedes that. The criterion is idealism, loyalty to the Torah, a *ben Torah*. Certainly there are better things than a professional.

But there's nothing wrong. Why should a man marry off his daughter to somebody who can barely support her and somebody who perhaps is not capable – maybe because of his inferior intellect and sometimes inferior character? These are usually the hallmarks of the failures. The failures are usually the people of inferior intelligence and sometimes inferior

Their daughters will be married to a talmid chacham, and in the years to come, their home will be a place of idealism and kedusha.

character. Usually the people who succeed in professions are people who have better intelligence and better character. Nothing wrong.

However, there's no question, parents should aspire to a son-in-law who is trained in the ways of the Torah, and therefore, their daughters will be married to a *talmid chacham,* and in the years to come, their home will be a place of idealism and *kedusha*. They'll have children, and there will be *bnei Torah* in the family and the family will increase and multiply with frum Jews and it'll be a blessing for the parents.

So therefore, there are all forms of decisions and choices that the parents should make. And the parents should make the very best choice that they can for their daughters.

January 1987

Chapter 18
The Jewish Home

Chapter Sponsor

לעילוי נשמת

פראג' בן תיירה מואדב ז"ל הי"ד

נלב"ע י"א מנחם אב תשנ"ד

צאלח בן ג'מילה חמדני עבאדי ז"ל

נלב"ע כ"א סיון תשס"ב

גאמאלו בת רבקה חמדני-עבאדי ז"ל

נלב"ע ביום הו"ר כ"א תשרי תשע"ז

עדית מואדב בת גאמאלו ז"ל

נלב"ע י"ד שבט תשפ"א

Contents

Chapter 18

The Jewish Home

Fancy Homes

Q/ Many *nashim tzidkaniyos* serve Hashem in their homes and therefore, they want to have nice kitchens and dining rooms. That's where they are all the time. But on the other hand, that goes against the ideal of living for the next world and it can make us very *megusham*. How do we, the husbands, and our wives, too, try to manage that?

A/ The desire for a nice home or a handsome dining room, is that a contradiction to Olam Haba?

The answer is no. If you desire Olam Haba, it doesn't mean you have to become a beggar, a wild man. No. Live a normal life. You can be happy. Hashem wants you to live a normal life and to be happy. He wants you to do that.

Hashem wants you to have a nice home, why not? Of course, to spend too much money – that's not necessary; you can give it to *tzedakah*. You can save it in the bank and marry off your children to *kollel* people. But whatever it is, if

You have to take home this Jew and feed him. It's a mitzvah.

it's not a matter of wastefulness of money, you're entitled to have Olam Hazeh; why not?

I'll give a *mashal*. Hillel Hazakein, in the morning when he left the yeshiva, they said to him, "Where are you going?"

He said, "I have to take care of a guest. I have to be *machnis orech.*"

"Who is the guest?" they asked.

"Myself."

You have to honor a Jew, and this Jew wants to eat. I'm taking this Jew home to eat. It's a mitzvah. You have to take home this Jew and feed him. It's a mitzvah.

And therefore, suppose you want to feed this Jew and also give him a nice room to sleep in; there's no harm if you make a nice room for him.

You're the Jew! Why not? You're justified in living a nice, normal life. Why not? Only don't forget the principle, that's all; don't forget the *ikar,* that we live for Olam Haba. After all, a person can be a beggar and a *batlan* and a *schlemazel* and still not believe in Olam Haba. One thing doesn't have to do with the other.

And therefore, live a normal happy life.

By the way, the best thing is if you'll spend time singing because of that: "I sing to You Hashem because You gave me a nice home. I sing to You Hashem, that you gave me a kitchen and a dining room. I sing to Hashem that I enjoy my supper. I sing to Hashem that I enjoy my good health. I sing to Hashem that I live in America and I don't live in China. I sing to Hashem that I can walk and talk. I'm normal. You give me sanity. You're the *Chonein daas.*"

If you sing to Hashem about all of the benefits He gives you, Hashem says, "Oh! I like to hear you sing. I'm going to let you continue singing in this world and in the World to Come too. And there you'll sing even more."

And therefore, the answer is that what is important is not to forget to serve Hashem, not to forget that there's another world. And that's the main purpose for which we were created.

November 1999

In a house full of children, it's not near impossible – it's impossible to have a spic and span house.

Clean Homes 1

Q/ Should religious Jews be careful to have neat and clean homes?

A/ Now pay attention to what I'm going to tell you. This subject, you must understand as follows – but don't be prejudiced by what I'm going to tell you in the beginning. There was a woman named Ilse Koch. Ilse Koch, *y'mach sh'mah,* was a famous Nazi woman. And in the concentration camps, she used to walk around with a whip and she would beat the dying inmates. She was called The Beast of Buchenwald. If you want a picture of one of the lowest characters in history, that's it.

Now, at her trial, there were Germans who spoke up for Ilse Koch and defended her. And what did they say in her defense? They said that her kitchen is spotless! And I believe it; I'm sure it was.

Keep that in mind while I give you the answer now, because it was the introduction to the answer.

Now, if you're going to have a Jewish house, it means you're going to have children. And if you have children, it means one, two, three, four, five, six; various ages. And in a house full of children, it's not *near* impossible – it's *impossible*

You walk into the house during the day at 2:00 in the afternoon; there's a man eating breakfast.

to have a spic and span house. If you're one of these women, one of these Modern Orthodox women who want to live a selfish life, you'll have one baby, and when this baby is already an old man, you'll have another one. So maybe that woman will succeed in having a nice clean house.

But if you're trying to raise a Jewish generation, it's impossible to expect such a thing. It's only in these castles of selfishness, where people live only for themselves, where the house is nice and clean – because there is nobody there to make it dirty. That's number one.

And the second thing is this: I was once in a Jewish house in Boro Park. And it was a house of love and warmth. Any wayfarer who would knock on the door at night and say, "I have no place to sleep," they wouldn't ask any questions. "Come in, there's a place here to sleep." Now, if you have a fancy home, you'd think, "Maybe this man is filthy; maybe he's a bearer of bedbugs." How can you let him sleep on your nice bed? You'll let him into your bathroom?! He'll contaminate your nice toilet seat. It's hard for a nice *baal habus* to allow a stranger into his fancy and clean home. So you say, "Go someplace else; go to the rabbi. Go to this one or go to that one." You send him away.

The Bostoner Rebbe, in Boston, has a big house. And anybody who wants can find lodging there – and food too. You walk into the house during the day at 2:00 in the afternoon; there's a man eating breakfast. He slept late, so he's eating breakfast. Nobody bothers him. The people in the house know that's the Rebbe's system. You walk in and they have a place to sleep for you always; there's always something to eat.

How could it be fancy, such a house? It can't be a spic and span house if people are always coming in, going out, coming in, going out. Even if you have fine guests, they bring in their baggage all over the floor. If your home is a place of *hachnasas orchim*, a place of hospitality, then it can't be fancy.

Now, in this home that I was in, in Boro Park, it always looked like they were moving. They weren't moving; but everything was in the wrong place. And that's because there were children all over the place. They had little children all over the place. You can't always give a child rubber diapers. He leaves an impression sometimes. And there were always guests in that place, wayfarers. Here's a *meshulach*, drinking a glass of tea. And the mother of the house, as soon as she finishes preparing the tea, she has to make lunch for somebody. She's packing up lunch. She can't take care of *everything*, so she's taking care of her children and the *meshulachim* instead of cleaning the walls. And therefore, we're seeing here that if it's a house of raising children and a house of hospitality, then it's impossible that it should be clean and neat all the time.

A shabby house is shabby! The linoleum is worn through!

And now, a third thing: If you're poor, if you don't invest a lot of money in your house, it's going to be shabby. Now, don't tell me this fairy tale, "poor but clean." A shabby house is shabby! The linoleum is worn through! And if the linoleum is worn through and there's a big hole in the linoleum, don't tell me that you get down on your knees three times a day and scrub the hole. Dust accumulates in that hole and that's it. There's a nail sticking out where the linoleum used to be. It's impossible!

I once walked into the house of Rav Aaron Kotler, *zichrono livracha*. Now, I'm not an expert on a neat house, so I'm not judging its neatness. But it was a poor house, a very poor house. And because of that, Rav Aaron rose in my eyes all the way up. I saw that he didn't take the money from the yeshiva and spend it on expensive things. He lived poorly. He lived very poorly. He gave the money to the boys in the yeshiva who were hungry. There were poor boys who needed it.

So if you want to have a spic and span home, that means that you'll invest in this world instead of the next world. Instead of charity, you're buying things for yourself, for the house, expensive things. Don't bother telling me fairy tales.

Should the homes of religious Jews be neat and clean? Absolutely.

It means expensive! It means investing a lot of money, besides investing a lot of time.

August 1976

Clean Homes 2

Q/ So you're saying a clean home is not important?

A/ Certainly it's good to have a clean home. Certainly. But anybody whose criterion of the quality of people in the home is if the home is clean or not, that person is a fool; he's an idiot. Why do I say that? Because he's a low *goy*. He has the head of a low *goy*. You know that there are some *goyim* who go to the cleaners every day. Cleaners tell me that. Their best customers are the low *goyim*! Why are the low *goyim* the best customers? They're the cleanest people – every day they're cleaning their clothing – because they have no ideals in life. So all they know is that they want to be clean and smell good.

And therefore, are we going to emulate them? We live for the purpose of spiritual achievement, for being kindly, for serving Hashem, for doing mitzvos. Certainly, the Gemara says that the house of a *talmid chacham* is well ordered. Certainly! Everything should be in place. Certainly everything should be *mesudar;* everything should be neat. But the question is, where is it on the list of virtues?

So along came some gentile with a new torah that cleanliness is next to you-know-what. And the Jews swallow this bait and they repeat the same thing. You know, people who say "Cleanliness is next to G-dliness," they are the people who hold that G-dliness is meaningless. It's a hundred percent rule.

So in answer to your question: Should the homes of religious Jews be neat and clean? Absolutely. But we have another question: Should the homes of religious Jews be full of little children? And should religious Jews and their homes be hospitable to the poor and needy?

So they let him stay a little longer. He's been sleeping there for ten years already. Ten years!

There's a home not far from here, and to that home a man once came; an old man who never married. He had no home, no family. So they let him in. He slept there one night and he said, "Can I sleep here a little longer?" So they let him stay a little longer. He's been sleeping there for ten years already. Ten years! He's been sleeping and eating for ten years in this home! Not far from here. I'll tell you privately where it is. And he's an old man, a demanding man. For breakfast, if you make his eggs not exactly the way he wants them, he tells the *balabuste.* And she and her husband take it. And they take it more. It's been ten years of taking it! Now, if you have an old bachelor at home and he sleeps in your living room or wherever, and he eats whenever he wants in your kitchen, it can't be fancy.

I'll tell you another story on this subject of being neat and clean. Once, a young man called me up from Grand Central Station. It was 11:00 at night. I asked him, "What do you want?" "Are you Rabbi Miller?" he said, "the one who wrote Rejoice O' Youth?"

So I said, "Yes." He tells me that he came from a city in the Midwest and he read my book and he decided he wanted to visit me. I said, "But it's 11:00 at night! And it'll take you another hour to get here!" He said he has no place else to go. I said "Do you have money?" "No, I have no money," he said.

So what can I do? He read my book after all, so he came to me. So it's 12:00 at night – and I go to sleep early, mind you – and he comes waltzing into my house. He comes with duffel bags, and all kinds of stuff. He's here to stay! I took a look and I saw *nit gut,* it's not good. I thought to myself, "Just tonight; one night, okay." So he slept in my house.

Now, this boy couldn't speak a word of Yiddish, and this man could barely speak English. But they under-stood each other.

You see, I'm not that kind of Jew. I'm talking about good Jews! So the next morning I called up one of our people in the shul who had a car and I said to him, "Take this young man with all of his stuff to the Satmarer *beis hamedrash*, and leave him there, right in the middle of the *beis hamedrash*, and don't worry about him." I know the Satmarer; I knew he'd be taken care of.

So he took him with all his duffel bags and his suitcase and everything else, he took him and he parked him in the Satmarer *beis hamedrash* in Williamsburg. A few minutes later, a Polish Jew came along – he davened there in the Satmarer *shtiebel* – and started talking to him. Now, this boy couldn't speak a word of Yiddish, and this man could barely speak English. But they understood each other. It's called "the language of the needy man." He needed a place to eat and sleep. So he took him to his house and he kept him for two weeks! It was hot; it was summertime. This was before there were air conditioners in the homes. His wife called me up finally. She says there's a stranger in her house; she can't take off her coat and she has to wear a sheitel all the time. She can't; it's very uncomfortable. There's a strange man in the house.

And they kept him for longer than two weeks, however. He remained. They didn't put him out on the street. For nothing, by the way; nobody paid them anything. And finally another Jew, a Williamsburg Jew, took him in hand and took him into his home, and he found him a job, and a place to eat for Shabbos. And for years he suffered from him. He suffered from him; he wasn't an easy fellow, this *baal teshuvah*.

And so, these are the people whose homes are not 'neat and clean' enough for you? At least you can get into their homes! Their homes are sanctuaries! If you want a neat and clean home, I'll tell you what you should do. Try coming without money to, let's say, Scarsdale. Spend your last nickel on carfare to Scarsdale; show up there at nine thirty at night or 10:00 at night, and start knocking on doors. Say, "I have no money. Can you give me some food and a place to sleep?" Now, I'm sure that the Scarsdale homes are fancy. There might be maids too. But they won't even open the door for you. They might even call the police.

And so, there are different ways of looking at this subject. But one thing is certain; if you have a lot of children spilling out all over the place, and you have a guest sprawled on the sofa, and you're trying with a broom and a brush to do the best you can, your house is the neatest and cleanest house that could be.

August 1976

Pets in the Home

What business do you have keeping a dog in your house?

Q/ Is there anything wrong with having a puppy in a Jewish house? Someone asked me and I didn't know what to say.

A/ Is it right to raise a dog in your house? I'm not going to answer that question directly, but in most cases, it's done as a form of demonstrating a certain unity with the environment; with a certain gentile attitude of having a dog. Jews usually don't have dogs, and people who like to walk with a dog in the street, or have a dog in the house – it's a sign that they're yielding to the environment.

Now, I'm not *paskening* any *halachos*, but it's a matter of *hashkafah* that we don't want to walk in the ways of the *goyim*. I once walked into a house to be *menachem avel*, and they knew my attitude about pets, so the dog was concealed. I heard scratching behind the door. They were very much embarrassed! They knew I'm against it.

Every Jewish home is of inestimable value to us

What business do you have keeping a dog in your house? It's not because it's a watchdog; no, it's not a watchdog at all. Some people have these little dogs – tiny fragile things – and the dogs themselves need protection. These little dogs, anyone can give it a good kick and kill it. And even if it's a bigger dog, in most cases, what it really means is, "I'm a *goy* like all the *goyim.*" That's what it really means in most cases. It's considered a form of yielding to the environment. That's why I say that in general, I disapprove of it.

February 1995

Home Insurance

Q/ What does it mean when it says that a house where the sound of the Torah is heard at night, that house will not be destroyed (*Eiruvin* 18b)?

A/ Now, that's like all the statements in the Scriptures and in the Gemara – preventing the destruction of a house depends on various factors, and this is one of the factors. Many times we suddenly see, *chas v'shalom,* it shouldn't happen, that a house is broken up. Sometimes an illness suddenly strikes, *chas v'shalom,* or another tragedy, and the parents are gone; both parents are gone. It happens. Sometimes, there's a breakup. A tragedy. One parent, the father runs away. It happens, *chas v'shalom.* There are all kinds of ways that a house can be attacked.

Now, a house is a very precious building block of our nation. Every Jewish home is of inestimable value to us, besides being the greatest value to the members of that house. And therefore, we have to utilize all factors available that will stabilize such a house. And one of the big factors is, if the sound of the Torah is heard there at night. Hakadosh Baruch

Hu is going to try to preserve a house like that; it means He has a personal interest in that house, so to speak. He is interested that this house should continue. And therefore, it's going to be protected against many vicissitudes which otherwise would come in and break up a house.

Chas v'shalom, when a house breaks up, a Jewish house, it's a *churban* of a little Beis Hamikdash. And one of the ways of ensuring the survival of that house is to take out a Gemara at night; if you don't know Gemara, take out a Chumash and say Torah aloud at night – even a little bit – at your table. You don't realize – the entire atmosphere changes in that house. And Hakadosh Baruch Hu already has a very big interest in preserving that house.

August 1976

Children should never have any oppor-tunity to have the slightest contact with the internet.

Computers in the Home

Q/ **Is a computer a danger to a Jewish home?**

A/ Now I can't tell you anything about it – I don't have a computer. But if it's used to connect to the internet, then it's *sakanas nefashos.* Children should never have any opportunity to have the slightest contact with the internet. The internet is *mamash* a poison, a deadly poison. Today, people are being ruined by connecting to the internet. They make contacts; wicked, sinful contacts. There's no question about that.

If you have a computer that you keep under lock and key, and you are the one who is *mashgiach* how it should be used and when it should be used, maybe. I don't see anything wrong there.

January 2001

The internet is Gehinom. That's what it is.

Internet in the Home

Q/ Can somebody have internet connection in the house for business? There are plenty of businesses that are on the internet today, and people want to know if they can have it in the house if they work from the house.

A/ If a person has an internet machine in his house, he should have it under lock and key; two locks! And he should have both of the keys. He shouldn't leave it unattended for even one evening. The internet is Gehinom. That's what it is. Even a computer in the house is a *sakanah*. Who knows what could happen! And therefore you have to keep it under lock and key! There's no alternative to that; there's no second choice.

April 2000

Shas in the Home

Q/ The Rav said during the *shiur* last week that people should buy a Shas for their homes, even if they won't use it. Can you explain the reason for that? And does it apply to an unmarried *bochur* as well?

A/ A Shas is an ornament; it's a most beautiful ornament for the Jewish people. And that's why it sometimes comes beautifully bound, and it's printed on nice, strong paper. It's our pride and joy, the Shas. Especially if you won't use it, it will always remain handsome. And you should be proud of that set of Gemaras on your shelf. When visitors come in, you should show it off to them; and when they say, "What are these big volumes?" you can tell them that the Shas is the pride and joy of the Jewish nation.

I was once in a man's house, and he took me into his room where he had his coin collection. He was so proud! He was showing me his African coins and his Chinese coins. What is there to be proud of?! I don't see anything in it. But when a man is proud of something, he shows it off.

The wise man is proud of the things that are worthy of pride.

The *Talmud Bavli*, now *that's* a collection. It's the masterpiece of our nation. Isn't it beautiful? It's a beautiful ornament to have on your shelf. Even if you don't read it, it's a masterpiece and it's something to talk about. It's a showpiece for your visitors. Take out the volumes and show them, "Look at this, and look at this one. Isn't it beautiful?" The wise man is proud of the things that are worthy of pride. And the fool is proud of his African coin collection.

The only question is: Suppose you are an unmarried young man, and you hope to get married eventually; so should you buy one right now, or should you wait for your future father-in-law to buy a set for you? I would answer as follows: Would you buy a bedroom set right now? No, you wait until you are married. So when you buy all your furniture, you'll buy a Shas as well.

A *bochur* has to keep moving; sometimes he has to go from one yeshiva to another. So you can't have a Shas around your neck and anchor yourself down. So wait until your father-in-law comes along and buys you a Shas, a set more expensive than you could afford anyhow. And when you do finally put that Shas on the bookshelf, you must know that it is the pride of the Jewish people.

March 1991

Always look ahead. A very important principle. Look ahead.

Videos in the Home 1

Q/ Can a person have a video machine in his home to show children educational video programs?

A/ We come now to a very important point, and that is what we say to the *nazir*. A *nazir* made a vow not to drink any wine and now you see him walking down the road, and you know that down there are grapevines hanging over the road. So the Gemara says that we tell him, "*Nazir nazir, sechor sechor! Nazir*, make a detour! *L'karma lo sikarev,* don't come close to the vineyard!"

So he says, "What do you mean? I'm a *yarei Shamayim.* You think I'm going to eat those grapes? Never mind. I would never eat them."

But the Torah says we don't trust him.

That's why the Torah says that a *nazir* cannot even eat the leaves of grapevines. What's wrong with leaves? Leaves don't make you intoxicated. The Gemara says no; *mikol* means anything of the vine; even the leaves you shouldn't eat. If the *nazir* eats leaves of a grapevine, it's a sin; he gets *malkus*. So you see how far you have to keep away from a sin. You can't trust yourself.

Now, let's say you have a video in your house. You will never show anything except very kosher programs. But suppose a child, without your knowledge, will buy a video in a certain kind of shop and he'll bring it when you're not home and play it. What will you do? You don't even know about it.

So it's best not to fool around. Don't fool around! That's my advice. Do what you want, but I'm telling you what's best for you.

In general, it's good to be a *roeh es hanolad,* someone who can see ahead. אֵיזֶהוּ חָכָם הָרוֹאֶה אֶת הַנּוֹלָד – *Who is a wise person? Someone who looks ahead* (*Tamid* 32a). Always look ahead. A very important principle. Look ahead. Think: What could happen eventually?

You can never be smart enough. You can never be careful enough with your children.

Let's say you moved into a place far away from a Torah center. You say, "Well, I'm going to keep my children strong with the best education," and so on. But you know, children play with their neighbors and they tend to be like the neighbor's children. Eventually, sooner or later, something's going to happen. You have to be a *roeh es hanolad.* You can never be smart enough. You can never be careful enough with your children.

And with yourself too. You can't trust yourself. And therefore, it's always better to beware of things that might be a temptation in the wrong direction.

September 1989

Videos in the Home 2

Q/ Can the Rav share with us a word of *chizuk* about videos?

A/ Forget about videos. A Jewish house shouldn't have any videos. That's all. No Jewish house should have videos. Because once you have videos, then you have all kinds of videos. Of course, TV is out of the question. Anybody who has a TV in his house should know he has no *chelek l'Olam Haba*. No question about it. The Gemara (*Sanhedrin* 100b) says הַקּוֹרֵא בִּסְפָרִים חִיצוֹנִיִּים אֵין לָהֶם חֵלֶק לָעוֹלָם הַבָּא. Now, *seforim chitzoniyim* are not as bad as TV. TV, you're looking in the faces of the *resha'im* and they're telling you their poison at your table. So anybody who

Please explain how magazines and newspapers are harmful in a frum home

has a TV in his house is risking his *neshamah*. No question about it. But this, people here know. I don't have to tell them about that. It's superfluous.

August 1997

Magazines in the Home

Q/ Please explain how magazines and newspapers are harmful in a frum home.

A/ I must tell you that although there might be a difference between this one and that one, in general, הַצַּד הַשָּׁוֶה שֶׁבָּהֶן שֶׁדַּרְכָּן לְהַזִּיק וּשְׁמִירָתָן עָלֶיךָ – *the common denominator between them is that they cause damage and it's your responsibility to guard yourself from them* (*Bava Kama* 2a).

None of them have a beneficial influence. Even the best ones are full of wrong ideas and they speak of ideals and pursuits that even if they're not harmful, are entirely unnecessary and they give people thoughts of pleasures or of pastimes that are nothing but a waste of one's life.

For instance; travel is always advertised and played up in the magazines. Now, it's not considered an immoral form of journalism to describe traveling in a foreign country. But actually, it's a hundred percent waste of life to travel. There's absolutely nothing to be gained by going to Florida! And I'm talking about the minimum in travel! I'm not talking about Hawaii. Hawaii?! When they show pictures of Hawaii, it falls flat on a sensible man's mind! It's meaningless. What's out there? It's only because it's being offered for sale, so some people have a reaction that they should buy what's offered for sale. They'll buy anything. They're attracted just because it's offered for sale. Going to Hawaii is a waste!

But even going to Florida is almost a hundred percent – I won't say entirely because maybe there are some people who must have a mild climate – but it's almost a hundred percent a waste. Not only is it a waste, but the bother of going to Florida is exacting, and many people get heart attacks just from packing and from traveling back and forth. Over here, you live in a comfortable apartment; you won't get the same apartment there. You're cramped and it's inconvenient and many times you'll go to a hotel and you want to get your money's worth, so you eat much more than you should eat. They sit down at the hotel table and they gobble up everything that's available. And so, at home, where you have all the requirements for a normal kind of life, you are much better off. Without any question.

Many people who would never have thought of going skiing are impelled to do so because of what they read in the papers.

Now, the newspapers, however, feed the people ideals of doing things. For instance, many people who would never have thought of going skiing are impelled to do so because of what they read in the papers. Now skiing, you have to know, is an excellent opportunity to get broken bones.

Many people are invited by the newspapers to travel on roads going to places. But traveling on these big highways is precarious. Very many people have lost their lives on the highways. It may sound old fashioned, but it's sensible. As much as possible, keep off the big highways.

Of course, you have to watch your step in the city too, but travel is costly. It's costly in terms of health. If you want to travel, travel on shoe leather. Walk in the streets – not in the nighttime though – and get fresh air and good exercise. It doesn't cost anything except the changing of your heels once in a while. But the ideal of traveling for the sake of broadening the mind and flattening your pocketbook is absolutely a false ideal.

Now, we come to music. I'm talking about the 'better' newspapers that play up the ideal of music. The ideal of music is as empty as could be. There's nothing to music. If

Keep your money in your pocket and you know what's doing.

someone finds consolation in a record or a tape, why not? But that it should be considered an ideal to aspire to and people clasp their hands and say, "Ooh" and "Ah"?! Like a certain writer, a scientific writer, I saw that he's *meshuga* right away. He said, "The world is full of wonders," he said. "Mankind has greatness in them," he said. "Especially Beethoven," he said. Beethoven?! What's in Beethoven?!

If you have music that you enjoy, why not? But to consider it an ideal and to declare that that's the greatness and the aspiration of mankind, it stamps the scientists as people who are mindless. They're fools and they're on the same level as the black man I saw standing in front of a music store and he's giving a jig to show how he loves music. There's nothing to these things.

Now, I'm talking about the innocent side of the newspapers, but today some newspapers play up wicked things. Today it's much worse!

Now, if you must, read the headlines as you pass by the candy store. Keep your money in your pocket and you know what's doing. Don't go through the bother of taking the garbage into your house.

Here I saw an old modern rabbi – he passed away already – he was already limping; he was so old. He was walking home Sunday morning with a big newspaper; a Sunday newspaper. It means he was going to waste his life that day reading a newspaper. A *meshugener!* An old rabbi; an American rabbi. He was limping. He didn't live long after that. He took it along with him in the next world; אַשְׁרֵי מִי שֶׁבָּא לְכָאן וְתַלְמוּדוֹ בְּיָדוֹ. That's a pity! A tragedy! A big newspaper like that means a whole day of reading on Sunday. Sunday! You can sit and learn that day! At least you can take a walk and get some fresh air and look at the *niflaos haborei* in nature! But to waste your time on that garbage! There's a mountain of *tzoah* in the newspaper!

And so, it certainly is an ideal if you can keep papers out of your house. Of course, if it means a battle with your wife, you have to use your judgment and buy the newspapers that are least harmful; but if possible, don't waste your life on newspapers.

If you get into the habit of reading at your meals, there are plenty of nice English Torah books to read. Today you have a choice. You can read English *seforim* if you wish, during a meal or other times.

January 1986

Think about the future when you won't be together anymore and try to enjoy life right now.

A Crowded Home

Q/ How can one happily accept the *nisayon* of a large family living in a small house?

A/ So let's picture forty years from now. All of your children are married and you are alone in that house. And now you look back to the good old days when everybody was together. Ohh! You yearn once more for the happiness of *yachad,* when the family was together.

Now your sons and daughters are all married and the house is empty. Even if they live near you – most of the time they don't live near you; they live in Lakewood; some in Yerushalayim – but even if they live near you, it's not the same. Once upon a time, every child was close to you; it's a *rachmanus* now on the old people. Now they look back and see how they didn't understand; *that* was the time to be happy. It was a small house? Alright, so you were close together; what about it?

And therefore, think about the future when you won't be together anymore and try to enjoy life right now.

May 1998

Chapter 19

The Jewish Father

Chapter Sponsor

Leilui Nishmat:

Zeev ben Yitschak Yaacov Z"L, Haim Shaul ben Sara Z"L
& Moshe Eliezer ben David Mordechai Z"L

For the hatzlacha of:

The Farberas family, The Thalenberg family
& Marat Crendel bat Hana
The Mandelbaum, Borer and Granatowicz families
לרפואה שלימה, פרנסה טובה ובריאות איתנה ואריכות ימים ושנים

Contents

Chapter 19

The Jewish Father

A Father's Role 1

What should the role of the father be in the home?

A/ He should contribute everything that he has to give. That's the plain and simple answer. Which means that when he comes home, before he even walks in, while he's still holding the doorknob, he should make it his business to dispel any crabbiness, any grouchiness that he acquired during the day. Because now begins his big career in life – the career of the home.

He has to expect anything from his wife when he comes in. Could be she is about to give a blast at him. "All day long you've been in a quiet office while I've been suffering from these kids." So while he's holding the doorknob, he should steel himself for that blast. He should be ready for anything and he should make up his mind, "No matter what is going to happen, יַעֲבֹר עָלַי הַכֹּל, but I'm going to play my role. I'm going to be a good actor." That's how he should prepare himself before he goes into the home.

Talking is the way of ruining your good reputation.

The only problem is if he's home all the time – what should he do then? On Shabbos – now that's hard! To act only in the evening, maybe, but all day Shabbos, that's a big job! And so, when he goes to shul on Shabbos he acts natural, and then when he comes home again, he should prepare again for the ordeal. And then he shouldn't remain in the house for long. He should quickly come back to the synagogue to learn. The less you're around, the easier it is to be an actor.

But that's only the beginning. There's a lot more to say about what a father should be contributing to the family. He has to put in a sense of humor into the house. A father must bring with him a sense of humor. Mothers are dealing with the children all day long, so they're worn out raw. And therefore, every little problem is magnified in her eyes. Little Chaim'l, he doesn't eat. It becomes such a major problem, that all the problems of the world are dwarfed in comparison. And so the father has to make a joke out of it. Of course, he has to be careful to do it in such a way that she doesn't become the butt of the joke. But it has to be a joke. "It's not so serious; Chaim will one day be a big fat rabbi anyhow."

April 1977

A Father's Role 2

How can a father gain favor in the eyes of his family?

A/ First of all, by not talking much. That's number one. Talking is the way of ruining your good reputation.

If people see your face, your face is *tzelem Elokim.* They respect your face. But when you open your mouth to bray, you do yourself betray. Because they see that it's not like your face; now they see that there's a donkey hiding inside that face.

And so, it's very important not to talk. Not to talk. People who give you credit looking at your face, give you credit for wisdom: "Oh, that's a smart fellow over there." But as soon as he opens his mouth, he gives himself away.

"Oh, that's a smart fellow over there." But as soon as he opens his mouth, he gives himself away.

That's number one. There are many other ways, but let's practice the first way, you'll see how effective it is.

Q/ Can you mention some of the other ways?

A/ He's pressing me so I won't refuse. Among the ways of gaining favor with your family are the ways of gaining favor with anybody else, and one is *sever ponim yafos* – have a pleasant cast of countenance. Don't come in with a sour face. Come in from the yeshiva, from the *kollel*, come in from your place of work, not like a sourpuss. Before you enter, you take hold of the doorknob and stop for a minute and take off the face that you had before and put on a mask, a pleasant face. Put on a smiling mask and walk in with a pleasant face. And don't talk. Say, "Good evening. How's everything?" You can say, "*Vos macht men?*" That's all. Keep quiet.

On Purim, sometimes a person puts on a mask and he looks very good; he looks more beautiful than he really is. So let's make it Purim always. Put on a mask, a nice mask on your face. That's another way.

However, there are many more things to do. Another way is to bring in money all the time when you work. Make sure you earn enough money! If you don't bring money home, there's trouble in the house.

September 1995

There are hundreds of things to do if you keep your eyes open for opportunities.

Helping at Home

Q/ When you spoke about הַצְנֵעַ לֶכֶת, about serving Hashem in secret, you mentioned a father in the home. Can you give an example of that?

A/ Let's say you walk into the house and your wife is not home. There are some dishes that have to be washed. Wash a few dishes. She doesn't know. She comes home. She thinks maybe there was a sink full of dishes but now she sees a half sinkful of dishes. She forgets about it. You should know you did a mitzvah. Don't tell her you washed them. Don't tell her.

I told this to one man and he said that he doesn't like this idea. All right, he's not satisfied with my idea; he's too lazy. There are other things you can do. Let's say, you're walking into the house and you see something, a piece of dirt on the floor. You know your wife will get busy. She's going to bring a broom and try to shovel it up. Kick it under the sofa, she shouldn't see it. She won't see it. It's saving her all that work.

You think it's a small idea? No, it's a good idea. Save people unnecessary work. *Hatznea leches*. There are hundreds of things to do if you keep your eyes open for opportunities.

April 1972

A Father's Chores 1

Should a husband help with the housework?

A/ Now, this is a question from the ladies' section and it's difficult to reply because there are husbands present. Truthfully however, to some extent, every husband should help. Especially when the mother is burdened with the task of children, when there's a sizable household, certainly there should be some help. The father and all the children should pitch in with the big job of maintaining the household chores.

Now, this is a question from the ladies' section and it's difficult to reply because there are husbands present.

But if it is an interference with his Torah program, if he has some time to study Torah, naturally, an idealistic wife would prefer to have the *zechus* of Torah study because she is a full partner.

And so, he cannot be expected to carry an equal share in the household work. After all, he has his work to do that he does all day, and in addition, he has his spiritual achievements that he must do in the evening. But to some extent, a helping hand can achieve a good deal, and he is expected to at least make a demonstration of participating in household things.

Again, this depends on individuals. It depends on the family. It depends on the environment in which you live and on customs, and it varies. But there's no question that some assistance must be lent to the wife in household chores.

November 1970

A Father's Chores 2

Q/ What is your opinion about a frum man who takes very little part in helping his wife and his children in the kitchen and so on?

A/ And the answer is, it depends on the circumstances. Sometimes a man works very hard for *parnassah* and he has to take a lot of ill treatment from his boss or from competitors or from customers. Sometimes, a man comes home so broken that the house is like a hospital for him. And therefore, he deserves a lot of consideration.

A father must shoulder that responsibility. A father must help out.

However, if it's a man who has a comparatively easy life and he comes home in good condition, there's no reason why he shouldn't help out a little bit. There should certainly be some token assistance, especially if the wife wants it.

Now, some women don't want the husband to putter around in the kitchen. They tell him to keep out of it. He's a lucky man. But even then, he should make some motions as if he's trying to help out until she tells him to go out.

But there's no question at all, everybody should feel it's his duty to help carry the burden of the house.

June 1983

Helping with Schoolwork

Q/ What is a father's responsibility when it comes to helping the younger children with their schoolwork?

A/ Now, I want to say this. When it comes to taking care of the children's Torah education, it's a very big error to let the burden fall on the wife. Some women have to take care of coaching the children in the Torah lessons from the yeshiva. A father must shoulder that responsibility. A father must help out.

Very many children need help. Even with *alef beis,* they need help. A father must help. Chumash, they need help. And some fathers neglect that and therefore, their children grow up feeling like failures, and sometimes they're dropouts from the yeshiva with the most terrible consequences, *chas v'shalom*. It's not the children's fault. The blame is on the father.

You must see to it that your children's learning is supervised.

If he cannot have patience to do it himself, he must spend money. He has to hire a boy to teach his little child, or a girl to teach his little daughter. You must see to it that your children's learning is supervised.

Don't rely on the yeshivos! Don't rely on the teachers. Day to day, check on your child if he's keeping up with the class. If he falls behind even in one lesson, it's a tragedy because the next day it will be two lessons. Then he'll be discouraged and he'll lose *cheishek, chalilah;* and sometimes he becomes an enemy of learning as a result.

So it's up to the father to constantly be on guard. This surely; he has to shoulder the responsibility of the *chinuch* of his children in *alef beis*, in Chumash, in learning Gemara. If he's not capable, he must hire help.

June 1983

Saving Up

Q/ Is it proper for a father to amass money in order to make sure that his children should be able to spend their lives studying Torah?

A/ Now, in the Gemara (*Kiddushin* 29b) it says as follows: הוּא לִלְמוֹד וּבְנוֹ לִלְמוֹד. There's a question being posed there. Who should learn? He should learn or his son should learn? And the answer given there is, הוּא קוֹדֵם – *he comes before his son.* If you have two persons, you and your son, and there's a certain fund that could support one of you in the *kollel*, what should you do? Should you say, "My son, you go learn"? Nothing doing! You

Your first job in this world is to make something from yourself, to achieve shleimus.

say, "My son, I'm going to make use of the money and you get busy and fend for yourself." Unless the father has no head, then it's a different story, but otherwise the father comes first.

July 1978

Retirement Savings

Q/ Is it important that when I save money for retirement, that I also should save to leave money for my children?

A/ It's permissible to save for yourself. You have to have money to live on.

However, when it comes to saving for your children, it depends. If you can save without sacrificing the purpose of your life, that's all right. Why not? But people who give away the time that they should be devoting for their own betterment, time they should be spending making something out of themselves, and instead they give that time towards saving for their children, then it's a one-hundred percent waste. Because your first job in this world is to make something from yourself, to achieve *shleimus.* And your child, when he comes into the world, he brings along an allowance that he takes with him from Heaven. Everybody is born with an allowance. My parents didn't set me up in business; they didn't leave me any money. And yet, *baruch Hashem*, I never had to borrow any money all my life.

And so, if you won't save up for your children – instead of working to save for them, you'll take off your evenings to study Torah, you'll do *tzedakah,* you'll give money to charity; so you'll be a success. Don't try to leave wealth for your children.

Of course, if you want to leave them Torah wealth and it costs money to send them to yeshivos, it costs money to keep even your married children in *kollel,* so that's yours – whatever you do for them is for you. It's an investment for your own self, to a certain extent.

Is it proper for someone to study Torah even though his family is in need?

But even so, you have to know what and when and how much. Suppose you're capable of sitting in a *kollel* and learning, but your son would like you to keep on slaving away to keep him in a *kollel.* So you should tell him, "If you wish, if you like this idea so much, then you can do it for me. I'll let you slave and support me in *kollel.*" Why not? The father has a right to be in a *kollel.*

Sometimes the father has a better head than the son has. The Gemara says, הוּא לִלְמוֹד וּבְנוֹ לִלְמוֹד הוּא קוֹדֵם לִבְנוֹ – *If there's a question who should learn, him or his son, he goes first* (*Kiddushin* 29b). So you don't give away your soul for your children. But, if you can do it without any big sacrifices of your time, you'll be able to make something out of yourself, but at the same time, leave a little bit for them, there's nothing wrong with that. Why not?

February 1976

A Father's Responsibilities

Q/ You mentioned an example of a *talmid chacham* who sits and learns when he has no money for his family; he's depending upon support from the outside. Is that the proper way for a husband to fulfill his responsibilities toward his family?

A/ Is it proper for someone to study Torah even though his family is in need?

And the answer is, it's a Gemara. On the words in *Shir Hashirim,* שְׁחוֹרוֹת כָּעוֹרֵב – *black like a raven,* the Gemara

When a person wants to succeed in Torah, he must make up his mind that he cannot have the things that others have.

(*Eiruvin* 22a) says like this: בְּמִי אַתָּה מוֹצְאָן [דִּבְרֵי תוֹרָה] – *By whom will you find success in learning Torah?* בְּמִי שֶׁמַּשְׁחִיר פָּנָיו עֲלֵיהֶן כָּעוֹרֵב – *By someone who blackens himself with affliction; he deprives himself so much that he becomes black like a raven.*

And then it goes on and says, רָבָא אָמַר – *Rava says,* בְּמִי שֶׁמֵּשִׂים עַצְמוֹ אַכְזָרִי עַל בָּנָיו וְעַל בְּנֵי בֵיתוֹ כָּעוֹרֵב – *The Torah will not be found* – it means nobody will succeed in studying Torah – *unless he is cruel upon his wife and children like the raven is cruel.*

Now what does that mean? It means that when a person wants to succeed in Torah, he must make up his mind that he cannot have the things that others have.

Now, if a person is willing to afflict himself, then he has a right to tell his family, "We're going to live on a meager scale of existence." But if a person is indolent; if he likes ease and he's not going to afflict himself studying Torah, then forget about it. Let's say he comes to the *kollel* at 10:30 in the morning after reading through the entire newspaper. And then at lunch, he takes off another hour-and-a-half or two hours, and then he loafs at night too. And you see him many times on the street in the middle of the *seder*. That fellow is being cruel to his family, but he's being very kindhearted to himself. He's living the life of Riley, not the life of a *kollel* man.

But if a person afflicts himself and he's willing to sit in poverty and study Torah, he has a right to expect his family to participate. Of course he can't starve them, but he has a right to be cruel to a certain extent.

Now, it doesn't mean he's actually hard-hearted towards them. He's a kindhearted father; he's a loving parent. There's no question about that. But he is not obligated to give his family more than the barest sustenance if he's doing it for the great ideal of studying Torah.

Again I say, that if a person is not putting his heart into Torah and he's merely using the *kollel* as an excuse to live a life of irresponsibility, then of course, he's nothing but a cruel and selfish fellow.

June 1980

What should a father do about training his children for a life of parnassah when his sons are learning in yeshiva?

Teaching a Profession 1

Q/ What did Chazal mean when they say (*Kiddushin* 82a) that a father should teach his son an *umnus kalah unekiyah*, a profession that's easy and clean?

A/ What did Chazal mean when they say teach your son an *umnus kalah unekiyah,* an easy and clean kind of *parnassah*?

It means this: A father can teach his son to be a sidewalk repairer. Why not? He can teach him how to pour and mix cement, how to repair sidewalks; but it's not such an easy *umnus* and it's not such a clean *umnus.*

If he can teach his son something that's easy and clean, then it's a *chesed* for his son, and the son is going to have a happier existence and be more respected in the community. And therefore, that father is bestowing a gift on the child.

Now, what is called today *umnus kalah unekiyah* is not what it used to be. It depends on the circumstances.

July 1982

Teaching a Profession 2

Q/ What should a father do about training his children for a life of *parnassah* when his sons are learning in yeshiva?

I'm not going to say anything right now. You can talk it over with some people. It's a delicate problem.

A/ That's a delicate question.

According to the Gemara (*Kiddushin* 29a), every father is *mechuyav* to teach his son a *parnassah*. However, some parents choose the way of one Tana who said אֵינִי מְלַמְּדוֹ אֶלָּא תּוֹרָה – I'll teach him only Torah (ibid.). There's an opinion like that. One Tana says that. And many parents choose that.

And therefore, I'm not going to say anything right now. You can talk it over with some people. It's a delicate problem.

Because it *is* a problem. Young men who are not going to become great *talmidei chachamim*, they deserve to have some training in some kind of *parnassah*. But exactly what to do and when to make a decision, I'll leave that open.

January 2000

A Father's Strength

Q/ In davening, we say כְּרַחֵם אָב עַל בָּנִים כֵּן תְּרַחֵם הַשֵּׁם עָלֵינוּ. We're asking Hashem to have mercy on us *like a father has mercy on his children.* Why doesn't it say "like the pity of a mother on her son"? Isn't it the mother who has more pity?

A/ The answer is like this. Let's say, one morning the father had to leave for work early and he's not home. And the mother goes into Chaim's room to wake him up for *cheder*. "Chaim," she says, "It's late. Get up quickly. You have to go to the yeshiva."

"You know, Ma, I'm really sick. I don't feel well. I can't go today." So the mother, she has a soft heart, so she says, "Alright, alright. Get some rest."

The father comes in and says, "What do you mean you don't feel well? What's the matter? Do you have a fever? We'll take your temperature."

"'No, I don't have a temperature."

"You have a sore throat?"

"No sore throat."

So the father is thinking, "If I let him stay home now, at 9:00, at 10:00 he'll become well and he'll go out in the street." No, I can't allow that. He says to the son, "Go straight to the yeshiva."

Now, had there been only a mother there, who knows what would have happened to this boy! Every second day Chaim would have a sore throat at 8:00 and he'd stay home from *cheder*. And by early afternoon, he'd be outside on the street. Who does he meet on the street? Bums. How do you think a boy bumps into drugs? He found them outside in the candy store when he was bumming around that day when he was off from yeshiva.

A father's mercies are generally better than the mother's mercies because you need a mercy that's firm

And therefore we say *kerachem av al banim,* because those are the mercies we need; a father's mercies are generally better than the mother's mercies because you need a mercy that's firm; it's *rachmanus* on the *neshamah*.

Of course you need the mother too. Let's say the boy got a *potch* and now the father walks out. The mother caresses him and says, "My sweet boy. I'm so sorry. Go to the yeshiva. Listen to your father." And she sends him off with a piece of cake or a cookie and he yields. He yields to the *potch* and the caress. Of course, everything should be done with *seichel*. The mother cannot be too yielding. The mother also has to worry about the child's future. She should always yield to him and make him feel good? No.

But it's the father in the home; he has an iron fist because he wants the children to toe the line. You need a father in the

A father must be firm; he must demand that the family walk in the ways of the Torah, in the ways of righteousness.

house, somebody to carry out the strictness. If there's a son who doesn't want to go to yeshiva, the father has to yank him out of bed. No such thing as pity on him. The mother can come along and give him a kiss, very good. But the father has to be a father. A son who doesn't want to learn; you have to force him to learn. Of course it doesn't mean you can't give him inducements. You should give him bribes too, certainly. But don't yield.

June 1996

A Firm Hand

Q/ What should I do in the home to make sure my children keep on the straight path? How firm do I have to be?

A/ You know, sometimes a father comes to me and he's describing a problem with a child. And as he's talking to me, I'm thinking, "What kind of milquetoast are you? That's a father?!" He should have laid down the law: "You're back in the house before dark, or else! You think you're going to hang out on the street? No way!" But he just can't bring himself to do that. He's a weakling. That's not a father. A father must be firm; he must demand that the family walk in the ways of the Torah, in the ways of righteousness.

I know it's not the style today, but sometimes the father even has to hit the child; that's also mercy. חוֹשֵׂךְ שִׁבְטוֹ שׂוֹנֵא בְנוֹ – *If you hold back the stick, you're an enemy of your son* (*Mishlei* 13:24). That's not mercy; it means you're his enemy.

Once upon a time even *goyim, l'havdil,* understood that. How many *goyim* were saved from ruining their lives? The father, an old Italian *goy*, took his boy in the backyard, into the woodshed, with a stick and gave him a drumming. And you know what? They didn't become criminals. Their lives were saved.

I once saw a write-up. It said like this: In which country in Europe – this was a long time ago – which place in Europe has the least juvenile delinquency? And it said there that Italy was the place. And the reason was because in Italy, of all the countries in Europe, the father was the boss. His word was law. And therefore, there was the least juvenile delinquency; because there was a fear of the father's *potch*.

Sometimes showing anger, displeasure, is more effective and stronger than hitting.

Only that today there are child abuse phone lines and snoopers. They see you hitting your child and they call up the child abuse committee and a woman comes down with a notebook, "What's it all about?"

There was a beautiful family, one of the most beautiful families in Brooklyn, and they had the best-behaved children. So an old gentile woman across the street mixed in and said there's child abuse. And she reported it to the headquarters and somebody came down to investigate it. A big nuisance. The *goyim* are *meshuga* today.

So we live in a *meshugene* world where they don't want us raising our children; there should be no fathers in the home, that's what they want. But we say no! We say that Hakadosh Baruch Hu planned the family that there should be a father in the home and we don't want to become *meshuga* like you.

And so certainly you must hit. Sometimes you must! Only you must employ wisdom. I can't give you easy solutions, but you must be a father! If you do it right, words will help much more than hitting. Sometimes showing anger, displeasure, is more effective and stronger than hitting. And so, if a father knows that the son is hurt by his father's displeasure, showing displeasure is sufficient. Whatever it is, the father's role is to make sure everyone is toeing the line.

Of course, the father has to be a man of consideration, but he has to be a man of principle too. The father must be

He knows what will happen in the long run if he allows the child to do as he wishes.

firm. He must demand that the family walk in the ways of the Torah, in the ways of righteousness. And sometimes he even has to take a stick and hit the child – it's not the style today, but that's unfortunate because if you hold back the stick, you're an enemy of your son.

Of course, the father also cannot be cruel and ignore the child's feelings, but after all, the father must be a man of principle. And he knows what will happen in the long run if he allows the child to do as he wishes.

June 1996

A Father's Potch 1

Q/ You spoke before about a man you know who learned how to live successfully because his father hit him when required. But doesn't it state in a certain *sefer* that one shouldn't hit a child with force?

A/ It could be. It depends on the circumstances.

I'll give you an example. If a child is addicted to the habit of running across the street through traffic and you hit him once and he still doesn't obey, then it's not enough to hit him as you did before. You have to hit him with force, with violence, because this is saving his life.

Suppose a child insists on going out in the street at night and coming back at all hours of the night; then you have to beat him within an inch of his life because you're saving his life. I know a father who yielded to his daughter and she started going out on the street at night. And I don't want to tell you what happened in the end. Had he beaten that daughter; had he said, "Nothing doing! You want to remain alive? Then you stay here!" he would have saved her life.

How many children have been killed – I don't mean just spiritually – because their parents gave them money and didn't ask any questions? You have to know where your child is. Is he hanging out with addicts? Who knows what your daughter is doing on the streets at night?

You have to know where your child is. Is he hanging out with addicts?

And therefore, there's no such thing as mild treatment when great peril is involved. Ordinarily, for smaller things, let's say a child broke a glass, a child even broke your watch, don't go into a rage over such things. It's not important. You might have to do something, but not in anger.

And therefore, the *seforim* say that you must always use discretion.

August 1982

A Father's Potch 2

Q/ How should daughters be punished, especially by their fathers?

A/ I was once speaking to a *menahel* of a girls' high school, a seminary. He said to me, "It's a good thing to punish girls." Don't think girls shouldn't be punished. He said, "First of all, you're doing a benefit to their future husbands." Girls can be spoiled, and it's good for a father sometimes, when necessary, to give a slap in the face.

Of course, girls are easier to handle, and in most cases it won't be necessary. But when it's necessary, once in a while, there's no harm.

What-ever it is, do not call him names. Leave that out!

Of course you have to be careful. Even a boy – if he's too big, the Gemara says, it's a sin, it's a *cheit* to hit a big son. And it's a *cheit* to hit a big daughter. But when they're in hittable ages, why not? A little bit is good. It's a medicine that helps.

December 1985

A Father's Encouragement

Q/ Since it's a father's job to discipline his son, how can he discipline him and also give encouragement at the same time?

A/ Now, this was mentioned here before briefly. Rather than continually knock the son and say, "You're no good," "You're rotten," "You good for nothing," it's better if you give him one smack if you see he's not doing his homework or he doesn't go to the yeshiva or if he was lazy to do his duty.

Whatever it is, do not call him names. Leave that out! You can force him to do what he has to do. Forcing is not bad, but to give him names, to convince him that he is a failure, to convince him that he's a low character, that's one of the worst things you could do.

And when he does a little bit, make it better than it is; let him feel that there's an incentive to do good. He'll know that there's *kavod*. Sometimes it's worth giving little prizes. Sometimes you can give great encouragement by giving little prizes.

January 1977

A Father's Blessings 1

A father's bracha is more genuine than a stranger's bracha and therefore it's very important.

Q/ When a father is blessing his children on Friday night, what should he have in mind? And also, what should the child who is receiving the blessing have in mind?

A/ A *bracha* is said by the parents because they love their children. So you're saying it *b'lev shaleim,* with a full heart. And therefore, Hakadosh Baruch Hu listens. He listens because it's being said with more *kavanah*. A *bracha* of a parent is more sincere. *Birchas av, barcheini avi.* A father's *bracha* is more genuine than a stranger's *bracha* and therefore it's very important.

Of course, you could always add even more *kavanah*. And what's the most important thought you should add? You have to know that it's not your *bracha*; it's the *bracha* of Hashem that you're asking for. You're asking Hashem, "Please Hashem, bless my children they should all be well and live long; they should all be *tzaddikim*; all should have the best *shidduchim*; all should be *talmidei chachamim* or the wives of *talmidei chachamim;* all should be healthy and they should have the most beautiful children; and after a long life, after 120 years, they should all go to Olam Haba." You want to add the last one? You can add it, there's no harm.

Now, what should the children think? Your children think, "Ribono Shel Olam, I don't know what my father is thinking, but I'm thinking all these *kavanos*." So the child puts all the *kavonos,* all these thoughts, into his father's words – and Hakadosh Baruch Hu is listening to his thoughts as well.

December 1995

Don't be ashamed to add words when you give blessings.

A Father's Blessings 2

Q/ What blessing should you bless girls on Friday night?

A/ You bless them they should be like our mothers, like Sara, Rivka, Rochel, and Leah. You can't find any better blessing than that.

If you want to add, nobody is limited – you can add whatever you want. Don't be ashamed to add words when you give blessings. If they're unmarried, bless them they should get good husbands, *talmidei chachamim*. And you can bless them that they should have many children. And you can also bless them that they should be rich. No harm. I remember my father-in-law, *zichrono livracha,* used to add to all the blessings, "And you should be rich, too." He said, "Why not?"

December 1978

QUESTIONS
On Any
SUBJECT

Chapter 20
The Jewish Mother

Chapter Sponsor

In honor of our dear and beloved mother,

Edythe Markowitz

A Jewish Mother in its truest sense

Whose sole goal is to make everyone else happy

Whose kochos seem to be endless
in all her chessed and devotion to our families

And someone who we all love, admire, appreciate
and truly look up to as the matriarch of our family.

May Hashem bentch you with arichas yamim v'shanim,
good health, happiness, and nachas from your family who love you so much.

Love,
All of your children, grandchildren and great grandchildren

Contents

Chapter 20

The Jewish Mother

A Mother's Role

Q/ Notwithstanding the three or four commandments given especially to women, it seems like men dominate our tradition. How do I know that we, the males, are not fooling our women and young girls into thinking that their mission in life is to be at home so that we can go out into the world, while they'll have to stay at home and cook and clean and wash diapers?

A/ How do we know that our sense of values as far as the mission of women in this world is not prejudiced by, we'll call it, male chauvinism?

So the question is this. How do we know that the mission of man in this world is to make a living and support a family? Maybe it's a plot by all the women so that they should be able to remain at home while the men have to go out of the house. Up until now, at least, that's how it was; only lately, they're becoming more generous and they're helping carry the load. But up until now, it was a woman's plot to send out the men to work hard in the fields.

A man, you should know, is like a bull. A man gets irritated too much.

You know, men didn't work in offices up until recently. They toiled in the fields. It was very heavy work. So the women's plot was that men should be the laborers; they should do all kinds of dirty work and grueling work, working outside in the freezing cold sometimes. Women, meanwhile, were home and they were protected. All they had to do was to take care of what was inside the house and they led a life of ease. And so, maybe it was just a plot, a plot of female chauvinism against the men.

And the answer is, nobody plotted anything; only Hashem plotted. Call it nature if you want, but it's Nature with a capital N. Hashem plotted it that way.

Because up until recently, women used to give birth to children. That's what their function was in life. Men up until now didn't have any breasts to nurse children and therefore they had to leave the job to the women.

Now, if a woman has children in the house, somebody has to take care of the children. And so, the one who can nurse the baby has to be there. Therefore she had to stay home to nurse the children.

She is also the one who has the most patience with children. Because a man, you should know, is like a bull. A man gets irritated too much. And therefore, she is the one fitted by nature to the task of raising little children. And since little children were in the house all the time until she was well past middle age, therefore, that's how it turned out by the plan of Hakadosh Baruch Hu that women were there.

But they had to eat. So the man had to go out on the fields and plow. And he was plowing all day under the hot sun. And when he was reaping, he was reaping under the hot sun. He brought back the flour after grinding it, and she baked it at home.

So therefore, it was a cooperation. She was home anyway and there was a stove there, so she baked the bread. She cooked the food that he brought back from hunting, let's say, or from raising livestock. And therefore, the cooperation was by the forces of nature which Hakadosh Baruch Hu created.

A woman has a nature. A man has a nature. And each nature has to be fulfilled

The truth is, nobody had it easy in the olden days. Everybody worked hard. The women worked all day long with big families. It was hard, but they achieved their purpose in life. And the more children they had, the more proud they were. It was accomplishing something for Hashem. And the men didn't have it easy, either. They slaved on the fields. They didn't have an eight-hour day. They worked from sunrise to sunset, even on the longest days. They toiled all the time. And therefore, nobody was privileged because of chauvinism.

It's only lately, since women decided that they don't want to have babies, they have nothing to do, so they say, "We want to compete with you in the offices."

So now they're going out to the offices and they're enjoying a childless life; a life where they're sitting in offices without fulfilling their purpose as mothers, without fulfilling their purpose of making a home. Their homes are nothing but an apartment on the West Side. They come home at night to a lonely apartment. Let's hope it's lonely.

So what do they have? A barren existence. A woman is not satisfied by being, let's say, an executive in a business. Don't deceive yourself. It's all fake. Even a woman who is elected, let's say, as a city councilwoman, so she comes home from the city hall to her apartment and she's thinking, "This is what I was created for?" She puts up a bluff, but she is dissatisfied.

A woman has a nature. A man has a nature. And each nature has to be fulfilled according to its own criteria. A woman's nature is most fully fulfilled when she has a family. By means of her children, that's where all the characteristics that are stored up within the depths of a woman's human nature come to the surface. She is kindly. She is full of *chesed*.

The world was created for chesed! For the doing of kindliness!

A woman becomes a creature of doing kindliness. Her whole life is devoted to kindliness. That's what she is for. Her voice is gentle and she is not rough. She is easily persuaded. It's easy to get along with her, more or less. And therefore, she fulfills her perfection through building a family.

And when the children grow up, she is busy helping raise her daughters' children. She helps them grow up. She is busy all the time with family. And it brings out the best in her nature: compassion. The desire to help. Charity. Unselfishness. All these qualities develop to the very best.

And when the time comes for her to return to the One who sent her, she goes back with the most *shleimus* that she could achieve. Instead of sitting in an office and not achieving the perfection of her character, she remains in a house full of children where there is family, where there are human beings, and there, she develops all the qualities that were implanted potentially in her nature. And when she finally comes back to Hakadosh Baruch Hu, she is perfect.

Even though she is not so wise. Even if she doesn't know Gemara. But she has achieved things that even the person who learned Gemara cannot achieve because the world was created for *chesed!* For the doing of kindliness! For the achievement of unselfish deeds of virtue. And a mother lives a life of unselfishness.

She sacrifices for her children. She doesn't sleep because of her children. She doesn't eat on time because of her children. She gives away from herself because of her children. She remains poor for the sake of her children; she wants to send them to *cheder*, to yeshiva.

And she gives up good times and luxuries for the sake of her children. Living a life of self-sacrifice for an ideal makes her ennobled. She's glorious! And a Jewish mother, when the time comes to come back to the next world, she comes with a crown on her head that many *tzaddikim* won't have.

And the Gemara says, גְּדוֹלָה הַבְטָחָה שֶׁהִבְטִיחוֹ הַקָּדוֹשׁ בָּרוּךְ הוּא לְנָשִׁים יוֹתֵר מִן הָאֲנָשִׁים – *How much greater is the promise that Hashem gave to women, even more than to men* (*Brachos* 17a). Because a man, let's say, who is a *rosh yeshiva*, he's a big *lamdan*, but who says that it's all for the service of Hashem? Who says it's unselfish?

How cruel it is to take her out of that home and put her into an office where she becomes not a woman!

After all, he gets glory and sometimes he gets money for it too. There's a certain exhilaration in being able to teach Torah to other people. Here's a wise man who writes *seforim*. How much is there of unselfish service to Hashem there? But a woman, it's all unselfishness.

Of course, you have to think about Hashem. If she forgets that He sent her, then it's like an Italian woman. But if she always remembers Hashem and she lives a life of dedicated unselfish *chesed,* then she has achieved the greatest she can achieve. There is nothing better you can do for her!

How cruel it is to take her out of that home and put her into an office where she becomes not a woman! She's a man there, and none of her qualities are able to develop anymore. And she remains barren. It's like a field that could have produced the most beautiful trees and fruits, and nothing grows there.

Because we don't need her in the office! Nothing is accomplished by her that couldn't be accomplished by just a plain automaton, a robot without feelings.

A man, however, goes out into the hard, bitter world of competition. He has to make a living. He has to fight his way with people. He also has certain tests. His tests are tests. Will he steal other people's money? Will he encroach on other people's rights? On people's properties? He has various tests of other kinds. And if he lives properly, he will also pass the test and develop the potential in his character.

But remember! Each one has a different nature. נָשִׁים עַם בִּפְנֵי עַצְמָן – *Women are a separate nation* (*Shabbos* 62a).

Do whatever you do and say, "I'm doing it for the service of Hashem."

They're actually a separate people and Hashem made them different. And they need a different kind of existence to create the perfection for which they were made.

December 1985

A Mother's Avodas Hashem

Q/ What is the best way for a woman to feel good while dealing with the pressures of childrearing and housework?

A/ Now, that's an important question because a great deal of time and effort is invested in that, and it pays to utilize these opportunities. First and foremost is to do whatever you do and say, "I'm doing it for the service of Hashem."

That sounds queer because people never thought of that. As you pick up a squalling baby, say, "I'm doesdoing it because Hashem says וְאָהַבְתָּ לְרֵעֲךָ כָּמוֹךָ, and so I love my fellow man." The baby is also your fellow man, after all. "It's my fellow man, this baby, and I want to help him." That's a *mitzvas aseih*. The little fellow man is sad; he's distressed and he's shrieking and you try to calm him. וְאָהַבְתָּ לְרֵעֲךָ כָּמוֹךָ. Think about that.

When you're handing out food to your family sitting at the table – they say, "Ma, give us some bread," and you think, נֹתֵן לֶחֶם לְכָל בָּשָׂר כִּי לְעוֹלָם חַסְדּוֹ – *Hashem is the One giving bread to mankind*. I am a *shaliach* of Hashem."

Your daughter wants a piece of bread – "Here's your slice of bread," and you're whispering to yourself, "Hashem is giving you the bread."

When you're baking, you're thinking: נֹתֵן לֶחֶם לְכָל בָּשָׂר. When you're doing anything in the kitchen, preparing food, you're imitating the *middah* of Hakadosh Baruch Hu. What's His *middah*? What's Hakadosh Baruch Hu doing? יוֹשֵׁב וְזָן – *He's sitting and feeding the world,* מִקַּרְנֵי רְאֵמִים עַד בֵּיצֵי כִנִּים – *from the biggest animal to the smallest insects* (*Avodah Zarah* 3b). Hashem is feeding the world, and He is the model for all the mothers who stand and labor in the kitchen; they're feeding *their* little world! That's how a person should think.

Whatever you do in the house, even when you're washing diapers, it's *l'sheim Shamayim*. You're serving Hakadosh Baruch Hu. And therefore a woman, if she has the right preparation, a little thought, she can transform all these menial tasks that a gentile girl can also do, and she transforms them into *avodas Hashem*.

Everything is transformed into gold; whereas otherwise, it remains nothing

And let me tell you, it's no less than a *kohen* in the Beis Hamikdash. Anybody who serves Hakadosh Baruch Hu with a *lev shaleim*, לַעֲשׂוֹת רְצוֹנוֹ וּלְעָבְדוֹ בְּלֵבָב שָׁלֵם – *To serve Him with a whole heart,* לְמַעַן לֹא נִיגַע לָרִיק – *in order that the labor shouldn't be in vain,* וְלֹא נֵלֵד לַבֶּהָלָה – *and so that we shouldn't be producing for no purpose,* is like a *kohen* doing the *avodah* in the Beis Hamikdash. It's a pity to 'waste' our lives in taking care of children and in cleaning the house when we could have done the same work as people who are working in the Beis Hamikdash – you're being *meshameish* like *levi'im* who are sweeping up in the *azarah.* You're serving Hakadosh Baruch Hu and therefore everything is transformed into gold; whereas otherwise, it remains nothing but tin – a waste of opportunity and a lost life.

September 1983

Compassion for Her Children

Q/ When a mother suffers pain because of her child's suffering, is it a positive or negative reaction?

True compassion is always a mitzvah. And therefore, you shouldn't be ashamed

A/ Any kind of commiseration, any kind of compassion is a mitzvah, because we are walking in the ways of Hashem. וְהָלַכְתָּ בִּדְרָכָיו – *You should walk in His ways* (*Devarim* 28:9). מָה הוּא רַחוּם אַף אַתָּה רַחוּם – *Just like He is merciful, you should also be merciful* (*Sotah* 14a). So therefore, a mother who has compassion on her child – or anybody who has compassion on anybody else – it's a good *middah*.

Of course, you have to be careful. כָּל הַמְרַחֵם עַל אַכְזָרִים – *Someone who has pity on cruel people,* like those liberals who have compassion on murderers, לְסוֹף נַעֲשָׂה אַכְזָרִי עַל רַחֲמָנִים – *in the end they are cruel to the kind people;* because they're doing harm to good people (*Midrash Tanchuma, Metzora*). But true compassion is always a mitzvah. And therefore, you shouldn't be ashamed and you don't need any justification.

However, if you add the ideal that you're emulating Hakadosh Baruch Hu, then you have a *mitzvas aseih*. וְהָלַכְתָּ בִּדְרָכָיו is a *mitzvas aseih*, one of the *taryag mitzvos*. So if you'll think, "I'm doing it because Hakadosh Baruch Hu wants me to emulate His ways," even better.

But whatever you do, you have to know, compassion, *rachmanus,* is a good *middah;* it's a Jewish *middah* because it's Hakadosh Baruch Hu's *middah*. Whether it's compassion of a mother or compassion on other people, not your own child, never be ashamed of compassion.

Of course, you should always do it within the *gidrei haTorah*. Never, because of compassion, should you allow your child to wheedle you into getting something that's wrong for the child.

The child begs his mother, "Ma, let me out on the street. Everybody is on the street at night. I have to stay in the house?"

No compassion! Stay inside the house. No streets for our children. Nighttime is a *sakanah*. Boys and girls in the house!

Always! Up until the time that they're ready to go out to get married. No boys and girls out on the street at night at all.

No compassion when it comes to wrong things.

The child begs and weeps. "But everybody else is doing it, Mama." Nothing doing!

I recall the case of the Lelover Rebbe. He tells the story of his mother. His mother used to get up every night in the middle of night for *chatzos* and she used to wake up the little children. And they were weeping – not for the Mikdash. But she didn't listen. She forced them to get up every night to say *tikkun chatzos*. An interesting story. That's how he became a *rebbe*. His mother made a *tzaddik* out of him.

Now, I'm not saying that mothers should go to that extent, but you cannot be compassionate to a child who wants bad things.

A child who doesn't want to go to *cheder* in the morning, "Ma, I don't feel like going to *cheder* today."

The answer is, "Nothing doing. You must go."

If you have compassion, you know what's going to happen? At 10:00, he'll be cured already. He'll be well by 10:00.

And so, nothing doing. No compassion when it comes to wrong things.

April 1986

On Washing Diapers

Q/ Is it better for a woman to wash diapers instead of using disposable pampers?

Everyone in the house should make the brachos out loud.

A/ This is a good question and it will need better heads than mine. There are a number of implications in this question, but they are so complicated that we'll leave this for somebody who is more capable.

January 1974

Reciting Brachos Out Loud

Q/ Is it proper for a mother to make *brachos* out loud so that her family will hear her and answer "Amen"?

A/ Absolutely. How else should you make a *bracha?* The Navi says, וְהַבֹּשֶׁת אָכְלָה אֶת יְגִיעַ אֲבוֹתֵינוּ – *The embarrassment, the bashfulness, ate up the work of our forefathers* (*Yirmiyahu* 3:24). To be embarrassed with Yiddishkeit?! וְהַבֹּשֶׁת אָכְלָה אֶת יְגִיעַ אֲבוֹתֵינוּ. Being bashful can sometimes eat away at your *avodas Hashem*. Don't be embarrassed! Certainly make a *bracha* out loud.

Of course, if there are men present, let's say *talmidei chachamim,* then you could make it quietly in another room. Nobody should make themselves conspicuous in front of *talmidei chachamim.* But among the family, why not?

Everyone in the house should make the brachos out loud. הוֹדוּ לַה' קִרְאוּ בִשְׁמוֹ – *Thank Hashem and make Him great by proclaiming His name* (*Tehillim* 105:1). You have to proclaim the name of Hashem and speak out loud His name.

March 1997

A Mother's Task

How much greater is the promise that Hashem gave to women, even more than to men

Q/ Why shouldn't a mother be able to learn Gemara?

A/ Gemara takes up a big part of your spare time and women can't afford to give all that time because women work all day long. A man's work is from sunrise to sunset usually, or from nine to five, but a woman's work is around the clock; they have to raise families and they can't afford to sit at the Gemara – otherwise, what would happen to the family? And therefore, whenever they get a chance, when they get a little crack in their schedule, they can get in something if they wish; there are plenty of good things to learn. But Gemara, anybody who knows anything about Gemara knows that it takes up a great deal of your time.

And therefore, Hakadosh Baruch Hu says to the women, "You will get reward in the next world for having beautiful, frum children with good *derech eretz*, and also as many as you can have." And Hakadosh Baruch Hu will reward you; you will be a millionaire in the next world. Your husband is going to be jealous of you.

גְּדוֹלָה הַבְטָחָה שֶׁהִבְטִיחוֹ הַקָּדוֹשׁ בָּרוּךְ הוּא לְנָשִׁים יוֹתֵר מִן הָאֲנָשִׁים – *How much greater is the promise that Hashem gave to women, even more than to men* (*Brachos* 17a). He promises it to them more easily; they go to Gan Eden more readily than men. Of course, you have the difficulties of raising your family in a kosher way, but it's not like the problems of a man. Men have various kinds of problems; they fight sometimes over *kavod* – glory, over who is a bigger *lamdan.* Oh yes! Competition in business, competition in the *beis hakneses.* Each one wants to be elected president and *gabbai;* all kinds of things happen among men. But the women are excused from that kind of competitive life.

How much pain and suffering must women be willing to endure for the sake of having children?

It's not so easy to be a man; it comes with a lot of baggage. Like I always say, the only reason we make the *bracha* of *shelo asani isha* is because a man has pockets in his suit; women don't have pockets. It's such a blessing to have pockets! So when you have pockets, that's why you can say *shelo asani isha* – "Baruch Hashem, I have pockets!" But women, mothers, can more readily have a contentment-filled ride through existence and be even more successful than men. That's גְּדוֹלָה הַבְטָחָה שֶׁהִבְטִיחָן הַקָּדוֹשׁ בָּרוּךְ הוּא לְנָשִׁים יוֹתֵר מִן הָאֲנָשִׁים – *How much greater is the promise that Hashem gave to women, even more than to men*. She'll be a very happy woman in Gan Eden.

January 1994

Children and Real Estate

Q/ How much pain and suffering must women be willing to endure for the sake of having children?

A/ Question: How much pain and suffering will you endure for the sake of having a very big apartment house a block long on Ocean Parkway; a beautiful, big, white apartment house? It brings enough *parnassah* to keep ten families going from the income. How much would you suffer for that apartment house?

I'm not able to tell you, but plenty, you would suffer plenty. I would suffer plenty even though I don't care for money that much, but I would suffer plenty.

I'd go into the mines if I knew that after a few weeks I'd get that apartment house. Others would do more.

Now compared to a child, an apartment house is nothing. A child is property. It's the greatest wealth. There's no wealth in the world – I'm talking about physical wealth – compared to having a child.

Of course, the child has to be utilized. If you buy an apartment house and then let bums move in, they'll wreck all the apartments. Of course, you have to watch it. A child has to be guarded. You have to let only the right ideas move into the child's mind. You have to give him the right training. But a child who grows up to be a frum Jewish man or woman, that's the greatest wealth that a parent can ever attain, and don't deceive yourself.

Billions of dollars, without an exaggeration, are nothing compared to one child.

Billions of dollars, without an exaggeration, are nothing compared to one child. And the more you have, the wealthier you become.

And here's the answer to women who complain that they're being knocked out by work because of children – ten children! They're making her crazy. The answer is, it pays to get crazy if you have ten apartment houses. Ten huge buildings! Every month, piles of checks come in! Every month, wealth comes in from every one of them.

And you have to know every child is endless wealth, *actual* endless wealth. כָּל הַמּוֹסִיף נֶפֶשׁ אַחַת מִיִּשְׂרָאֵל כְּאִלּוּ הוֹסִיף עוֹלָם מָלֵא. The Rambam (*Ishus* 15:16) says this *lashon*. A whole world! A child is a world! There's no measure to the value of one more person of the Am Hashem you bring into the world.

So how much should you take? You should take as much as you're able to take. And that means you should never give up the hope of having another one.

September 1984

A Mother's Gehinom

Q/ It says in the *seforim* that כָּל מִי שֶׁיֵּשׁ לוֹ צַעַר גִּדּוּל בָּנִים אֵינוֹ רוֹאֶה פְּנֵי גֵּהִינּוֹם **– *If you suffer from raising children you won't have to go to Gehinom.* Does that**

It's a remarkable thing, what happens to a mother of children.

mean that everyone who has a family won't see Gehinom?

A/ The question is, it states that a person who endures the difficulties of raising children won't see even the beginning of Gehinom. What does that mean?

Now I have to explain that to you.

What's the purpose of Gehinom? Gehinom is to prepare a person for Olam Haba. If he has certain *mumim*, certain blemishes in his character, Gehinom will burn them out of him, it will clean them out of him. It's not so easy, however. Gehinom is terrible. You have to know that Gehinom is terrible! If you can avoid Gehinom, even a little part of Gehinom, it pays to do anything in the world to avoid it. But if it's needed, it does a good cleaning job.

And when one is finally clean of all the faults that he has, he comes out of Gehinom. He's pale. He's worn out from his sufferings, but he's there. He's a *maamin*, he's a frum Jew, so now he's ready to go to Gan Eden and get his reward for his mitzvos forever and ever. Forever and ever.

Now, bringing up children – we're talking about having a whole houseful of children, a frum house – is not easy. But when she does that, you know what happens to her? It's a remarkable thing, what happens to a mother of children.

You know, the mother was a selfish girl once upon a time. Here she was a selfish girl who thought only about herself. Now she's married and her whole life is devoted to others; to caring for her children, for her husband, for the family. And there are a lot of children. There are boys who are fighting all the time and she has to make *shalom*. She has to have patience with them. They don't obey. It's a tremendous *nisayon*.

And she is bringing them up properly. She has patience. She learns to be a *sovel!* Self-control! And self-control for the sake of *chesed*, for kindness! She's bringing up a generation of *avdei Hashem*.

So she does not *need* Gehinom to make her perfect. She went through so many things in life. She sacrificed her own good times for her children. Instead of buying clothing for herself, she bought for her children. When there was some candy or cake in the house, she didn't eat it. She gave it to the children.

She does not need any-thing to make her purified. She goes straight to Gan Eden.

Everything was for the children in order to bring them up *b'derech haTorah*. She suffered. At night she didn't sleep because of the children.

So Hakadosh Baruch Hu says, "Look. You gave everything you had for the sake of My service. You're bringing up servants for Hakadosh Baruch Hu. Then you don't need Gehinom because you went through everything already and you're purified and you go straight to Gan Eden after a hundred and twenty years."

Of course, it's talking about a case where she makes sure that after all the children are married, she continues to live a life of *yiras Shamayim*. Sometimes a woman, when she has more spare time, she's thinking of going places, having a more wealthy home. She can spoil after that too. But suppose she didn't spoil and she continued with all the *shleimus*, the perfection that she acquired as a result of *tzaar gidul banim* then there's no question that she does not need anything to make her purified. She goes straight to Gan Eden.

March 1996

Physical vs. Spiritual Safety

Q/ What is more important for a mother to study: first aid, like how to save a child's life, or *hashkafah*, the attitudes of *emunah* and *middos tovos*?

It's so important for parents to think about their children in the most common sense terms.

A/ And the answer is both. What's more important, the brain or the heart? You can't get along without either of them.

And therefore, it certainly is worthwhile to learn *pikuach nefesh,* but that doesn't mean that a person's time is so occupied that he can't learn matters of *emunah* and *middos tovos*.

And by the way, while we're on the subject of *pikuach nefesh*, most of the matters of *pikuach nefesh* are not things that need much study. The precautions to save the lives of children are much more simple than the study of *hashkafos*. And it's because of negligence, *batlanus,* just plain downright carelessness, that children's lives are sacrificed constantly.

It's unforgivable in a frum house that a child should fall out of a window and lose his life. And it's happened again and again. It's unforgivable. That doesn't need any studying. Just plain common sense.

It's common sense that you shouldn't let children play on the sidewalk without being supervised; they're playing with a ball and they'll run out into the street to pick up the ball. It's so important for parents to think about their children in the most common sense terms.

Or a *menahel* of a yeshiva who allows boys to sit on windows on the top floor; boys are sitting on the window sills and he passes by and says nothing. He thinks it's not his *kavod* to say such *gashmiusdig* things. He should take action immediately! There must be either window guards or strict punishment for sitting on windows.

Batlanus, carelessness, is a matter of life and death. And that's something that we could teach. We should speak about it and practice it, and it doesn't take up much time.

November 1988

The Last Laugh

Everybody is weeping, but the righteous are laughing.

Q/ What does it mean when we praise the *eishes chayil* that she's וַתִּשְׂחַק לְיוֹם אַחֲרוֹן – *she'll laugh on the last day* (*Mishlei* 31:25)? Who's going to laugh as they're dying?

A/ The Gemara describes the death of a righteous person as follows: יָצְאוּ צַדִּיקִים לְקַבֵּל שְׂכָרָם – *When the righteous leave this world, they are going out to receive their reward* (*Bava Metzia* 83b). Everybody is weeping, but the righteous are laughing.

It doesn't mean that they're laughing before they die. Before they die, they try to hold on. "Please Ribono Shel Olam, another year! At least another month. Maybe another day." They try to hold on.

But as soon as it's too late and Hakadosh Baruch Hu gives them a gentle push and He throws them out of this world, they find themselves immediately in the great banquet hall which is illuminated with the brilliant lights of Olam Haba, and then they come with the greatest happiness.

That's what it means "she laughs on the last day." Others are busy laughing before the last day. They sit in front of television sets and they laugh all evening; but when it's all over, there's nothing to laugh about. It's not a laughing matter. They go to theaters and sit and laugh at the clowns, but the lights go out and they go out on the dark street and it's all over. And then the lights of life will go out, and then it's waiting for them – a nice, well-illuminated grave, a brilliant grave. It's a lot of fun in the grave. There are a lot of entertainers there. There are a lot of worms. It will make them happy as the worms bite into them. So these people will not laugh on the last day.

This pious woman, her clothing is strong and beautiful.

But the pious woman, she didn't laugh at television in her day. She didn't laugh in theaters. She was busy. She was busy with her children. She was busy having *nachas* from a big family. She was busy washing diapers. She was busy cooking meals for her husband and her sons who were going to the yeshiva to learn Torah. She was busy day and night. She had no time to fool around.

And so עֹז וְהָדָר לְבוּשָׁהּ – *Her garments are strong and beautiful* (*Mishlei* 31:25). This pious woman, her clothing is strong and beautiful. You know, when you buy a garment, if you are a prudent person, you look for good qualities in a garment. It should be lasting, it should be strong, and it should be beautiful.

All the garments that we purchase in this world are neither. They're surely not lasting. And whether they're beautiful or not, today they're beautiful but tomorrow they're old fashioned. It's ridiculous. You're ashamed to walk out in the street because the fashion is out of style. So nothing in this world is both עוֹז, strong, and הָדָר, beautiful.

But the pious woman – she wears, let's say, not such fashionable garments; but they're beautiful because they are beautiful forever. The style never goes out of fashion. In the next world, they last forever, these garments of precious character attributes, of *tznius*, of modesty, of piety, of charity, of industry, of obedience to her husband – oooh, it's out of style over here in America; I'll say it again, of obedience to her husband. Ah! What a beautiful garment that is. And all these beautiful garments, they last forever and they endure.

And therefore, וַתִּשְׂחַק לְיוֹם אַחֲרוֹן – *she laughs on the last day.* Before she dies, the pious woman, she's lying on her bed, an old *bubby,* an old grandmother. She takes out her *Tz'ena Urena.* There's a big *Vidui* in the back, pages and pages of confessions; confessions of sins she never even thought about. The great men who drew up this *Vidui* wanted to cover all contingencies, all the things that you can imagine. She confesses and sheds tears and she leaves this world purified with tears of repentance.

And she leaves behind her family sorrowing, they're all weeping, but as she crosses the border, she begins to laugh. וַתִּשְׂחַק לְיוֹם אַחֲרוֹן because she's carrying those precious garments. There are sequins set into her dress, diamonds sewed into her dress, all the diamonds of good deeds.

This dress will never go out of style. It will be admired no end in the next world. In the next world the *tzaddikim* look at women's dresses, and they'll encounter all the sequins; and they're real sequins, all the diamonds, all the doubloons, real gold sewed into her dresses. And therefore, the Jewish mother, the *eishes chayil,* she's going to laugh forever in the next world.

This dress will never go out of style. It will be admired no end in the next world.

January 1973

QUESTIONS *On Any* SUBJECT

Chapter 21

The Childless Righteous

Chapter Sponsor

In memory or our parents

ר' **שמעון גדליה** בן החבר ר' **שלום** הכהן ז"ל

ומרת **מלכה** בת ר' **יצחק** ע"ה

Walter and Amelia Marlene Neuman

ר' **משה אהרן** ב"ר **דוד** הלוי ז"ל

ומרת **זעלדא** בת ר' **יצחק** ע"ה

Morris and Sylvia Zharnest

By Leon and Faye Zharnest and family

Contents

Chapter 21

The Childless Righteous

Sensitivity Toward the Childless

Q/ How do we understand the principle of *ayin hara*, that some people who have large families are careful about not showing them off or something like that, especially in front of those who are childless?

A/ It was explained here once but I'll explain it again. What is the evil eye? The evil eye is as follows: If you are proud of your possessions and you practice ostentation – you display your wealth or your success – then you cause a certain sorrow to other people who don't have that success. That is why Jewish mothers who have a brood of a lot of children, they make it their business that when somebody comes into the house, they shoo the children out. The visitor may be a childless person or somebody who doesn't have that much *nachas;* why should he or she be pained to see how successful you are in building your family?

Now, you have to know that even though it's not your fault – on the contrary, you are doing a great thing by raising a big family – nevertheless, Hakadosh Baruch Hu takes into account the distress of every individual. It

That is ayin hara, that is a bad eye, because people look at you with an eye and they feel bad,

doesn't mean that there will be some drastic action, but there could be some kind of penalty for causing distress to people.

And that is why it is always good to cover up your success. Don't display your wealth with expensive diamonds, expensive necklaces – you can never know what is going to happen. Maybe Hakadosh Baruch Hu will cause a bum to come along and snatch it off of you. And that would be the easiest way to get away with it! Sometimes, a physician might have to take that necklace off of you in the operating room.

And so, it's always good to not display your success. Try to be as plain as you can. That is why it is good for wealthy people to teach their children to live plainly; not to give them too much money to spend; they should try to act like people of the poor. You wealthy people, see to it that your children are always like poor children. They shouldn't have things to display and come among other children in the yeshiva to show expensive watches or expensive toys to others. It hurts the poor boy or poor girl who can't afford it. And Hakadosh Baruch Hu doesn't keep quiet. That is *ayin hara,* that is a bad eye, because people look at you with an eye and they feel bad, and Hakadosh Baruch Hu will take some action.

And so, it's important to be careful with the feelings of those who don't have children. Of course, the best thing is to daven for them. Always, always daven for them.

But also, besides putting time into prayer for your fellow Jew who is childless and waiting for children, do your best to not hurt his feelings by displaying your good fortune.

Now, the things that people do to ward off *ayin hara* are all foolish things. The best way is not to be ostentatious, not to display your success. Because if you are displaying it, it's not going to help you if you put a piece of garlic in your pocket.

June 1982

Praying for Children

Why are some righteous people deprived of having children?

Q/ Why are some righteous people deprived of having children?

A/ Righteous and not righteous.

But one reason I can tell you immediately, why righteous people sometimes don't have children. Because the Gemara (*Yevamos* 64a) asks, why did Sara not have children? And why did Yitzchak and Rivka not have children? And why was Rochel deprived of children?

And the Gemara says an interesting reason. Because Hakadosh Baruch Hu wanted them to pray more fervently. שֶׁהַקָּדוֹשׁ בָּרוּךְ הוּא מִתְאַוֶּה לִתְפִלָּתָן שֶׁל צַדִּיקִים, it's because He wants them to pray.

Prayer is a very big achievement because it makes you more aware of Hakadosh Baruch Hu. דַּע לִפְנֵי מִי אַתָּה עוֹמֵד – *Know in front of Whom you're standing* (*Brachos* 28b). *Daas!* To be aware, that's the highest achievement. יִרְאַת ה' רֵאשִׁית דָּעַת – *The highest wisdom is yiras Hashem* (*Mishlei* 1:7). It doesn't mean merely to be afraid. It means to be *aware* of Hashem, to know that Hashem is watching over us.

Now therefore, people who have trouble with having children should follow that pattern, and they must pour out their hearts in prayer. Of course you should go to *tzaddikim* and ask them to pray for you. But it's a mistake if you rely on that alone. It's a very big mistake! Hakadosh Baruch Hu wants you to pour out your heart.

Now, even if eventually you'll have children, you have to know that your best children are your own prayers. אֵלֶּה תּוֹלְדֹת נֹחַ נֹחַ אִישׁ צַדִּיק. The best child of Noach was Noach himself. If you're a *tzaddik,* that's your best child. You are your best child. Of course you'll have *nachas* from all your children, but your best child is you.

Make yourself your best child. From yourself you'll have nachas.

So if you pray your heart out like Yitzchak and Rivka did – they had a lot of children, a lot of descendants, but of all their descendants, do you know who the best child of Yitzchak and Rivka was? Two children named Yitzchak and Rivka. And the best child that Noach had was not Shem; it was Noach.

So in case you have trouble at home and you can't succeed with children – it happens sometimes that you don't succeed; maybe your wife is in the way or there are other causes, or you started too late – don't give up, because you're still around. And make yourself your best child. From yourself you'll have *nachas.* When you'll come to the next world, you'll take along this *kaddish'l* of yours with you – that's yourself. And he'll give you so much *nachas* without end.

And that's why Hakadosh Baruch Hu sometimes visits people with these difficulties. So that they should pray. And pray and pray and pray. Not once in a while say a halfhearted weak, pale prayer. Pour out your hearts with tears to Hakadosh Baruch Hu.

And thereby, if they'll have children, well and good. And if *chas v'shalom* they'll remain childless, they're not childless. כֹּה אָמַר ה' לַסָּרִיסִים – *So said Hashem to the childless ones*: וּבָחֲרוּ בַּאֲשֶׁר חָפַצְתִּי – *these people who choose what I desire;* it means you choose what Hashem desires, even though you can't always carry it out. But in your heart you long to do it! וּבָחֲרוּ בַּאֲשֶׁר חָפַצְתִּי – *they choose what Hashem wants them to do* (*Yeshayahu* 56:4).

They'd like to have twenty children, and all of them *tzaddikim, bnei Torah,* frum boys and girls. They'd love it! And they pour out their hearts with tears. So Hakadosh Baruch Hu says, "Then you have them already." וְנָתַתִּי לָהֶם בְּבֵיתִי וּבְחוֹמֹתַי יָד וָשֵׁם – *I will give these childless people in My house and upon My walls a place and a name. Their names will be engraved forever,* טוֹב מִבָּנִים וּבָנוֹת – *better than sons and daughters* (ibid.).

Sometimes there will be sons and daughters too. That's certainly good!

And that's one of the reasons why some people are childless, one of the purposes.

January 1976

But we don't question the plans of Hashem. He has His reasons.

Difficult Fortunes

Are childless people less fortunate?

A/ Absolutely. What about people who, *chalilah*, die young? Are they less fortunate? People who have children are immensely more fortunate than those who don't.

But we don't question the plans of Hashem. He has His reasons.

Now sometimes, Hakadosh Baruch Hu had that in mind when they were born, that they should be childless. Sometimes it's a result of something that they once did. I'm not able to tell you exactly each case, but there's no question, there's a *yosher* in every kind of arrangement.

May 1997

The Childless Tzaddik

Q/ **You quoted a *maamar Chazal* that Hashem makes *tzaddikim* childless because He wants them to pray and gain the achievement of awareness of Hashem and *bitachon* and *emunah.* Does that mean that when a person is childless, he's a *tzaddik?***

Hashem listens to our prayers with mercy.

A/ No, absolutely not. It depends how he reacted to it. If he reacted in the proper way, he can become a *tzaddik.*

Of course, it depends on the amount of prayers and *avodah*. If he cries out to Hakadosh Baruch Hu properly, certainly he becomes enlightened and the greatness of his heart issues and makes him what he was supposed to be.

But otherwise, there are plenty of childless people that are *resha'im gemurim,* and that's one of the reasons why they're childless. Hakadosh Baruch Hu says better they shouldn't transmit their wickedness to another generation.

January 1979

Does Prayer Help?

Q/ Does praying help, besides helping me gain awareness? Will it help me gain children?

A/ Absolutely it could help gain you children; what's the question? וְהַנְיָא בָּעְוּתָא – *Tefillah helps* (*Akdamus*, Shavuos). We have a lot of pull with Hakadosh Baruch Hu. כִּי אַתָּה שׁוֹמֵעַ תְּפִלַּת עַמְּךָ יִשְׂרָאֵל בְּרַחֲמִים – *Hashem listens to our prayers with mercy.*

Here's a man who thought he would never have any children. A true story. He came to me many years ago, over twenty years ago, and he was very sad. No children! But what could I do for him? I can't help him. I'm not an עוֹשֶׂה פֶלֶא. I'm not a *baal mofeis.*

So I told him he should take care of himself, he should go to sleep on time, and eat three meals a day on time, and he should take walks, and he should drink a lot of water. "And pray to Hakadosh Baruch Hu," I told him, "Pray all the time to Hakadosh Baruch Hu for children."

Twenty years later he came to me. He called me on the phone and said he needs to speak to me about something. He wants to come over.

When he came, he said, "You know, I have a problem. I have too many children."

I said, "I can't help you. I can't help you."

So absolutely, you have to keep on praying to Hashem. And Hakadosh Baruch Hu should answer your prayers among all of the prayers of the Am Yisroel.

September 1994

There are all kinds of good deeds in the world for you to do.

The Successful Childless

Q/ What should those who have no children do?

A/ אַל יֹאמַר הַסָּרִיס הֵן אֲנִי עֵץ יָבֵשׁ – *The childless one shouldn't say I'm a dry tree* (*Yeshayahu* 56:3). No, a person can have children even without having children. Your good deeds are your children. Your *ma'asim tovim* are your children. There are all kinds of good deeds in the world for you to do.

I know one *gadol b'Torah* who became a *gadol* only because he didn't have any children. He had no need to waste any time. He gave all his life only to learn. He became a great man as a result. I won't mention his name, but he's a well-known, big *talmid chacham*. He didn't have any children and he became very great because of that. And his good deeds, his accomplishments, they became his children. If you learn a *masechta*, that's a *ben yachid*, a beautiful boy. *Bava Kama*

Women can go out and do mitzvos for other people. There are so many things to do.

is a beautiful little boy to have. Believe me. Or even *Maseches Megillah; Maseches Megillah* is a beautiful little boy. So you have plenty of children.

And women can do tremendous things. Women can go out and do mitzvos for other people. There are so many things to do. People need help constantly. If you help other people, those *ma'asim tovim* are your children.

January 2000

Adopting Gentile Children

Q/ Should childless people adopt gentile orphans and convert them?

A/ They should certainly *not* do it. If they feel well-disposed towards gentile orphans, let them give money to homes where such orphans are raised. But to bring in gentiles into Jewish homes and to confer upon them the status of Jews is adulterating the Jewish people. We have no right to do it.

September 1971

Maximizing One's Childlessness 1

Q/ Is a childless marriage a punishment from Hashem, and if so, can anything be done by the couple?

A/ Now, why Hakadosh Baruch Hu does anything is His business. But one purpose we surely understand, and that is to cause them to pray.

If they pray all their lives and no children result, then they have not lived in vain, because אֵלֶּה תּוֹלְדוֹת נֹחַ נֹחַ – *These are the children of Noach, Noach.* If you yourself become a firm servant of Hashem, a loyal servant of Hashem, then you are your most beloved child.

Don't think your life is childless. If you and your wife have produced two fine people who have wept many years to Hashem and asked Him and He didn't see fit to grant your request, then you have to know you have lived for a purpose because *emunah* is the prime achievement.

You have to know you have lived for a purpose because emunah is the prime achievement.

If in addition, if you utilize your extra leisure time to do good things, very good. Here there was a *gaon* who didn't have any children; he was able to learn more. If he had children he would have had to go to work, he wouldn't have become a *gadol b'Yisroel.*

You could learn more Torah in your time. The women can do more mitzvos. There are so many people who need more help in this world. Patients in hospitals, various individuals who need help.

And so, if in addition to praying to Hashem they utilize the extra time to do good deeds, then they have children. תּוֹלְדוֹתֵיהֶם שֶׁל צַדִּיקִים אֵלּוּ מַעֲשֵׂיהֶם – *Who are the children of tzaddikim? Their good deeds.* כֹּה אָמַר ה' לַסָּרִיסִים – *So said Hashem to the childless ones who keep My Shabbos and fulfill My laws,* וְנָתַתִּי לָהֶם בְּבֵיתִי וּבְחוֹמוֹתַי יָד וָשֵׁם – *I will give you in My house and upon My walls a place and a name,* טוֹב מִבָּנִים וּבָנוֹת – *better than sons and daughters* (*Yeshayahu* 56:5). You hear that?! *Better than sons and daughters!*

And so, when you will earn a place and a name with Hashem, you are blessed with a great family of your own children; and children from which you have the most *nachas*; that's your good deeds.

January 1986

Some people have become very great as a result of childlessness; such greatness that they would never have attained otherwise.

Maximing One's Childlessness 2

Q/ If the very purpose of *nisayon* is to improve a person and to help him come to achieve in this world, what about those kinds of *nisyonos* which by their very nature, prevent a person from making achievements, for example the inability to have children or brain damage?

A/ Now those are two different kinds of *nisyonos* that you mentioned. If you mention brain damage, *chalilah,* it's like saying death. That's not a *nisayon;* that's the end of a person's activity. Only that if the brain damage doesn't interfere with a person's freewill, then certainly he has *nisyonos*. He has opportunities; he can do very many good things. He has his whole career of serving Hashem in his heart; he can serve Hashem with thinking, with *emunah*, with *bitachon* – certainly. All the *Chovos Halevavos* are available to a man like that. If, however, he loses the opportunity to function entirely, then it is death; he's *chashuv k'meis.*

The *nisayon* of lacking children? Absolutely, it's an opportunity for achievement. It's a different achievement than having children but it's an opportunity nonetheless. Some people have become very great as a result of childlessness; such greatness that they would never have attained otherwise.

I don't want to point out *gedolim,* but there are *gedolim* that I recall, close to this generation, who had no children, and therefore, all the Jewish nation became their children. They gave their time for everybody.

I will just mention one, however – Reb Chaim Ozer, *zichrono livracha*. His house was open to everybody. Men and women used to come, and he sat like a father and gave them advice. He had no other things to bother himself with. He could have learned all day long, but he became a father. That's what happens to a lot of people who are great in character; the Jewish nation becomes their children.

Like we mentioned here once, Devorah, Devorah Haneviah: עַד שַׁקַּמְתִּי דְּבוֹרָה – *Until I, Devorah, arose,* שַׁקַּמְתִּי אֵם בְּיִשְׂרָאֵל – *that I became a mother in Yisroel* (*Shoftim* 5:7). She became a mother to the Jewish people. Her love that a mother has for her children, she extended to the entire Jewish people, and therefore, she was a mother to her people.

And so these people sometimes attain much greatness.

There is another couple I know. They weren't *gedolei Yisroel* and they weren't wealthy people either, but they spent their lives doing *tzedakah v'chesed*, he and his wife, for the Jewish people.

They spent their lives doing tzedakah v'chesed, he and his wife, for the Jewish people.

And these people became great just because they were childless. That's what the Navi says, וְנָתַתִּי לָהֶם בְּבֵיתִי וּבְחוֹמֹתַי יָד וָשֵׁם – *I will give them in My house and in My walls,* it means in the World to Come, *a place and a name,* טוֹב מִבָּנִים וּמִבָּנוֹת – *better than sons and daughters* (*Yeshayahu* 56:5). It means they will accomplish a better name for themselves than if they had sons and daughters.

Because as a result of their deprivation, they dedicated themselves to the great task of helping the Jewish nation by serving Hashem and helping His children.

December 1981

Entertainment for the Childless

What should a couple who don't have children do?

You know some people are not fit to be rich? You have to be a decent man to get rich.

A/ Everything. All good things they should do.

But they shouldn't say, "Because we don't have children, we are able to save more money." No! They should spend that money for good purposes.

They shouldn't say, "We have more time to travel around and to waste our lives on amusements and entertainment." No. All the time that they would have given on raising children and all the trouble – there is a lot of trouble raising children – they should invest that trouble and that time in doing good deeds.

December 1985

Becoming Worthy of Having Children

Q/ For what sins does one not have children, and what could someone do about it?

A/ Now that's a question that I wouldn't talk about in public. But in general, if a person suspects that it is due to certain iniquities that he's not having children, he should do *teshuvah*. That's the plain answer. And not only for those sins. He should do *teshuvah* all along the line, and Hakadosh Baruch Hu might decide that now this person is so much better, and therefore he or she will be a good parent.

Otherwise, some people are not fit to be parents. You know some people are not fit to be rich? You have to be a decent man to get rich. Now, it seems queer to hear that. Some people, when they're rich, they're intolerable. And therefore Hakadosh Baruch Hu says, let them remain poor.

And in general, if a childless person suspects that it's due to his or her sins, they should do *teshuvah,* and hope that Hakadosh Baruch Hu will answer their prayers.

July 1980

Are we little girls who need baby dolls? Something to play with?

The Privileged Childless

Q/ **How can someone who is constantly sad because they have no children be thankful to Hashem?**

A/ And the answer is, the *Chovos Halevavos* says that if you are one of the privileged ones who has no children, you should thank Hashem always. You should be grateful that He absolved you from the obligation of children.

Now pay attention.

What do you need children for? Are we little girls who need baby dolls? Something to play with? It's irrational. And it's selfish. Is that what children are for?

Children are given to us by Hashem as a responsibility. However, it's our job not to dodge it. Certainly you have to marry young and have as many as you can because that's Hakadosh Baruch Hu's command. פְּרוּ וּרְבוּ! You must do that.

And as they come and the obligations are raining down upon you, you're going crazy from even one child; so go crazy from ten. It's the same thing. It's a big mistake; women think if they don't have more, they won't go crazy. I've seen woman who claim they are crazy from one baby. So you might as well go crazy over a lot.

Don't waste your life mourning because that shows that you don't under-stand the purpose of life.

But suppose Hakadosh Baruch Hu didn't give; it's silly for a person to waste his life in sadness. On the contrary, breathe a sigh of relief, like the *Chovos Halevavos* says, and be grateful; now you can go ahead and do the great things in life.

How many women have time to read the *Kuzari* or to read the *Chovos Halevavos*? You can read it in translation too. A woman can become great now that she has no children. She's not of that bent of mind? She can become great in *gemilas chasadim*. There are careers in helping other people; a lot of things to do that mothers of families cannot do.

Now, mothers of families, תָּבוֹא עֲלֵיהֶם בְּרָכָה – blessed should they be with all their chores; certainly Hakadosh Baruch Hu will reward them. But the *Chovos Halevavos* says that you should thank Hashem when you have no children because He has exonerated you from those obligations, and now you can do a lot of things that people with children cannot do. And don't waste your life mourning because that shows that you don't understand the purpose of life.

The purpose of life is to serve Hakadosh Baruch Hu. How do you serve Him? In whatever manner He requires of you. So if he deposits children on your doorstep, so that's what's required of you. And if He doesn't, so He requires other things. And there are so many requirements in life that there's never any spare time. Never do you have any leisure time to take off from *avodas Hashem*.

And so, people should always be busy in serving Hashem in one way or the other. To utilize life for its purpose; whether it's by raising children or by raising somebody else's children or by raising money for Torah causes, or by raising your mind to heights of *avodas Hashem* by creating a mind filled with all the attitudes and ideals of the Torah.

May 1983

The Childless Build the Nation

They wanted one thing in life. They wanted to build up a nation to serve Hashem.

Q/ Is being childless a tragedy? The Imahos, even though they were childless for a long time, had children at the end. But what about someone who never has children?

A/ If it happens that there's a childless couple, of course it's a tragedy for them. It's sad for them. But you must know it's really a fundamental mistake to think that our Forefathers wanted children like people today want children. People today want children like a little girl wants a doll. Her heart yearns for a doll. Parents yearn for a doll. That's what it is today.

But our Avos and Imahos didn't want children in that sense. They wanted one thing in life. They wanted to build up a nation to serve Hashem. The Rambam says that their only purpose in life was to build up a nation to serve Hashem. And you have to have material to build that, so they wanted children for that. That's all they wanted. They didn't weep for a doll. They wept for a nation.

But now that there's already a nation, the childless can build up the nation even without having their own children. It happens sometimes; they're not capable of having children, so there are substitutes. They have to do things to make up for it.

Suppose a person doesn't have children. If he's a *talmid chacham*, וְשִׁנַּנְתָּם לְבָנֶיךָ אֵלּוּ הַתַּלְמִידִים – teaching children or teaching *talmidim*, that's like having children, because you create minds, and minds are just as important as bodies. Or helping other children go to learn Torah. If you can pay *s'char limud* for poor children, you could be *mekarev* children to the Torah, that's important. That's why our Avos and Imahos

Did the Chazon Ish feel the same way about not having children?

prayed and cried for children, because they wanted to build a nation. So you can build up the nation in other ways.

Q/ Did the Chazon Ish feel the same way about not having children?

A/ The Chazon Ish didn't tell me anything. I can't tell you anything about him; I don't know anything.

So you'll say, how can I tell you about the Avos? They didn't tell me anything either. But the Rambam told us. The Rambam says in *Moreh Nevuchim* that the reason the Avos wanted children was only because they wanted to set up a nation that would serve Hashem.

And so, even though it can be considered a tragedy because how happy are those who have children, how happy are those who can fulfill וּרְאֵה בָנִים לְבָנֶיךָ – to see your children having their own children, but if Hakadosh Baruch Hu chose a couple to not have children, they can accomplish just as much in this world, because we know that there are certain substitutes for children. תּוֹלְדוֹתֵיהֶם שֶׁל צַדִּיקִים אֵלּוּ מַעֲשֵׂיהֶם (*Rashi*, *Bereishis* 6:9). And so the childless have to be t*zaddikim* and do good deeds. The childless people have to learn more Torah and do more mitzvos, all kinds of things to make up; and these will serve in lieu, in place of children.

And so, if a person is childless, *chalilah*, he should know he shouldn't feel brokenhearted. He should know Hakadosh Baruch Hu has chosen him for a special achievement and he has to create a different type of children. אֵלֶּה תּוֹלְדוֹת נֹחַ נֹחַ, Who are the children of Noach? Noach himself was the best child.

So you have to be the best child of yourself with your good deeds. And that's a very big achievement. וְאַל יֹאמַר הַסָּרִיס הֵן אֲנִי עֵץ יָבֵשׁ – *The saris shouldn't say he's a dry piece of wood* (*Yeshayahu* 56:3). Let's say a man who lost his genitals, a gentile who was castrated and now he became a *ger*, but he's just sorry he can't have any children. So Yeshaya says to him, "Don't say, 'I am an *eitz yavesh*, a dry piece of wood.' No!" אָמַר ה' לַסָּרִיסִים – And He quotes what Hashem says to the childless. He said to those people who will keep My Shabbosos and all My commandments, Hakadosh Baruch Hu will give you a permanent place, וְנָתַתִּי לָהֶם בְּבֵיתִי וּבְחוֹמֹתַי יָד וָשֵׁם – *I will give them in the World to Come, a place and a name,* טוֹב מִבָּנִים וּמִבָּנוֹת – *that is even better than sons and daughters.* If they want, they can have a place in Olam Haba that is greater than those with children.

If they want, they can have a place in Olam Haba that is greater than those with children.

And therefore, it's not an exaggeration to say that a person without children can accomplish sometimes more than others who do have children.

August 1995

QUESTIONS *On Any* SUBJECT

Chapter 22

Life After Death

Chapter Sponsor

L'eluy Neshmat

Rena Bat Shefika

ר'נה בת שפ'קה

Renee Hazan A"H

By Ralph Hazan and Family

Contents

Chapter 22

Life After Death

Posthumous Regrets

Q/ When a person dies, does he immediately recognize all the truths that are concealed in this world?

A/ I must tell you that I don't know. We'll have to wait and find out.

But one truth he *will* recognize. And that is that he will groan in anguish at the lost opportunities. *Now* he realizes what it meant to be alive.

And so when the hearse comes with his body in front of the synagogue for the last farewell – they open the doors in the back and somebody comes out and says a prayer, קֵל מָלֵא רַחֲמִים, he would like to leap out for one last minute to the synagogue, one last visit!

But he can't come out. It's too late. He's lying there and he regrets it terribly. He regrets it! His life is gone forever. "That's the way I should have spent my life. I should have visited the *beis hamedrash* more often."

That truth he surely realizes; but it's too late now.

April 1991

There are people who claim that they actually died; they experienced that someone took them away

A Visit to the Next World

Q/ How does Rabbi Miller explain the people who claim that they died and came back to life again? Did they actually experience anything?

A/ Can you tell me the name of the someone who claimed that – besides for the famous one?

Q/ There are people who claim that they actually died; they experienced that someone took them away; a *malach hamaves* came and took them away. And then they came back to life.

A/ Well, we have a right to be skeptical. It's almost certain that every instance is nothing but imagination or fraud. People who die usually tend to remain dead.

August 1976

Autopsies and Organ Donation

Q/ If we benefit from all of the medical advancements that are achieved by means of the study of dead bodies, why are Jews not permitted to allow our bodies, upon death, to be used for research in order to maintain and save lives?

A/ So the question is, since we see that Hashem has encouraged progress in the field of medicine, and that it was done by the use of donated bodies or organs for research, why doesn't the Jewish nation permit the donation of bodies or organs?

And the answer is that when a president passes away, nobody considers taking his body for experimenting. The president's body is never taken for the purpose of experiment. It's buried in state. And that's because of the reverence we have for a president. And we *should* have a reverence for a president – even for a dead president; even for a dead ex-president.

The Jewish nation, however, has been accorded a special status by Hashem.

Now, where will you get bodies for scientific research? On the Bowery. They're dropping dead every day on the Bowery. They are homeless people and there is nobody to claim their bodies, and so there's no reason why they shouldn't be used. Also in India, there are masses of people who die and their families are happy to sell their bodies for $25. And so, there is no lack of bodies on which to do experiments.

The Jewish nation, however, has been accorded a special status by Hashem. We are a מַמְלֶכֶת כֹּהֲנִים וְגוֹי קָדוֹשׁ – *A kingdom of priests and a holy nation* (*Shemos* 19:6). It's not our fault. We didn't choose that name – He gave it to us. What can we do? We are a holy people.

And therefore, even more than a president, a Jewish body is inviolate. It's sacred. We cannot do anything, except to honor it and bury it without making the slightest use for no matter what purpose.

And so, you can have Orthodox Jewish doctors – if they're not *kohanim* – and they can cut up bodies merrily and do research. You can get plenty of bodies; it's only a matter of a few dollars. But to make use of the *am kadosh,* no; that can't be helped. We are in a different class. And it will take a long time for us to appreciate that.

It's not that we Jews are proud or we Jews try to classify ourselves as superior. It's a principle that the Torah has taught us. Hakadosh Baruch Hu told us that. We are superior, and it can't be helped. And therefore our bodies are not for experiment.

June 1976

A Jewish body is kadosh. And you have to respect it with the greatest derech eretz.

The Holiness of a Jewish Body

Q/ What should I think when I go to the mitzvah of *taharas meisim* and I see a dead body lying there on the bed?

A/ You have to think a number of thoughts; I'll tell you one thought, however, that most people don't think about: טוֹב לָלֶכֶת אֶל בֵּית אֵבֶל מִלֶּכֶת אֶל בֵּית מִשְׁתֶּה – *Better to go to a house of mourning rather than to go to a house of rejoicing,* וְהַחַי יִתֵּן אֶל לִבּוֹ – *because the living man should put something into his mind* (*Koheles* 7:2). He gains a certain thought from this experience.

Now what thought does he gain? A number of thoughts, but one thought he has to have in mind is, "*Baruch Hashem,* I'm not lying on that bed. *Baruch Hashem,* I'm alive!"

Also another thought, if you still have time after that – there's so much to think about in the first thought, but if you still have room in your mind for another thought, then add this, too: Think that the body is *kadosh*. A Jewish body is *kadosh.* And you have to respect it with the greatest *derech eretz*. Hakadosh Baruch Hu declares that we are a holy nation, *physically* a holy nation.

That, by the way, is why Hakadosh Baruch Hu gave us the mitzvah of *korban Pesach* when we first became a nation. The *korban Pesach* is the first *korban* in history that was eaten by anybody. Never before was there such a thing. A *korban* always meant that you slaughtered whatever you had to slaughter, you put it on the *mizbei'ach* and burned it up as a form of allegiance of devotion to Hakadosh Baruch Hu. But to eat from it? It wouldn't even enter somebody's mind, such a concept. A human being should have the audacity to put a *korban Hashem* into his mouth? Nobody even dreamed of such a possibility.

And then came Pesach. וְאָכְלוּ אֶת הַבָּשָׂר בַּלַּיְלָה הַזֶּה – *And they should eat from the meat of the sacrifice* (*Shemos* 12:8). Every Jewish body is now elevated to the status of an altar! And instead of burning the offering on the fire of a *mizbei'ach,* it was consumed in the body of an Israelite in order to demonstrate that we can put the *korban* into our mouths just like you can burn an *olah* on the *mizbei'ach*. The *korban Pesach* means that the body of a Jew is declared holy by Hakadosh Baruch Hu! A Jewish body is *kodesh kadoshim*. Even a dead body is *kodesh kadoshim*.

November 1995

When you see death staring in your face, it's a contradiction to emunah in Olam Haba.

The Tumah of a Jewish Body

Q/ You said that the Jewish body, even a dead body, is *kodesh kadoshim.* So why is the *meis* so *tamei* then? If it's *kodesh kadashim,* why is *tumas meis* such a severe *tumah*?

A/ Because *tumas meis* is the biggest falsehood in the world. It's the biggest *sheker* in the world because it makes people forget Olam Haba; death makes you forget Olam Haba. When you're alive, yes, there's Olam Haba, but when you see death staring in your face, it's a contradiction to *emunah* in Olam Haba. The biggest contradiction to *emunah* is the sight of a dead person. That's the end! Oy! It's over!

And therefore, it's that *sheker* that makes the *tumah.* The Torah says that being under the same roof as a *meis* is *metamei*. Get out! Get rid of him as soon as possible. קָבוֹר תִּקְבְּרֶנּוּ בַּיּוֹם הַהוּא – *Bury the body right away* (*Devarim* 21:23). Get rid of him because a *meis* causes *apikorsus*.

It looks like he's dead, but he's still alive.

The *Chovos Halevavos* says that of all the *sfeikus* that the *yetzer hara* tries to persuade a person the most prevalent *safek* is not to believe in Olam Haba. That's the biggest *safek* there is, not to believe in Olam Haba. And that's why we have to get the *meisim* out of our sight as soon as possible. Because they discourage us. He looks dead but actually, it's a *sheker*! He *didn't* die! That man *didn't* die. He's alive! It looks like he's dead, but he's still alive. And that's why you have to get rid of him as soon as possible.

So therefore, when you look at a dead body, you have to fight against the *yetzer hara*. You have to remind yourself now that that person is not dead. And therefore, you respect him more and more because he's still alive. Now he's *really* living.

November 1995

The Chevrah Kadisha

Q/ If seeing a dead body is a contradiction to the *emunah*, what should the *chevrah kadisha* do? They're burying people every day! And what is an *eitzah* that we can counsel them?

A/ The Gemara says that if a man is afraid of doing a sin, if his *yetzer hara* is tempting him, so the Gemara gives him various kinds of counsel on what to do to get out of the influence of the *yetzer hara*. But if nothing helps, the Gemara (*Brachos* 5a) says, יַזְכִּיר לוֹ יוֹם הַמִּיתָה – *Let him remind himself of the day of death.* Oh! That's the most powerful antibiotic there is, to think of the day of death. It accomplishes the job. It kills the germs of the *yetzer hara*.

So a person once asked Rav Yisroel Salanter the following question. He said that the gentlemen of the *chevrah kadisha* who bury people every day, they should be the most frum people around. And it happens that they weren't. Maybe today they are because today it's all volunteers of frum Jews, but even today, I don't think that the people who run the funeral parlors are the most pious people. I doubt it. On the outside, they're all glum and they dress conservatively. But inside, when no customers are around, who knows what they do? When the telephone rings, he says, "Sam! Close the radio. Sam, answer the telephone but quick, close the radio before you answer, so they shouldn't hear any music playing here." The ones who deal with the dead aren't always the most frum. But they should be; that's what this person asked Rav Yisroel.

When people have no heads, they're the same as the horses – nothing is going to help.

So Rav Yisroel answered. He said, "Why are you asking about the funeral people, why they don't have *yiras Shamayim*? Ask about the horses who pull the hearse. Where is their *yiras Shamayim*?" The horses should be the *frummest* in the world. Every day they're pulling the hearse.

The answer is, horses have no heads. And when people have no heads, they're the same as the horses – nothing is going to help.

It means, if a man has some intellect and he's willing to use his thoughts, if you mention the *yom hamisah* to him, it'll have an effect. But if you have no head, it won't help.

And therefore, the *chevrah kadisha* and the funeral people, if they are people who think into it, no question, every day they become *frummer* and *frummer*. But if they don't think about it, nothing happens.

What's the *eitzah*? The *eitzah* is that they should learn *Mesilas Yesharim*. They should learn *Chovos Halevavos*. That's the *eitzah*. They won't do it, however. And therefore, there's no *eitzah* except to go into the grocery business instead.

June 1980

In ancient times, Jews used to aspire to burial in Eretz Yisroel.

Burial in Eretz Yisroel 1

Q/ Why do so many *tzaddikim* want to be buried in Eretz Yisroel?

A/ Why do *tzaddikim* want to be buried in Eretz Yisroel?

First of all, why not? Isn't Eretz Yisroel the best place in the world? It's common sense.

There are other reasons too, but why go into mystical reasons. I think this is the very best reason – to be close! That your remains should be close to the place of the Shechinah!

Now, I could tell you what *seforim* say, but that's a very good reason you just heard.

December 1978

Burial in Eretz Yisroel 2

Q/ Why do we hear so much of *kevurah* in Eretz Yisroel today, and what is its significance?

A/ Now it's not only today. In ancient times, Jews used to aspire to burial in Eretz Yisroel. The Jews who lived in far-off countries used to aspire to *kevurah* in Bavel – Bavel was like a Jewish country – but the Jews of Bavel aspired to *kevurah* in Eretz Yisroel.

Every year, a huge convoy came from Bavel to Eretz Yisroel to bring the shekel money, the *machtzis hashekel* money, and they had a big army. The Jews hired mercenaries, and so, a big army came along to protect that money.

Along with that convoy came many *bnei yeshiva* who wanted to study Torah in Eretz Yisroel. In those days, you couldn't travel on the road by yourself safely so every year, they traveled together.

And along with that convoy came many coffins of Jews who were to be buried in Eretz Yisroel because of the love of Eretz Yisroel; the earth of Eretz Yisroel is so precious that Jews aspire to be buried there.

Now, before it became a style for airplanes to transport the dead to Eretz Yisroel, they used to send earth from Eretz Yisroel. It was sold in the *moicher seforim* stores. And they sprinkled Eretz Yisroel earth on the coffin when they buried a Jew in America or in Russia, wherever it was.

וְכִפֶּר אַדְמָתוֹ עַמּוֹ – *The earth of it will be an atonement for the people* (*Devarim* 32:43). It means to be buried with the earth of Eretz Yisroel is an atonement. The *pasuk* doesn't mean that, but that's how Jewish nation understood it.

But the idea of being one with the soil of Eretz Yisroel, the holy soil on which the Forefathers trod, is an ideal from ancient times, as far as we can remember, even from the days of the Chumash: וּנְשָׂאתַנִי מִמִּצְרַיִם וּקְבַרְתַּנִי בִּקְבֻרָתָם – *And you should carry my remains from Mitzrayim and bury me in the burial place of my ancestors* (*Bereishis* 47:30). Yaakov Avinu requested burial in Eretz Yisroel and so did Yosef, and both of them achieved their desires.

Yaakov Avinu requested burial in Eretz Yisroel and so did Yosef, and both of them achieved their desires.

August 1981

Burial in Eretz Yisroel 3

Who should strive to be buried in Eretz Yisroel?

If death is no reason to be sad, why do we have mourning, aveilus?

A/ And the answer is, anybody who strives to be buried in Eretz Yisroel is worthy of being buried there. If a Jew understands that, then even though he might have lived a wicked life, but since he would like his remains to be interred in Eretz Yisroel, that's a form of atonement for him. וְכִפֶּר אַדְמָתוֹ עַמּוֹ – *The earth will be an atonement for him* (*Devarim* 32:43).

Of course, it's a pity, it's a tragedy. If only he had come to Eretz Yisroel, even in his last days, and had lived there piously! He would have walked the streets of Yerushalayim like a humble, pious Jew, serving Hashem. That would have been a million times better than sending his unclean remains, the dead body, to be *metamei* the land. But if it's his wish to do that, then his wish is also a form of *teshuvah.*

However, if a man dies a *rasha* – if he remained a *rasha* until his last day and he didn't desire it – just that his children want to send him to Eretz Yisroel, I don't approve of that. No, I don't approve of that at all. I think that they should just dump him somewhere on Long Island – in a Jewish cemetery of course – and that's good enough for him. But to send his remains to Eretz Yisroel when he didn't ask for it? I don't know what the *gedolim* would say, but personally, I don't approve of it.

January 1978

On Sadness and Mourning

Q/ If the happiness of Olam Haba that you described is true, then why are we sad when somebody dies?

A/ If death is no reason to be sad, why do we have mourning, *aveilus*?

Now let me explain something. We should not be hypocrites. When that man died, was he sorry he died? There's no question, he didn't want to die. He ran around to all the specialists in order to save his life. So we have to show sympathy for him. If we'll just get together and say we're rejoicing now that he's in Gan Eden and he's happy there, no, that's not the way. You have to have sympathy with him.

Do you want to be in the next world? Are you in a hurry to be there?

And therefore, we have to go to his *levayah.* We have to weep with him. He's weeping. He wanted to continue to live. יָפָה שָׁעָה אַחַת שֶׁל תְּשׁוּבָה וּמַעֲשִׂים טוֹבִים בָּעוֹלָם הַזֶּה – *Better to live in this world a little bit and be able to do good things, good deeds,* מִכָּל חַיֵּי הָעוֹלָם הַבָּא – *than all the happiness of the next world* (*Avos* 4:17).

Of course, he's in the world of happiness. But now he realizes what he missed. He looks back now, "Oh, why didn't I do that? Why didn't I do this?" And therefore, we have to have sympathy with him.

There's a Gemara that says if a man died, a *tzaddik* died, let's say, and people don't appreciate the fact that he died, Hashem is going to punish them. Because if they feel that the *tzaddik* is still alive, that it's okay because he's in the next world, Hakadosh Baruch Hu says, "What do you mean it's okay because he's in the next world? Do you want to be in the next world? Are you in a hurry to be there?" And therefore, the fact that you're not sympathetic with him shows that you are a man of cruelty.

And that's why the Ramban says in *Sefer Hagemul* when he talks about *hilchos aveilus,* that there are two separate considerations. One is the *emes* that Olam Haba is the place of great happiness, and the second is the consideration of having a soft heart, not a stony heart like the Greeks.

The Greeks had stony hearts. They were philosophers. "He died? Now he's better off," they said. "Now he's in the heavens among the idols, the *pessilim.* He's enjoying the

We have to always be aware of both consid-erations and we shouldn't let one thing interfere with the other.

pleasures of the *ovdei avodah zarah.*" That's what the Greeks said. That's a stony heart.

So the Ramban says in *Sefer Hagemul* that we shouldn't have a stony heart like the Greeks. We have to have a soft heart with sympathy. And that's why we have to show *aveilus.* But in our heart of hearts we have to know, the truth is that there is *simcha*.

I'll tell a little story, I told it to you already. Once in Vilna there was a *mageifah,* it shouldn't happen, of cholera, a *mageifah* of *cholerya.* It was an epidemic and people were dying. When it came to Yom Kippur, Rav Yisroel Salanter said that nobody should fast. And he went up in the big *shul* to the *bimah* with a bottle of wine and cake to make *kiddush.* People were astounded when they saw that. *Kiddush* on Yom Kippur! And he said it's *assur* to fast because when you're weakened, the epidemic can more readily overtake the person.

And he also said as follows: "When people die because of the epidemic, don't mourn for them, don't be *mis'abel* for them. They're better off. They're in Gan Eden. They're happy. Only that ordinarily it's a mitzvah to mourn, but now that mourning won't be good for our health – it will make us susceptible to the disease – now we have to talk only logic. And therefore if a man dies, we should say he's better off; he's a *tzaddik* and he's better off now and so nobody should be *mis'abel* for him in the middle of the epidemic."

That's what he said. So he *paskened* no *aveilus,* because the *emes* is that the man is better off.

Ay, but there's a mitzvah of *aveilus?* That's the question. What about the second consideration, having a soft heart?

So the answer is that the mitzvah of *pikuach nefesh* is *docheh* the mitzvah of *aveilus.*

And therefore, we have to always be aware of both considerations and we shouldn't let one thing interfere with the other.

And Hakadosh Baruch Hu wants us to keep in mind always – despite the fact of death, despite the fact of *aveilus,* despite the sympathy, we must have not the slightest question in our mind that this person, because he was a Jew who kept mitzvos, he's going to a very great era of endless happiness.

December 1992

You must mourn, chas v'shalom, when the time comes, but distress is something else.

Distress vs. Mourning

Q/ What's the difference between *tzaar* and *aveilus*, distress and mourning?

A/ Mourning is a formality. You must mourn, *chas v'shalom*, when the time comes, but distress is something else.

Distress means disturbance. צער and ערץ are the same same letters. *Aritz* means to break; it's a broken person. You're not supposed to be broken in *aveilus.*

A man, in the midst of his *aveilus, nit keinem gedacht,* is still full of confidence. He can even enjoy the three meals that he's eating. He can even enjoy the vacation he's getting during *shivah*. He can enjoy it. But he doesn't forget the purpose. The purpose is, it's a demonstration, a demonstration of appreciation of the one who left; a demonstration of sadness that he's not here.

But it has nothing to do with *tzaar*. That's a different thing.

February 1980

The Purpose of Mourning

Should a man neglect his health or even become depressed? Chas v'shalom!

Q/ Why is there such a thing as mourning?

A/ I want to tell you what *Rashi* says about mourning. *Rashi* (*Sukkah* 25a) says it's not a mitzvah to have *tzaar,* to have distress, when a man is an *avel.* It's only a mitzvah to go through the procedures of mourning.

So Rashi is making a big distinction. *Tzaar* is not a mitzvah. It's not a mitzvah to be broken up, *rachmana litzlan,* by *aveilus.* It's a mitzvah to go through the ceremonies, the dealings, the procedures of mourning.

And the purpose of it is *teshuvah.* The purpose is repentance. נַחְפְּשָׂה דְרָכֵינוּ וְנַחְקֹרָה וְנָשׁוּבָה עַד ה' – *Let us search out our ways and return to Hashem* (*Eichah* 3:40). מַה זֹּאת עָשָׂה אֱלוֹקִים לָנוּ – *What is that that Elokim has done to us? What is the purpose?* (*Bereishis* 42:28). But to be broken up by mourning? That's a sin.

Should a man neglect his health or even become depressed? *Chas v'shalom!* That's very important.

June 1973

Consolation for a Mourner 1

Q/ What is the best consolation to give someone who is sitting *shiva, lo aleichem v'lo aleinu?*

A/ To console people, the best thing is to come and show yourself. That's the consolation. Just by honoring him by coming, that's already a consolation.

Now, if it's somebody who's really broken up, then you have to use words that are suited to the occasion. But you cannot give one prescription that suits everybody. If a person is of a philosophical bent of mind, talk to him about Olam Haba and about this world being only a temporary place; you can talk about how a man who deserves reward was taken by Hakadosh Baruch Hu to Gan Eden, and he's now being treated to all the great promises that Hakadosh Baruch Hu promised to those who serve Him. Whatever it is, there are ways and means of consoling each person according to his *seichel*.

Some people are obtuse; they're not intelligent, so you can't tell them anything. So all you can say is, "*Vus machstu,* cousin Jake?" That's all you can say. Now, *vus machstu* you shouldn't say because that's *sh'eilas shalom,* it's a greeting (see *Yoreh Dei'ah* 385:1), but you speak to him about mundane ordinary things, and that's the only consolation you can give a man without any brains. So it all depends, according to his *seichel*.

September 1982

Consolation for a Mourner 2

You stated that in the ancient days it was a custom to comfort the mourner with wine. Why don't we do that today?

Q/ You stated that in the ancient days it was a custom to comfort the mourner with wine. Why don't we do that today?

A/ We don't use that method today because we're not capable of handling it. It would be drunkenness, that's all.

But the truth is that even though today we don't comfort him with wine, we do come to him, and our mere presence is

Whatever it is that can console the mourner is a mitzvah to say.

a consolation. The fact that others come and show respect for him, that's a consolation for him.

If they are capable of saying words of wisdom to speak about the great issues of life, very good. If they can speak to him about the reward that the deceased is now enjoying in the afterlife, and they can mention the good deeds that the *niftar* accomplished for which he is now receiving recompense, excellent. That's also a consolation.

Also – this is the lower level, the simple way of talking – if they can talk about the fact that life is short and everyone must walk the same path and therefore they shouldn't be broken up by it, that's also a consolation. Whatever it is that can console the mourner is a mitzvah to say.

And even today it's possible to give him some *gashmius* too, some wine. You can give him something to drink. It's only when he's an *onen* before the burial that he can't drink any wine, but subsequently, an *avel* can drink *mashkeh* and there's certainly nothing wrong. He shouldn't do it in public because then it's a demonstration that he doesn't take his loss seriously, but he can excuse himself from the company and retire for a moment, and he can get a little encouragement on his own.

There's nothing wrong with consoling a mourner with *gashmius.* Only we try to be careful שֶׁלֹּא יַסִּיחַ דַּעְתּוֹ מִן הָאֲבֵלוּת, that he shouldn't forget that he's an *avel* (*Y.D.* 390). That's important. But you can console him within the framework of that and talk about Olam Haba and the reward of the *niftar* and his good deeds and other forms of consolation including, by the way, urging the *aveilim* to take care of their health. That's very important by the way. *Nit eingedacht,* in the *beis avel* it's important to urge the *aveilim* not to neglect their health. They should eat on time and sleep on time despite their loss.

And all these things we do today too.

June 1975

What should a person think about when he leaves a shivah house?

Nichum Aveilim

Q/ What should a person think when he goes for *nichum aveilum* and he says הַמָּקוֹם יְנַחֵם אֶתְכֶם בְּתוֹךְ שְׁאָר אֲבֵלֵי צִיּוֹן וִירוּשָׁלָיִם?

A/ When a person goes, *lo aleichem*, *lo aleinu*, to *tanchumei aveilim*, he's going to say these words. He mumbles the words הַמָּקוֹם יְנַחֵם אֶתְכֶם. Unfortunately, he doesn't think what he's saying and they don't think what he's saying, but these are very important words.

He's saying we're all *aveilim*. We're all *aveilim*; we're mourning for Yerushalayim! How can we be happy if Yerushalayim is in the hands of the gentiles? The Beis Hamikdash is not in existence, the *Malchus Beis Dovid* is not there, the Shechinah departed from us. We're all mourning.

It's a very important lesson! So when you console him, that's part of the consolation. After all, צָרַת רַבִּים חֲצִי נֶחָמָה – *If everyone else is suffering too that's already a partial consolation.* If everybody else is suffering, then your suffering is just part of the natural, universal suffering of our nation. We're all sad.

September 1995

The Purpose of Nichum Aveilim

Q/ What should a person think about when he leaves a *shivah* house?

As long as I'm still alive, I'm going to prepare for my station in the World to Come.

A/ Do you ever go to a *shivah* house and you have nothing to talk about? You come in, you sit a few minutes, you say הַמָּקוֹם יְנַחֵם אֶתְכֶם and you walk out. It's something, it's still a mitzvah, but there's something more you can accomplish still. You can accomplish after you walk out.

It says, טוֹב לָלֶכֶת אֶל בֵּית אֵבֶל מִלֶּכֶת אֶל בֵּית מִשְׁתֶּה – *It's better to go to the house of an avel than to go to a wedding* (*Koheles* 7:2). When you go to a wedding, some people come out of the wedding drunk, and some come out confused; they were wasting time, *leitzanus*. Of course it doesn't have to be that way, but it could be. When you go to a house of an *avel*, however, וְהַחַי יִתֵּן אֶל לִבּוֹ – *you learn the lesson of life,* that this world is only a *prozdor* before Olam Haba*;* this world is only a vestibule, a lobby before the World to Come. That's a tremendous lesson; that no matter how many times you hear the lesson, it's not enough – the tremendous lesson that we're in this world only to prepare for our career; our main career is only in the World to Come. And when you go to the house of an *avel*, that lesson hits you right between the eyes.

And so, as you walk out of the house of the *avel*, think, "From now on, I'm going to get busy. As long as I can still walk, I can still talk, I'm going to accomplish something for myself. As long as I'm still alive, I'm going to prepare for my station in the World to Come." That's the first thought when you walk out.

Now pay attention to the next thought. When you walk out of the house of the *avel*, הַחַי יִתֵּן אֶל לִבּוֹ – *the one who is still alive* should put that into his mind. You should think, "How lucky I am that I'm alive!" You hear the *chiddush*? When you're *menachem avel*, as soon as you walk out, on the steps, going down the steps to the street, think: "*Baruch Hashem* I'm alive." Even better, say it. I'm serious. That's how you walk down the block when you leave. "*Baruch Hashem*, I'm alive!" He just discovered the happy news that he's alive. It's a *simcha,* a real happiness!

And breathe deeply! "Aah!" It's a pleasure to breathe air! A pleasure to see the sunlight! טוֹב לָעֵינַיִם לִרְאוֹת אֶת הַשָּׁמֶשׁ (*Koheles* 11:7)! A pleasure to be alive! The happiness of life! When you go out of the *beis avel*, get a new lease on life, a new understanding of the *simchas hachaim*.

It's a pleasure to walk! A great taanug to walk! Walking is fun! Walking is happiness!

Now most people wouldn't like that idea – to walk out of the house of an *avel* and to gain *simcha?* But that's one of the great lessons. If you don't understand how lucky you are that you're alive in this world, then you're missing the great lesson of *chasdei Hashem*, of עָלֵינוּ לְשַׁבֵּחַ.

And therefore, if it ever happens – it shouldn't happen until 120 years – that you go to a *beis avel*, when you walk outside, first think, "Time is short. I only have a hundred more years to live. I'll get busy and accomplish all I can."

And then as you start walking, בָּרוּךְ אַתָּה ה'... הַמֵּכִין מִצְעֲדֵי גָבֶר – it's a pleasure to walk! It's a pleasure to walk! A great *taanug* to walk! Walking is fun! Walking is happiness! הַמֵּכִין מִצְעֲדֵי גָבֶר!

And looking around with your two eyes – two camcorders; you're looking around and seeing pictures with your eyes. *Pokei'ach ivrim*! What a *simcha* it is to be able to see!

And your computer mind is working! Every second your mind is taking up impulses, thousands of impulses from all over the body, and recording it in your mind. Your mind is the most complicated computer that mankind can ever think of making.

So you thank Hashem, בָּרוּךְ אַתָּה ה'... חוֹנֵן הַדָּעַת! Do you know what it means? *Baruch Hashem,* I'm not in an insane asylum! *Baruch Hashem* I'm not *meshuga*! *Baruch Hashem!* You see a *meshugener* woman standing on the street corner, it's a *rachmanus* on her. She's in rags. She's muttering to himself. Her life is a *gehinom*. *Baruch Hashem,* you're a happy person!

Most people never dreamed what the truth is. The secret of aveilus is teshuvah.

Your computer is working perfectly! You know how to live! Ah! Ah! Ah! חוֹנֵן הַדָּעַת! *Baruch Hashem,* I'm not insane!

And there are so many things to be happy about. So when you walk out of the *beis ha'avel,* הַחַי יִתֵּן אֶל לִבּוֹ! He should pay attention to how happy he is! And from now on, he should get busy on טוֹב לְהוֹדוֹת לַה'!

September 1995

Shivah: A Form of Teshuvah

Q/ What is the reason that *aveilim,* mourners, change their seat in *shul* for one year?

A/ We have to understand what the secret of *aveilus* is. And most people never dreamed what the truth is. The secret of *aveilus* is *teshuvah.* Rav Simcha Zissel says that when a man *rachmana litzlan* is observing *shivah,* it's *teshuvah.* It's repentance.

So you say, "What does he have to repent for? His father lived until 110 years, so what's the misfortune? How long did he expect him to live?"

And the answer is, death is a misfortune. Death is a punishment. It's a curse. And as long as it continues to come, no matter how long a man lives, even if he lives a thousand years, the day of death is an occasion to remember that it was because of an iniquity, a trespass, that death happened. And therefore we have to do *teshuvah.*

And moving from your place to a new place is a form of *teshuvah.*

July 1979

Reciting Kaddish

Why should a son say kaddish for his father?

Q/ Why should a son say *kaddish* for his father?

A/ The answer is, when you say *kaddish,* you're making a *kiddush Hashem*. Of course, you have to think what you're saying: יִתְגַּדֵּל וְיִתְקַדֵּשׁ שְׁמֵיהּ רַבָּא – *His great name should be exalted and sanctified.*

It's a tremendous thing! *Kaddish* is a tremendous thing if you say it with *kavanah;* you want Hashem's name to be exalted in this world. And the father in Gan Eden is gathering *nachas* from the fact that his son is working on the principle of *kiddush Hashem*.

And therefore, it's important to be *mechavein,* to think what you're saying; it shouldn't be just a formality. And then, when he says יִתְגַּדֵּל וְיִתְקַדֵּשׁ שְׁמֵיהּ רַבָּא and everybody answers "Amen!" you're making a *kiddush Hashem* which is a *nachas* for the father in Gan Eden.

February 2000

Lighting Candles for a Niftar

A/ What's the benefit of lighting a candle on a person's *yahrtzeit*?

A/ When someone is *niftar* and candles are lit for that person, it is a *kavod* for the *meis.* And that's because a candle is a beautiful symbol. A flame is a beautiful thing, and even today it's hard to explain exactly how it works. The physical materials – the wick, the

The light of the candle is a beautiful symbol.

wax, the oil – turn into light. That symbolizes the *neshamah* that was enclosed in a *guf* and is now only *neshamah.* It's now *ohr*. Like the *ohr* of the candle that has been transformed from physical materials into light, the *guf* has been transformed into *neshamah.* And the *neshamah* is now *ohr*, shining in Olam Haba. And when we light the candle and show that we recognize this truth, it gives *nachas* to the *neshamah.*

When someone passes away, that person doesn't stop existing. The *neshamah* is real and it exists in Olam Haba. And the *neshamah* can still feel and recognize these things. The *nifter* is honored by the family when they light a *yahrzeit* candle; it is a *nachas ruach* for the *neshamah.* The symbol of the light that comes from the wax and the wick is an important thing.

And therefore, the light of the candle is a beautiful symbol. It's a symbol for the *neshamah* that has turned from *gashmius* into *ruchnius*. And the *neshamah* in the next world is happy that people are lighting the candle and recognizing the truth of the next world. It's a *nachas ruach* for the *neshamah*.

November 2000

The bookmark for this sefer
is dedicated Leilui Nishmas

R' Hirsh Berel
Ben R' Avraham Leib

Nessie Feigela
Bas R' Yehudah

And their daughter

Chaya Rivka
Bas Nessie Feigela

And Lehavdil Bein Chaim L'chaim
as a zechus for

Yisrael Issur
Ben R' Hirsh Berel

Dedicated to my parents

Ya'akov Dovid ben Eliyahu

and

Etel bas Aleksander

Who instilled in me a passionate quest for the truth, in every subject, no matter where it would lead me. They were very patient with me to let this journey take place, in spite of their misgivings. I have found Rabbi Avigdor Miller's writings much later in my life, but they continue to inspire contemplation and spiritual growth. I hope they will do the same for readers of this compendium.

Akiva Pearlman

לעילוי נשמת

In memory of our father

Harav Yitzchok Singer זצ"ל

הרה"ג ר' יצחק אהרן בן הרה"ג ר' אליהו זינגער זצ"ל

נפטר י"ג טבת תשס"א

Multitudes knew him as an extraordinary talmid chacham and a masterful orator. But that was only the outer manifestation of his inner greatness. He brought honor to the rabbinate, comfort to the afflicted, and inspiration to the downtrodden.

הרה"ג ר' יצחק אהרן בן הרה"ג ר' אליהו זינגער זצ"ל
וזוגתו הרבנית רייזל בת הרה"ח ר' יששכר דוב ע"ה

הרה"צ ר' ישראל אריה ליב האלפערן
בן הרה"צ ר' ברוך מסאקאליוקא זצ"ל
וזוגתו הרבנית שבע בת הרה"ג ר' אריה ליבוש ע"ה

And in memory of our mother

Rebbetzin Bluma Singer ע"ה

She was a quintessential aishes chayil ... wise, warm, and dedicated to the many who relied on her. She was an equal partner with our father זצ"ל, in his work for klal yisroel and any individual who needed his help.

Our mother was actually aware of her responsibility to carry on the great messorah of her forbearers and indeed she is a credit to our distinguished yichus.

רבות בנות עשו חיל ואת עלית על כלנה

Baruch and Susie Singer and Yitzchak Ahron
Rabbi Eli Hersh and Rivky Singer
Rabbi Nussie and Ruchy Singer
Yossie and Surie Singer
Sruly Singer

In Memory of

Irwin J. Betesh A"H

By his Family

לעילוי נשמת

אהרן יצחק בן משה
יענטל לאה בת ר' חיים יוסף יהודה
אטי' בת ישראל זאב
יעקב שלום בן שלמה

משפחת גליקסמאן

In honor of

my wife

Claire Louzeh

and our kids,

Yosef, Chaim, David Abraham

and Elisheva

Liuly nishmas

Dovid Chaim Ben

Shmuel Yosef HaKohen

who taught us
never to let go of Hashem.

To my wife

Dalya

who personifies the
Ashes Chayil that Rabbi Miller
always spoke about

In Memory of

Rivka Bas Reb Pinchas A'H

Pinchas Ben Avrohom Moshe

Liba Bas Shalom

Yom Tov Ben Nissim

Matilda Bat Yaakov

לעילוי נשמת

ר' יצחק שלום
בן ר' שאול ע"ה

מרת אסתר דבורה
בת ר' מרדכי אליעזר ע"ה

נדבת
משפחת ראזענבלום

לעילוי נשמת

ר' משה ב"ר חיים שמואל ע"ה

מרת באשע בת ר' ישראל ע"ה

ר' דוד ב"ר יצחק אריה ע"ה

Made in the USA
Columbia, SC
08 July 2025

13768f16-fc8c-44c0-9c8e-b0b47226dda0R03